HIMSS Dictionary
of Health Information
and Technology
Terms, Acronyms and
Organizations,

Fifth Edition

HIMSS Dictionary
of Health Information and Technology Terms, Acronyms and Organizations,

Fifth Edition

CRC Press is an imprint of the
Taylor & Francis Group, an **informa** business

CRC Press
Taylor & Francis Group
6000 Broken Sound Parkway NW, Suite 300
Boca Raton, FL 33487-2742

© 2019 by Taylor & Francis Group, LLC
CRC Press is an imprint of Taylor & Francis Group, an Informa business

No claim to original U.S. Government works

Printed and bound by CPI Group (UK) Ltd, Croydon, CR0 4YY on acid-free paper

International Standard Book Number-13: 978-1-138-47750-6 (Hardback)
International Standard Book Number-13: 978-0-367-14864-5 (Paperback)
International Standard Book Number-13: 978-1-351-10452-4 (e-Book)

Visit the Taylor & Francis Web site at
http://www.taylorandfrancis.com

and the CRC Press Web site at
http://www.crcpress.com

Contents

About HIMSS

As a mission driven non-profit, HIMSS offers a unique depth and breadth of expertise in health innovation, public policy, workforce development, research and analytics to advise global leaders, stakeholders and influencers on best practices in health information and technology. Through our innovation companies, HIMSS delivers key insights, education and engaging events to healthcare providers, governments and market suppliers, ensuring they have the right information at the point of decision.

As an association, HIMSS encompasses more than 72,000 individual members and 630 corporate members. We partner with hundreds of providers, academic institutions and health services organizations on strategic initiatives that leverage innovative information and technology. Together, we work to improve health, access and the quality and cost-effectiveness of healthcare.

Headquartered in Chicago, Illinois, HIMSS serves the global health information and technology communities with focused operations across North America, Europe, United Kingdom, the Middle East and Asia Pacific.

To learn more about HIMSS and to find out how to join us and our members in advancing our cause, please visit our website at www.himss.org.

HIMSS Vision

Better health through information and technology.

HIMSS Mission

Globally lead endeavors optimizing health engagements and care outcomes through information and technology.

Foreword

Constant change continues to impact the ecosystem of health and healthcare as we experience consolidation, expansion, and disruption all at the same time. HIMSS' focus is evolving as well with a renewed intent to enhance value to our members while advancing the content direction of the industry through our thought leadership. What hasn't changed, however, is the importance of staying informed and remaining credible.

The fifth edition of HIMSS Dictionary of Health Information and Technology Terms, Acronyms and Organizations is an essential resource. It reflects HIMSS' acknowledgment of the value of combining the best use of information and technology. New organizations are forming, terms are evolving, technologies are being disrupted, and much of that innovation is reflected in this new edition.

Innovation will continue to identify opportunities to improve everything from cost efficiency to the patient experience and clinical outcomes. Organizations of the future must have a vision capable of fluid change in a dynamic environment. New roles will be created while care models and services will evolve. This is the re-imagined becoming reality through asking, trying, and measuring the "what if" of tomorrow. We invite you to leverage this trusted resource to equip you with the knowledge needed to embark on this journey toward a value-driven health landscape.

Joyce Sensmeier MS, RN-BC, CPHIMS, FHIMSS, FAAN

Joyce Sensmeier is Vice President of Informatics at HIMSS where she is responsible for clinical informatics, standards, and interoperability programs and initiatives.

Steve Wretling is Chief Technology & Innovation Officer at HIMSS

As CTIO, Steve serves as HIMSS senior technical leader and advisor, driving our thought leadership on technical innovation and best practices.

Foreword

Introduction

Welcome to the fifth edition of the *HIMSS Dictionary of Health Information and Technology Terms, Acronyms and Organizations*, which follows the anniversary of the dictionary's first publication in June 2006, the second edition in 2009, the third edition in 2013, and the fourth edition in 2016.

The fifth edition encompasses many terms found in the previous four editions, but also includes updates to reflect the continuing evolution occurring within the health information and technology (HIT) industry. As new technologies and stakeholders emerge, the list of terms included in the dictionary has changed. The current terminology included in this fifth edition, reflects, to the best of our efforts, the current state of healthcare and health information technology.

The changes made in this edition reflect a careful process of collection, review, refinement, and, finally, compilation, and include input from stakeholders from across the HIT industry. The book includes an appropriate reference for each term.

This fifth edition contains 3400+ entries. Professional credentialing and organizational terms are separated from the main terms of the dictionary via appendices. Acronyms are incorporated into the alphabetical organization of the main terms to simplify searches for terms. A separate acronym reference list is included should the user need to conduct a quick search of the acronym's full name. In summary, we hope our audience of HIT professionals, students, and others who are engaged in HIT activities will find this edition to be a useful tool.

We would like to thank HIMSS for undertaking the 2019 revision and publication of this valuable resource. Thank you to the numerous individuals who collaborated with us, gave us new ideas on content, and suggested improvements to this edition. Thank you also to those who purchased and used previous editions of this book. Your past and continued support will ensure that future editions are accessible to the industry. Without your support, this edition would not have happened.

Christine A. Hudak, PhD, CPHIMS, FHIMSS
Gary W. Ozanich, PhD

Acknowledgments

HIMSS sincerely thanks the student volunteers, led by Christine Hudak and Gary Ozanich, and HIMSS subject matter experts for the time and effort dedicated to the development of the fifth edition of this dictionary. Without their leadership, expertise, and consideration, this dictionary would not have become a reality.

Christine Hudak, PhD, CPHIMS, FHIMSS
Professor and Director, Health Informatics
Kent State University
Kent, Ohio

Gary W. Ozanich, PhD
Director, Health Informatics
College of Informatics
Northern Kentucky University
Highland Heights, Kentucky

HIMSS Staff

Joyce Sensmeier MS, RN-BC, CPHIMS, FHIMSS, FAAN
Vice President
Informatics

Katie Crenshaw, MPA
Manager
Informatics

Mari Greenberger, MPPA
Director
Informatics

Jessica Bird, CAE
Manager
Strategic Relations

Jeff Coughlin, MPP
Senior Director
Federal & State Affairs

Mara Daiker, MS, CPHIMS, RHIA, SHIMSS
Director
Professional Development

Rich Delort, VP
Information Technology

Stephanie Denvir, CAE
Senior Director
Strategic Relations

Audrey Garnatz, PhD, CAPM
Program Manager
Informatics

James Gaston, FHIMSS, MBA
Senior Director
Healthcare Advisory Services Group
HIMSS Analytics

Lee Kim, BS, JD, CISSP, CIPP/US, FHIMSS
Director, Privacy and Security

Michael Kirwan
Vice President
Continua
Personal Connected Health Alliance

JoAnn Klinedinst, MEd, CPHIMS, PMP, DES, FHIMSS
Vice President
Professional Development

Rod Piechowski, MA, CPHIMS
Senior Director
Health Information Systems

John Sharp, MSSA, PMP, FHIMSS
Senior Manager, Personal Connected Health Alliance

DonVielle Young
Senior Associate
Professional Development

A

AA (Attribute authority): A directory or database in which systems can securely add, modify, and save attributes. An attribute authority is a trusted source of data for attribute-based access control (ABAC) decisions.[21]

AAA (Authentication, authorization, and accounting): A principle that is the cornerstone of security, whether IT or otherwise, and is comprised of access control, authentication, and accounting.[422] *See* **Authentication**, **Authorization**, and **Accounting**.

ABAC (Attribute-based access control): A logical access control model that is distinguishable because it controls access to objects by evaluating rules against the attributes of the entities (subject and object) actions and the environment relevant to a request.[1]

ABC (Activity-based costing): An accounting technique that allows an organization to determine the actual cost associated with each product and service produced by the organization, without regard to organizational structure. A cost accounting approach concerned with matching costs with activities (called cost drivers) that cause those costs. It is a more sophisticated kind of absorption-costing and replaces labor-based costing systems. ABC states that (1) products consume activities, (2) it is the activities (and not the products) that consume resources, (3) activities are the cost drivers, and (4) activities are not necessarily based on the volume of production. Instead of allocating costs to cost centers (such as manufacturing, marketing, finance), ABC allocates direct and indirect costs to activities such as processing an order, attending to a customer complaint, or setting up a machine.[4]

ABC codes (Alternative billing codes): Terminology to describe alternative medicine, nursing, and other integrative healthcare interventions that include relative value units and legal scope of practice information. ABC codes are five-digit Health Insurance Portability and Accountability Act (HIPAA) compliant alpha codes (e.g., AAAAA) used by licensed and non-licensed healthcare practitioners on standard healthcare claim forms (e.g., CMS 1500 Form) to describe services, remedies, and/or supply items provided and/or used during patient visits.[40]

Abend: Abnormal termination of software. **1.** A type of system error in which a task or program fails to execute properly (i.e., "ab-normally ends"). The term is also used as the name for a type of error message that indicates such a failure has occurred. **2.** ABnormal END or ABortive END. System crash or other abnormal termination of a computer program caused by memory conflict or some other (usually unidentifiable) glitch.[6,4]

Abort: In data transmission, an *abort* is a function invoked by a sending station to cause the recipient to discard or ignore all bit sequences transmitted by the sender since the preceding flag sequence. To terminate a program or process abnormally and usually suddenly, with or without diagnostic information.[8,135]

Abstract message: The basic level of definition within HL7 is that of the abstract message associated with a particular trigger event. The abstract message includes the data fields that will be sent within a message, the valid response messages, and the treatment of application level errors or the failure of the underlying communications system. An HL7 abstract message is defined in terms of HL7 segments and fields.[9]

Abstract syntax: A form of representation of data that is independent of machine-oriented structures and encodings and also of the physical representation of the data. Abstract syntax is used to give a high-level description of programs being compiled or messages passing over a communications link.[8]

Abstract syntax notation: *See* **ASN**.

Abstracting: An application that facilitates the collection and maintenance of coded patient information with selected patient demographic, clinical, and admissions data from the medical record, usually post-discharge. This information can be used for internal control, analysis, regulatory reports, etc.[2]

Abstraction: 1. The process of extracting essential properties while omitting unessential details. **2.** The process of taking away or removing characteristics from something in order to reduce it to a set of essential characteristics. In object-oriented programming, abstraction is one of three central principles (along with encapsulation and inheritance). Through the process of abstraction, a programmer hides all but the relevant data about an object in order to reduce complexity and increase efficiency.[11,2] *See* **Encapsulation** and **Inheritance**.

ACA (Affordable Care Act): On March 23, 2010, President Obama signed the Patient Protection and Affordable Care Act, which sought to extend healthcare coverage to more individuals and makes coverage more affordable for many others. Section 1561 requested the U.S. Department of Health & Human Services (HHS), in consultation with the Health Information Technology (HIT) Policy Committee, and the HIT Standards Committee (the Committees), to develop interoperable and secure standards and protocols that facilitate electronic enrollment of individuals in federal and state health and human services programs.[12]

Acceptable downtime: *See* **Maximum tolerable period of disruption** and **MAO**.

A

Acceptable risk: Level of risk at which, given costs and benefits associated with risk reduction measures, no action is deemed to be warranted at a given point in time.[13]

Acceptable use policy: *See* **AUP.**

Acceptance testing: A user-run testing event that demonstrates an application's ability to meet business objectives and system requirements. Also known as beta testing.[2]

Access: The ability and means to communicate with or otherwise interact with a system, to use system resources to handle information, to gain knowledge of the information the system contains, or to control system components and functions.[15]

Access control: The process of granting or denying specific requests for or attempts to (1) obtain and use information and related information processing services; and (2) enter specific physical facilities.[15]

Access control decision function: *See* **ADF.**

Access control enforcement function: *See* **AEF.**

Access control information: *See* **ACI.**

Access control list: *See* **ACL.**

Access control policy: The way an organization will manage access control and under which rules users have access to which systems and information. It also defines the access control model that an organization may use.[423]

Access level: A category within a given security classification limiting entry or system connectivity to only authorized persons.[1]

Access mode: A distinct operation recognized by the protection mechanisms as a possible operation on an object. Read, write, and append are possible modes of access to a file, while execute is an additional mode of access to a program.[16]

Access point: A device that allows wireless devices to connect to a wired network using Wi-Fi or related standards.[1]

Access provider: *See* **ISP.**

Access to radiology information: *See* **ARI.**

Accountability: Refers to identifying the healthcare party (i.e., individuals, organizations, business units) or agent (e.g., software, device, instrument, monitor) that is responsible for data origination, amendment, verification, translation, stewardship, access and use, disclosure, and transmission and receipt.[17]

Accountable Care Organization: *See* **ACO.**

Accounting: Systematic and comprehensive recording of financial transactions pertaining to a business. Also refers to the process of summarizing, analyzing, and reporting these transactions to oversight agencies and tax collection entities.[18]

Accounting of disclosures: Individuals have a right to receive an accounting of disclosures of protected health information made by a covered entity in the six years prior to the date on which the accounting is required, subject to certain exceptions as set forth in 45 CFR 164.528.[424]

Accreditation: 1. Formal declaration by a designated approving authority that an information system is approved to operate in a particular security mode using a prescribed set of safeguards at an acceptable level of risk. **2.** A process of review that healthcare organizations participate in to demonstrate the ability to meet predetermined criteria and standards established by a professional accrediting agency. Accreditation represents agencies as credible and reputable organizations dedicated to ongoing and continuous compliance with the highest standard of quality.[100,22]

ACDF (Access control decision function) or ADF: A specialized function that makes access control decisions by applying access control policy rules to an access request, access control decision information (of initiators, targets, access requests, or that retained from prior decisions), and the context in which the access request is made.[16]

ACG (Ambulatory care group): Also known as an *adjusted clinical group*. A method of categorizing outpatient episodes: preventative, diagnostic, therapeutic, surgical, and/or rehabilitative that are based on resource use over time and are modified by principal diagnosis, age, and sex.[23] *See* **ADG** and **APG**.

ACI (Access control information): Information used for access control purposes, including contextual information. An ACI controls user access by defining the access privileges of an ITIM group or ACI principal. Members of an ITIM group or an ACI principal can view and perform operations on attributes within a target class (context) as defined by the scope of the ACI.[24,25]

ACID (Atomicity, consistency, isolation, and durability): An acronym and mnemonic device for learning and remembering the four primary attributes ensured to any transaction by a transaction manager (which is also called a transaction monitor). The ACID concept is described in ISO/IEC 10026-1:1992 Section 4. Each of these attributes can be measured against a benchmark.[2] *See* **Atomicity**, **Consistency**, **Isolation**, and **Durability**.

ACK (General acknowledgment message): In data networking, an acknowledgment is a signal passed between communicating processes or computers to signify acknowledgment, or receipt, of response, as part of a communications protocol. The ACK message is used to respond to a message where there has been an error that precludes application processing or where the application does not define a special message type for the response.[9]

ACL (Access control list): A list of permissions associated with an object. The list specifies who or what is allowed to access the object and what operations are allowed to be performed on the object.[1]

ACO (Accountable care organization): Groups of doctors, hospitals, and other healthcare providers, who come together voluntarily to give coordinated high-quality care to the patients they serve. Coordinated care helps ensure that patients, especially the chronically ill, get the right care at the right time, with the goal of avoiding unnecessary duplication of services and preventing medical errors. When an ACO succeeds in both delivering high-quality care and spending healthcare dollars more wisely, it will share in the savings it achieves.[26]

Acquisition modality: A system that acquires medical images, waveforms, or measurements while a patient or specimen is present (e.g., a computed tomography scanner, a specimen microscope, or a hemodynamic measurement system).[27]

Acquisition modality importer: A system that integrates a non-DICOM-ready modality into workflows.[27]

Active directory: *See* **AD**.

Active server pages: *See* **ASP**.

Activity-based costing: *See* **ABC**.

Activity tracker: A device or application for monitoring and tracking fitness-related metrics such as distance walked or run, calorie consumption, heartbeat, and quality of sleep. Most often refers to dedicated electronic monitoring devices that are synced to a computer or smartphone for long-term data tracking.[52] *See* **Wearable technology**.

Acute physiology and chronic health evaluation: *See* **APACHE**.

AD (Active directory): A system that automates network management of user data, security, and distributed resources.[2]

AD (Addendum): New documentation used to add information to an original entry. Addenda should be timely and bear the current date and reason for the additional information being added to the health record.[28]

Addendum: *See* **AD**.

Address resolution protocol: *See* **ARP**.

ADE (Adverse drug event): An injury resulting from the use of a drug. Under this definition, the term ADE includes harm caused by the drug (adverse drug reactions and overdose) and harm from the use of the drug (including dose reductions and discontinuations of drug therapy). Adverse drug events may result from medication errors, but most do not. ADEs are injuries resulting from drug-related medical interventions. ADEs can occur in any healthcare setting, including: inpatient, such as acute care hospitals, outpatient, and long-term care settings, such as nursing homes.[31,67,32]

ADG (Ambulatory diagnostic group): A method of categorizing outpatient episodes. *See* **ACG** and **APG**.[23]

Ad hoc query: 1. A query that is not determined prior to the moment it is run against a data source. **2.** A nonstandard inquiry created to obtain information as the need arises and contrasts with a query that is predefined and routinely processed.[71]

Administrative code sets: Code sets that characterize a general business situation, rather than a medical condition or service. Under HIPAA, these are sometimes referred to as nonclinical, or nonmedical, code sets. Compare to code sets and medical code sets.[26]

Administrative record: A record concerned with administrative matters, such as length of stay, details of accommodation, and billing.[4]

Administrative safeguards: Administrative actions, policies and procedures to manage the selection, development, implementation, and maintenance of security measures to safeguard electronic protected health information; and to manage the conduct of the covered entity's or business associate's workforce in relation to the protection of that information.[79]

Administrative services only: *See* **ASO.**

Administrator user access level: Administrator accounts are generally for users who require full access to the computer system.[425]

Admission date: The date the patient was admitted for inpatient care, outpatient service, or start of care.[26]

ADPAC (Automated data processing application coordinator): The person responsible for implementing a set of computer programs (application package) developed to support a specific functional area such as Immunology Case Registry, PIMS, etc.[37]

ADR (Adverse drug reaction): An unwanted response to a therapeutic drug. Health professionals must report all adverse reactions related to drugs or medical devices to the manufacturer and the FDA to aid in monitoring the safety of marketed medical products.[38]

ADR (ADT response message): Admission, discharge, and transfer response message.[9]

ADSL (Asymmetric digital subscriber line): A type of DSL broadband communications technology used for transmitting digital information at a high bandwidth on existing phone lines to homes and businesses. Unlike dial-up phone services, ADSL provides continuously available, "always on" connection. ADSL is asymmetric in that it uses most of the channel to transmit downstream to the user and only a small part to receive information from the user. ADSL simultaneously accommodates analog (voice) information on the same line.[2]

ADT (Admission, discharge, and transfer): Admission, discharge, and transfer message for patients in a healthcare facility.[9]

ADT response message: *See* **ADR.**

Advance directive: A document by which a person makes provision for healthcare decisions in the event that he or she becomes unable to make those decisions. There are two main types of advance directive—the "Living Will" and the "Durable Power of Attorney for Health Care." There are also hybrid documents that combine elements of the Living Will with those of the Durable Power of Attorney.[81]

Advanced analytics: The autonomous or semi-autonomous examination of data or content using sophisticated techniques and tools, typically beyond those of traditional business intelligence, to discover deeper insights, make predictions, or generate recommendations. Advanced analytic techniques include those such as data/text mining, machine learning, pattern matching, forecasting, visualization, semantic analysis, sentiment analysis, network and cluster analysis, multivariate statistics, graph analysis, simulation, complex event processing, and neural networks.[142]

Advanced APM (Advanced Alternative Payment Model): A track in the CMS Quality Payment Program where Eligible Clinicians (ECs) can earn a 5 percent incentive payment for achieving a threshold level of payments or patients that are achieved through a specific, designated APM. If ECs achieve these thresholds, they become a Qualifying APM Participant (QP) and are excluded from the Merit-based Incentive Payment Systems (MIPS) reporting requirements and payment adjustment under QPP.[26]

Advanced persistent threat: *See* **APT**.

Advanced technology attachment: *See* **ATA**.

Adverse drug event: *See* **ADE**.

Adverse drug reaction: *See* **ADR**.

Adverse event: *See* **AE**.

AE (Adverse event/adverse experience): Any untoward medical occurrence associated with the use of a drug or a medical product in humans, whether or not considered drug related. Pre-marketing: Any untoward medical occurrence in a patient or clinical investigation subject administered a pharmaceutical product and which does not necessarily have a causal relationship with this treatment. Post-marketing/US: Any adverse event associated with the use of a drug in humans, whether or not considered drug related, including the following: An adverse event occurring in the course of the use of a drug product in professional practice; an adverse event occurring from drug overdose; an adverse event occurring from drug withdrawal; and any failure of expected pharmacologic action. Post-marketing/European Union: Any undesirable experience occurring to a patient treated with a pharmaceutical product whether or not considered related to the medicinal product.[9,41]

AE Title (Application entity title): An identifier utilized by picture archiving and communication systems (PACS) to uniquely name devices that can send and/or receive information to the imaging/PACS system.[42]

AEF (Access control enforcement function): A specialized function that is part of the access path between an initiator and a target on each access request and enforces the decision made by the access control decision function.[16]

Affinity domain policy: Clearly defines the appropriate uses of the Integrating the Healthcare Enterprise (IHE) Cross-Enterprise Document Sharing (XDS) affinity domain. Within this policy is a defined set of acceptable use privacy consent policies that are published and understood.[27]

Affordable Care Act: *See* **ACA**.

Aggregate: The collection or gathering of elements into a mass or whole.[29]

Aggregate data: 1. Data elements assembled into a logical format to facilitate comparisons or to elicit evidence of patterns. **2.** A data type composed of multiple elements. An aggregate can be homogeneous (all elements have the same type), e.g., an array, a list in a functional language, a string of characters, a file; or it can be heterogeneous (elements can have different types), e.g., a structure. In most languages, aggregates can contain elements which are themselves aggregates, e.g., a list of lists.[43,44]

Aggregation logics: Logic for aggregating detailed data into categories.[45]

AHT (Average handling time/average handle time): The average duration of a call handled by a customer service associate.[2]

AI (Artificial intelligence): The theory and development of computer systems able to perform tasks normally requiring human intelligence, such as visual perception, speech recognition, decision-making, and translation between languages.[107]

AIDC (Automatic identification and data capture): A broad category of technologies used to collect information from an individual, object, image, or sound without manual data entry. AIDC systems are used to manage inventory, delivery, assets, security, and documents. Sectors that use AIDC systems include distribution, manufacturing, transportation, medicine, government, and retail, among many others. AIDC applications typically fall into one of a few categories: identification and validation at the source, tracking, and interfaces to other systems. The actual technologies involved, the information obtained, and the purpose of collection vary widely. Current AIDC technologies include: barcodes, 2D barcodes, magnetic strips, smart cards, optical character recognition, radio frequency identification, biometrics applications including finger scanning, and voice recognition.[2]

AIMS (Anesthesia information management system): An information system that allows integrated communication with other hospital and provider systems throughout the perioperative period (such as clinical information systems used by nurses, clinical data repositories used by hospitals, and professional billing systems). AIMS are a specialized form of electronic health record (EHR) systems that allow the automatic and reliable collection, storage, and presentation of patient data during the perioperative period. In addition to providing basic record-keeping functions, most AIMS also allow end users to access information for management, quality assurance, and research purposes. AIMS typically consist of a combination of hardware and software that interface with intraoperative monitors, and in many cases hospital clinical data repositories or EHRs. Although the primary role of an AIMS is to capture data during the intraoperative phase, most systems also can incorporate pre- and postoperative patient information.[47]

AIS (Automated information system): An assembly of computer hardware, software, firmware, or any combination of these, configured to automatically accomplish specific information handling operations, such as communication, computation, dissemination, processing, and storage of information. Included are computers, word processing systems, networks, or other electronic information handling systems, and associated equipment.[109]

Alert: Written or acoustic signal to announce the arrival of messages and results and to avoid possible undesirable situations, such as contradictions, conflicts, erroneous entry, tasks that are not performed in time, or an exceptional result. A passive alert will appear on the screen in the form of a message. An active alert calls for immediate attention, and the appropriate person is immediately notified (e.g., by electronic pager).[34] *See* **Decision support system.**

Alert fatigue: Multiple false alarms by smart technology or computer programs that cause workers to ignore or respond slowly to them.[48]

Algorithm: Step-by-step procedure for problem-solving or calculating; a set of rules for problem-solving. In data mining, it defines the parameters of the data mining model.[2]

ALOS (Average length of stay): Refers to the average number of days that patients spend in hospital. It is generally measured by dividing the total number of days stayed by all inpatients during a year by the total number of admissions or discharges. Day cases, such as same day surgeries, are excluded.[49]

Alpha/beta testing: A pre-production development stage comprised of an initial trial (alpha test) by a select set of users. This initial test is to ensure that the system is stable enough for a rigorous trial (beta test) by additional users, or in a variety of settings.[50,51] *See* **Beta testing.**

Alternative payment models: *See* **APMs.**

ALU (Arithmetic logic unit): A major component of the central processing unit (CPU) of a computer system. It does all processes related to arithmetic and logic operations that need to be done on instruction words. In some microprocessor architectures, the ALU is divided into the arithmetic unit and the logic unit.[2]

Ambulatory care: Clinical care, including diagnosis, observation, treatment, and rehabilitation that is provided on an outpatient basis. Ambulatory care is given to persons who are able to ambulate or walk about.[96]

Ambulatory care group: *See* **ACG.**

A

Ambulatory care information system: Information systems used to improve the quality of care and promote business systems integration in the ambulatory care setting.[53]

Ambulatory EHR: The electronic health record (EHR) that supports the ambulatory/clinic/physician office environments. Provides all of the functions of an EHR, which may include: clinical documentation, order entry, clinical data repository, practitioner order entry, physician or nurse clinical documentation, etc.[2]

Ambulatory medical record: *See* **AMR**.

Amendments and corrections: Documentation meant to clarify health information within a health record. An amendment is made after the original documentation has been completed by the provider. All amendments should be timely and bear the current date of documentation. A correction is a change in the information meant to clarify inaccuracies after the original electronic document has been signed or rendered complete.[28]

American Recovery and Reinvestment Act of 2009: *See* **ARRA**.

American standard code for information interchange: *See* **ASCII**.

AMR (Ambulatory medical record): An electronic or paper-based medical record used in the outpatient or ambulatory care setting.[53]

Analog: Representing data by measurement of a continuous physical variable, as voltage or pressure, as opposed to digital, which represents data as discrete units.[39]

Analog signal: In telecommunications, an analog signal is one in which a base carrier's alternating current frequency is modified in some way, such as by amplifying the strength of the signal or varying the frequency, in order to add information to the signal.[2] *See* **Digital signal**.

Analog-to-digital conversion: An electronic process in which a continuously variable (analog) signal is changed, without altering its essential content, into a multi-level (digital) signal.[2]

Analytics: A process that uses mathematics, statistics, predictive modeling and machine learning techniques to find meaningful patterns and knowledge in recorded data.[116]

Analytics Competency Center: A cross-functional organizational team that has defined tasks, roles, responsibilities, and processes for supporting and promoting the effective use of business intelligence and/or analytics across an organization.[7]

Analytics strategy: A formal document presenting an organizational plan that outlines the goals, methods, and responsibilities for achieving analytics maturation.[10]

Ancillary care: Refers to the wide range of healthcare services. These services can be classified into three categories: diagnostic, therapeutic, and custodial. Diagnostic services include laboratory tests, radiology, genetic testing, diagnostic imaging, and more. Therapeutic services range from rehabilitation to physical and occupational therapy, as well as massage, chiropractic services, and speech therapy. Custodial services include hospice care, long term past acute care (LTPAC). urgent care and nursing facility care.[54]

Anesthesia information management system: *See* **AIMS.**

ANN (Artificial neuron network): An artificial neuron network (ANN) is a computational model based on the structure and functions of biological neural networks. Information that flows through the network affects the structure of the ANN because a neural network changes—or learns, in a sense—based on that input and output. ANNs are considered nonlinear statistical data modeling tools where the complex relationships between inputs and outputs are modeled or patterns are found, and are among the main tools used in machine learning.[52]

Anonymization: A process that removes or replaces identity information from a communication or record. Communications and records may be made pseudonymous, in which case the same subject will always have the same replacement identity, but cannot be identified as an individual.[56]

Anti-tearing: The process or processes that prevent data loss when a smartcard is withdrawn during a data operation.[2]

Anti-virus software: A program specifically designed to detect many forms of malware and prevent them from infecting computers, as well as cleaning computers that have already been infected.[1]

APACHE (Acute physiology and chronic health evaluation): 1. A severity-of-disease classification scoring system widely used in the United States. APACHE II is the most widely studied version of this instrument (a more recent version, APACHE IV, is proprietary, whereas APACHE II is publicly available); it derives a severity score from such factors as underlying disease and chronic health status. Other points are added for 12 physiologic variables (e.g., hematocrit, creatinine, Glasgow Coma Score, mean arterial pressure) measured within 24 hours of admission to the ICU. The APACHE II score has been validated in several studies involving tens of thousands of ICU patients. **2.** A widely used web server platform written by the Apache Software Foundation (ASF). The Apache web server browser had a key role in the initial growth of the World Wide Web.[58]

APC (Ambulatory payment class): A payment type for outpatient prospective payment system (PPS) claims.[59]

APG (Ambulatory patient group): A reimbursement methodology developed by 3M Health Information Systems for the Health Care Financing Administration (HCFA); APGs are to outpatient procedures as DRGs are to inpatient days; APGs provide for a fixed reimbursement to an institution for outpatient procedures or visits and incorporate data regarding the reason for the visit and patient data; APGs prevent unbundling of ancillary services; *see also* **ACG** and **ADG.**[60]

API (Application program interface): 1. A set of standard software interrupts, calls, functions, and data formats that can be used by an application program to access network services, devices, applications, or operating systems. **2.** A set of pre-made functions used to build programs. APIs ask the operating system or another application to perform specific tasks. A variety of types of APIs exist, including messaging APIs for e-mail, telephony APIs for calling systems, Java APIs, and graphics APIs, such as DirectX.[2] *See* **Socket**, **SSL**.

APMs (Alternative payment models): Models that offer healthcare providers added incentive payments to deliver high-quality and cost-efficient care. APMs are outlined in MACRA as a path for participation in MACRA's Quality Payment Program (QPP). Accountable Care Organizations (ACOs), Patient Centered Medical Homes (PCMH), and bundled payment models are some examples of APMs.[26] *See* **MACRA, ACO**.

Application: A software program or set of related programs that provide some useful healthcare capability or functionality.[132]

Application architecture: Defines how applications are designed and how they cooperate; promotes common presentation standards to facilitate rapid training and implementation of new applications and functions. Good application architecture enables a high level of system integration, reuse of components, and rapid deployment of applications in response to changing business requirements.[57]

Application entity title: *See* **AE title**.

Application integration: Sometimes called *enterprise application integration* or EAI; the process of bringing data or a function from one application program together with that of another application program. Where these programs already exist, the process is sometimes realized by using middleware, either packaged by a vendor or written on a custom basis. A common challenge for an enterprise is to integrate an existing (or legacy) program with a new program or with a web service program of another company. In general, for new applications, the use of object-oriented programming and actual or de facto standard development tools and interfaces (such as Java or .NET) will help ensure that new application programs can be easily integrated with those that may be needed in the future. The Extensible Markup Language (XML) promises to serve as a tool for exchanging data among disparate programs in a standard way.[2]

Application layer: *See* **OSI**. Layer 7 of the OSI (open systems interconnection) model. Responsible for information transfer between two network applications. This involves such functions as security checks, identification of the two participants, availability checks, negotiating exchange mechanisms, and most importantly initiating the exchanges themselves.[52]

Application metadata: *See* **Metadata**.

Application program interface: *See* **API**.

Application protocol services: These are services supporting application level protocols. Simple object access protocol (SOAP) will be supported. Other remoting protocols, such as remote method invocation, DICOM, etc., can be plugged into the application protocol service.[57]

Application role: A characteristic of an application that defines a portion of its interfaces. It is defined in terms of the interactions (messages) that the role sends or receives in response to trigger events. Thus, it is a role played by a healthcare information system component when sending or receiving health information technology messages; a set of responsibilities with respect to an interaction.[9]

Application server: 1. Program on a distributed network that provides business logic and server-side execution environment for application programs. **2.** A computer that handles all operations between a company's back-end applications or databases and the users' computers' graphical user interface or web browsers. **3.** The device that facilitates the hosting and delivery of applications, used by multiple and simultaneously connected local and remote users.[2,10,52]

Appointment: An appointment represents a booked slot or group of slots on a schedule, relating to one or more services or resources. Two examples might include a patient visit scheduled at a clinic, and a reservation for a piece of equipment.[9]

Appropriate Use Criteria: *See* **AUC.**

APT (Advanced persistent threat): An adversary that possesses sophisticated levels of expertise and significant resources which allow it to create opportunities to achieve its objectives by using multiple attack vectors (e.g., cyber, physical, and deception). These objectives typically include establishing and extending footholds within the information technology infrastructure of the targeted organizations for purposes of exfiltrating information; undermining or impeding critical aspects of a mission, program, or organization; or positioning itself to carry out these objectives in the future. The advanced persistent threat: (i) pursues its objectives repeatedly over an extended period of time; (ii) adapts to defenders' efforts to resist it; and (iii) is determined to maintain the level of interaction needed to execute its objectives.[1]

Archetype: 1. A named content type specification with attribute declarations. **2.** Model (or pattern) for the capture of clinical information—a machine-readable specification of how to store patient data.[61,62]

Archetype instance: Metadata class instance of an archetype model, specifying the clinical concept and the value constraints that apply to one class of record component instances in an electronic health record extract.[63]

Archetype model: Information model of the metadata to represent the domain-specific characteristics of electronic health record entries, by specifying values or value constraints for classes and attributes in the electronic health record reference model.[63]

Archetype repository: Persistent repository of archetype definitions accessed by a client authoring tool, or by a run-time component within an electronic health record service.[63]

Architecture: 1. A term applied to both the process and the outcome of specifying the overall structure, logical components, and the logical interrelationships of a computer, its operating system, a network, or other conception. **2.** A framework from which applications, databases, and workstations can be developed in a coherent manner, and in which every part fits together without containing a mass of design details. Normally used to describe how a piece of hardware or software is constructed and which protocols and interfaces are required for communications. Network architecture specifies the function and data transmission needed to convey information across a network.[134]

Archive: Long-term, physically or digitally separate storage.[64]

Archiving: Data archiving is the process of moving data that is no longer actively used to a separate storage device for long-term retention. Archive data consists of older data that is still important to the organization and may be needed for future reference, as well as data that must be retained for regulatory compliance. Data archives are indexed and have search capabilities so files and parts of files can be easily located and retrieved.[2]

Arden syntax: A language created to encode actions within a clinical protocol into a set of situation-action rules for computer interpretation, and to facilitate exchange between different institutions.[65]

Argonaut Project: A private sector initiative to advance industry adoption of modern, open interoperability standards. The purpose of the Argonaut Project is to rapidly develop a first-generation FHIR-based API and Core Data Services specification to enable expanded information sharing for electronic health records and other health information technology based on Internet standards and architectural patterns and styles.[138]

ARI (Access to radiology information): Specifies a number of query transactions providing access to radiology information, including images and related reports, in a DICOM format, as they were acquired or created. Such access is useful, both to the radiology department and to other departments, such as pathology, surgery, and oncology.[27]

Arithmetic logic unit: *See* **ALU.**

ARP (Address Resolution Protocol): Performs a required function in IP routing. ARP finds the hardware address, also known as Media Access Control (MAC) address with its associated IP address.[2]

ARRA (American Recovery and Reinvestment Act of 2009): An economic stimulus bill enacted by the 111th United States Congress and signed into law by President Barack Obama created the Health Information Technology for Economic and Clinical Health (HITECH) Act, which provided $30 billion for various health information technology investments, including funding incentives for acute care hospitals and physicians in private practice to adopt certified EHRs.[139]

Array: A set of sequentially indexed elements having the same intrinsic data type. Each element of an array has a unique identifying index number.[68]

Artificial Intelligence: *See* **AI.**

Artificial Neuron Network: *See* **ANN.**

ASA (Average speed of answer): The average amount of time (measured in seconds) from when a caller calls customer service (enters the customer service queue) to when the caller begins speaking to a customer service associate.[155]

ASCII (American standard code for information interchange): Bit standard information processing code that represents 128 possible standard characters used by PCs. In an ASCII file, each alphabetic, numeric, or special character is represented with a 7-bit number (a string of seven 0s or 1s), which yields the 128 possible characters.[2]

ASN (Abstract syntax notation): The International Organization of Standardization (ISO), the International Electrotechnical Commission (IEC), and the International Telecommunications Union-Telecommunications Sector (ITU-T) (formerly known as the International Telegraph and Telephone Consultative Committee [CCITT]) have established Abstract Syntax Notation One (ASN.1) and its encoding rules as a standard for describing and encoding messages. ASN.1 is a formal notation for abstractly describing data to be exchanged between distributed computer systems. Encoding rules are sets of rules used to transform data specified in the ASN.1 notation into a standard format that can be decoded by any system that has a decoder based on the same set of rules.[2]

ASO (Administrative services only): Sometimes referred to as an administrative services contract (ASC); a contract between an insurance company and a self-funded plan where the insurance company performs administrative services only and does not assume any risk; services usually include claims processing but may include other services such as actuarial analysis and utilization review.[23] An arrangement in which an organization funds its own employee benefit plan such as a pension plan or health insurance program but hires an outside firm to perform specific administrative services.[18]

ASP (Active server pages): Server-side scripting environment for creating dynamic and interactive web pages and applications.[68]

Assembly services: A business request may include calls to various components providing multiple result sets. These result sets will be assembled together in the appropriate output format by the assembly service. This service will use assembly templates to carry out its function.[57]

Association: Linking a document with the program that created it so that both can be opened with a single command (e.g., double-clicking a ".doc" file opens Microsoft® Word and loads the selected document).[9]

Assurance: The grounds for confidence that the set of intended security controls in an information system are effective in their application.[1]

Asymmetric cryptographic algorithm: Algorithm for performing encryption or the corresponding decryption, in which the keys used for encryption and decryption differ.[72,170]

Asymmetric digital subscriber line: *See* **ADSL**.

Asymmetric keys: A combination of public and private keys used to encrypt and decrypt data. The public key is shared with others and the complementary private key is kept secret. The public key may be used to encrypt the data and the associated private key may be used to decrypt the data. Also known as public key cryptography.[2]

Asymmetric multiprocessing: Technique involves master-slave relationship among the processors. There is one master processor that controls remaining slave processor. The master processor allots processes to slave processor, or they may have some predefined task to perform.[69]

Asynchronous communication: Communication in which the reply is not made immediately after the message is sent, but when the recipient is available. E-mail is an example of asynchronous communication.[66]

Asynchronous transfer mode: *See* **ATM**.

ATCB (Authorized testing and certification body): An entity that tests and certifies that certain types of electronic health record (EHR) technology (base EHRs and EHR modules) are compliant with the standards, implementation specifications, and certification criteria adopted by the U.S. Department of Health & Human Services Secretary and meet the definition of certified EHR technology.[26]

ATM (Asynchronous transfer mode): A high-performance, cell-oriented, switching, and multiplexing technology that utilizes fixed-length packets to carry different types of traffic.[74] *See* **Frame relay**, **SONET**.

Atomic concept: 1. Primitive concept. **2.** Concept in a formal system whose definition is not a compositional definition.[75,76]

Atomic data (atomic level data): Data elements that represent the lowest level of possible detail in a data warehouse. The elemental, precise data captured at the source in the course of clinical care, can be manipulated in a variety of ways. These data are collected once, but used many times.[2]

Atomicity: Atomicity is a feature of database systems dictating where a transaction must be all-or-nothing. That is, the transaction must either fully happen or not happen at all. It must not complete partially. Atomicity is part of the ACID model (Atomicity, Consistency, Isolation, Durability), which is a set of principles used to guarantee the reliability of database transactions. Atomicity is usually achieved by complex mechanisms such as journaling or logging, or via operating system calls. The definition of what constitutes an atomic transaction is decided by its context or the environment in which it is being implemented.[52] *See* **ACID.**

Attachment unit interface: *See* **AUI.**

Attack vectors: Means by which an unauthorized person or entity gains access to a target (e.g., system, network, or otherwise).[2]

Attenuation: The measurement of how much a signal weakens over distance on a transmission medium. The longer the medium, the more attenuation becomes a problem without the regeneration of the signal.[2]

Attribute: An attribute expresses characteristics of a basic elemental concept. Attributes are also known as *roles* or *relationship types*. Semantic concepts form relationships to each other through attributes. Attributes are abstractions of the data captured about classes. Attributes capture separate aspects of the class and take their values independent of one another. Attributes assume data values that are passed in HL7 messages.[9,77]

Attribute authority: *See* **AA.**

Attribute certificate: 1. Data structure, digitally signed by an attribute authority, which binds some attribute values with identification about its holder. **2.** A digital document containing attributes associated to the holder by the issuer.[72]

Attribute relationship: Consists of two semantic concepts related to each other through an attribute. When an attribute-value pair has been assigned to a concept, that relationship becomes part of the concept's logical definition. For this reason, attribute relationships are called "defining characteristics" of semantic concepts.[77]

Attribute type: The last part of an attribute name (suffix). Attribute type suffixes are rough classifiers for the meaning of the attribute.[9] *See* **Data type** for contrast in definition.

Attribute-value pair: The combination of an attribute with a value that is appropriate for that attribute. Assigning attribute-value pairs to semantic concepts is known as "authoring" or "modeling" and is part of the process of semantic content development. Attributes and values are always used together as attribute-value pairs. Sometimes the entire relationship is referred to as an object-attribute-value triple, or "OAV" triple.[77]

AUC (Appropriate use criteria): Criteria that are evidence-based (to the extent feasible) and assist professionals who order and furnish applicable imaging services to make the most appropriate treatment decisions for a specific clinical condition. The AUC Program is established under CMS to promote the use of AUC for advanced diagnostic imaging services, as directed by Section 218(b) of the Protecting Access to Medicare Act of 2014 Title XVIII of the Social Security Act.[26]

Audit: Independent review and examination of records and activities to assess the adequacy of system controls; to ensure compliance with established

A

policies and operational procedures; and to recommend necessary changes in controls, policies, or procedures.[132]

Audit repository: Stores audit events.[27]

Audit trail: 1. Chronological record of system activity which enables the reconstruction of information regarding the creation, distribution, modification, and deletion of data. **2.** Documentary evidence of monitoring each operation of individuals on health information. May be comprehensive or specific to the individual and information. Audit trails are commonly used to search for unauthorized access by authorized users.[132]

Auditing: Specific activities that make up an audit. This can be manual, automated, or a combination.[20]

AUI (Attachment unit interface): The AUI (attachment unit interface) is the 15-pin physical connector interface between a computer's network interface card (NIC) and an Ethernet cable.[2]

AUP (Acceptable use policy): Provides guidance to employees and other workforce members regarding the appropriate use of a healthcare organization's information technology resources and data.[53]

Authentication: Security measure, such as the use of digital signatures, to establish the validity of a transmission, message, or originator, or a means of verifying an individual's authorization to receive specific categories of information. The process of proving that a user or system is really who or what it claims to be. It protects against the fraudulent use of a system, or the fraudulent transmission of information.[2]

Authenticity: Assurance that a message, transaction, or other exchange of information is from the source it claims to be from. Authenticity involves proof of identity.[78]

Authority certificate: Certificate issued to a certification authority or to an attribute authority. A certificate authority (CA) is a trusted entity that issues electronic documents that verify a digital entity's identity on the Internet. The electronic documents, which are called digital certificates, are an essential part of secure communication and play an important part in the public key infrastructure (PKI).[2,72]

Authorization: A security mechanism used to determine user/client privileges or access levels related to system resources, including computer programs, files, services, data, and application features. Authorization is normally preceded by authentication for user identity verification.[52]

Authorized testing and certification body: *See* **ATCB**.

Automated data processing application coordinator: *See* **ADPAC**.

Availability: Timely, reliable access to data and information services for authorized users.[1]

A

Average handling time: *See* **AHT**.
Average length of stay: *See* **ALOS**.
Average speed of answer: *See* **ASA**.
AVR (Analysis, visualization, and reporting): Ability to analyze, display, report, and map accumulated data, and share data and technologies for analysis and visualization with other public health partners.[80]

B

B2B (Business-to-business): On the Internet, B2B (business-to-business), also known as e-biz, is the exchange of products, services, or information (aka e-commerce) between businesses, rather than between businesses and consumers.[2]

B2B2C (Business-to-business-to-consumer): An emerging e-commerce model that combines business-to-business (B2B) and business-to-consumer (B2C) for a complete product or service transaction. B2B2C is a collaboration process that, in theory, creates mutually beneficial service and product delivery channels.[2]

B2C (Business-to-consumer): An Internet and electronic commerce (e-commerce) model that denotes a financial transaction or online sale between a business and consumer. B2C involves a service or product exchange from a business to a consumer, whereby merchants sell products to consumers.[2]

BA (Business associate): As set forth in 45 CFR 160.103, on behalf of such covered entity or of an organized healthcare arrangement in which the covered entity participates, but other than in the capacity of a member of the workforce of such covered entity or arrangement, creates, receives, maintains, or transmits protected health information for a HIPAA function or activity regulated by this subchapter, including claims processing or administration, data analysis, processing, or administration, utilization review, quality assurance, patient safety activities listed at 42 CFR 3.20, billing, benefit management, practice management, and repricing; or performs, or assists in the performance of: (A) A function or activity involving the use or disclosure of individually identifiable health information, including claims processing or administration, data analysis, processing or administration, utilization review, quality assurance, billing, benefit management, practice management, and repricing; or (B) Any other function or activity regulated by this subchapter; or (C) Provides, other than in the capacity of a member of the workforce of such covered entity, legal, actuarial, accounting, consulting, data aggregation, management, administrative, accreditation, or financial services to or for such covered entity, or to or for an organized healthcare arrangement in which the covered entity participates, where the provision of the service involves the disclosure of individually identifiable protected health information from such covered entity or arrangement, or from another business associate of such covered entity or arrangement, to the person.[35] *See* **Covered entity, BAA.**

B

BAA (Business associate agreement): Also known as HIPAA business associate agreement (BAA). Identified under the U.S. Health Insurance Portability and Accountability Act, a contract between a HIPAA covered entity and a HIPAA business associate (BA). The contract safeguards protected health information (PHI) in accordance with HIPAA guidelines.[2,35] *See* **Covered entity**.

Back-door: Typically, unauthorized hidden software or hardware mechanism used to circumvent security controls.[1]

Backbone: The high-speed, high-performance main transmission path in a network; a set of paths that local or regional networks connect to as a node for interconnection. The top level in a hierarchical network. Stub networks and transit networks which connect to the same backbone are guaranteed to be interconnected.[8]

Background: A task running in the background (a background task) is detached from the terminal where it was started (and often running at a lower priority); opposite of foreground. This means that the task's input and output must be from/to files (or other processes).[8]

Background process: A program that is running without user input. A number of background processes can be running on a multitasking operating system, such as Linux, while the user is interacting with the foreground process. Some background processes, such as daemons, for example, never require user input. Others are merely in the background temporarily while the user is busy with the program presently running in the foreground so that other processes can be sleeping and taking up swap space, until activated, which thus makes it currently a background process.[33]

Backup: A copy of files and programs made to facilitate recovery, if necessary.[1]

Backup domain controller: *See* **BDC**.

BAN (Body area network): The interconnection of multiple computing devices worn on, affixed to, or implanted in a person's body. A BAN typically includes a smartphone in a pocket or bag that serves as a mobile data hub, acquiring user data and transmitting it to a remote database or other system.[2]

Bandwidth: The difference between the highest and lowest frequencies of a transmission channel (the width of its allocated band of frequencies). The term is often erroneously used to mean data rate or capacity.[8]

Bar code: A printed horizontal strip of vertical bars of varying widths, groups of which represent decimal digits and are used for identifying products or parts. Bar codes are read by a bar code reader and the code is interpreted either through software or a hardware decoder.[8]

Bar code medication administration: *See* **BCMA**.

Bar coding: Using barcode symbols to identify an item. Bar coding is the most common form of automatic identification used in automatic data capture technologies. Bar codes track virtually everything: from retail goods to medical records, and machinery to human beings.[4]

Baseband: A transmission medium through which digital signals are sent without frequency shifting. In general, only one communication channel is available at any given time.[8]

Baseline: Hardware, software, and relevant documentation for an information system at a given point in time.[1]

Baseline configuration: A set of specifications for a system, or Configuration Item (CI) within a system, that has been formally reviewed and agreed on at a given point in time, and which can be changed only through change control procedures. The baseline configuration is used as a basis for future builds, releases, and/or changes.[1]

Basic input output system: *See* **BIOS.**

Batch file: A text file containing operating system commands which are executed automatically by the command-line interpreter. Batch files can be used as a simple way to combine existing commands into new commands.[60]

Batch job: A batch job in SAP (Systems, Applications, and Products) is a scheduled background program that usually runs on a regular basis without any user intervention. Batch jobs are provided with more allocated memory than the ones that are done in the foreground. They are used to process high volumes of data that would normally consume long-term memory if run in the foreground, as well as for running programs that require less user interaction.[52]

Batch processing: A system that takes a sequence (a "batch") of commands or jobs, executes them, and returns the results, all without human intervention. This contrasts with an interactive system where the user's commands and the computer's responses are interleaved during a single run.[8]

BCMA (Bar code medication administration): An inventory control system that uses barcodes to prevent human errors in the distribution of prescription medications. The goal of BCMA is to make sure that patients are receiving the correct medications at the correct time by electronically validating and documenting medication administration. The information encoded in barcodes allows for the comparison of the medication being administered with what was ordered for the patient.[2]

BCP (Business continuity plan): The documentation of a predetermined set of instructions or procedures that describe how an organization's mission/business functions will be sustained during and after a significant disruption.[1]

BEC (Business email compromise): A sophisticated scam targeting businesses working with foreign suppliers and/or businesses that regularly perform wire transfer payments.[426]

Behavioral health: *See* **BH.**

Behavioral health outcome management: *See* **BHOM.**

Behavioral Risk Factor Surveillance System: *See* **BRFSS.**

Benchmarking: Refers to testing a product or service against a reference point to quantify how much better or worse it is compared to other products. Benchmarking is the standard way of comparing one product to another. With technology in particular, benchmarking against competing products is often the only way to get an objective measure of quality. This is because many technology products increase rapidly in measures such as speed and storage size when compared to the previous version from the same company, making comparisons between the versions virtually useless.[52]

Best of breed system: The best system in its referenced niche or category. Although it performs specialized functions better than an integrated system, this type of system is limited by its specialty area. To fulfill varying requirements, organizations often use best of breed systems from separate vendors. However, maintaining multiple systems provides little cross connectivity, which creates maintenance and integration challenges.[52]

Best practice: A technique or methodology that, through experience and research, has proven to reliably lead to a desired result.[52]

Beta testing: The final stage in the testing of new software before its commercial release, conducted by testers other than its developers.[84]

BH (Behavioral health): A branch of interdisciplinary health which focuses on the reciprocal relationship between the holistic view of human behavior and the well-being of the body as a whole entity.[85]

BHOM (Behavioral health outcome management): Involves the use of behavioral health outcome measurement data to help guide and inform the treatment of each individual patient.[7]

BIA (Business impact analysis): An analysis of an information system's requirements, functions, and interdependencies used to characterize system contingency requirements and priorities in the event of a significant disruption.[1]

Big data: Any voluminous amount of structured, semi-structured, and unstructured data that can be mined for information. Big data can be characterized by the volume of data, the variety of types of data, and the velocity at which the data must be processed.[2]

Big data storage: A storage infrastructure that is designed specifically to store, manage, and retrieve massive amounts of data, or big data. Big data storage enables the storage and sorting of big data in such a way that it can easily be accessed, used, and processed by applications and services working on big data. Big data storage is also able to flexibly scale as required.[52]

Binary base two: A numeric system that only uses two digits—zero and one. Computers operate in binary, meaning they store data and perform calculations using only zeros and ones.[73]

Binding: Process of associating two related elements of information. An acknowledgment by a trusted third party that associates an entity's identity with its public key.[1]

BinHex: A Macintosh format for representing a binary file using only printable characters. The file is converted to lines of letters, numbers, and punctuation. Because BinHex files are simply text, they can be sent through most electronic mail systems and stored on most computers. However, the conversion to text makes the file larger, so it takes longer to transmit a file in BinHex format than if the file was represented some other way.[8]

Bioinformatics: The use of computer science, statistical modeling, and algorithmic processing to understand biological data.[52]

Biomedical informatics: The interdisciplinary field that studies and pursues the effective uses of biomedical data, information, and knowledge for scientific inquiry, problem-solving, and decision-making, motivated by efforts to improve human health.[175]

Biomedical Translational Research Information System: *See* **BTRIS**.

Biometric authentication: A user identity verification process that involves biological input, or the scanning or analysis of some part of the body, such as fingerprints or iris scans. Biometric authentication methods are used to protect many different kinds of systems—from logical systems facilitated through hardware access points to physical systems protected by physical barriers, such as secure facilities and protected research sites.[52]

Biometric identifier: Biologically unique data that identify a person. Under the provisions of the Health Insurance Portability, and Accountability Act, biometric identifiers are protected health information that must be held in strict confidence by healthcare agencies and professionals.[123]

Biometric system: A technological system that uses information about a person (or other biological organism) to identify that person. Biometric systems rely on specific data about unique biological traits in order to work effectively. A biometric system will involve running data through algorithms for a particular result, usually related to a positive identification of a user or other individual.[52]

Biometric verification: An identity authentication process used to confirm a claimed identity through uniquely identifiable biological traits, such as fingerprints and hand geometry. Designed to allow a user to prove his or her identity by supplying a biometric sample and associated unique identification code in order to gain access to a secure environment.[52]

Biometrics: 1. A physical or behavioral characteristic of a human being. **2.** Pertaining to the use of specific attributes that reflect unique personal characteristics, such as a fingerprint, an eye blood-vessel print, or a voice print, to validate the identity of a person. **3.** Biometrics is a technological and scientific authentication method based on biology and used in information assurance. Biometric identification authenticates secure entry, data, or access via human biological information such as DNA or finger-prints. Biometric systems include several linked components for effective functionality. The biometric system connects an event to a single person, whereas other ID forms, such as a personal identification number (PIN), may be used by anyone.[1,36,52]

BIOS (Basic input output system): A set of computer instructions in firmware which control input and output operations.[107]

BioSense Platform: At the core of CDC's National Syndromic Surveillance Program (NSSP) is its BioSense Platform. It provides public health offi-cials a common cloud-based health information system with standardized tools and procedures to rapidly collect, evaluate, share, and store infor-mation. Health officials can use the BioSense Platform to analyze and exchange syndromic data—improving their common awareness of health threats over time and across regional boundaries. They can exchange information faster and better coordinate community actions to protect the public's health. The BioSense Platform was developed through an active collaboration of CDC and other federal agencies, state and local health departments, and public health partners. The platform hosts an array of user-selected tools and has features that are continually being enhanced to reflect their needs.[80]

Biosurveillance: The process of gathering, integrating, interpreting, and com-municating essential information that might relate to disease activity and threats to human, animal, or plant health. Activities range from standard epidemiological practices to advanced technological systems, utilizing complex algorithms.[176] *See* **Surveillance.**

Bit: A contraction of the term Binary Digit. The smallest unit of information in a binary system of notation.[1]

Bitcoin: Virtual currency that has an equivalent value in real currency, or that acts as a substitute for real currency, is referred to as "convertible" virtual cur-rency. Bitcoin is one example of a convertible virtual currency. Bitcoin can be digitally traded between users and can be purchased for, or exchanged into, U.S. dollars, Euros, and other real or virtual currencies.[427]

Bit depth: The number of bits used to represent each pixel in an image, determin-ing its color or tonal range.[7]

Bitmap: A data file or structure which corresponds bit-for-bit with an image dis-played on a screen, probably in the same format as it would be stored in the display's video memory or maybe as a device independent bitmap. A bitmap is characterized by the width and height of the image in pixels and the number of bits per pixel which determines the number of shades of gray or colors it can represent. A bitmap representing a colored image (a "pixmap") will usually have pixels with between one and eight bits for each of the red, green, and blue components, though other color encod-ings are also used. The green component sometimes has more bits than the other two to cater to the human eye's greater discrimination in this component.[8]

Bits per second: *See* **BPS**.

Blacklisting: The process of the system invalidating a user ID based on the user's inappropriate actions. A blacklisted user ID cannot be used to log on to the system, even with the correct authenticator. Blacklisting and lifting of a blacklisting are both security-relevant events. A control to prevent unwanted applications and programs from gaining access to an organization's computing resources. Blacklisted users can refer to a process, application, or human user associated with an ID.[1,2]

Blanket Purchasing Agreement: *See* **BPA**.

BLE (Bluetooth low energy): A power-conserving variant of Bluetooth personal-area network technology, designed for use by Internet-connected machines and appliance.[2]

Blockchain: A technology for transactional applications that can be used to share a ledger across a business network. This ledger is the source of all transactions across the business network and is shared among all participants in a secure, encrypted environment. This technology grew out of the Bitcoin technological innovation. Blocks, or transaction records, are added to the chain in a linear, chronological order. Each node (or participant connected to the network) gets a copy of the blockchain, which gets downloaded automatically upon joining.[89,18]

Blockchain node: A device on a blockchain network, which is in essence the foundation of the technology, allowing it to function and survive. Nodes are distributed across a widespread network and carry out a variety of tasks. The role of a node is to support the network by maintaining a copy of a blockchain and, in some cases, to process transactions. Nodes are often arranged in the structure of trees, known as binary trees. Nodes are the individual parts of the larger data structure that is a blockchain.[178]

Bluetooth: A specification for radio links between mobile devices, mobile phones, digital cameras, and other portable devices.[8]

Bluetooth low energy: *See* **BLE**.

Body area network: *See* **BAN**.

Boolean logic/Boolean algebra: Form of logic seen in computer applications in which all values are expressed either as true or false. Symbols used to designate this are often called Boolean operators. They consist of equal to (=), more than (>), less than (<), and any combination of these, plus the use of "AND," "OR," and "NOT."[8]

Boot partition: Partition that contains the operating system files.[2]

Born in the cloud: Refers to a specific type of cloud service that does not involve legacy systems, but was designed only for cloud delivery. This category of cloud services is instructive in changing how companies view reliance on cloud vendors.[52]

Bot: Software that performs an automated task over the Internet. More specifically, it is an automated application used to perform simple and repetitive tasks that are time-consuming, mundane, or impossible for a human to perform. Bots are also frequently used for malicious purposes.[52]

Bounce: An electronic mail message that is undeliverable and returns an error notification (a "bounce message") to the sender is said to "bounce."[8]

Bourne shell: A shell command-line interpreter for Unix or Unix-like operating systems.[8]

BPA (Blanket purchasing agreement): A method of acquiring a variety of goods and services under an agreement when an order is issued. It is not a contract; BPAs are used by government agencies and organizations for simplifying the government purchasing process.[161]

BPM (Business process management): A systematic approach to making an organization's workflow more effective, more efficient and, more capable of adapting to an ever-changing environment.[2]

BPS (Bits per second): The basic unit of speed associated with data transmission.[2]

BRE (Business rules engine): A software component that allows non-programmers to add or change business logic in a business process management (BPM) system.[2]

Breach of security: The acquisition, access, use, or disclosure of protected health information in a manner not permitted or compromises the security or privacy of the protected health information as set forth in 45 CFR 164.402.[35]

BRFSS (Behavioral Risk Factor Surveillance System): The nation's premier system of health-related telephone surveys that collect state data about U.S. residents regarding their health-related risk behaviors, chronic health conditions, and use of preventive services. Established in 1984 with 15 states, BRFSS now collects data in all 50 states as well as the District of Columbia and three U.S. territories.[80]

Bridge: A device which forwards traffic between network segments based on data link layer information. These segments would have a common network layer address. Every network should only have one root bridge.[8]

Bridging router: *See* **Brouter.**

Bring your own cloud: *See* **BYOC.**

Bring your own device: *See* **BYOD.**

Broadband: A class of communication channels capable of supporting a wide range of frequencies, typically from audio up to video frequencies. A broadband channel can carry multiple signals by dividing the total capacity into multiple, independent bandwidth channels, where each channel operates only on a specific range of frequencies.[8]

Broadcast: A transmission to multiple, unspecified recipients. On Ethernet, a broadcast packet is a special type of multicast packet which all nodes on the network are always willing to receive.[8]

Broadcast storm: Result of the number of broadcast messages on the network reaching or surpassing the bandwidth capability of the network. A broadcast on a network that causes multiple hosts to respond by broadcasting themselves, causing the storm to grow exponentially in severity.[8]

Brouter (Bridging router): A device that bridges some packets (i.e., forwards based on data link layer information) and routes other packets (i.e., forwards based on network layer information). The bridge/route decision is based on configuration information.[8]

Browser: A program that allows a person to read hypertext. The browser gives some means of viewing the contents of nodes (or "pages") and of navigating from one node to another.[8]

Browsing: Act of searching through information system storage or active content to locate or acquire information without necessarily knowing the existence or format of information being sought.[1]

Brute force attack: In this attack, the adversary tries every possible value for a password until they succeed. A brute force attack, if feasible computationally, will always be successful because it will essentially go through all possible passwords given the alphabet used (lower case letters, upper case letters, numbers, symbols, etc.) and the maximum length of the password.[429]

BTRIS (Biomedical Translational Research Information System): A resource available to the U.S. Department of Health and Human Services' National Institutes of Health (NIH) intramural community that brings together clinical research data from the Clinical Center and other NIH Institutes and Centers. BTRIS provides clinical investigators with access to identifiable data for subjects on their own active protocols, while providing all NIH investigators with access to data without personal identifiers across all protocols. Data are available from 1976 to the present.[183]

Buffer: An area of memory used for storing messages. Typically, a buffer will have other attributes such as an input pointer (where new data will be written into the buffer), and output pointer (where the next item will be read from) and/or a count of the space used or free. Buffers are used to decouple processes so that the reader and writer may operate at different speeds or on different sized blocks of data.[8]

Bug: An unwanted and/or unintended property of a program, other software or operating system component, or piece of hardware. In addition, a bug may be an operational bug or a security bug.[8]

Bus: 1. A structure that is used for connecting processors and peripherals, either within a system or in a local area network (LAN). **2.** The internal wiring between and within the central processing unit (CPU) and other motherboard subsystems. **3.** A set of electrical conductors (wires, PCB tracks, or connections in an integrated circuit) connecting various "stations," which can be functional units in a computer or nodes in a network. A bus is a broadcast channel, meaning that each station receives every other station's transmissions and all stations have equal access to the bus.[8]

Business associate. *See* **BA.**

Business continuity plan: *See* **BCP.**

Business impact analysis: *See* **BIA.**

Business intelligence: Represents the tools and systems that play a key role in the strategic planning process of the corporation. These systems allow a company to gather, store, access, and analyze corporate data to aid in decision-making.[39] *See* **Decision support system.**

Business interruption: Anticipated interruption to normal business, functions, operations, or processes such as due to a strike or unanticipated such as due to a power failure.[4]

Business process management: *See* **BPM.**

Business rules engine: *See* **BRE.**

Business-to-business: *See* **B2B.**

Business-to-business-to-consumer: *See* **B2B2C.**

Business-to-consumer: *See* **B2C.**

BYOC (Bring your own cloud): A concept/trend in which employees are allowed to use public or private third-party cloud services to perform certain job roles. BYOC often involves the piecing together of enterprise and consumer software—both in the cloud and on the premises—to get the job done.[52]

BYOD (Bring your own device): An enterprise policy used to permit partial or full integration of user-owned mobile devices for business purposes.[52]

Byte: A component in the machine data hierarchy larger than a bit and usually smaller than a word; now nearly always eight bits and the smallest addressable unit of storage. A byte typically holds one character.[8]

C

CA (Certificate authority): An independent licensing agency that vouches for a patient/person's identity in encrypted electronic communication. Acting as a type of electronic notary public, a certified authority verifies and stores a sender's public and private encryption keys and issues a digital certificate, or seal of authenticity, to the recipient.[57] Also referred to as Certification authority.

CA (Corrective Action): Identification and elimination of the causes of a problem, thus preventing their recurrence.[4]

Cache: 1. An area of temporary computer memory storage space that is reserved for data recently read from a disk, which allows the processor to quickly retrieve it, if it is needed again. A part of random access memory (RAM). **2.** A small, fast memory holding recently accessed data, designed to speed up access.[57]

Cache server: A dedicated network server or service acting as a server that saves Web pages or other Internet content locally. By placing previously requested information in temporary storage, or cache, a cache server both speeds up access to data and reduces demand on an enterprise's bandwidth. Cache servers also allow users to access content offline, including rich media files or other documents. A cache server is sometimes called a "cache engine."[2]

CAD (Computer-aided detection): Combining elements of artificial intelligence and digital image processing with radiological image processing to assist in the interpretation of medical images. Designed to decrease observational oversights, thus reducing false negative rates.[91] Also known as computer-aided diagnosis (CADx).

CAH (Critical-access hospital): Rural community hospitals that receive cost-based reimbursement. To be designated a CAH, a rural hospital must meet defined criteria that were outlined in the Conditions of Participation 42 CFR 485 and subsequent legislative refinements to the program through the Balanced Budget Refinement Act of 1999 (BBRA), Benefits Improvement and Protection Act (BIPA, 2000), the Medicare Modernization Act, the Medicare Improvements for Patients and Providers Act (MIPPA, 2008), and the Patient Protection and Affordable Care Act (ACA, 2010).[92]

CAL (Computer-assisted learning): Any use of computers to aid or support the education or training of people. CAL can test attainment at any point, can provide faster or slower routes through the material for people of different aptitudes, and can maintain a progress record for the instructor.[56] *See* **CBL**.

Canadian Health Outcomes for Better Information and Care: *See* **C-HOBIC**.

CAP (Common alerting protocol): A digital format for exchanging emergency alerts with a single, consistent message that are simultaneously delivered over many different communications systems.[93]

CAP (Corrective action plan): A step-by-step plan of action that is developed to achieve targeted outcomes for resolution of identified errors.[4]

Capability: Conceptual elements that define what a technology can do, and are used to understand whether two types of technology are fundamentally doing the same thing and to identify duplication in a technology portfolio.[219]

Capacity: 1. The ability to run a number of jobs per unit of time. **2.** The maximum amount or number that can be received or contained.[57,44]

Capacitor: A passive electronic component that stores energy in the form of an electrostatic field.[2]

Capitation: Pre-established payment of a set dollar amount to a provider on a per member basis for certain contracted services, for a given period of time. Amount of money paid to provider depends on number of individuals registered to their patient list, not on volume or type of service provided.[46]

Capture: Input of data, not as a direct result of data entry but instead as a result of performing a different but related activity. Barcode reader equipped supermarket checkout counters, for example, capture inventory related data while recording a sale.[4]

Card reader: The generic term for an input device that reads flash memory cards. It can be a standalone device that connects to a computer via USB or it may be integrated into a computer, printer, or multifunction device. In fact, most multifunction printer/scanner/copiers now have built-in card readers.[73]

Cardiac catheterization workflow: *See* **CATH**.

Cardinality: 1. The number of rows in a table, or the number of indexed entries in a defined index. **2.** The number of elements in a set.[9] *See* **Multiplicity**.

Care coordination: The deliberate organization of patient care activities between two or more participants (including the patient) involved in a patient's care to facilitate the appropriate delivery of healthcare services. Organizing care involves the marshaling of personnel and other resources needed to carry out all required patient care activities, and is often managed by the exchange of information among participants responsible for different aspects of care.[94]

Care management: A set of activities that assures that every person served by the treatment system has a single approved care (service) plan that is coordinated, not duplicative, and designed to assure cost-effective and good outcomes. Care managers will oversee a patient's journey through treatment.[95]

Care plan: *See* **Plan of care**.

Care transitions: The various points where a patient moves to, or returns from, a particular physical location or makes contact with a healthcare professional for the purposes of receiving healthcare. This includes transitions between home, hospital, residential care settings, and consultations with different healthcare providers in out-patient facilities. Every change from provider or setting is another care transition.[184]

Carrier sense multiple access with collision detection: *See* **CSMA/CD.**

CASE (Computer-assisted software engineering): A computer-assisted method to organize and control the development of software. CASE allows developers to share a common view, allow checkpoint process, and serves as a repository.[2]

Case mix: The relative numbers of various types of patients being treated as categorized by disease-related groups, severity of illness, rate of consumption of resources, and other indicators; used as a tool for managing and planning healthcare services.[123]

CAT (Computerized axial tomography): An x-ray procedure that combines multiple x-ray images with the aid of a computer to generate cross-sectional views and, if needed, three-dimensional images of the internal organs and structures of the body.[96] Also known as CT.

Categorization: Process by which an individual information product can be associated with other products, using vocabularies designed to help individuals locate and access information. There can be multiple attributes assigned to a product (e.g., multiple categorizations). Categorization is used to provide context to a specific product, and to define relationships across a group of information products.[97] *See* **Classification.**

Cause and effect diagram: A display of the factors that are thought to affect a particular problem or system outcome. The tool is often used in a quality improvement program or in brainstorming to group people's ideas about the causes of a particular problem in an orderly way. Also known as the fishbone diagram because of the shape that it takes when illustrating the primary and secondary causes.[99]

CCC (Clinical care classification): Standardized, coded nursing terminology system that identifies the discrete elements of nursing practice. CCC provides a unique framework and coding structure for capturing the essence of patient care in all healthcare settings.[101]

CCD (Continuity of care document): An implementation guide for sharing Continuity of Care Record (CCR) patient summary data using the HL7 Version 3 Clinical Document Architecture (CDA), Release 2. CCD establishes a rich set of templates representing the typical sections of a summary record, and expresses these templates as constraints on CDA. These same templates for vital signs, family history, plan of care, and so on can then be reused in other CDA document types, establishing interoperability across a wide range of clinical use cases. CCD is an XML-based markup standard intended to specify the encoding, structure, and semantics of a patient summary clinical document for exchange, used for sharing patient summary data.[9]

C-CDA (Consolidated clinical document architecture): Implementation guide developed through joint efforts of Health Level Seven (HL7), Integrating the Healthcare Enterprise (IHE), the Health Story Project, and the Office of the National Coordinator (ONC) in order to consolidate CDA implementation guides from various Standards Development Organizations (SDOs) conflicting information. C-CDA specifies a library of templates and prescribes their use for a set of specific document types. CCD is an example of a C-CDA document template.[9] *See* **CDA, CCD.**

CCDS (Common Clinical Data Set): A set of data elements specified in 2014 and 2015 Edition EHR Certification Criteria, which focuses on the representation of clinical data during exchange. It specifies a list of data elements and the standards for expressing those data. In 2017, this data set was absorbed into the U.S. Core Data for Interoperability (USCDI).[12]

CCM (Chronic care management): The non-face-to-face services provided to Medicare beneficiaries who have multiple (two or more), significant chronic conditions.[430]

CCMM (Continuity of Care Maturity Model): A HIMSS Analytics eight stage (0-7) Maturity Model created to demonstrate the evolution of communication between clinicians in different settings, with limited or no electronic communication to an advanced, multi-organizational, knowledge-driven community of care.[10]

CCO (Chief compliance officer): Role responsible for legal processes and procedures, maintaining industry standards, and ensuring compliance with healthcare regulations.[10]

CCR (Continuity of care record): 1. A standard specification developed jointly by ASTM International, the Massachusetts Medical Society (MMS), the Healthcare Information and Management Systems Society (HIMSS), the American Academy of Family Physicians (AAFP), and the American Academy of Pediatrics (AAP). It was intended to foster and improve continuity of patient care, reduce medical errors, and assure at least a minimum standard of health information transportability when a patient is referred or transferred to, or is otherwise seen by another provider. **2.** An XML document standard for a summary of personal health information that clinicians can send when a patient is referred, and that patients can carry with them to promote continuity, quality, and safety of care.[103]

CDA (Clinical document architecture): 1. An XML-based document markup standard that specifies the structure and semantics of clinical documents for the purpose of exchange. **2.** Known previously as the patient record architecture, CDA provides an exchange model for clinical documents, such as discharge summaries and progress notes, and brings the healthcare industry closer to the realization of an electronic medical record. By leveraging the use of XML, the HL7 Reference Information Model (RIM), and coded vocabularies, the CDA makes documents both machine readable (so documents are easily parsed and processed electronically) and human readable so documents can be easily retrieved and used by the people who need them.[9,10]

CDMA (Code division multiple access): A spread spectrum technology for cellular networks. Unlike the GSM and TDMA technologies, CDMA transmits over the entire frequency range available. It does not assign a specific frequency to each user on the communications network. Because CDMA does not limit each user's frequency range, there is more bandwidth available.[73]

CDPD (Cellular digital packet data): A specification for supporting wireless access to the Internet and other public packet-switched networks. Cellular telephone and modem providers that offer CDPD support make it possible for mobile users to get access to the Internet at up to 19.2 kbps. Because CDPD is an open specification that adheres to the layered structure of the Open Systems Interconnection (OSI) model, it has the ability to be extended in the future. CDPD supports both the Internet Protocol and the ISO Connectionless Network Protocol (CLNP).[2]

CDR (Clinical data repository): 1. A structured, systematically collected store house of patient-specific clinical data. **2.** A centralized database that allows organizations to collect, store, access, and report on clinical, administrative, and financial information, collected from various applications within or across the healthcare organization that provides an open environment for accessing/viewing, managing, and reporting enterprise information.[68]

CDS (Clinical decision support): The use of automated rules based on clinical evidence to provide alerts, reminders, clinical guidelines, and other knowledge to assist users in healthcare delivery.[43]

CDS (Core Data Services): An infrastructure layer introduced by SAP for defining semantically rich data models, which are represented as CDS views. CDS allows developers to define entity types (such as orders, business partners, or products) and the semantic relationships between them, which correspond to foreign key relationships in traditional entity relationship (ER) models. CDS is defined using a SQL-based data definition language (DDL) that is based on standard SQL with some additional concepts, such as associations, which define the relationships between CDS views, and annotations, which direct the domain-specific use of CDS artifacts.[431]

CDSS (Clinical decision support system): An application that uses pre-established rules and guidelines that can be created and edited by the healthcare organization, and integrates clinical data from several sources to generate alerts and treatment suggestions.[432]

CDT (Current dental terminology): Official coding system for dentists to report professional services and procedures to third parties for payment. CDT is produced by the American Dental Association (ADA).[43]

CDW (Clinical data warehouse): Grouping of data accessible by a single data management system, possibly of diverse sources, pertaining to a health system or subsystem; and enabling secondary data analysis for questions relevant to understanding the functioning of that health system, and hence can support proper maintenance and improvement of that health system.[104]

CE (Coded element): A data type that transmits codes and the text associated with the code.[9]

CEHRT (Certified EHR technology): Technology that meets the standards and criteria for structured data, established by the U.S. Centers for Medicare and Medicaid Services (CMS) and the Office of the National Coordinator for Health Information Technology (ONC), to qualify for use in CMS Promoting Interoperability (PI) programs. CEHRT gives assurance that an EHR system or module offers the necessary technological capability, functionality, and security to help users meet the meaningful use criteria. Certification also helps healthcare providers and patients be confident that the electronic health IT products and systems they use are secure, can maintain data confidentially, and can work with other systems to share information.[26]

Cellular digital packet data: *See* **CDPD.**

CEN (European Committee for Standardization): Major provider of European standards and technical specifications. CEN is the only recognized European organization for the planning, drafting, and adoption of European standards in all areas of economic activity with the exception of electrotechnology (CENELEC) and telecommunication (ETSI).[105]

Centers for Medicare & Medicaid Services (CMS) Promoting Interoperability Programs: Programs that provide Medicare incentive payments to eligible clinicians, eligible hospitals, and critical-access hospitals (CAHs) as they adopt, implement, upgrade, or demonstrate meaningful use of certified EHR technology as well as payment adjustments for providers that fail to meet the criteria.[26]

Central processing unit: *See* **CPU** and **Microprocessor.**

Centralized computing: A type of computing architecture where all or most of the processing/computing is performed on a central server. Centralized computing enables the deployment of all of a central server's computing resources, administration and management. The central server, in turn, is responsible for delivering application logic, processing and providing computing resources (both basic and complex) to the attached client machines.[52]

CERT (Computer emergency response team): A trusted authority and team of system specialists and other professionals, who are dedicated to improving the security and resilience of computer systems and networks, and are a national asset in the field of cybersecurity.[106]

Certificate: An electronic document that allows a person, system or organization to exchange information securely in an electronic format, using public key infrastructure (PKI) to verify identity and ownership of a public key.[2] Also known as digital certificate or identity certificate. See **Public key certificate.**

Certificate Authority: *See* **CA**.

Certificate distribution: Act of publishing certificates and transferring certificates to security subjects.[72]

Certificate extension: Extension fields (known as extensions) in X.509 certificates that provide methods for associating additional attributes with users or public keys, and for managing the certification hierarchy. Note: Certificate extensions may be either critical (i.e., a certificate-using system has to reject the certificate if it encounters a critical extension it does not recognize) or noncritical (i.e., it may be ignored if the extension is not recognized).[72]

Certificate generation: Act of creating certificates.[72]

Certificate issuer: Authority trusted by one or more relying parties to create and assign certificates and which may, optionally, create the relying parties' keys.[72] Note 1: Adapted from ISO 9594-8:2001. Note 2: "Authority" in the Certificate Authority (CA) term does not imply any government authorization; it only denotes that the certificate authority is trusted. Note 3: *CA* is more widely used.

Certificate management: Procedures relating to certificates (i.e., certificate generation, certificate distribution, certificate archiving, and revocation).[72]

Certificate policy: *See* **CP**.

Certification: 1. Comprehensive evaluation of the technical and nontechnical security features of an IT system and other safeguards, made in support of the accreditation process, to establish the extent that a particular design and implementation meets a set of specified requirements. **2.** Procedure by which a third party gives assurance that all, or part of, a data processing system conforms to specified requirements. **3.** A defined process to ensure that EHR technologies meet the adopted standards, certification criteria, and other technical requirements to achieve meaningful use of those records in systems.[12,1,72]

Certification practices statement: *See* **CPS**.

Certification profile: Specification of the structure and permissible content of a certificate type.[72]

Certification revocation: Act of removing any unreliable link between a certificate and its related owner (or security subject owner) because the certificate is not trusted any more, even though it is unexpired.[72]

Certified EHR technology: *See* **CEHRT**.

Certified Health IT Product List: *See* **CHPL**.

CF (Conditional formatting/coded formatted element): 1. A tool that allows a user to apply formats to dynamically style a cell or range of cells and have that formatting change, depending on the value of the cell or the value of a formula. **2.** Coded element with formatted values data type. This data type, outlined in HL7, transmits codes and the formatted text associated with the code.[108,9]

CGI (Common gateway interface): A standard or protocol for external gateway programs to interface with information servers, such as HTTP servers. Part of the overall HTTP protocol.[73]

Chain of trust: A linked path of verification and validation to ensure SSL/TLS certificates utilize a chain of trust. The trust anchor for the digital certificate is the root certificate authority (CA). An ordered list of certificates, containing an end-user subscriber certificate and intermediate certificates that enables the receiver to verify that the sender and all intermediates certificates are trustworthy.[188]

Channel: A path for the transmission of signals between a transmitting and receiving device.[2]

Channel sharing unit/data service unit: *See* **CSU/DSU.**

CHAP (Challenge handshake authentication protocol): An authentication protocol used to log in a user to an Internet access provider.[7]

Character: A member of a set of elements that is used for representation. Organization or control of data.[36]

Character-based terminal: A type of computer terminal and system that supports only alphabetical or numeric characters, with the visual displays and "mouse"-driven, bitmap software that most systems now utilize; the opposite of graphical user interface (GUI).[7]

Characteristic: Abstraction of a property of an object or a set of objects.[75]

Check digit: Number added to a code (such as a bar code or account number) to derive a further number as a means of verifying the accuracy or validity of the code as it is printed or transmitted. A code consisting of three digits, for example, such as 135 may include 9 (sum of 1, 3, and 5) as the last digit and be communicated as 1359.[4]

Chief compliance officer: *See* **CCO.**

Chief information/informatics officer: *See* **CIO.**

Chief medical information/informatics officer: *See* **CMIO.**

Chief nursing informatics/information officer: *See* **CNIO.**

Chief security officer: *See* **CSO.**

Chief technology and innovation officer: *See* **CTIO.**

Chief technology officer: *See* **CTO.**

Child document: Subordinate to another, such as a parent document.[9]

Children's Health Insurance Program: *See* **CHIP.**

CHIP (Children's Health Insurance Program): An insurance program under the Centers for Medicare and Medicaid Services (CMS), CHIP provides low-cost health coverage to children in families that earn too much money to qualify for Medicaid. In some states, CHIP covers pregnant women. Each state offers CHIP coverage, and works closely with its state Medicaid program.[218]

C-HOBIC (Canadian Health Outcomes for Better Information and Care): Joint project between the Canadian Nurses Association (CNA) and Canada Health Infoway to begin the process of collecting standardized clinical outcomes that are reflective of nursing practice for inclusion in electronic health records.[110]

CHPL (Certified Health IT Product List): The comprehensive and authoritative listing of all certified Health Information Technology which has been successfully tested and certified by the ONC Health IT Certification program. All products listed on the CHPL have been tested by an ONC-Authorized Testing Labs (ONC-ATLs) and certified by an ONC-Authorized Certification Body (ONC-ACB) to meet criteria adopted by the U.S. Secretary of the Department of Health and Human Services (HHS).[88]

Chronic care model: Model developed by Edward Wagner and colleagues that provides a solid foundation from which healthcare teams can operate. The model has six dimensions: community resources and policies; health system organization of healthcare; patient self-management supports; delivery system redesign; decision support; and clinical information system. The ultimate goal is to have activated patients interact in a productive way with well-prepared healthcare teams. Three components that are particularly critical to this goal are adequate decision support, which includes systems that encourage providers to use evidence-based protocols; delivery system redesign, such as using group visits and same-day appointments; and use of clinical information systems, such as disease registries, which allow providers to exchange information and follow patients over time.[111]

Chronic care management: *See* **CCM.**

Chronic disease: An illness that is long-lasting or recurrent. Examples include diabetes, asthma, heart disease, kidney disease, and chronic lung disease.[111]

CHV (Consumer health vocabulary initiative): Open-access, collaborative initiative that links everyday words and phrases about health to technical terms or jargon used by healthcare professionals.[112]

CIA (Confidentiality/integrity/availability): The *CIA triad* is a model designed to guide policies for information security within an organization. The model is also sometimes referred to as the AIC triad (availability, integrity and confidentiality) to avoid confusion with the acronym for the Central Intelligence Agency. The elements of the triad are considered the three most crucial components of security.[2]

CIO (Chief information officer/chief informatics officer): Executive responsible for overseeing people, processes and technologies within a company's IT organization to ensure they deliver outcomes that support the goals of the business. The CIO plays a key leadership role in the critical strategic, technical, and management initiatives that mitigate threats and drive business growth.[142]

Cipher text: Data produced through the use of encipherment, the semantic content of which is not available.[72]

Circuit switched: A type of network in which a physical path is obtained for and dedicated to a single connection between two end points in the network for the duration of the connection.[2] *See* **Packet switching**.

CIS (Clinical information system): A system dedicated to collecting, storing, manipulating, and making available clinical information important to the delivery of healthcare. Clinical information systems may be limited in scope to a single area (e.g., lab system, ECG management system) or they may be comprehensive and cover virtually all facets of clinical information (e.g., electronic patient; the original discharge summary residing in the chart, with a copy of the report sent to the admitting physician, another copy existing on the transcriptionist's machine).[57]

CISC (Complex instruction set computer or computing): Computers designed with a full set of computer instructions that were intended to provide needed capabilities in the most efficient way. Later, it was discovered that, by reducing the full set to only the most frequently used instructions, the computer would get more work done in a shorter amount of time for most applications. Since this was called Reduced Instruction Set Computing (RISC), there was a need to have something to call full-set instruction computers, which resulted in the term CISC.[2]

Claim attachment: Any variety of hardcopy forms or electronic records needed to process a claim, in addition to the claim itself.[113]

Claim status category codes: A national administrative code set that indicates the general category of the status of healthcare claims. This code set is used in the Accredited Standards Committee (ASC) X12 248 claim status notification transaction, and is maintained by the healthcare code maintenance committee.[113]

Claim status codes: A national administrative code set that identifies the status of healthcare claims. This code set is used in the Accredited Standards Committee (ASC) X12 277 claim status notification transaction, and is maintained by the healthcare code maintenance committee.[113]

Class: A term used in programs written in the object-oriented paradigm. A blueprint, template, or set of instructions to build a specific type of object.[191]

Classification: The systematic placement of things or concepts into categories that share some common attribute, quality, or property. A classification structure is a listing of terms that depicts hierarchical structures.[192]

Clear text: *See* **Plain text**.

Client: A single term used interchangeably to refer to the user, the workstations, and the portion of the program that runs on the workstation. If the client is on a local area network (LAN), the client can share resources with another computer (server).[57]

Client application: A system entity, usually a computer process acting on behalf of a human user, which makes use of a service provided by a server.[64]

Client records: All personal information that has been collected, compiled, or created about clients, which may be maintained in one or more locations and in various forms, reports, or documents; including information that is stored or transmitted by electronic media.[13]

Client registry: The area where a patient/person's information (i.e., name, date of birth, Social Security number, health access number) is securely stored and maintained.[57]

Client/server model: A distributed communication framework of network processes among service requestors, clients, and service providers. The client-server connection is established through a network or the Internet. Web technologies and protocols built around the client-server model are include Hypertext Transfer Protocol (HTTP), Domain Name System (DNS), and Simple Mail Transfer Protocol (SMTP).[52]

Clinical algorithm: Flow charts to which a diagnostician or therapist can refer for a decision on how to manage a patient with a specific clinical program.[94]

Clinical care classification: *See* **CCC.**

Clinical data: All relevant clinical and socioeconomic data disclosed by the patient and others, as well as observations, findings, therapeutic interventions, and prognostic statements, generated by the members of the healthcare team.[195]

Clinical data repository: *See* **CDR.**

Clinical data warehouse: *See* **CDW.**

Clinical decision support: *See* **CDS.**

Clinical decision support system: *See* **CDSS.**

Clinical document architecture: *See* **CDA.**

Clinical documentation system: An application that allows clinicians to chart treatment, therapy, and/or health assessment results for a patient. This application provides the flow sheets and care plan documentation for a patient's course of therapy.[10]

Clinical informaticist: A person who evaluates clinical data, information systems, and technology relative to improving patient safety, clinical outcomes, and protocols and guidelines for clinical services. The functions are usually performed by people with clinical degrees.[10] Also known as clinical informatician.

Clinical informatics: 1. Promotes the understanding, integration, and application of information technology in healthcare settings to ensure adequate and qualified support of clinician objectives and industry best practices. **2.** The application of informatics and information technology to deliver healthcare services. Clinical informatics is concerned with information use in healthcare by clinicians. It includes a wide range of topics ranging from clinical decision support to visual images (e.g., radiological, pathological, dermatological, ophthalmological, etc.); from clinical documentation to provider order entry systems; and from system design to system implementation, adoption, and optimization issues.[53,86]

Clinical laboratory information system: *See* **LIS**.

Clinical observation: Information compiled by doctors, nurses, or other healthcare providers that documents the conditions they encounter, treatments provided and outcomes of those treatments.[197]

Clinical observation access service: *See* **COAS**.

Clinical pathway: A patient care management tool that organizes, sequences, and times the major interventions of nursing staff, physicians, and other departments for a particular case type, subset, or condition.[99]

Clinical performance measure: A method or instrument to estimate or monitor the extent to which the actions of a healthcare practitioner or provider conform to practice guidelines, medical review criteria, or standards of quality.[26]

Clinical practice guidelines: A set of systematically developed statements, usually based on scientific evidence, to assist practitioners and patient decision-making about appropriate healthcare for specific clinical circumstances.[207]

Clinical protocol: A set of rules defining a standardized treatment program or behavior in certain circumstances.[221]

Clinical Quality Language: *See* **CQL**.

Clinical quality measures: *See* **CQM**.

Clinical record: *See* **EHR**.

CMET (Common message element type): Common, reusable, standardized model fragments produced by a particular work group within HL7 that are intended to be building blocks that domains can use or include in their design. The use of CMETs can reduce the effort to produce a domain-specific design while maintaining similar content across several domains.[9]

CMIO (Chief medical information officer/chief medical informatics officer): A person that provides overall leadership in the ongoing development, implementation, advancement, and optimization of electronic information systems that impact patient care. Works in partnership with the organization's IT leadership to translate clinician requirements into specifications for clinical and research systems.[10]

CNIO (Chief nursing information officer/chief nursing informatics officer): Leads the strategy, development, and implementation of information technology to support nursing, nursing practice, and clinical applications, collaborating with the chief nursing officer on the clinical and administration decision-making process.[10]

COAS (Clinical observations access service): Standardizes access to clinical observations in multiple formats, including numerical data stored by instruments, or entered from observations.[118]

COB (Coordination of benefits): 1. The process by which a payer handles claims that may involve other insurance companies (i.e., situations in which an insured individual is covered by more than one insurance plan). **2.** Process of determining which health plan or insurance policy will pay first and/or determining the payment obligations of each health plan, medical insurance policy, or third-party resource when two or more health plans, insurance policies, or third-party resources cover the same benefits.[119,26]

Code: 1. Concept identifier that is unique within a coding system. **2.** A representation assigned to a term so that the term may more readily be electronically processed.[43,76]

Code 128: A one-dimensional bar code symbology, using four different bar widths, used in blood banking and other healthcare and non-healthcare applications.[433] *See* **ISBT 128.**

Code division multiple access: *See* **CDMA.**

Code meaning: Element within a coded set.[120]

Code set: 1. A set of elements which is mapped onto another set according to a coding scheme. **2.** Clinical or medical code sets identify medical conditions, and the procedures, services, equipment, and supplies used to deal with them. Nonclinical or nonmedical or administrative code sets identify, or characterize, entities and events in a manner that facilitates an administrative process.[36,121]

Code set maintaining organization: Under the Health Insurance Portability and Accountability Act (HIPAA), this is an organization that creates and maintains the code sets adopted by the HHS Secretary for use in the transactions for which standards are adopted.[113,121]

Code value: Result of applying a coding scheme to a code meaning.[120]

Codec (Compression/decompression): An algorithm, or specialized computer program that reduces the number of bytes consumed by large files and programs.[117]

Coded element: *See* **CE.**

Coded formatted elements: *See* **CF.**

Coded with exceptions: *See* **CWE.**

Coding: The creation of computer programming code. More generally, the act of assigning a classification to something.[52]

Coding scheme: The collection of rules that maps the elements of one set onto the elements of a second set.[36]

Coding system: Combination of a set of concepts (coded concepts), a set of code values, and at least one coding scheme mapping code values to coded concepts.[76]

Cognitive computing: Type of computing that addresses human kinds of problems that are complex, ambiguous, and uncertain. In these situations, the data are dynamic, information-rich, shifting and change frequently and can be conflicting. This type of computing allows for the synthesis of information sources, influences, contexts, and insights and allows the systems to make decisions that are the "best" for a given situation versus "right". Cognitive computing allows for the system to compute the context of a situation and make a decision based on the information available at a given time and/or place. Cognitive computing may serve as an assistant or coach for the user (e.g. Amazon Alexa) and may act autonomously in some or many problem-solving situations.[222] *See* **Artificial intelligence**.

Collect and communicate audit trails: Means to define and identify security-relevant events and the data to be collected and communicated, as determined by policy, regulation, or risk analysis.[20]

Collect/collection: The assembling of information through interviews, forms, reports, or other information sources.[20]

Collision detection: *See* **CSMA/CD**.

Command: A specific action assigned to a program to perform a specific task.[52]

Committee draft: *See* **CD**.

Common alerting protocol: *See* **CAP**.

Common Clinical Data Set: *See* **CCDS**.

Common Criteria: An international set of guidelines and specifications developed for evaluating information security products, specifically to ensure they meet an agreed-upon security standard for government deployments. Common Criteria is more formally called "Common Criteria for Information Technology Security Evaluation."[2]

Common gateway interface: *See* **CGI**.

Common message element type: *See* **CMET**.

Common object request broker architecture: *See* **CORBA**.

Common services: A type of software service that can be shared across multiple applications. These include services such as messaging, security, logging, auditing, mapping, etc. Common services are part of the health information access layer.[224]

Common vulnerabilities and exposures: *See* **CVE**.

Common weakness enumeration: *See* **CWE**.

Communication bus: Part of the health information access layer that allows applications to communicate according to standard messages and protocols.[57]

Communication network: Configuration of hardware, software, and transmission facilities for transmission and routing of data carrying signals between electronic devices.[192]

Communities of interest: Inclusive term to describe collaborative groups of users who must exchange information in pursuit of shared goals, interests, missions, or business process; and must have a shared vocabulary for the information exchanged. Communities provide an organization and maintenance construct for data.[122]

Community health information network: *See* **CHIN**.

Comparability: The ability of different parties to share precisely the same meaning for data.[43]

Compatibility: Suitability of products, processes, or services for use together under specific conditions to fulfill relevant requirements without causing unacceptable interactions.[226] *See* **Forward compatibility**.

Compiler: 1. Programs written in high-level languages are translated into assembly language or machine language by a compiler. Assembly language programs are translated into machine language by a program called an assembler. Every CPU has its own unique machine language. Programs must be rewritten or recompiled, therefore, to run on different types of computers. **2.** A software that translates a program written in a high-level programming language to a machine-language program, which can then be executed. [39,52,227] *See* **Assembler**.

Complex instruction set computer processor: *See* **CISC**.

Compliance: Adherence to those policies, procedures, guidelines, laws, regulations, and contractual arrangements to which the business process is subject.[13]

Compliance date: Under the Health Insurance Portability and Accountability Act (HIPAA), this is the date by which a covered entity must comply with a standard, an implementation specification, or a modification. This is usually 24 months after the effective date of the associated final rule for most entities; 36 months for small health plans. For future changes in the standards, the compliance date would be at least 180 days after the effective date, but can be longer for small health plans or for complex changes.[113]

Component: An object-oriented term used to describe a reusable building block of GUI applications. A software object that contains data and code. A component may or may not be visible.[2]

Component object model: Used by developers to create reusable software components, link components together to build applications, and take advantage of Windows® services.[52]

Composite message: *See* **CM**.

Comprehensive Primary Care Initiative: *See* **CPC**.

Comprehensive Primary Care Plus Initiative: *See* **CPC+**.

Compression/decompression: *See* **Codec**.

Compromise: Disclosure of information to unauthorized persons, or a violation of the security policy of a system in which unauthorized intentional or unintentional disclosure, modification, destruction, or loss of an object may have occurred.[64]

Computer-aided detection: *See* **CAD**.

Computer-assisted coding: Software solutions using natural language processing (NLP), which is an exclusive patented algorithmic software to electronically analyze entire medical charts to pre-code with both CPT procedure and ICD diagnostic nomenclatures.[53]

Computer-assisted learning: *See* **CAL.**

Computer-assisted medicine: Use of computers directly in diagnostic or therapeutic interventions (e.g., computer-assisted surgery).[123]

Computer-assisted software engineering: *See* **CASE.**

Computer emergency response team: *See* **CERT.**

Computer-on-wheels: *See* **COW.**

Computer security: The protection of data and resources from accidental or malicious acts, usually by taking appropriate actions.[36]

Computer Security Incident Response Team: *See* **CSIRT.**

Computer system: An integrated arrangement of computer hardware and software operated by users to perform prescribed tasks.[52]

Computer telephony integration: *See* **CTI.**

Computerized axial tomography: *See* **CAT.**

Computerized practitioner order entry: *See* **CPOE.**

Computing environment: The total environment in which an automated information system, network, or a component operates. The environment includes physical, administrative, and personnel procedures, as well as communication and networking relationships, with other information systems.[1]

Concentrator: Network device where networked nodes are connected. Used to divide a data channel into two or more channels of lower bandwidth.[2] *See* **Hub.**

Concept: 1. An abstraction or a general notation that may serve as a unit of thought or a theory. In terminology work, the distinction is made between a concept and the terms that reference the concept. Where the concept is identified as abstract from the language and the term is a symbol that is part of the language.[236] **2.** A clinical idea to which a unique concept has been assigned. Each concept is represented by a row in the concepts table. Concept equivalence occurs when a post-coordinated expression has the same meaning as a pre-coordinated concept or another post-coordinated expression.[77]

Concept harmonization: Activity for reducing or eliminating minor differences between two or more concepts that are closely related to each other.[236] Note: Concept harmonization is an integral part of standardization.

Concept identifier: Concept name, code, or symbol, which uniquely identifies a concept.[31]

Concept status: A field in the concepts table that specifies whether a concept is in current use. Values include "current," "duplicate," "erroneous," "ambiguous," and "limited."[77]

Concept unique identifier: *See* **CUI.**

Concepts table: A data table consisting of rows, each of which represents a concept.[77]

Concurrent versioning system: *See* **CVS**.

Conditional formatting: *See* **CF**.

Confidentiality: 1. Obligation of an entity that receives identifiable information about an individual as part of providing a service to that individual to protect that data or information; including not disclosing the identifiable information to unauthorized persons, or through unauthorized processes. **2.** A property by which information relating to an entity or party is not made available or disclosed to unauthorized individuals, entities, or processes.[20,36]

Confidentiality/integrity/availability: *See* **CIA**.

Configuration: The components that make up a computer system, including the identity of the manufacturer, model, and various peripherals; the physical arrangement of those components (what is placed and where, as in online or on premises configurations). The software settings that enable two computer components to communicate with each other.[7]

Configuration control: Process of controlling modifications to an IT system's hardware, firmware, software, and documentation to ensure the system is protected against improper modifications prior to, during, and after system implementation.[21]

Configuration management: Management of security features and assurances through control of changes made to hardware, software, firmware, documentation, test, test fixtures, and test documentation, throughout the lifecycle of the IT.[21]

Configuration manager: The individual or organization responsible for configuration control or configuration management.[21]

Configuration services: This service is used to configure an electronic health record (EHR). This includes configuration of the EHR data repository, the system, the metadata, the service components, EHR indexes, schema support, security, session, caching mechanism, etc.[57]

Conformance: The precise set of conditions for the use of options which must be implemented in a standard. There are two types of conformance: dynamic and static. Dynamic conformance requirements of a standard are all those requirements (including options) which determine the possible behavior permitted by the standard. Static conformance is a statement of what conforming implementation should be capable of doing (i.e., what is implemented).[36]

Conformance assessment process: The complete process of accomplishing all conformance testing activities necessary to enable the conformance of an implementation or system to one or more standards to be assessed.[243]

Conformance testing: Testing to determine whether a system meets some specified standard. To aid in this, many test procedures and test setups have been developed, either by the standard's maintainers or external organizations, specifically for testing conformance to standards. Conformance testing is often performed by external organizations, sometimes the standards body itself, to give greater guarantees of compliance. Products tested in such a manner are then advertised as being certified by that external organization as complying with the standard.[247]

Connected health: The use of technology to connect the various pieces of the healthcare system (people, tools, facilities, and so on) in a way that enables delivery of ongoing, virtual care as needed across a patient population.[249]

Connectivity: The process of connecting various parts of a network to one another, through the use of routers, switches and gateways.[2]

Consensus: General agreement, characterized by the absence of sustained opposition to substantial issues by any important part of the concerned interests, and by a process that involves seeking to take into account the views of all parties concerned, and to reconcile any conflicting arguments.[250]

Consensus algorithm: A process in computer science used to achieve agreement on a single data value among distributed processes or systems. Consensus algorithms are designed to achieve reliability in a network involving multiple nodes.[2]

Consensus standards: These are standards developed or adopted by consensus standards bodies, both domestic and international. Such work and the resultant standards are usually voluntary.[36]

Consent: Under the HIPAA Privacy Rule, consent is made by an individual for the covered entity to use or disclose identifiable health information for treatment, payment, and healthcare operations purposes only. This is different from consent for treatment, which many providers use and which should not be confused with the consent for use or disclosure of identifiable health information. Consent for use and/or disclosure of identifiable health information is optional under the HIPAA Privacy Rule, although it may be required by state law, and may be combined with consent for treatment unless prohibited by other law.[20]

Consent directive: The record of a healthcare consumer's privacy policy that grants or withholds consent for: one or more principals (identified entity or role); performing one or more operations (e.g., collect, access, use, disclose, amend, or delete); purposes, such as treatment, payment, operations, research, public health, quality measures, health status evaluation by third parties, or marketing; certain conditions (e.g., when unconscious); specified time period (e.g., effective and expiry dates); and certain context (e.g., in an emergency).[20]

Consenter: An author of a consent directive; and may be the healthcare consumer or patient, a delegate of the healthcare consumer (e.g., a representative with healthcare power of attorney), or a provider with legal authority to either override a healthcare consumer's consent directive, or create a directive that prevents a patient's access to protected health information (PHI) until the provider has had an opportunity to review the PHI with the patient.[20]

Consistency: The transaction takes the resources from one consistent state to another.[7] *See* **ACID**.

Consistent presentation of images: *See* **CPI**.

Consistent time: *See* **CT**.

Consumer health vocabulary initiative: *See* **CHV**.

Content profile: An Integrating the Healthcare Enterprise (IHE) content profile specifies a coordinated set of standards-based information content, exchanged between the functional components of communicating healthcare IT systems and devices. An IHE content profile specifies a specific element of content (e.g., a document) that may be conveyed through the transactions of one or more associated integration profiles.[124]

Continua Design Guidelines: Open implementation framework for authentic, end-to-end interoperability of personal connected health devices and systems. The Continua Design Guidelines are based on common international standards defined by recognized standards development organizations.[254]

Continuity: Strategic and tactical capability, preapproved by management, of an organization to plan for and respond to conditions, situations, and events in order to continue operations at an acceptable predefined level.[87]

Continuity of care document: *See* **CCD**.

Continuity of Care Maturation Model: *See* **CCMM**.

Continuity of care record: *See* **CCR**.

Continuity strategy: Approach by an organization intended to ensure continuity and ability to recover in the face of a disruptive event, emergency, crisis, or other major outage.[87]

Control: Means of managing risk, including policies, procedures, guidelines, practices, or organizational structures, which can be of an administrative, technical, management, or legal nature.[125]

Control chart: A graphic display of the results of a process over time and against established control limits. The dispersion of data points on the chart is used to determine whether the process is performing within prescribed limits, and whether variations taking place are random or systematic.[98]

Control unit: *See* **CU**.

Controlled medical vocabulary: An approved list of terms coded in a fashion that facilitates the use of the computer. Controlled vocabularies are essential if clinical applications are to function as intended. Widely used systems include the American College of Radiology (ACR) Code, Current Procedural Terminology (CPT), Diagnostic and Statistical Manual of Mental Disorders (DSM-IV), and the International Classification of Diseases, Ninth Revision (ICD-9).[142]

Convergence: The end point of any algorithm that uses iteration or recursion to guide a series of data processing steps. An algorithm is usually said to have reached convergence when the difference between the computed and observed steps falls below a predefined threshold.[127]

Cookies: A small amount of data generated by a web site and saved to the web browser or in another location. The purpose is to remember information about the web session, similar to a preference file created by a software application. This data may be persistent or temporary.[73]

Coordination of benefits: *See* **COB.**

Coprocessor: A supplementary processor unit or an entirely different circuitry that is designed to complement the central processing unit (CPU) of a computer. Its basic functionality is to offload other processor-intensive tasks from the CPU in order to achieve accelerated system performance, by allowing the CPU to focus on tasks essential to the system.[52]

CORBA (Common object request broker architecture): A standard developed by the Object Management Group (OMG) to provide interoperability among distributed objects. It is a design specification for an Object Request Broker (ORB), where an ORB provides the mechanism required for distributed objects to communicate with one another, whether locally or on remote devices, written in different languages, or at different locations on a network.[256]

Core-based statistical area: *See* **CBSA.**

Core Data Services: *See* **CDS.**

Corporate executives or C-level: *See* **CxO.**

Corrective action plan: *See* **CAP.**

Cost-benefit analysis: A comparison of the costs of a proposed course of action with its benefits, considering tangible and intangible economic impacts, and the time value of money.[50]

Cost containment: The process of planning in order to keep costs within certain constraints.[4]

Cost-effectiveness: A system contributing to cost savings in healthcare by efficiently collecting, storing, and aggregating data; and by providing decision support and augmented practices with appropriate and timely information.[4]

Countermeasure response administration: *See* **CRA.**

Covered entity: Health plans, healthcare clearinghouses, and healthcare providers who transmit any health information in electronic form, in connection with a transaction that is subject to Health Insurance Portability and Accountability Act (HIPAA) requirements, as those terms are defined and used in the HIPAA regulations, 45 CFR Parts 160 and 164.[261]

Covered function: Functions that make an entity a health plan, a healthcare provider, or a healthcare clearing house.[113]

COW (Computer-on-wheels): Allows a single computer to operate in multiple places around the hospital or other healthcare setting. This method is used to save space as there is minimal space to accommodate a computer in every patient room.[128]

CP (Certificate policy): Named set of rules that indicates the applicability of a certificate to a particular community and/or class of application with common security requirements.[72,266]

CPC (Comprehensive Primary Care Initiative): A four-year multi-payer Centers for Medicare and Medicaid Services (CMS) initiative designed to strengthen primary care. CMS collaborates with commercial and State health insurance plans in U.S. regions to offer population-based care management fees and shared savings opportunities to participating primary care practices to support the provision of a core set of five "Comprehensive" primary care functions. These five functions are: (1) Risk-stratified Care Management; (2) Access and Continuity; (3) Planned Care for Chronic Conditions and Preventive Care; (4) Patient and Caregiver Engagement; (5) Coordination of Care across the Medical Neighborhood. CPC serves as the foundation for Comprehensive Primary Care Plus (CPC+). *See* **CPC+.**[26]

CPC+ (Comprehensive Primary Care Plus Initiative): A five-year advanced primary care medical home model launched in January 2017. CPC+ integrates many lessons learned from CPC, including insights on practice readiness, the progression of care delivery redesign, actionable performance-based incentives, necessary health information technology, and claims data sharing with practices. *See* **CPC.**[26]

CPOE (Computerized practitioner order entry): 1. An order entry application specifically designed to assist practitioners in creating and managing medical orders for patient services and medications. This application has special electronic signature, workflow, and rules engine functions that reduce or eliminate medical errors associated with practitioner ordering processes. **2.** A computer application that accepts the provider's orders for diagnostic and treatment services electronically, instead of the clinician recording them on an order sheet or prescription pad.[10] Also known as computerized physician order entry, computerized patient order entry, and computerized provider order entry.

CPR (Computer-based patient record): *See* **EHR.**

CPRS (Computer-based patient record system): *See* **EHR.**

CPS (Certification practices statement): Statement of the practices that a certification authority employs in issuing certificates.[72]

CPT (Current procedural terminology): 1. The official coding system for physicians to report professional services and procedures to third parties for payment. It is published by the American Medical Association.[46] **2.** A medical code set, maintained and copyrighted by the AMA, that has been selected for use under HIPAA for non-institutional and non-dental professional transactions.[43,121,267]

CPU (Central processing unit): Main system board (motherboard) integrated chip that directs computer operations. The component in a digital computer that interprets and executes the instructions and data contained in software. Microprocessors are CPUs that are manufactured on integrated circuits, often as a single-chip package. Performs the arithmetic, logic, and controls operations in the computer.[268]

CQL (Clinical Quality Language): A Health Level Seven International (HL7) authoring language standard that's intended to be human readable. It is part of the effort to harmonize standards used for electronic clinical quality measures (eCQMs) and clinical decision support (CDS). CQL provides the ability to express logic that is human readable yet structured enough for processing a query electronically.[88]

CQM (Clinical quality measures): Tools that measure and track the quality of healthcare services provided by eligible clinicians, eligible hospitals, and critical-access hospitals (CAHs) within the U.S. healthcare system.[26]

CRA (Countermeasure response administration): Systems that manage and track measures taken to contain an outbreak or event, and to provide protection against a possible outbreak or event. This public health information network (PHIN) functional area also includes multiple dose delivery of countermeasures: anthrax vaccine and antibiotics; adverse events monitoring; follow-up of patients; isolation and quarantine; and links to distribution vehicles (such as the Strategic National Stockpile).[80]

Crash: An event wherein the operating system or computer application stops functioning properly. It typically occurs when hardware fails in a non-recoverable fashion, operating system data is corrupted or recovery from an error is not possible without loss of data. An application crash can result in an unexpected exit from the applications whereas a system crash can result in the freezing of the computer.[52]

Crawler: *See* **Web crawler.**

Credential: Evidence attesting to one's right to credit or authority; in this standard, the data elements associated with an individual that authoritatively binds an identity (and, optionally, additional attributes) to that individual.[64]

Crisis management team: Group of individuals functionally responsible for directing the development and execution of the response and operational continuity plan, declaring an operational disruption or emergency/crisis situation, and providing direction during the recovery process, both pre- and post-disruptive incident. The crisis management team may include individuals from the organization, as well as immediate and first responders, stakeholders, and other interested parties.[87]

Critical-access hospital: *See* **CAH.**

Critical path: A tool that supports collaborative, coordinated practices. It provides for multidisciplinary communication, treatment and care planning, and documentation of caregiver's evaluations and assessments.[50]

Criticality assessment: A process designed to systematically identify and evaluate an organization's assets based on the importance of its mission or function, the group of people at risk, or the significance of a disruption on the continuity of the organization.[87] *See* **Risk assessment.**

CRM (Customer relationship management): 1. A computerized system for identifying, targeting, acquiring, and retaining the best mix of customers. **2.** In healthcare, CRM is an organization-wide strategy for managing an organization's interactions with its patients and their supporting infrastructure, suppliers, providers, and/or employees using CRM technologies. IT seeks to optimize the way we establish and nurture meaningful and sustainable relationships in efforts to enhance patient experience, improve population health, reduce costs and improve the work life of healthcare providers - ultimately leading to increased trust in and loyalty to the organization.[4,53]

Cross-enterprise document sharing: *See* **XDS**.

Cross map: A reference from one concept in one terminology to another in a different terminology. A concept may have a single cross map or a set of alternative cross maps.[77]

Cross-platform: A product or system that can work across multiple types of platforms or operating environments. Different kinds of cross-platform systems include both hardware and software systems, as well as systems that involve separate builds for each platform, as well as other broader systems that are designed to work the same way across multiple platforms.[52]

Crosstalk: A disturbance caused by the electric or magnetic fields of one telecommunication signal affecting a signal in an adjacent circuit.[2]

Crosswalk: *See* **Data mapping**.

CRUD (Create, read, update, and delete): The basic processes that are applied to data.[2,60]

Cryptocurrency: *See* **Bitcoin**.

Cryptographic algorithm cipher: Method for the transformation of data in order to hide its information content, prevent its undetected modification, and/or prevent its unauthorized use.[72]

Cryptography: The act of creating written or generated codes that allow information to be kept secret. Cryptography converts data into a format that is unreadable for an unauthorized user, allowing it to be transmitted without unauthorized entities decoding it back into a readable format, thus compromising the data.[52]

CSIRT (Computer Security Incident Response Team): *See* **CERT**.

CSMA/CD (Carrier sense multiple access with collision detection): 1. A network control protocol in which a carrier-sensing scheme is used; and a transmitting data station that detects another signal while transmitting a frame stops transmitting that frame, transmits a jam signal, and then waits for a random time interval (known as "backoff delay" and determined using the truncated binary exponential backoff algorithm) before trying to send that frame again. Ethernet is the classic CSMA/CD protocol. **2.** A protocol for carrier transmission access in Ethernet networks. On Ethernet, any device can try to send a frame at any time. Each device senses whether the line is idle and therefore available to be used. If it is, the device begins to transmit its first frame. If another device has tried to send at the same time, a collision is said to occur and the frames are discarded. Each device then waits a random amount of time and retries until successful in getting its transmission sent.[2,7]

CSO (Chief security officer): The person in an organization with the responsibility for the security of the paper-based and electronic information, as well as the physical and electronic means of managing and storing that information.[129]

CSU/DSU (Channel sharing unit/data service unit): A channel service unit (CSU) is a device that connects a terminal to a digital line. A data service unit (DSU) is a device that performs protective and diagnostic functions for a telecommunications line. Typically, the two devices are packaged as a single unit, CSU/DSU.[89]

CTI (Computer telephony integration): Systems that enable a computer to act as a call center, accepting incoming calls and routing them to the appropriate device or person.[2]

CTIO (Chief technology and innovation officer): A person in a company who is primarily responsible for managing the process of innovation and change management in an organization, as well as being in some cases the person who originates new ideas and/or recognizes innovative ideas generated by others.[7]

CTO (Chief technology officer): 1. Executive with overall responsibility for managing technical vendor relationships and performance, as well as the physical and personnel technology infrastructure, including technology deployment, network and systems management, integration testing, and developing technical operations personnel. **2.** Develops technical standards and ensures compatibility for the enterprise-wide computer environment.[10]

CTS (Common terminology services): Specification developed as an alternative to a common data structure.[9]

CU (Control unit): Portion of the CPU that handles all processor control signals. It directs all input and output flow, fetches code for instructions from microprograms and directs other units and models by providing control and timing signals.[52]

CUI (Concept unique identifier): An identifier leveraged by the Unified Medical Language System (UMLS) to uniquely represent a meaning or sense.[269]

Cure letter: A letter sent by one party to another, proposing or agreeing to actions that a party will take to correct legal errors or defects that have occurred under a contract between the parties or other legal requirement.[13]

Current procedural terminology: *See* **CPT.**

Custom, customized: Software that is designed or modified for a specific user or organization; may refer to all or part of a system.[7]

Customer-centric: Placing the customer at the center or focus of design or service.[4]

Customer-driven: Strategies, offerings, or systems focused on user acceptance; focused on customer demands or requirements.[4]

Customer relationship management: *See* **CRM.**

CVE (Common vulnerabilities and exposures): A list of standardized names for vulnerabilities and other information security exposures. CVE aims to standardize the names for all publicly known vulnerabilities and security exposures.[24]

CVS (Concurrent versioning system): Keeps track of all work and changes in a set of files.[7]

CWE (Coded with exceptions): Specifies a coded element and its associated detail. The CWE data type is used (1) when more than one table may be applicable or (2) when the specified HL7 or externally defined table may be extended with local values or (3) when the text is in place, the code may be omitted.[130]

CWE (Common weakness enumeration): A community-developed formal list of software weaknesses, idiosyncrasies, faults, and flaws.[24]

CxO (Corporate executives or C-level or C-Suite): A short way to refer, collectively, to corporate executives at what is sometimes called the C-level, whose job titles typically start with "Chief" and end with "Officer."[2]

Cyberattack: An attack, via cyberspace, targeting an enterprise's use of cyberspace for the purpose of disrupting, disabling, destroying, or maliciously controlling a computing environment/infrastructure; or destroying the integrity of the data or stealing controlled information.[1]

Cybersecurity: The practice of keeping computers and electronic information safe and secure by preventing, detecting, and responding to attacks or unauthorized access against a computer system and its information.[12]

Cyberspace: The realm of communications and computation. A term used to refer to the electronic or virtual universe of information.[73]

D

DaaS (Data as a service): A cloud strategy used to facilitate the accessibility of business-critical data in a well-timed, protected, and affordable manner. DaaS depends on the principle that specified, useful data can be supplied to users on demand, irrespective of any organizational or geographical separation between consumers and providers.[52]

Daemon: A long-running background process that answers requests for services. The term originated with Unix, but most operating systems use daemons in some form or another. In Unix, the names of daemons conventionally end in "d". Some examples include inetd, httpd, nfsd, sshd, named, and lpd.[435]

DAF (Data access framework): HL7 initiative that identifies and recommends standards for the interoperable representation and transmission of data using the notion of a Query Stack which modularizes the various layers of the Data Access Framework. The DAF FHIR Implementation Guide provides requirements and implementation guidance for the various layers of the DAF Query Stack which includes: Queries including structure, vocabularies, and value sets; Query Results including structure, vocabularies, and value sets; Transport Requirements; and Security and Privacy controls required for data access.[9]

DAG (Directed Acyclic Graph): In mathematics, a graph that travels in one direction without cycles connecting the other edges, meaning that it is impossible to traverse the entire graph by starting at one edge. It is a form of distributed ledger technology in which transactions are represented as a node in a graph. These transactions are "directed" (the links point in the same direction) and "acyclic" (a transaction cannot loop back on itself after linking to another transaction).[436]

DApp (Decentralized application): Application that runs on a P2P (peer-to-peer) network of computers rather than a single computer. A type of software program designed to exist on the Internet in a way that is not controlled by a single entity. DApps can be defined by four characteristics: decentralized (all records of operation and app transactions are stored on a public ledger, and run on blockchain or blockchain-like cryptographic networks with no central server or network hierarchy); incentivized (consists of a reward system to encourage network nodes to participate and collectively perform the duties of a central server); open source (source codes are available to the public); and consensus mechanism (a working protocol is required for achieving the consensus with the DApp blockchain. Any and every decision within the DApp is subject to such a protocol and it is usually implemented in the form of cryptographic hashing protocol).[270,271] Also known as dApp, Dapp.

DAM (Domain analysis model): An abstract representation of a subject area of interest, complete enough to allow instantiation of all necessary concrete classes needed to develop child design artifacts.[9]

Dashboard: A user interface or web page that gives a current summary, usually in graphic, easy-to-read form, of key information relating to progress and performance, especially of a business or website.[44]

Data: 1. Factual information used as a basis for reasoning, discussion, or calculation. **2.** Discrete entities that are described objectively without interpretation.[2,29]

Data access: Refers to a user's ability to access or retrieve data stored within a database or other repository. Users who have data access can store, retrieve, move, or manipulate stored data, which can be stored on a wide range of hard drives and external devices.[2]

Data access framework: *See* **DAF**.

Data aggregation: 1. A process by which information is collected, manipulated, and expressed in summary form. **2.** Combining protected health information by a business associate, on behalf of more covered entities than one, to permit data analysis related to the healthcare operations of the participating covered entities.[20,131]

Data analytics: The systematic use of data to drive fact-based decision-making for planning, management, measurement, and learning. Analytics may be descriptive, predictive, or prescriptive. In healthcare, data analytics is being used to drive clinical and operational improvements to meet business challenges. Data analytics focuses on inference, the process of deriving a conclusion based solely on what is already known by the researcher.[89] *See* **Analytics**.

Data architecture: A set of rules, policies, standards, and models that govern and define the type of data collected and how data are used, stored, managed, and integrated within an organization and its database systems. It provides a formal approach to creating and managing the flow of data and how data are processed across an organization's IT systems and applications.[2]

Data as a service: *See* **DaaS**.

Data capture: The retrieval of information from a document using methods other than data entry. The utility of data capture is the ability to automate this information retrieval where data entry would be inefficient, costly, or inapplicable.[133]

Data center: 1. A centralized repository, either physical or virtual, for the storage, management, and dissemination of data and information organized around a particular body of knowledge or pertaining to a particular business. **2.** Computer facility designed for continuous use by several users, and well-equipped with hardware, software, peripherals, power conditioning, backup, communication equipment, security systems, etc.[2,4]

Data circuit-terminating equipment: *See* **DCE**.

Data classification: Conscious decision to assign a level of sensitivity to data as they are being created, amended, enhanced, stored, or transmitted. The classification of the data, whether established by federal or state law or by the entity holding the data, will determine the extent the data need to be protected, controlled, and/or secured, and is indicative of its value in terms of information assets.[20]

Data cleaning/cleansing: Also known as data scrubbing. A process of amending or removing data that are incorrect, incomplete, improperly formatted, or duplicated.[2]

Data collection: A systematic approach to gathering information from a variety of sources to get a complete and accurate picture of an area of interest.[2]

Data compression: A reduction in the number of bits needed to represent data. Compressing data can save storage capacity, speed file transfer, and decrease costs for storage hardware and network bandwidth.[2]

Data condition: The rule that describes the circumstances under which a covered entity must use a particular data element or segment.[20]

Data content: All the data elements and code sets inherent to a transaction, and not related to the format of the transaction.[113]

Data corruption: A deliberate or accidental violation of data integrity.[1]

Data definition language: *See* **DDL**.

Data dictionary: A collection of descriptions of the data objects or items in a data model for the benefit of programmers and others who need to refer to them.[2]

Data diddling: Unauthorized data alteration; also known as tampering or false data entry.[253]

Data element: 1. The smallest named unit of information in a transaction or database. **2.** A unit of data for which the definition, identification, representation, and permissible values are specified by means of a set of attributes.[36,113]

Data elements for emergency department systems: *See* **DEEDS**.

Data entry: Direct input of data in the appropriate data fields of a database, through the use of a human data-input device such as a keyboard, mouse, stylus, or touch screen, or through speech recognition software. *See* **Data capture** and **Data logging**.[4]

Data exchange: The sharing of data between systems, organizations and individuals. During this process, the information content or meaning assigned to the data is not altered during transmission.[2]

Data field: In the structure of a database, the smallest component under which data is entered through data capture or data entry. All data fields in the same database have unique names, several data fields make up a data record, several data records make up a data file, and several data files make up a database.[4]

Data flow diagram: *See* **DFD**.

Data governance: The overall management of the availability, usability, integrity, and security of the data employed in an enterprise. A sound data governance program includes a governing body or council, a defined set of procedures, and a plan to execute those procedures.[2]

Data granularity: *See* **Granularity**.

Data integration: A process in which heterogeneous data are retrieved and combined as an incorporated form and structure. Data integration allows different data types (such as data sets, documents, and tables) to be merged by users, organizations, and applications, for use as personal or business processes and/or functions.[52]

Data integrity: 1. Assurance of the accuracy, correctness, or validity of data, using a set of validation criteria against which data are compared or screened. **2.** The property that data have not been altered or destroyed in an unauthorized manner or by authorized users; it is a security principle that protects information from being modified or otherwise corrupted, either maliciously or accidentally.[43,50]

Data interchange: The process of transferring data from an originating system to a receiving system.[52] *See* **EDI**.

Data leakage: The unauthorized transfer of classified, sensitive, proprietary, or otherwise private information from a computer, device or datacenter to the outside world.[150]

Data linkage: The merging of information from two or more sources of data with the object of consolidating facts.[434]

Data link layer: Second layer in the Open Systems Interconnection (OSI) architecture model. It is the protocol layer in a program that handles the moving of data into and out of a physical link in a network. Consists of logical link control (LLC) and media access control (MAC) sublayers. Handles data flow control, the packaging of raw data in its frames, or frames into raw data bits, and retransmits frames as needed.[2]

Data logging: The process of using a computer to collect data through sensors, analyze the data and save and output the results of the collection and analysis. Data logging also implies the control of how the computer collects and analyzes the data.[39]

Data manipulation language: *See* **DML**.

Data mapping: A process used in data warehousing by which different data models are linked to each other using a defined set of methods to characterize the data in a specific definition. This data linking follows a set of standards, which depends on the domain value of the data model used.[52]

Data mart: 1. A repository of data that serves a particular community of knowledge workers. The data may come from an enterprise-wide database or a data warehouse. **2.** Collection of data focusing on a specific topic or organization unit or department created to facilitate strategic business decisions. **3.** The access layer of the data warehouse environment that is used to get data out to users. It is a subset of the data warehouse, usually oriented to a specific business line or team.[2,136,7]

Data messaging: *See* **Messaging**.

Data migration: The process of transferring data between data storage systems, data formats, or computer systems.[2]

Data mining: The process of finding anomalies, patterns, and correlations within large data sets to predict outcomes and solve outcomes through data analysis.[2,116]

Data model: 1. A conceptual model of the information needed to support a business function or process. **2.** Describes the organization of data in an automated system. The data model includes the subjects of interest in the system (or entities) and the attributes (data elements) of those entities. It defines how the entities are related to each other (cardinality) and establishes the identifiers needed to relate entities to each other. A data model can be expressed as a conceptual, logical, or physical model.[57,113]

Data modeling: A method used to define and analyze data requirements needed to support the business functions of an enterprise. Data modeling defines the data elements, their relationships, and their physical structure in preparation for creating a database.[7]

Data object: A collection of data that has a natural grouping and may be identified as a complete entity.[120]

Data origin authentication: Corroboration that the source of data is received as is claimed.[1]

Data originator: The person, organization, or system who generates data, such as the patient for symptoms, the physician for examination and decisions, the nurse for patient care, medical devices, EHRs, etc.[41]

Data processing: The converting of raw data to machine-readable form and its subsequent processing (as storing, updating, rearranging, or printing out) by a computer.[29]

Data provenance: 1. The ability to trace and verify the creation of data, how it has been used or moved among different databases, as well as altered throughout its lifecycle. **2.** Information about the source of the data and processing/transitions the data has undergone.[137,12]

Data quality: 1. Perception or assessment of data's ability to serve its purpose in a given context, determined by factors such as accuracy, completeness, reliability, relevance, and how up to date it is. **2.** The features and characteristics that ensure data are accurate, complete, and convey the intended meaning.[2,43]

Data registry: An information resource by a registration authority that describes the meaning and representational form (metadata) of data units, including data element identifiers, definitions, units, allowed value domains, etc. HIPAA's standards for electronic transactions call for a master data dictionary to be developed and maintained to ensure common data definitions across standards selected for implementation.[43]

Data repository: *See* **Repository** and **Data warehouse.**

Data segmentation for privacy: *See* **DS4P.**

Data service unit: *See* **DSU.**

Data set: A collection of discrete items of related data that may be accessed individually or in combination or managed as a whole entity such as Uniform Hospital Discharge Data Set (UHDDS). Analyzing data sets during data mining can discover patterns and use those patterns to forecast or predict the likelihood of future events.[2,52] *See* **PNDS, NMDS**, and **NMMDS.**

Data standards: Consensual specifications for the representation of data from different sources and settings; necessary for the sharing, portability, and reusability of data.[140]

Data structure: Interrelationships among data elements that determine how data are recorded, manipulated, stored, and presented by a database.[4]

Data subject: The person whose information is collected, stored or processed.[272]

Data synchronization: The process of maintaining the consistency and uniformity of data instances across all consuming applications and storing devices. It ensures that the same copy or version of data is used in all devices—from source to destination.[52]

Data tagging: A formatted word that represents a wrapper for a stored value. The data tag is a small piece of scripting code, typically JavaScript, which transmits page-specific information via query string parameters. The process begins when a page containing a data tag is requested from the server. The tag is a piece of scripting code executed when the page is loaded into the browser. The data tag constructs the query string by scanning the document source for HTML, beginning with a specific identifier.[141]

Data terminal ready: *See* **DTR.**

Data transformation: The process of converting data or information from one format to another, usually from the format of a source system into the required format of a new destination system. The usual process involves converting documents, but data conversions sometimes involve the conversion of a program from one computer language to another to enable the program to run on a different platform. The usual reason for this data migration is the adoption of a new system that is totally different from the previous one.[52]

Data type: 1. A category of data. The broadest data types are alphanumeric and numeric. Programming languages allow for the creation of several data types, such as integer (whole numbers), floating point, date, string (text), logical (true/false), and binary. Data type usually specifies the range of values, how the values are processed by the computer, and how the data type is stored. **2.** The categories of data that will be persisted in the EHR.

They include voice, waveforms, clinical notes, and summaries, diagnostic imaging, lab, and pharmacy information.[273,57]

Data use agreement: *See* **DUA.**

Data validation: A process used to determine if data are accurate, complete, or meet specified criteria. Data validation may include format checks, check key tests, reasonableness checks, and limit checks.[36]

Data visualization: The presentation of data in a pictorial or graphical format. It enables decision makers to see analytics presented visually, so they can grasp difficult concepts or identify new patterns or trends.[116]

Data warehouse: 1. A central repository where historical and current data from disparate sources (clinical, administrative, and financial) are stored together for later retrieval within an enterprise. Data warehouses are used for creating analytical reports for knowledge workers throughout an enterprise.[10]

Database: 1. A collection of information that is organized to be easily accessed, managed, and updated. The basic database contains fields, records, and files; a field is a single piece of information, a record is one complete set of fields, and a file is a collection of records.[2]

Database administrator: *See* **DBA.**

Database design: This includes logical (entity relationship) and physical (table, column, and key) design tools for data. Physical data modeling is becoming almost mandatory for applications using relational database management systems (RDBMSs).[142]

Database management system: *See* **DBMS.**

Database schema: The organization of data as a blueprint of how the database is constructed (divided into database tables in the case of relational databases).[10]

Datum: Any single observation or fact. A medical datum generally can be regarded as the value of a specific parameter (e.g., a patient, at a specific time).[274]

Daughterboard: A circuit board that attaches to another board, such as the motherboard or an expansion card.[2]

DaVinci Project: Initiative working to accelerate the adoption of HL7 Fast Healthcare Interoperability Resources (FHIR) as the standard to support and integrate value-based care (VBC) data exchange across communities. Initial use cases focus on exchange between payer and provider trading partners.[9]

DBA (Database administrator): The person responsible for the creation, maintenance, backup, querying, security, and user rights assignment of a database system.[52]

DBMS (Database management system): 1. A program that lets one or more computer users create and access data in a database. On personal computers, Microsoft® Access® is a popular example of a single or small group user DBMS. Microsoft's SQL server is an example of a DBMS that serves database requests from a larger number of users. **2.** A set of programs used to define, administer, store, modify, process, and extract information from a database.[10]

DCM (Detailed clinical models): An information model designed to express one or more clinical concept(s) and their context in a standardized and reusable manner, specifying the requirements for clinical information as a discrete set of logical clinical data elements.[70]

DCM (Dynamic case management): The handling of case-related work through the use of technologies that automate and streamline aspects of each case. In this context, a case is a collection of information about a particular instance of something, such as a person, company, incident, or problem.[2]

DDI (Design, develop, implement): A team-based learning design process that is activity based, iterative, forward-looking, and grounded in everyday educational practices. The DDI process is situated in a supported social learning environment—a "habitat"—providing program teams the space and time to explicitly integrate the language, practice and tools for learning design with access to expertise required for that context. The program teams collaborate to develop design patterns that work with what is practical in context, rather than on a theoretical view of what could be effective in theory in the future.[275]

DDL (Data definition language): A language used to define data structures and modify data. For example, DDL commands can be used to add, remove, or modify tables within a database. DDLs used in database applications are considered a subset of SQL, the Structured Query Language. However, a DDL may also define other types of data, such as XML.[73] Also known as data description language.

Debugging: The process of discovering and eliminating abnormalities errors and defects, or bugs, in program code.[52]

Decision support (analytics): Recommendations for intervention based on computerized care protocols.[48]

Decision support system: *See* **DSS**.

Decision tree: A schematic, tree-shaped diagram used to determine a course of action or show a statistical probability. Each branch represents a possible decision, occurrence of reaction.[18]

Decompression: The expansion of compressed image files.[2] *See* **Lossless compression** and **Lossy**.

Decryption: The process of transforming encrypted data back to its original, unencrypted form. A system of extracting and converting garbled data and transforming them to text and/or images that are human and/or machine readable.[52]

Dedicated line: A telephone or data line that is always available. This line is not used by other computers or individuals, is available 24 hours a day, and is never disconnected.[276]

DEEDS (Data elements for emergency department systems): The recommended data set for use in emergency departments; it is published by the Centers for Disease Control and Prevention (CDC). Subsequently Health Level Seven (HL7) Data Elements for Emergency Department Systems (DEEDS) was created to improve interoperability of emergency care data.[80,9]

Deep learning: An area of machine learning research, introduced with the objective of moving machine learning closer to one of its original goals of artificial intelligence.[277]

Default gateway: An access point or IP router that a networked computer uses to send information to a computer in another network or the Internet. Default simply means that this gateway is used by default, unless an application specifies another gateway.[52] *See* **Gateway**.

Default route: The route that takes effect when no other route is available for an IP destination address.[278]

Definition: Statement that describes a concept and permits differentiation from other concepts within a system.[36]

Degaussing: Exposure to high magnetic fields. One method of destroying data on a hard drive, USB thumb drive, smartphone, or floppy disk. Also commonly used to improve the picture resolution on electronic displays. Many display manufacturers include an internal coil that will degauss the display when it is turned on. Display monitors and televisions with cathode ray tube (CRT) technology are particularly subject to the buildup of magnetic fields.[2]

De-identified health information: Removal of individual identifiers so that the corresponding information cannot be used to identify an individual. De-identified health information is not protected by HIPAA. Health information that meets the standard and implementation specifications for de-identification under 45 CFR § 164.514(a) and (b) is considered not to be individually identifiable health information, i.e., de-identified.[20]

Deliverable: Any tangible outcome that is produced by the project. These can be documents, plans, computer systems, buildings, aircraft, etc. Internal deliverables are produced as a consequence of executing the project, and are usually only needed by the project team. External deliverables are those that are created for clients and stakeholders.[68]

Delivery System Reform Incentive Payment: *See* **DSRIP**.

Demodulation: Reverse of modulation. The act of extracting the original information-bearing signal from a modulated carrier wave or signal. The conversion from analog signals to digital signals occurring in a modem at a receiving site. Analog signals are used to transfer data over phone lines. Digital signals are in a format that can be used by a computer.[7]

Demographic data: Data that describe the characteristics of enrollee populations such as within a managed care entity. Demographic data include but are not limited to age, sex, race/ethnicity, and primary language.[26]

Denial of service attack: An attack in which a user or a program attempts to prevent legitimate users from accessing the service by increasing traffic or taking up so much of a shared resource that the network or server is busy or none of the resource is left for other users or uses.[52]

Derivative: Any reuse of information at the application level. Captures the notion of "collect once, use many times." For example, detailed data information from an accounting system can be used for financial planning. Loosely adapted from mathematics, investing.[4]

Derivative file: A subset from an original identifiable file.[26]

Description logics: A family of knowledge representation languages that can be used to represent the terminological knowledge of an application domain in a structured and formally well-understood way. The name *description logic* refers, on the one hand, to concept descriptions used to describe a domain; and, on the other hand, to the logic-based semantics which can be given by a translation into first-order predicate logic.[143]

Descriptor: The text defining a code in a code set.[114]

Design: 1. Phase of software development following analysis and concerned with how the problem is to be solved. **2.** The process and result of describing how a system or process is to be automated. Design must thoroughly describe the function of a component and its interaction with other components. Design usually also identifies areas of commonality in systems and optimizes reusability.[57]

Designated approving authority: Official with the authority to formally assume the responsibility for operating a system or network at an acceptable level of risk.[21]

Designated code set: A medical code set or an administrative code set that is required to be used by the adopted implementation specification for a standard transaction.[26]

Designated record set: A group of records maintained by or for a covered entity that comprises the medical records and billing records about individuals maintained by or for a covered healthcare provider; enrollment, payment, claims adjudication, and case or medical management record systems maintained by or for a health plan; or other records that are used, in whole or in part, by or for the covered entity to make decisions about individuals.[35]

Designated standard maintenance organization: *See* **DSMO**.

DFD (Data flow diagram): A two-dimensional diagram that explains how data is processed and transferred in a system. The graphical depiction identifies each source of data and how it interacts with other data sources to reach a common output. This type of diagram helps business development and design teams visualize how data are processed and identify or improve certain aspects.[4]

DHCP (Dynamic host configuration protocol): Standard protocol used to automatically and centrally manage the distribution of network IP addresses, alleviating manual static IP address assignment.[203]

DI (Diagnostic imaging): Also called medical imaging. The use of digital images and textual reports prepared as a result of performing diagnostic studies, such as x-rays, CT scans, MRIs, etc.[144]

Diagnostic and Statistical Manual: *See* **DSM**.

DICOM (Digital imaging and communications in medicine): 1. A standard for the electronic communication of medical images and associated information. DICOM relies on explicit and detailed models of how patients, images, and reports involved in radiology operations are described and how the above are related. The DICOM standards contain information object definitions, data structure, data dictionary, media storage, file format, communications formats, and print formats. **2.** An ANSI-accredited standards development organization that has created a standard protocol for exchanging medical images among computer systems.[43] *See* **RIS**.

Dictionary: In computer science programming languages, a dictionary is an abstract data type storing items or values. A value is accessed by an associated key. Basic operations are new, insert, find, and delete.[145]

Digital: Data is in terms of two states: positive and nonpositive. Positive is expressed or represented by the number 1 and nonpositive by the number 0. Thus, data transmitted or stored with digital technology are expressed as a string of 0's and 1's. Each of these state digits is referred to as a bit and a string of bits that a computer can address individually as a group is a byte.[2]

Digital certificate: An electronic "passport" that allows a person, computer, or organization to exchange information securely over the Internet using the public key infrastructure (PKI). A digital certificate may also be referred to as a public key certificate. Just like a passport, a digital certificate provides identifying information, is forgery resistant, and can be verified because it was issued by an official, trusted agency. The certificate contains the name of the certificate holder, a serial number, expiration dates, a copy of the certificate holder's public key (used for encrypting messages and digital signatures), and the digital signature of the certificate authority (CA) so that a recipient can verify that the certificate is real.[2]

Digital envelope: Data appended to a message that allow the intended recipient to verify the integrity of the content of the message.[36]

Digital health: An umbrella term for the use of technology in healthcare, which includes medical devices and information systems used in doctors' offices and hospitals, personal fitness, DNA testing, and the future of medicine.[150]

Digital Health Collaborative: An open source initiative whose goal is to use the power of community to accelerate the adoption and implementation of innovative health solutions.[439]

Digital imaging and communications in medicine: *See* **DICOM**.

Digital radiography: A form of radiography, using a digital x-ray detector to automatically acquire images and transfer them to a computer for viewing. This system is additionally capable of fixed or mobile use. Given its

D

high-volume capabilities it is often the choice for larger or busier clinics or health systems.[279]

Digital signal: Transmission signal that carries information in the discrete value form of 0 and 1.[69]

Digital signature: A mathematical technique used to validate the authenticity and integrity of a message, software, or digital document.[2] *See* **Private key** and **Public key**.

Digital signature standard: Specifies algorithms for applications requiring a digital signature, rather than a written signature. A digital signature is represented in a computer as a string of bits. A digital signature is computed using a set of rules and a set of parameters that allow the identity of the signatory and the integrity of the data to be verified. Digital signatures may be generated on both stored and transmitted data. Signature generation uses a private key to generate a digital signature; signature verification uses a public key that corresponds to, but is not the same as, the private key. Each signatory possesses a private and public key pair. Public keys may be known by the public; private keys are kept secret. Anyone can verify the signature by employing the signatory's public key. Only the user that possesses the private key can perform signature generation.[146]

Digital subscriber line: *See* **DSL**.

Digital subscriber line access multiplexer: *See* **DSLAM**.

Digital therapeutics: A class of digital tools that helps people make positive and sustainable behavior change that can be as effective as taking a medication or in some cases, more effective.[280]

Digitize: To convert something, such as data or an image to digital form.[29]

Digitized signature: *See* **Electronic Signature**.

Dimension table: A building block of a star schema data model; it contains the descriptive data regarding the objects in a fact table.[2]

Direct address: A direct address is similar to a typical email address which can be issued to an individual, organization, or machine but is different because a direct address serves as a secure messaging system that provides for identity management and message encryption to enable the secure sending and receiving of personal health information and other sensitive communication exchange.[147]

Direct connection: A situation where one computer is directly linked to another computer by a cable instead of via a network connection.[52]

Direct exchange: Describes the push of health information from a sender to a known receiver, similar to a how an email or fax is pushed from one endpoint to another.[147]

Direct memory access: *See* **DMA**.

Direct messaging: One type of secure messaging that is generally recognized as an effective, secure, encrypted communication mechanism for use in the point-to-point exchange of sensitive clinical and administrative data.[147]

DIRECT Project: Launched in March 2010 as a part of the Nationwide Health Information Network, the DIRECT Project was created to specify a simple, secure, scalable, standards-based way for participants to send authenticated, encrypted health information directly to known, trusted recipients over the Internet. Participants include EHR and PHR vendors, medical organizations, systems integrators, integrated delivery networks, federal organizations, state and regional health information organizations, organizations that provide health information exchange capabilities, and health information technology consultants. Two primary DIRECT Project specifications are the Applicability Statement for Secure Health Transport and the XDR and XDM for Direct Messaging.[12]

Direct sequence spread spectrum: *See* **DSSS.**

Directed acyclic graph: *See* **DAG.**

Directory: An organizing unit in a computer's file system for storing and locating files.[44]

Directory services markup language: *See* **DSML.**

Disclosure history: Under the Health Insurance Portability and Accountability Act (HIPAA), this is a list of any entity that has received personally identifiable healthcare information for uses unrelated to treatment and payment.[35]

Disclosure/disclose: The release, transfer, provision of, access to, or divulging in any other manner of information outside the entity holding the information.[20]

Discovery/e-discovery: Electronic discovery, or e-discovery, is a type of cyber forensics (also referred to as computer or digital forensics) and describes the process whereby law enforcement or attorneys can obtain, secure, search, and process any electronic data for use as evidence in a legal proceeding or investigation. Electronic discovery may be limited to a single computer or a network-wide search.[39]

Discrete data: Information that can be categorized into a classification. Discrete data are based on counts. Only a finite number of values is possible, and the values cannot be subdivided meaningfully. For example, the number of parts damaged in shipment.[148]

Disease registry: A large collection or registry that contains information on different chronic health problems affecting patients within the system. A disease registry helps to manage and log data on chronic illnesses and diseases. All data contained within the disease registry are logged by healthcare providers and are available to providers to perform benchmarking measures on healthcare systems.[12]

Disease staging: A classification system that uses diagnostic findings to produce clusters of patients based on etiology, pathophysiology, and severity. It can serve as the basis for clustering clinically homogeneous patients to assess quality of care, analysis of clinical outcomes, utilization of resources, efficacy of alternative treatments, and assignment of credentials for hospital privileges. Staging was also designed as a quality assurance tool for evaluating ambulatory care by comparing levels of severity at the time of hospitalization for patients receiving their health benefits from government and private insurers.[149] *See* **Severity system**.

Disk striping: The process of dividing a body of data into blocks and separating the data blocks across multiple storage devices.[2]

Disk striping with parity: Fault-tolerant storage technique that distributes data and parity across three or more physical disks. Storage technique that stripes data and parity in 64K blocks across all disks in the array. Striping provides fast data transfer and protection from a single disk failure by regenerating data for a failed disk through the stored parity. Minimum of three physical disks are required for disk striping with parity.[1] Also known as RAID 5.

Disk striping without parity: Storage technique that distributes data across two or more physical disks in 64K blocks across all disks in the array. Striping provides fast data transfer. Minimum of two physical disks are required for disk striping without parity. This technique is not fault-tolerant.[2] Also known as RAID 0.

Distinguished name: A name given to a person, company, or element within a computer system or network that uniquely identifies it from everything else.[150]

Distributed computing environment: Technology for setting up and managing computing and data exchange in a system of distributed computers.[2]

Distributed database: A database in which portions are stored in more than one physical location and processing is distributed among multiple database nodes.[2] *See* **Federated Database**.

Distributed ledger: A database held and updated independently by each participant (or node) in a large network. Records are not communicated to various nodes by a central authority, but instead are independently constructed and held by each node. Every node on the network processes every transaction, coming to consensus with all nodes on the conclusions related to that transaction. Also known as **Distributed ledger technology** or **DLT**.[281]

Distributed processing: The distribution of computer processing work among multiple computers to run an application. Often refers to local area networks (LANs) designed so a single program can run simultaneously at various sites.[39]

DLC (Data link control): A service that ensures reliable network data communication by managing frame error detection and flow control. DLC is based on the Data Link layer of the Open Systems Interconnection (OSI) model.[52]

DLL (Dynamic link library): A collection of small programs that can be loaded when needed by larger programs and used at the same time. The small program lets the larger program communicate with a specific device, such as a printer or scanner. It is often packaged as a DLL program, which is usually referred to as a DLL file.[2]

DLT (Distributed ledger technology): *See* **Distributed ledger**.

DMA (Direct memory access): Method that allows an input/output device to send or receive data directly to/from the main memory, bypassing the CPU to speed up memory operations. The process is managed by an integrated computer chip, known as the DMA controller.[52]

DME (Durable medical equipment): Equipment and supplies ordered by a healthcare provider for everyday or extended use. Coverage for DME may include: oxygen equipment, wheelchairs, crutches, or blood testing strips for diabetics.[218]

DML (Data manipulation language): A family of computer languages, including commands permitting users to manipulate data in a database. This manipulation involves inserting data into database tables, retrieving existing data, deleting data from existing tables, and modifying existing data. DML is most often incorporated into structured query language (SQL) databases.[52]

DNS (Domain name server): A database of public IP addresses and their associated host names. It serves to resolve or translate those common host names to IP addresses as requested. This server allows for the translation of host names to IP addresses and vice versa to allow for mapping between human-readable names and machine-readable IP addresses to access websites.[203]

DNSSEC (Domain name system security extension): A set of Internet Engineering Task Force (IETF) standards created to address vulnerabilities in the Domain Name System (DNS) and protect it from online threats. The purpose of DNSSEC is to increase the security of the Internet as a whole by addressing DNS security weaknesses. Essentially, DNSSEC adds authentication to DNS to make the system more secure.[2]

Document management: Software systems allowing organizations to control the production, storage, management, and distribution of electronic documents, yielding greater efficiencies in the ability to reuse information and to control the flow of the documents, from creation to archiving.[10]

Document type definition: *See* **DTD**.

Documentation and procedures test: A testing event that evaluates the accuracy of user and operations documentation and determines whether the manual procedure will work correctly as an integral part of the system.[50]

Documentation integrity: The accuracy of the complete health record. It encompasses information governance, patient identification, authorship validation, amendments, and record corrections. It also includes auditing the record for documentation validity when submitting reimbursement claims.[26]

D

Domain: A domain contains a group of computers that may be accessed and administered with a common set of rules.[73]

Domain analysis model: *See* **DAM**.

Domain information model: The model providing a view for an entire domain, commonly constructed in diagrams to represent semantics of an entire domain using language that subject matter experts understand.[282]

Domain name server: *See* **DNS**.

Dot pitch: A measurement (in millimeters) of the distance between dots on a monitor. The lower the number, the higher the clarity of the display.[2]

Dots per square inch: *See* **DPI**.

Download: To copy data from one computer system to another, typically over the Internet.[107]

DPI (Dots per square inch): A measure of the resolution of a printer, scanner, or monitor. It refers to the number of dots per inch. The more dots per inch, the higher the resolution.[73]

Draft international standard: *See* **DIS**.

Draft standard for trial use: *See* **DSTU**.

Draft supplement for public comment: A specification candidate for addition to an IHE Domain Technical Framework (e.g., a new profile) that is issued for comment by an interested party.[124]

Draft technical report: *See* **DTR**.

DRAM (Dynamic random access memory): A type of memory used for data or program code that a processor needs to function. A common type of random access memory (RAM) that must refresh every few milliseconds, by rewriting the data to the module. It accesses memory directly, holds memory for a short period and loses its data when power is shut off.[52]

DRG (Diagnosis related group): A classification system that groups patients according to diagnosis, type of treatment, age, and other relevant criteria. Under the prospective payment system, hospitals are paid a set fee for treating patients in a single DRG category, regardless of the actual cost of care for the individual.[26]

Drilldown: Exploration of multidimensional data allows moving down from one level of detail to the next, depending on the granularity of data in the level.[104]

Driver: A piece of software that enables an external device, such as a printer, hard disk, CD-ROM drive, or scanner to work with a computer's operating system.[73]

Drop-down list (or menu): A menu of commands or options that appears when you select an item with a mouse. The item you select is generally at the top of the display screen, and the menu appears just below it, as if you had it dropped down or you had pulled it down.[29]

Drug information system: A computer-based system that maintains drug-related information, such as information concerning appropriate dosages and side effects, and may access a drug interaction database. A drug information system may provide, by way of a directed consultation, specific advice on the usage of various drugs.[236]

Drug interaction database: Database containing information on drug interactions.[236]

Drug reference terminology: A collection of drug concepts and information such as definitions, hierarchies, and other kinds of knowledge and relationships related to the drug concepts.[43]

Drug therapy: The use of drugs to cure a medical problem, to improve a patient's condition, or to otherwise produce a therapeutic effect.[236]

DS4P (Data segmentation for privacy): Standard that allows a provider to tag a Consolidated-Clinical Document Architecture (CCDA) document with privacy metadata that expresses the data classification and possible re-disclosure restrictions placed on the data by applicable law. This aids in the electronic exchange of this type of health information.[12]

DSA (Digital signature algorithm): *See* **Digital signature**.

DSG (Document digital signature): *See* **Digital signature**.

DSL (Digital subscriber line): A communications medium used to transfer digital signals over standard telephone lines. Along with cable Internet, DSL is one of the most popular ways ISPs provide broadband Internet access.[73]

DSL (Domain-specific language): A small expressive programming language custom designed for specific tasks. Unlike a general-purpose language (GPL) such as C# or UML, DSL is designed to express statements in a particular problem space, or domain. Well-known DSLs include regular expressions and SQL.[30]

DSLAM (Digital subscriber line access multiplexer): A device used by Internet Service Providers (ISPs) to route incoming DSL connections to the Internet. Since a "multiplexer" combines multiple signals into one, a DSLAM combines a group of subscribers' connections into one aggregate Internet connection.[73]

DSM (Diagnostic and Statistical Manual of Mental Disorders): Manual produced by the American Psychiatric Association. Used by clinicians and researchers to diagnose and classify mental disorders. The criteria are concise and explicit, intended to facilitate an objective assessment of symptom presentations in a variety of clinical settings—inpatient, outpatient, partial hospital, consultation-liaison, clinical, private practice, and primary care.[151]

DSML (Directory services markup language): A proposed set of rules for using extensible markup language (XML) to define the data content and structure of a directory and maintain it on distributed directories. It permits XML and directories to work together, enabling applications to use directories efficiently.[52]

DSMO (Designated standard maintenance organization): An organization, designated by the Secretary of the U.S. Department of Health & Human Services, to maintain standards adopted under Subpart I of 45 CFR Part 162. A DSMO may receive and process requests for adopting a new standard or modifying an adopted standard.[26]

DSRIP (Delivery System Reform Incentive Payment): A Medicaid delivery system reform program, providing states with funding that can be used to support hospitals and other providers in changing how they provide care to Medicaid beneficiaries.[230]

DSSS (Direct sequence spread spectrum): Also known as direct sequence code division multiple access (DS-CDMA), one of two approaches to spread spectrum modulation for digital signal transmission over the airwaves. In direct sequence spread spectrum, the stream of information to be transmitted is divided into small pieces, each of which is allocated to a frequency channel across the spectrum. A data signal at the point of transmission is combined with a higher data-rate bit sequence (also known as a chipping code) that divides the data according to a spreading ratio. The redundant chipping code helps the signal resist interference and also enables the original data to be recovered if data bits are damaged during transmission.[2]

DSTU (Draft standard for trial use): A standard or implementation specification released to allow implementers to test the standard. At the end of the trial period, the standard may be balloted, revised, or withdrawn.[2,152]

DSU (Data service unit): A device used for interfacing data terminal equipment (DTE) to the public telephone network.[153]

DSU/CSU (Data service unit/channel service unit): A hardware device about the size of an external modem that converts a digital data frame from the communications technology used on a local area network (LAN) into a frame appropriate to a wide area network (WAN) and vice versa. For example, if you have a web business from your own home and have leased a digital line (perhaps a T-1 or fractional T-1 line) to a phone company or a gateway at an Internet service provider, you have a CSU/DSU at your end and the phone company or gateway host has a CSU/DSU at its end.[2]

DT (Date data type) (YYYY-MM-DD): International format defined by ISO (ISO 8601) to define a numerical date system as follows: YYYY-MM-DD where YYYY is the year (all the digits, i.e., 2012), MM is the month (01 [January] to 12 [December]),DD is the day (01 to 31).[61]

DTD (Document type definition): A specific document defining and constraining definition or set of statements that follow the rules of the Standard Generalized Markup Language (SGML) or of the Extensible Markup Language (XML), a subset of SGML. A DTD is a specification that accompanies a document and identifies what the markup codes are that, in the case of a text document, separate paragraphs, identify topic headings, and so forth and how each is to be processed. By mailing a DTD with a document, any location that has a DTD "reader" (or "SGML compiler") will be able to process the document and display or print it as intended. This means that a single standard SGML compiler can serve many different kinds of documents that use a range of different markup codes and related meanings. The compiler looks at the DTD and then prints or displays the document accordingly.[2]

DTE (Data terminal equipment): An end instrument that converts user information into signals for transmission or reconverts the received signals into user information.[153]

DTR (Draft technical report): Standards that are in the process of review but are implementable in their current form.[154]

DUA (Data use agreement): Contractual, confidentiality agreement between a covered entity and the recipient of health information in a limited data set.[20]

Dual-use technology: Technology that has both civilian and military applications (e.g., cryptography).[7]

Dumb terminal: Device that consists of a keyboard and a monitor, and a connection to a server PC, minicomputer, or a mainframe computer. Dumb terminals have no "intelligence" (data processing or number crunching power) and depend entirely on the computer to which they are connected for computations, data storage, and retrieval. Dumb terminals are used by airlines, banks, and other such firms for inputting data to, and recalling it from, the connected computer.[4]

Durability: A database property that ensures transactions are saved permanently and do not accidentally disappear or get erased, even during a database crash. This is usually achieved by saving all transactions to a nonvolatile storage medium. Durability is part of the ACID acronym, which stands for atomicity, consistency, isolation, and durability. ACID is a set of properties guaranteeing the reliability of all database transactions.[52] *See* **ACID.**

Durable medical equipment: *See* **DME.**

DVD (Digital video disk or digital versatile disk): A type of optical media used for storing digital data. It is the same physical size as a CD, but has a larger storage capacity. Some DVDs are formatted specifically for video playback, while others may contain different types of data, such as software programs and computer files.[73]

Dynamic host configuration protocol: *See* **DHCP.**

Dynamic link control: *See* **DLC.**

Dynamic link library: *See* **DLL.**

Dynamic RAM: *See* **DRAM.**

E

e-[text] or e-text: Short for "electronic," "e" or "e" is used as a prefix to indicate that something is Internet-based, not just electronic. The trend began with e-mail in the 1990s, and now includes eCommerce, eHealth, e-GOV, etc.[29]

E-1 (European digital signal): Digital transmission format devised by the ITU-TS and given the name by the Conference of European Postal and Telecommunication Administration (CEPT). It's the equivalent of the North American T-carrier system format. E2 through E5 are carriers in increasing multiples of the E1 format.[2]

EAI (Enterprise application integration): 1. The use of software and architectural principles to bring together (integrate) a set of enterprise computer applications. It is an area of computer systems architecture that gained wide recognition from about 2004 onward. EAI is related to middleware technologies, such as message-oriented middleware (MOM), and data representation technologies, such as eXtensible markup language (HTML, XML). Newer EAI technologies involve using web services as part of service-oriented architecture as a means of integration. **2.** A presentation-level integration technology that provides a single point of access to conduct business transactions that utilize data from multiple disparate applications.[52] *See* **System integration**.

EAP (Extensible authentication protocol): A general protocol for authentication that also supports multiple authentication methods, such as token cards, one-time passwords, certificate, public key authentication, and smartcards.[2]

EAV (Entity-Attribute-Value) model: A data model that is often used in instances where the amount of attributes, properties, or parameters that can be used to define an entity are potentially limitless, however the number that will apply to the entity is somewhat modest. Also sometimes referred to at the Object-Attribute-Value Model, or even the Open Schema.[71]

Early event detection: *See* **EED**.

EBCDIC (Extended binary coded decimal interchange code): A character set coding scheme that represents 256 standard characters. IBM mainframes use EBCDIC coding, while personal computers use American Standard Coding for Information Interchange (ASCII) coding. Networks that link personal computers to IBM mainframes must include a translating device to mediate between the two systems.[283]

EC (Eligible clinician): According to the Centers for Medicare & Medicaid Services (CMS), an individual physician or healthcare practitioner that is eligible to participate in, or is subject to, mandatory participation in a payment incentive adjustment or quality reporting program. For the purposes of the Merit-based Incentive Payment System (MIPS), a MIPS-eligible clinician (for 2017 and 2018 program years) includes physicians, physician assistants, nurse practitioners, clinical nurse specialists, and certified registered nurse anesthetists.[284]

EC (Electronic commerce): Consists of the buying and selling of products or services over electronic systems such as the Internet and other computer networks.[156] Also known as *eCommerce*.

ECN (Explicit congestion notification): An extension to the Transmission Control Protocol (TCP) packet that notifies networks about congestion with the goal of reducing packet loss and delay by making the sending device decrease the transmission rate until the congestion clears, without dropping packets.[278]

eCQI (Electronic clinical quality improvement): The use of common standards and shared technologies to monitor and analyze the quality of healthcare provided to patients and patient outcomes.[88]

eCQM (Electronic clinical quality measures): The use of data from electronic health records (EHR) and/or health information technology systems to measure healthcare quality. The Centers for Medicare & Medicaid Services (CMS) use eCQMs in a variety of quality reporting and incentive programs. eCQMS are seen as an improvement over traditional quality measure collection because if the EHRs are not used, the work to gather the data from medical charts, e.g., "chart-abstracted data," is very resource intensive and subject to human error.[88]

ED (Encapsulated data): The coupling or encapsulation of the data with a select group of functions that defines everything that can be done with the data.[52]

EDC (Electronic data capture system): A computerized system designed for the collection of clinical data in electronic format for use mainly in human clinical trials.[285]

EDDS (Electronic document digital storage): Document management systems available online.[29]

EDI (Electronic data interchange): 1. Even before HIPAA, the American National Standards Institute (ANSI) approved the process for developing a set of EDI standards known as the X12. EDI is a collection of standard message formats that allows businesses to exchange data via any electronic messaging service. **2.** The electronic transfer of data between companies using networks to include the Internet. Secure communications are needed in healthcare to exchange eligibility information, referrals, authorization, claims, encounter, and other payment data needed to manage contracts and remittance.[19] *See* **X12 Standard.**

EDI Gateway (Electronic data interchange gateway): An electronic process to send data (claims, membership, and benefits) back and forth between providers and insurance companies.[46]

E

EDIT: In the Centers for Medicare & Medicaid Services, the logic within the Standard Claims Processing System (or PSC Supplemental Edit Software) that selects certain claims, evaluates or compares information on the selected claims or other accessible source, and, depending on the evaluation, takes action on the claims, such as pay in full, pay in part, or suspend for manual review.[13]

EED (Early event detection): This component of the Public Health Information Network (PHIN) preparedness uses case and suspect case reporting, along with statistical surveillance of health-related data, to support the earliest possible detection of events that may signal a public health emergency.[80]

EDXL (Emergency data exchange language): A standard message distribution framework for data sharing among emergency information systems.[157]

EDXLHAVE (Emergency data exchange language–hospital availability exchange): Describes a standard message for data sharing among emergency information systems using the XML-based Emergency Data Exchange Language (EDXL).[157]

EEPROM (Electronically erasable programmable read only memory): A reprogrammable memory chip that can be electronically erased and reprogrammed through the application of higher than normal electronic voltage without having to remove the chip from the computer for modification.[2]

Effective date: This is the date that a federal agency final rule is effective, which is usually 60 days after it is published in the *Federal Register.*[113]

E-GOV: The E-Government Act of 2002 was signed into law by President George W. Bush in July 2002. It aims to enhance the management and promotion of electronic Government services and processes by establishing a Federal Chief Information Officer within the Office of Management and Budget, and by establishing a broad framework of measures that require using Internet-based information technology to enhance citizen access to Government information and services, and for other purposes.[286]

eHealth (also written e-health): A broadly defined term for healthcare practice which is supported by information and communication technologies; the term eHealth encompasses a whole range of services that is at the edge of medicine/healthcare and information technology, including electronic medical records, telemedicine, and evidence-based medicine.[7]

EHR (Electronic health record): 1. A longitudinal electronic record of patient health information generated by one or more encounters in any care delivery setting. Included in this information are patient demographics, progress notes, problems, medications, vital signs, past medical history, immunizations, laboratory data, and radiology reports and images. The EHR automates and streamlines the clinician's workflow. The EHR has the ability to generate a complete record of a clinical patient encounter, as well as supporting other care-related activities directly or indirectly via interface; including evidence-based decision support, quality management, and outcomes reporting. **2.** Health-related information on an individual that conforms to nationally recognized interoperability standards and that can be created, managed, and consulted by authorized clinicians and staff across more than one healthcare organization. *See* **EMR**.[12,53]

EIDE (Enhanced or extended integrated drive electronics): A standard interface for high-speed disk drives that operates at speeds faster than the standard Integrated Drive Electronics (IDE) interface. It has since been replaced by other standards that offer faster transfer rates.[52]

EIN (Employer identification number): 1. Employers, as sponsors of health insurance for their employees, often need to be identified in healthcare transactions, and a standard identifier for employers would be beneficial for electronically exchanged transactions. Healthcare providers may need to identify the employer of the participant on claims submitted electronically to health plans. **2.** The HIPAA standard is the EIN, the taxpayer-identifying number for employers that is assigned by the Internal Revenue Service. This identifier has nine digits with the first two digits separated by a hyphen, as follows: 00-000000.[113]

EIP (Enterprise information portal): 1. A framework for integrating information, people, and processes across organization boundaries. Provides a secure unified access point. **2.** An Internet-based approach to consolidate and present an organization's business intelligence and information resources through a single access point via an intranet.[2] Also known as an Internet portal enterprise portal.

EIS (Enterprise information system): Large-scale computing system that offers high quality of service, managing large volumes of data and capable of supporting large organizations.[287]

eLTSS (Electronic long-term services and supports): Initiative within the U.S. Office of the National Coordinator for Health IT (ONC) to facilitate the development of basic elements for inclusion in electronic standards. These standards will enable the creation, exchange, and reuse of interoperable service plans by beneficiaries, community-based long-term services and supports providers, payers, healthcare providers, and the individuals they serve.[12]

Electromagnetic interference: *See* **EMI**.

Electronic certificate: *See* **Digital certificate**.

Electronic claim: Any claim submitted for payment to a health plan by a central processing unit, tape diskette, direct data entry, direct wire, dial-in telephone, digital fax, or personal computer download or upload.[10] *See* **EDI Gateway**.

Electronic clinical quality improvement: *See* **eCQI**.

Electronic clinical quality measures: *See* **eCQM**.

Electronic commerce: *See* **EC** and **eCommerce**.

Electronic data: Recorded or transmitted electronically, while non-electronic data would be everything else. Special cases would be data transmitted by fax and audio systems, which are, in principle, transmitted electronically, but which lack the underlying structure usually needed to support automated interpretation of its contents.[113]

Electronic data capture system: *See* **EDC.**

Electronic data interchange: *See* **EDI.**

Electronic data interchange gateway: *See* **EDI Gateway.**

Electronic forms management: A software system that automatically generates forms and can be populated by importing data from another system and/or can export data that have been entered into another system.[10]

Electronic health record: *See* **EHR.**

Electronic health record provider: Entity in legitimate possession of electronic health record data, and in a position to communicate that data to another appropriate entity.[63]

Electronic long-term services and supports: *See* **eLTSS.**

Electronic media: 1. Electronic storage media, including memory devices in computers (hard drives) and any removable/transportable digital memory media, such as magnetic tapes or disks, optical disks, or digital memory cards. **2.** Transmission media used to exchange information already in electronic storage media; including, for example, the Internet (wide open), extranet (using Internet technology to link a business with information accessible only to collaborating parties), leased lines, dial-up lines, private networks, and the physical movement of removable/transportable electronic storage media. Certain transmissions, including paper via facsimile and voice via telephone, are not considered to be transmissions via electronic media because the information being exchanged did not exist in electronic form before the transmission.[13]

Electronic media claims: *See* **EMC.**

Electronic medical record: *See* **EMR.**

Electronic medical record adoption model: *See* **EMRAM.**

Electronic medication administration record: *See* **eMAR.**

Electronic patient record: *See* **EHR.**

Electronic personal health record: *See* **ePHR** and **PHR.**

Electronic prescribing: *See* **E-prescribing.**

Electronic prescriptions for controlled substances: *See* **EPCS.**

Electronic prior authorization: *See* **ePA.**

Electronic protected health information: *See* **ePHI.**

Electronic remittance advice: *See* **ERA.**

Electronic signature: Also known as e-signature. **1.** An electronic indication of a person's intent to agree to the content of a document or a set of data to which the signature relates. Like its handwritten counterpart in the offline world, an electronic signature is a legal concept capturing the signatory's intent to be bound by the terms of the signed document. **2.** A digital version of a traditional pen and ink signature, often providing the same legal commitment as a handwritten signature. The terms e-signature and digital signature are often confused and used incorrectly as synonyms by laymen. A digital signature is a type of e-signature that uses mathematics to validate the authenticity and integrity of a message, software, or digital document.[288,2]

Electronic text: *See* **e-[text]** or **e-text**.

Electronically erasable programmable read-only memory: *See* **EEPROM**.

Eligible clinician: *See* **EC**.

Eligibility-based billing: *See* **EBB**.

E-mail (Electronic mail): The exchange of computer-stored messages via telecommunication. These messages are usually encoded in ASCII text but can include non-text files, such as graphic images and sound files.[2]

eMAR (Electronic medication administration record): An electronic record-keeping system that documents when medications are given to a patient during a hospital stay. This application supports the five rights of medication administration (right patient, right medication, right dose, right time, and right route of administration) and can be used with bar coding functionality, although bar coding is not required. eMAR functionality is normally found within a nursing documentation application.[10]

EMC (Electronic media claims): This term usually refers to a flat file format used to transmit or transport claims.[113]

Emergency: Sudden demand for action; a condition that poses an immediate threat to the health of the patient.[20,66]

Emergency access: Granting of user rights and authorizations to permit access to protected health information and applications in emergency conditions outside of normal workflows. Emergency room access is considered to be a normal workflow.[20]

Emergency care system: An application that assists emergency department clinicians and staff in the critical task of managing patients quickly and efficiently; directs each step of the patient management/patient flow and patient documentation process, including triage, tracking, nursing and physician charting, disposition, charge capture, and management reporting.[10]

Emergency data exchange language: *See* **EDXL**.

Emergency permission: Permission granted to certain caregivers in advance that allows self-declaration of an emergency and assumption of an emergency role. Emergency permissions defined in standard ways, compliant with appropriate ANSI standards and Health Level Seven (HL7) healthcare permission definitions, are suitable for federated circumstances, where the person declaring the emergency is not a member of the organization possessing the requested information.[20]

Emergency repair disk: *See* **ERD**.

Emergency respond data architecture: *See* **ERDA**.

EMI (Electromagnetic interference): Any disruption of operation of an electronic device caused by electromagnetic waves.[2]

Emissions security: *See* **EMSEC.**

Emoticons: A combination word for "emotional icon," it is a small picture created with the normal keys on a keyboard meant to denote the writer's mood in a message.[66]

EMPI (Enterprise master patient index): A system that maintains consistent and accurate information about each patient registered by a healthcare organization. It may link several smaller MPIs together, such as those from outpatient clinics and rehabilitation facilities. It can also aggregate patient data from separate systems within one facility.[2]

Employee Retirement Income and Security Act: *See* **ERISA.**

Employee welfare benefit plan: A plan, fund, or a program maintained by an employer, or an employee organization, that provides medical, surgical, or hospital care.[20]

Employer identification number: *See* **EIN.**

EMR (Electronic medical record): 1. An application environment that is composed of the clinical data repository, clinical decision support, controlled medical vocabulary, order entry, computerized practitioner order entry, and clinical documentation applications. This environment supports the patient's electronic medical record across inpatient and outpatient environments, and is used by healthcare practitioners to document, monitor, and manage healthcare delivery. **2.** Health-related information on an individual that can be created, gathered, managed, and consulted by authorized clinicians and staff within one healthcare organization.[10,12] *See* **EHR.**

EMRAM (Electronic medical record adoption model): A tool developed by HIMSS Analytics guiding hospitals to improved clinical outcomes.[10]

EMSEC (Emanations security): Measures taken to deny unauthorized persons information derived from intercept and analysis of compromising emanations from crypto-equipment of an IT system.[21]

Emulation: A software program that allows a computer to imitate another computer with a differing operating system.[2]

EN (European standard): Developed by the European Committee for Standardization (CEN). CEN is a major provider of European standards and technical specifications.[289]

EN 46000 Medical device quality management systems standard: Technically equivalent to ISO 13485: 1996, an international medical device standard. The two are similar enough that if an organization is prepared to comply with one, it could easily comply with the other.[159]

Encapsulated data type: *See* ED.

Encapsulation: In object-oriented programming, the inclusion within a program object of all the resources needed for the object to function—basically, the methods and the data. The object is said to "publish its interfaces." Other objects adhere to these interfaces to use the object without having to be concerned with how the object accomplishes it. An object can be thought of as a self-contained atom. The object interface consists of public methods and instantiated data.[2]

Encoded data: Data represented by some identification of classification scheme, such as a provider identifier or a procedure code.[59]

Encoder: This application enables health information management personnel to find and use complete and accurate codes and code modifiers for procedures and diagnosis to optimize billing and reimbursement. For example, 1234 is bronchitis, whereas 1235 is bronchitis with asthma, and 1236 is bronchitis with stomach flu.[10]

Encoding-decoding services: This service will encode and/or decode messages from and to different coding formats, such as Unicode, UTF-8, Base64, etc.[57]

Encounter: 1. An instance of direct provider/practitioner to patient interaction, regardless of the setting, between a patient and practitioner vested with primary responsibility for diagnosing, evaluating, or treating the patient's condition, or both, or providing social worker services. **2.** A contact between a patient and practitioner who has primary responsibility for assessing and treating the patient at a given contact, exercising independent judgment. Encounter serves as a focal point linking clinical, administrative, and financial information. Encounters occur in many different settings—ambulatory care, inpatient care, emergency care, home healthcare, field, and virtual (telemedicine).[103]

Encounter data: Detailed data about individual services provided by a capitated managed care entity. The level of detail about each service reported is similar to that of a standard claim form. Encounter data are also sometimes referred to as "shadow claims."[26]

Encryption: 1. An application/technology that provides the translation of data into a secret code. Encryption is the most effective way to achieve data security. To read an encrypted file, you must have access to a secret key or password that enables you to decrypt it. Unencrypted data are called plain text; encrypted data are referred to as cipher text. **2.** Means of securing data by transforming/generating them into apparently meaningless random characters between source and destination. A process by which a message is encoded so that its meaning is not obvious. It is transformed into a second message using a complex function and a special encryption key.[10]

Encryption-decryption services: This encrypts and decrypts messages. It could use X.509 certificates and other cryptography mechanisms.[57]

End user: In information technology, the person for whom a hardware or software product is designed by the developers, installers, and servicers of the product.[2]

End user license agreement: *See* **EULA**.

Enhanced or extended integrated drive electronics: *See* **EIDE**.
Enhanced Oversight Accountability Rule: *See* **EOA**.
Enhanced small device interface: *See* **ESDI**.
Enterprise: A business organization.[29]
Enterprise application integration: *See* **EAI**.
Enterprise architecture: 1. A strategic resource that aligns business and technology, leverages shared assets, builds internal and external partnerships, and optimizes the value of information technology services. **2.** A business-focused framework developed in accordance with the Clinger-Cohen Act of 1996 that identifies the business processes, systems that support processes, and guidelines and standards by which systems must operate.[12,160]
Enterprise architecture integration: Tools and techniques that promote, enable, and manage the exchange of information and distribution of business processes across multiple application systems, typically within a sizeable electronic landscape, such as large corporations, collaborating companies, and administrative regions.[57]
Enterprise information portal: *See* **EIP**.
Enterprise information system: *See* **EIS**.
Enterprise master patient index: *See* **EMPI**.
Enterprise master person index: A system that coordinates client identification across multiple systems, namely, by collecting and storing IDs and person-identifying demographic information from source system (track new persons, track changes to existing persons). These systems also take on several other tasks and responsibilities associated with client ID management.[57]
Enterprise network: An enterprise's communications backbone that helps connect computers and related devices across departments and workgroup networks, facilitating insight and data accessibility. An enterprise network reduces communication protocols, facilitating system and device interoperability, as well as improved internal and external enterprise data management.[52]
Enterprise resource planning: *See* **ERP**.
Enterprise scheduling: Ability to schedule procedures, exams, and appointments across multiple systems and/or locations spanning an entire jurisdiction.[57]
Enterprise user authentication: *See* **EUA**.
Entity: Something that has a distinct, separate existence, though an entity needs not be a material existence. In some usages, an entity is close in meaning to "object."[2]
Entity identity assertion: Ensures that an entity is the person or application that claims the identity provided.[20]
Entity relationship diagram: *See* **ERD**.
Entries: Health record data in general (clinical observations, statements, reasoning, intentions, plans, or actions) without particular specification of their

formal representation, hierarchical organization, or of the particular record component class(es) that might be used to represent them.[63]

EOA (Enhanced Oversight Accountability Rule): This rule finalizes modifications and new requirements under the ONC Health IT Certification Program, including provisions related to the Office of the National Coordinator for Health Information Technology (ONC)'s role. The final rule creates a regulatory framework for ONC's direct review of health information technology (health IT) certified under the Program, including, when necessary, requiring the correction of non-conformities found in health IT certified under the Program and suspending and terminating certifications issued to Complete EHRs and Health IT Modules. The final rule also sets forth processes for ONC to authorize and oversee accredited testing laboratories under the Program. In addition, it includes provisions for expanded public availability of certified health IT surveillance results.[12]

EOB (Explanation of benefits): A document detailing how a claim was processed according to the insured's benefits.[46]

EOP (Explanation of payment): Generated to the provider in reply to a claim submission.[46]

ePA (Electronic prior authorization): An electronic process established in the National Council for Prescription Drug Programs (NCPDP) SCRIPT Standard that enables patient and drug-specific prior authorization criteria and a real-time approval for medication prior authorization.[290]

EPCS (Electronic prescriptions for controlled substances): A technology solution to help address prescription drug abuse in the United States. The rule "Electronic Prescriptions for Controlled Substances", provides practitioners with the option of writing and transmitting prescriptions for controlled substances electronically. The regulations also permit pharmacies to receive, dispense, and archive these electronic prescriptions. The technology addresses the problem of forged or stolen prescriptions by requiring authentication of prescribers, improving security standards, and auditing activity on EPCS platforms.[291]

ePHI (Electronic protected health information): Any protected health information (PHI) that is created, stored, transmitted, or received electronically.[20]

ePHR (Electronic personal health record): A universally accessible, layperson comprehensible, lifelong tool for managing relevant health information, promoting health maintenance, and assisting with chronic disease management via an interactive, common data set of electronic health information and eHealth tools. The ePHR is owned, managed, and shared by the individual or his or her legal proxy(s) and must be secure to protect the privacy and confidentiality of the health information it contains. It is not a legal record unless so defined, and is subject to various legal limitations.[53] *See* **PHR.**

Episode of care: Services provided by a healthcare facility or provider for a specific medical problem or condition or specific illness during a set time period. Episode of care can be given either for a short period or on a continuous basis or it may consist of a series of intervals marked by one or more brief separations from care.[161]

E-prescribing (Electronic prescribing): The computer-based electronic generation, transmission and filling of a prescription.[292]

ERA (Electronic remittance advice): Any of several electronic formats for explaining the payments of healthcare claims.[113]

Erasable programmable memory: *See* **EPROM.**

ERD (Entity relationship diagram): A type of diagram that illustrates how entities, such as people, objects, or concepts relate to each other within a system. Also known as ER diagrams.[293]

ERDA (Emergency respond data architecture): A data architecture developed to support real-time information sharing and interoperability during emergency situations of all types.[162]

ERISA (Employee Retirement Income and Security Act of 1975): Most group health plans covered by ERISA are also health plans under the Health Insurance Portability and Accountability Act.[20]

ERP (Enterprise resource planning): Management information systems that integrate and automate many of the business functions associated with the operations or production aspects of an enterprise, such as general ledger, budgeting, materials management, purchasing, payroll, and human resources.[11]

Error chain: Generally, refers to the series of events that led to a disastrous outcome, typically uncovered by a root cause analysis. A more specific meaning of error chain, especially when used in the phrase "break the error chain," relates to the common themes or categories of causes that emerge from root cause analyses. These categories go by different names in different settings, but they generally include (1) failure to follow standard operating procedures; (2) poor leadership; (3) breakdowns in communication or teamwork; (4) overlooking or ignoring individual fallibility; and (5) losing track of objectives. Used in this way, "break the error chain" is shorthand for an approach in which team members continually address these links as a crisis or routine situation unfolds; the checklists that are included in teamwork training programs have categories corresponding to these common links in the error chain (e.g., establish team leader, assign roles and responsibility, monitor your teammates).[94]

Error proofing: Used to ensure products and processes are completed correctly the first time. Often relies on mechanisms built into tools or systems that automatically signal when problems occur or prevent the process from continuing until the proper conditions are met.[159] Also known as *mistake proofing.*[92]

eRX: *See* **e-prescribing.**

ESS (Executive support system): A class of decision support systems that provide predefined data presentation and exploration functionality to top-level executives. The system is intended to facilitate and support the information and decision-making needs of senior executives by providing ready access to both internal and external information relevant to meeting the strategic goals of the organization. Commonly considered a specialized form of decision support systems (DSS). The emphasis of ESS is on graphical displays with reporting and drilldown capabilities. In general, an ESS is an enterprise-wide DSS that allows executives to analyze, compare, and highlight trends and important variables, as well as monitor performance and identify opportunities and problems.[10]

Ethereum: A decentralized blockchain application platform that runs smart contracts, applications that run exactly as programmed without the possibility of downtime, censorship, fraud or third-party interference. These applications run on a custom built blockchain creating an environment for developers to create markets, store registries, move funds, etc. without a middleman or counterparty risk.[294]

Ethernet: 1. The most common type of connection computers use within a local area network (LAN). An Ethernet port looks much like a regular phone jack, but it is slightly wider. This port can be used to connect the computer to another computer, a local network, or an external DSL or cable modem. **2.** A family of computer networking technologies and protocols for local area networks (LANs) commercially introduced in 1980. **3.** A frame-based computer networking technology for LANs. The name comes from the physical concept of ether. It defines wiring and signaling for the physical layer and frame formats and protocols for the media access control (MAC)/data link layer of the Open Systems Interconnection (OSI) model. Ethernet is mostly standardized as IEEEs 802. It has become the most widespread LAN technology in use during the 1990s to the present.[166]

ETL (extraction, transformation, loading): Short for **e**xtract, **t**ransform, **l**oad, three database functions that are combined into one tool to pull data out of one database and place it into another database. Extract is the process of reading data from a database. Transform is the process of converting the extracted data from its previous form into the form it needs to be in so that it can be placed into another database. Transformation occurs by using rules or lookup tables or by combining the data with other data. Load is the process of writing the data into the target database. ETL is used to migrate data from one database to another, to form data marts and data warehouses, and also to convert databases from one format or type to another.[39]

EULA (End user license agreement): An agreement between a software application licensor and the end user of the application. Also referred to as a software license.[2]

European committee for standardization: *See* **CEN**.

European digital signal: *See* **E-1**.

European standard: *See* **EN**.

Event: Action or activity that occurs within a system and/or network scope, inclusive of its boundaries.[20]

Event aggregation: Consolidation of similar log entries into a single entry, containing a count of the number of occurrences of the event.[20]

Event correlation: Relationships between two or more log entries.[20]

Event filtering: Suppression of log entries from analysis, reporting, or long-term storage because their characteristics indicate that they are unlikely to contain information of interest.[20]

Event reduction: Removal of unneeded data fields from all log entries to create a new log that is smaller.[20]

Evidence documents: *See* **ED**.

Evidence-based medicine: 1. The conscientious, explicit, judicious and reasonable use of modern, best evidence in making decisions about the care of an individual. It integrates clinical experience and patient values with best available research information.[163] **2.** Evidence-based medicine follows four steps: formulate a clear clinical question from a patient's problem; search the literature for relevant clinical articles; evaluate (critically appraise) the evidence for its validity and usefulness; and implement useful findings in clinical practice.[295]

Evidence-based practice: *See* **Evidence-based medicine**.

Exceeds authorized access: To access a computer with authorization and to use such access to obtain or alter information in the computer that the accessor is not entitled to obtain or alter.[16]

Exception: In programming, an unplanned event, such as invalid input or a loss of connectivity, that occurs while a program is executing and disrupts the flow of its instructions.[2]

Exchange format: The interim data format for converting from one file or database structure to another. Also called a data interchange format.[150]

Exclusive branching: Splits a process in several branches, only one of which can be selected, based on the fulfillment of a condition associated with a given branch.[164]

Exclusive choice: The divergence of a branch into two or more branches, such that when the incoming branch is enabled, the thread of control is immediately passed to precisely one of the outgoing branches, based on a mechanism that can select one of the outgoing branches.[165] *See* **Simple merge**.

Executive information system: *See* **EIS**.

Expert system: Artificial intelligence based system that converts the knowledge of an expert in a specific subject into a software code. This code can be merged with other such codes (based on the knowledge of other experts) and used for answering questions (queries) submitted through a computer.

Expert systems typically consist of three parts: (1) a knowledge base which contains the information acquired by interviewing experts, and logic rules that govern how that information is applied; (2) an inference engine that interprets the submitted problem against the rules and logic of information stored in the knowledge base; and an (3) interface that allows the user to express the problem in a human language such as English.[4]

Explanation of benefits: *See* **EOB.**

Explanation of payment: *See* **EOP.**

Explicit congestion notification: *See* **ECN.**

Expression: The textual means to convey a concept to the user. It can be a major concept, a synonym, or a lexical variant.[29]

Extended ASCII (Extended American standard code for information interchange): Extensively used 8-bit standard information processing code with 256 characters.[39]

Extended binary coded decimal interchange code: *See* **EBCDIC.**

Extensibility: 1. System design feature that allows for future expansion without the need for changes to the basic infrastructure. **2.** The ability to economically modify or add functionality.[57,136]

Extensible authentication protocol: *See* **EAP.**

Extensible markup language: *See* **XML.**

Extensible stylesheet language: *See* **XSL.**

External customer: A person or organization that receives a product, service, or information; not part of the organization supplying the product, service, or information.[60]

Extraction, transformation, loading: *See* **ETL.**

Extranet: Restricted network of computers that allows controlled access to a firm's internal information to authorized outsiders (customers, suppliers, joint venture partners, etc.) by connecting them (usually via Internet) to the firm's intranet.[4]

F

Fact table: In data warehousing, a fact table is the primary table that contains quantitative or factual data of a business. It may also contain textual attributes to limit the usage of dimension tables. In a dimensional database, there can be multiple business processes that are used, which can warrant the use of many fact tables.[296,297]

Failback: The process of restoring operations to a primary machine or facility after it has been shifted to a secondary machine, or facility during failover.[2]

Failover: A backup operational mode in which the functions of a system component (such as a processor, server, network, or database, for example) are assumed by secondary system components when the primary component becomes unavailable through either failure or scheduled downtime. Used to make systems more fault-tolerant, failover is typically an integral part of mission-critical systems that must be constantly available.[2]

Failsafe: Incorporating some feature for automatically counteracting the effect of an anticipated possible source of failure.[29]

Family set: Group of backup tapes consisting of a single run of backup information.[36]

FAR (False acceptance rate): A statistic used to measure biometric performance when operating in the verification task. The percentage of times a system produces a false accept, which occurs when an individual is incorrectly matched to another individual's existing biometric.[14]

Fast healthcare interoperability resources: *See* FHIR.

FAT Client: A networked computer with most resources installed locally, rather than distributed over a network as is the case with a thin client. Also called thick, heavy, or rich client.[2]

Fat protocol: A network protocol that uses commands and identifiers that are typically text based and rather wordy and consume more bandwidth than a "thin" protocol. For example, SOAP, which is used to invoke processing on a remote server, is considered fat compared to CORBA or DCOM. While the Internet stack is composed of thin protocols, blockchain application stack is composed of fat protocols.[150,298]

FCOE (Fiber channel over Ethernet): An encapsulation of fiber channel frames over Ethernet networks. This allows a fiber channel to use 10 gigabit Ethernet networks (or higher speeds) while preserving the fiber channel protocol.[10]

FDDI (Fiber distributed data interface): A set of ANSI and ISO standards for data transmission on fiber optic lines in a local area network (LAN) that can extend in range up to 200 km (124 miles). The FDDI protocol is based on the token-ring protocol. In addition to being large geographically, an

FDDI local area network can support thousands of users. FDDI is frequently used on the backbone for a wide area network (WAN). FDDI is a type of physical network based on fiber optics. It is supported by the Digital Imaging and Communications in Medicine (DICOM) standard.[2]

Federal financial participation (FFP): *See* **FFP.**

FFP (Federal financial participation): The U.S. Federal Government's share of a state's expenditures under the Medicaid program. This funding can be provided through different funding methods including 90/10, 50/50, and 75/25.[299]

Federal Information Security Management Act: *See* **FISMA.**

Federated database: A system in which several databases appear to function as a single entity. Each component database in the system is completely self-sustained and functional. When an application queries the federated database, the system figures out which of its component databases contains the data being requested and passes the request to it.[2]

Fee-for-service: *See* **FFS.**

Feeder systems: Operational systems that will feed patient/person data to the EHR in the form of real-time single messages, multiple messages, or batch file uploads.[57] *See* **Source systems**. These systems may also be known as legacy systems and are often involved in extract-transform-load processes.[50] *See* **ETL.**

FFS (Fee-for-service): A type of payment in which a person or a system pays a specific amount of money for medical treatment according to the type of treatment received regardless of the outcome achieved. Federal payment systems are continuing to attempt to shift providers toward value-based care delivery and away from the FFS reimbursement model.[26,135]

FHIR (Fast healthcare interoperability resources): A next generation standards framework created by HL7®, FHIR combines the best features of HL7's V2, HL7 V3, and CDA product lines that leverage emerging web standards which apply a tight focus on ease of implementation. Furthermore, it defines a set of resources for health that represent granular clinical concepts that can be exchanged to quickly and effectively solve problems in healthcare and related processes. The resources cover the basic elements of healthcare—patients, admissions, diagnostic reports, medications, and problem lists, with their typical participants. In addition the resources support a range of richer and more complex clinical models. The simple direct definitions of the resources are based on thorough requirements gathering, formal analysis, and extensive cross-mapping to other relevant standards.[9]

FHIR resource: The basic building block in the FHIR standard. All exchangeable content is defined as a resource. Resources all share the following set of characteristics: a common way to define and represent them, building them from data types that define common reusable patterns of elements, a common set of metadata, and a human-readable part.[9]

Fiber channel: A gigabit-speed network technology primarily used for storage networking.[10]

Fiber channel over Ethernet: *See* **FCOE.**

Fiber distributed data interface: *See* **FDDI.**

Fiber optic cable: A pure glass cable used for the high-speed transmission of digital signals. Data are transmitted through the cable via rapid pulses of light. The receiving end translates the light pulses into binary values. The cables are less susceptible to noise and interference compared to copper wires or telephone lines.[73]

Fiber optics: High-speed communications technology that uses glass or plastic medium to transmit light pulses produced by LEDs or ILDs to represent data. Fiber optics are immune to electronic magnetic interference, but susceptible to chromatic dispersion. Information is transmitted through the fiber as pulsating light. The light pulses represent bits of information. Fiber optics give users of telecommunications added capacity, better transmission quality, and increased clarity.[2,300]

Fiber optic transceiver: Device that converts fiber optic signals to digital signals and vice versa. Usually used to make a connection from a fiber run to an Ethernet segment.[52]

Field: The smallest component under which data are entered through data capture or data entry.[4]

Field components: Makes up the discernible parts or components of a field entry. For example, the patient's name is recorded as last name, first name, and middle initial, each of which is a distinct entity separated by a component delimiter.[9]

Field level security: Data protection and/or authorization of specified fields or data elements within files, rather than of entire files.[301]

FIFO (First in, first out): A data buffer approach to handling program requests from queues or stacks so that the oldest request is handled next.[2]

File: A collection of data stored in one unit. Files have unique names and entities that allow for them to be stored, moved, and edited. Types of files include documents, pictures, audio, video, data library, or application. Often, a file's extension describes its type, such as a Microsoft document file (.doc) or an audio file (MP3, WAV, etc.).[73]

File extension: A file extension is an identifier used as a suffix to a name of the computer file in an operating system such as Microsoft Windows®. It can be categorized as a type of metadata. A file extension helps the operating system to understand the characteristics of the file, and to some extent, its intended use.[52]

File server: A networked computer that provides file handling and storage for users with network access. A computer that each computer on a network can use to access and retrieve files that can be shared among the attached computers. Access to a file is usually controlled by the file server software, rather than by the operating system of the computer that accesses the file.[2]

File transfer protocol: *See* **FTP.**

Filmless radiology: Use of devices that replace film by acquiring digital images and related patient information, and transmit, store, retrieve, and display them electronically.[167]

Filter: A program that accepts a certain type of data as input, transforms the data in some manner, and then outputs the transformed data. Also defined as a pattern through which data are passed. Only data that match the pattern are allowed to pass through the filter.[39]

FIPS (Federal information processing standard): Under the Information Technology Management Reform Act (Public Law 104-106), the Secretary of Commerce approves standards and guidelines that are developed by the National Institute of Standards and Technology (NIST) for federal computer systems. These standards and guidelines are issued by NIST as Federal Information Processing Standards (FIPS) for use government wide. NIST develops FIPS when there are compelling federal government requirements such as for security and interoperability and there are no acceptable industry standards or solutions.[168]

Firewall: A system designed to prevent unauthorized access to or from a network. Firewalls can be implemented in both hardware and software, or a combination of both.[1]

Firmware: Software programs or computer instructions written to a hardware device on how a device communicates with various hardware components. It is typically stored in the flash ROM of a hardware device, meaning it can be erased and rewritten because it is a type of flash memory.[18]

First in, first out: *See* **FIFO.**

FISMA (Federal Information Security Management Act): U.S. legislation that defines a comprehensive framework to protect government information, operations and assets against natural or man-made threats. FISMA was signed into law part of the Electronic Government Act of 2002.[2]

Fixed wireless: The point-to-point transmission over the air between stationary devices. Fixed wireless is typically used for "last mile" connectivity to buildings, and it implies high-speed (broadband) transmission. Contrast with mobile wireless.[150]

Flash drive: A small, ultra-portable storage device which, unlike an optical drive or a traditional hard drive, has no moving parts. Flash drives connect to computers and other devices via a built-in USB Type-A plug, making a flash drive a kind of combination USB device and cable.[203]

Flash memory: Nonvolatile, rewritable storage chip. Comprised of cells that hold a charge without power, flash memory is extremely durable and used in just about every electronic device, including cameras, smartphones, tablets, music players and USB drives.[150]

Flat files: 1. Files in which each record has the same length, whether or not all the space is used. Empty parts of the record are padded with a blank, or zero, depending on the data type of each field. **2.** Refers to a file that consists of a series of fixed-length records that include some sort of record type code.[113]

Flat table: One data element per field, tables are in the simplest form.[50]

Flexibility: The ability to support architectural and hardware configuration changes.[57]

Flexible spending account: *See* **FSA**.

Flip-flop: An electronic circuit that maintains its 0 or 1 state and is used in static memories and hardware registers.[150]

Flow chart: A diagram that combines symbols and abbreviated narratives to describe a sequence of operations and/or a process. The flow chart is a tool typically associated with the waterfall methodology of software development.[2]

Flow sheet: A tabular summary of information that is arranged to display the values of variables as changed over time.[302]

Foreground: Contains the applications the user is working on.[150] *See* **Background**.

Foreign key: In relational databases, it is a field in one table that is indexed in another. Foreign keys provide the building blocks for relating tables.[150] *See* **Primary key**.

Formal system: In a concept representation, a set of machine processable definitions in a subject field.[169]

Format: Specifications of how data or files are to be characterized.[59]

Forward compatibility: Ability of an IT system to be compatible with or to support a similar version of itself in the future. Also known as upward compatibility, future-time compatibility, or newer-version compatibility.[52]

Foundational interoperability: Refers the building blocks of information exchange between disparate systems by establishing the inter-connectivity requirements needed for one system or application to share data with and receive data from another. It does not outline the ability for the receiving information technology system to interpret the data without interventions from the end user or other technologies.[53] *Definition current as of December 2018. To review any updates to this definition please visit the HIMSS website. See* **Interoperability**

FQDN (Fully qualified domain name): A phrase that describes a concept uniquely and in a manner that is intended to be unambiguous. In the context of networking, the term fully qualified domain name may be used similarly. A fully qualified domain name (FQDN) is the complete domain name for a specific computer, or host, on the Internet. Also known as fully specified name.[14,77]

FQHC (Federally Qualified Health Centers): Community-based healthcare providers that receive funds from the Health Resources and Services Administration (HRSA) Health Center Program to provide primary care services in underserved areas. They must meet a stringent set of requirements, including providing care on a sliding fee scale based on ability to pay and operating under a governing board that includes patients. FQHCs may be Community Health Centers, Migrant Health Centers, Health Care for the Homeless, and Health Centers for Residents of Public Housing.[181]

Frame: A unit of data. A frame works to help identify data packets used in networking and telecommunications structures. Frames also help to determine how data receivers interpret a stream of data from a source. Frame is a term used to refer to the existence of data at the Data Link Layer of the OSI Model.[39,52] *See* **OSI**.

Frame relay: A high-speed packet switching protocol used in wide area networks (WANs). Providing a granular service of up to DS3 speed (45 Mbps), it has become popular for LAN to LAN connections across remote distances, and services are offered by most major carriers.[150] *See* **ATM** and **SONET**.

Framework: 1. A structured description of a topic of interest, including a detailed statement of the problem(s) to be solved and the goals to be achieved. An annotated outline of all the issues that must be addressed while developing acceptable solutions to the problem(s). A description and analysis of the constraints that must be satisfied by an acceptable solution, and detailed specifications of acceptable approaches to solving the problem(s). **2.** The ideas, information, and principles that form the structure of an organization or plan.[135]

Free text: Unstructured, uncoded representations of information in text format (e.g., sentences describing the results of a patient's physical condition).[302]

FTP (File transfer protocol): A standard high-level protocol for transferring files between computers over a TCP/IP network. FTP is a client-server protocol that relies on two communications channels between client and server: a command channel for controlling the conversation and a data channel for transmitting file content. Clients initiate conversations with servers by requesting to download a file. Using FTP, a client can upload, download, delete, rename, move, and copy files on a server.[2]

Full duplex: Data transmission that occurs in both directions on a signal carrier at the same time.[2]

Fully qualified domain name: *See* **FQDN**.

Functional requirements: A declaration of intended function of a system and its components. Based on the functional requirements, an engineer determines the behavior or output that a device or software is expected to exhibit given a certain input.[52]

G

Gantt chart: A type of bar chart used in process or project planning, and control to display planned work targets for completion of work in relation to time. Typically, a Gantt chart shows the week, month, or quarter in which each activity will be completed, and the person or persons responsible for carrying out each activity.[303]

Gap analysis: The comparison of a current condition to the desired state. Gap analysis is a term also used within process analysis to describe the variance between current and future state processes.[159]

Garbage in, garbage out: *See* **GIGO**.

Gateway: 1. A computer or a network that allows access to another computer or network. **2.** A phrase used by web masters and search engine optimizers to describe a web page designed to attract visitors and search engines to a particular web site. A typical gateway page is small, simple, and highly optimized. **3.** A technical term for the software interface between a web-based shopping cart (or order form) and a merchant account.[304] *See* **Electronic commerce**.

GB (Gigabyte): Approximately one billion (1024 megabytes) bytes. Unit of computer storage capacity.[2]

GBps (Gigabits per second): Transmission of a billion bits per second.[73]

GDPR (General Data Protection Regulation): European Union (EU) regulation designed to harmonize data privacy laws across the EU, to protect and empower all EU citizen data privacy and to reshape the way organizations approach data privacy. It replaces the Data Protection Directive 95/46/EC. The regulation applies to all companies processing the personal data of data subjects residing in the EU, regardless of the company's location.[305]

GELLO (Guideline expression language, object oriented): An object-oriented query and expression language for clinical decision support.[102] Note: GELLO is an HL7 standard.[171]

General Data Protection Regulation: *See* **GDPR**.

General order message: The function of this message is to initiate the transmission of information about an order. This includes placing new orders, cancellation of existing orders, discontinuation, holding, etc. Messages can originate with a placer, filler, or interested third party.[15] Also known as ORM messages.

Genomics: The study of all of a person's genes (the genome), including interactions of those genes with each other and with the person's environment. Genomics includes the scientific study of complex diseases that are typically caused more by a combination of genetic and environmental factors than by individual genes.[172] *See* **Precision medicine.**

GIF (Graphics interchange format): An image file format used for images on the web and graphics in software programs. Unlike JPEG, GIF uses lossless compression that does not degrade the image quality.[73]

GIG (Global information grid): A globally interconnected, end-to-end set of information capabilities, associated processes, and personnel for collecting, processing, storing, disseminating, and managing information on demand.[160]

Gigabit: One billion bits; commonly used for measuring the amount of data transferred in a second between two telecommunication points.[2]

Gigabits per second: *See* **Gbps.**

Gigabyte: *See* **GB.**

Gigahertz: One billion cycles per second, commonly used to measure computer processing speeds.[73]

GIGO (Garbage in, garbage out): Synonymous with the entry of inaccurate or useless data and processed output of worthless/useless information. A concept common to computer science and mathematics: the quality of output is determined by the quality of the input.[2]

Global information grid: *See* **GIG.**

Global system for mobile communications: *See* **GSM.**

Global unique device identification database: *See* **GUDID.**

Global unique identifier: *See* **GUID.**

Graduated security: A security system that provides several levels of protection based on threats, risks, available technology, support services, time, human concerns, and economics.[64]

Granular: 1. An expression of the relative size of a unit. The smallest discrete information that can be directly retrieved. In security, it is the degree of protection. Protection at the file level is considered coarse granularity, whereas protection at the field level is finer granularity. **2.** Refers to a high degree of detail. In particular, a vocabulary that is highly granular provides names and definitions for the individual data elements within the context of a broader concept.[43]

Granularity: The level of depth represented by the data in a fact or dimension table in a data warehouse. High granularity means a minute, sometimes atomic grade of detail, often at the level of the transaction. Low granularity zooms out into a summary view of data and transactions.[173]

Graphical user interface: *See* **GUI.**

Grid computing: Uses the resources of many separate computers connected by a network (usually the Internet) to solve large-scale computation problems. Also known as Beowulf computing.[306]

GSM (Global system for mobile communications): 1. A worldwide digital mobile telephony system widely used in Europe and other parts of the world. GSM uses a variation of time division multiple access (TDMA). It digitizes and compresses data, then sends it down a channel with two other streams of user data, each in its own time slot. GSM typically operates at either the 900 MHz or 1800 MHz frequency band.[2]

GS1 standards: Set of standards that provide a common language and help to create seamless work processes that allow businesses to identify, capture, and share information the same way all over the world. A common standard from the GS1 organization is the UPC barcode.[307]

GUDID (Global unique device identification database): A Food and Drug Administration (FDA) publicly accessible database that would hold information about each medical device marketed in the United States.[41]

GUI (Graphical user interface): 1. User interface that employs graphical elements such as windows, icons, and buttons as opposed to text-based command-line entry to execute programs, commands or resources.[73]

GUID (Global unique identifier): A Microsoft® term for a number that its programming generates to create a unique identity for each entity. GUIDs are widely used in Microsoft products to identify interfaces, replica sets, records, and other objects.[308]

Guideline expression language, object oriented: *See* **GELLO**.

G

H

Hacker: Unauthorized user who attempts to or gains access to an information system.[1]

Hacktivist/hacktivism: A computer hacker whose activity is aimed at promoting a social or political cause.[309]

Hadoop: An open source software framework for storing data and running applications on clusters of commodity hardware. It provides massive storage for any kind of data, large processing power, and the ability to handle virtually limitless concurrent tasks or jobs.[116]

Half duplex: The transmission of data in both directions, but only one direction at a time. For example, two-way radio (push-to-talk phones) use half-duplex communications. When one party speaks, the other party listens.[150]

HAN (Health alert network): To ensure that each community has rapid and timely access to emergent health information; a cadre of highly trained professional personnel; and evidence-based practices and procedures for effective public health preparedness, response, and service on a 24/7 basis.[80]

Handheld: A portable computer that is small enough to hold in one's hand. Used to refer to a variety of devices ranging from personal data assistance, such as smartphones, to more powerful devices that offer many of the capabilities of desktop or laptop computers. Handhelds are used in clinical practice for such tasks as ordering prescriptions, accessing patients' medical records, and documenting patient encounters.[52]

Hard copy: Printed output.[150]

Hard disk: Part of a unit, often called a "disk drive" or "hard disk drive," that stores and provides relatively quick access to large amounts of data on an electromagnetically charged surface or set of surfaces.[2]

Hardware: The physical equipment of a computer system, including the central processing unit, data storage devices, terminals, and printers.[52]

Harmonization: The prevention or elimination of differences in the technical content of standards having the same scope, particularly differences that may cause hindrances to trade. The coordination processes by standard development organizations to make standards work together. Processes to achieve harmonization include convergence, modeling, mapping, translation, and other techniques.[43]

Hash function: A type of cryptography algorithm in which a fixed-length hash value is computed based on the plaintext, making it impossible for either the contents or length of the plaintext to be recovered.[310]

Hash value: A numeric value of fixed length that uniquely identifies data or the contents of a file. It serves as a digital fingerprint of a message's contents, which ensures that the message has not been altered by an intruder, virus or other means. If the data or contents are modified in any way the hash value will also change significantly.[310,311]

Hashing: Iterative process that computes a hash value from a particular data unit using a mathematical function. It enables security during the process of message transmission. A formula generates a hash value to protect against tampering.[52] *See* **Hash function**.

Hashtag: A type of label or metadata tag used on social network and blogging services to make it easier for users to find messages with a specific theme or content or community.[6] Users create and use hashtags by placing the hash character "#" in front of a word or un-spaced phrase. Hashtags tie public conversation from different users into a single stream that can be found by searching for a hashtag, clicking on one, or using a third-party monitoring tool.[174]

HCPCS (Healthcare Common Procedure Coding System): For Medicare and other health insurance programs to ensure that healthcare claims are processed in an orderly and consistent manner, standardized coding systems are essential. The HCPCS Level II Code Set is one of the standard code sets used for this purpose. The HCPCS is divided into two principal subsystems, referred to as level I and level II of the HCPCS.[26]

hData: A specification for lightweight, scalable information exchange. hData creates network-facing interfaces based on REST and Atom that can enable interactions with existing health data systems.[9]

Heads-up display: *See* **HUD**.

Health alert network: *See* **HAN**.

Health informatics: The intersection of clinical informatics and public health informatics. It is one of several fields which compose the interdisciplinary field known as biomedical informatics. Health informatics is the interdisciplinary study of the design, development, adoption and application of IT-based innovations in healthcare services delivery, management and planning.[86]

Health information: Information, whether oral or recorded in any form or medium, that (1) is created or received by a healthcare provider, health plan, public health authority, employer, life insurer, school or university, or healthcare clearinghouse; and (2) relates to the past, present, or future physical or mental health or condition of an individual; the provision of healthcare to an individual; or the past, present, or future payment for the provision of healthcare to an individual.[20]

Health information exchange: *See* **HIE**.

Health information organization: *See* **HIO**.

Health information privacy: An individual's right to control the acquisition, uses, or disclosures of his or her identifiable health data.[20] *See* **HIPAA**.

Health information security: Refers to physical, technological, or administrative safeguards or tools used to protect identifiable health data from unwarranted access or disclosure.[20]

Health information service provider: *See* **HISP.**

Health information system: Computer systems that capture, store, process, communicate, and present any healthcare information, including patient medical record information (PMRI).[43]

Health information technology: *See* **HIT.**

Health Information Technology Advisory Committee: *See* **HITAC.**

Health Information Technology for Economic and Clinical Health Act: *See* **HITECH Act.**

Health insurance exchange: *See* **HIEx.**

Health Insurance Portability and Accountability Act of 1996: *See* **HIPAA.**

Health interoperability ecosystem: Comprises individuals, systems and processes that want to share, exchange, and access all forms of health information, including discrete, narrative and multimedia. Individuals, patients, providers, hospitals/health systems, researchers, payers, suppliers, and systems are potential stakeholders within this ecosystem. Each is involved in the creation, exchange and use of health information and/or data. An efficient health interoperability ecosystem provides an information infrastructure that uses technical standards, policies, and protocols to enable seamless and secure capture, discovery, exchange, and utilization of health information.[53]

Health IT: *See* **HIT.**

Health outcome: *See* **Outcome.**

Health plan identifier: *See* **HPID.**

Health Quality Measure Format: *See* **HQMF.**

Healthcare Clearinghouse: Organization that processes health information received from another entity in a nonstandard format or containing nonstandard data content, into standard data elements or a standard transaction, or vice versa.[20]

Healthcare Common Procedure Coding System: *See* **HCPCS.**

Healthcare data card: A machine-readable card conformant to ISO 7810, intended for use within the healthcare domain.[120]

Healthcare effectiveness data and information set: *See* **HEDIS.**

Healthcare evaluation: Critical assessment, through rigorous processes, of an aspect of healthcare to assess whether it fulfills its objectives.[312]

Healthcare terminology: A collective term used to describe the continuum of code set, classification, and nomenclature (or vocabulary). A code is a representation assigned to a term so that it may more readily be processed. A classification arranges or organizes like or related terms for easy retrieval. A nomenclature, or vocabulary, is a set of specialized terms that facilitates precise communication by eliminating ambiguity. The term *controlled vocabulary* suggests only the set of individual terms in the vocabulary. A *structured vocabulary*, or *reference terminology*, relates terms to one another (with a set of relationships) that qualifies them (with a set of attributes) to promote precise and accurate interpretation.[43]

HealthKit: Apple's software platform for collecting data from various health and fitness apps, and then making that data easily available to Apple users through the company's new Health app.[177]

HEDIS (Healthcare effectiveness data and information set): A tool used by health plans to measure performance on important dimensions of care and service. Altogether, HEDIS consists of 81 measures across 5 domains of care.[179]

Hexadecimal: Base 16 numbering system where 4 bits are used to represent each digit. Uses the 0–9 digits and A–F letters for the representations of the 10–15 digits.[313]

HIE (Health information exchange): 1. The sharing action between any two or more organizations with an executed business/legal arrangement that have deployed commonly agreed-upon technology with applied standards for the purpose of electronically exchanging health-related data between the organizations. **2.** A catch-all phrase for all health information exchanges, including RHIOs, QIOs, AHRQ-funded communities, and private exchanges. **3.** A concept evolved from the community health information exchanges of the mid-1990s. HIE provides the capability to electronically move clinical information among disparate healthcare information systems, and maintain the meaning of the information being exchanged. The goal of HIE is to facilitate access to and retrieval of clinical data to provide safer, more timely, efficient, effective, equitable, patient-centered care. HIE is also used by public health authorities to assist in the analysis of the health of populations.[12,46,53]

HIEx (Health insurance exchange): A set of state-regulated and standardized healthcare plans in the United States from which individuals may purchase health insurance eligible for federal subsidies. All exchanges must be fully certified and operational by January 1, 2014, under federal law outlined in the Affordable Care Act (ACA).[314] Also referred to as a health insurance marketplace.

Hijacking: 1. A type of network security attack in which the attacker takes control of communication. **2.** An attack in which the Attacker is able to insert himself or herself between a Claimant and a Verifier subsequent to a successful authentication exchange between the latter two parties. The Attacker is able to pose as a Subscriber to the Verifier or vice versa to control session data exchange. Sessions between the Claimant and the Relying Party can also be similarly compromised.[2,1]

HIO (Health information organization): An organization that oversees and governs the exchange of health-related information among organizations according to nationally recognized standards. The purpose of an HIO is to perform oversight and governance functions for health information exchanges (HIEs).[12]

HIPAA (Health Insurance Portability and Accountability Act of 1996): Title I of HIPAA protects health insurance coverage for workers and their families when they change or lose their jobs. Title II of HIPAA, the Administrative Simplification (AS) provisions, requires the establishment of national standards for electronic healthcare transactions and national identifiers for providers, health insurance plans, and employers. The AS provisions also address the security and privacy of health data. The standards are meant to improve the efficiency and effectiveness of the nation's healthcare system by encouraging the widespread use of electronic data interchange in healthcare. Also known as the Kennedy-Kassebaum Bill, K2, Public Law 104-91.[20]

HIPAA administrative code sets: Code sets that characterize a general business situation, rather than a medical condition or service.[20] Also called nonmedical code sets.

HIPAA administrative simplification: HIPAA, Title II, Subtitle F, gives the U.S. Department of Health & Human Services the authority to mandate the use of standards for the electronic exchange of healthcare data; specify what medical and administrative code sets should be used within those standards; require the use of national identification systems for healthcare patients, providers, payers (or plans), and employers (or sponsors); and specify the types of measures required to protect the security and privacy of personally identifiable healthcare information.[20]

HIPAA clearinghouse (or healthcare clearinghouse): Under HIPAA, this is a public or private entity that reformats health information, especially billing transactions, from a nonstandard format into a standard and approved format.[20]

HIPAA data dictionary: A data dictionary that defines and cross-references the contents of all X12 transactions included in the HIPAA mandate. The dictionary is maintained by the X12N/TG3.[20]

HIPAA Privacy Rule: Establishes national standards to protect individuals' medical records and other personal health information and applies to health plans, healthcare clearinghouses, and those healthcare providers that conduct certain healthcare transactions electronically. The Rule requires appropriate safeguards to protect the privacy of personal health information, and sets limits and conditions on the uses and disclosures that may be made of such information without patient authorization. The Rule also gives patients' rights over their health information, including rights to examine and obtain a copy of their health records, and to request corrections. The Privacy Rule is located at 45 CFR Part 160 and Subparts A and E of Part 164.[35]

HIPAA Security Rule: Establishes national standards to protect individuals' electronic personal health information that is created, received, used, or maintained by a covered entity. The Security Rule requires appropriate administrative, physical, and technical safeguards to ensure the confidentiality, integrity, and security of electronic protected health information. The Security Rule is located at 45 CFR Part 160 and Subparts A and C of Part 164.[35]

HIPAA standard: Any data element or transaction that meets each of the standards and implementation specifications adopted or established by the Secretary of the U.S. Department of Health & Human Services.[20]

HIPAA standard setting organization: An organization accredited by the American National Standards Institute (ANSI) to develop information transactions or data elements for health plans, clearinghouses, and/or providers.[20]

HIPAA unique identifier: A standard unique health identifier for each employer, health plan, and healthcare provider, for use in the healthcare system.[26]

HIS (Health information system): Any system that captures, stores, manages, or transmits information related to the health of individuals or activities of organizations that work within the health sector.[315]

HISP (Health information service provider): Term used by the DIRECT project to describe both a function (the management of security and transport for directed exchange) and an organizational model (an organization that performs HISP functions on behalf of the sending or receiving organization or individual).[180]

HIT (Health information technology): An area of information technology (IT) that involves the design, development, creation, use, and maintenance of information systems for the health and healthcare markets.[2] It involves the application of information processing with both computer hardware and software that deals with the storage, retrieval, sharing, and use of health and healthcare data, information, and knowledge for communication and decision-making. As an industry, it has gained prominence in the last several years as healthcare has modernized to adopt IT. Enterprise resource planning, revenue cycle management, and other business applications have been joined by electronic health records (EHRs), population health platforms, personal health devices, and other health-oriented applications to represent health IT.[181]

HITECH Act (Health Information Technology for Economic and Clinical Health Act): Part of the American Recovery and Reinvestment Act of 2009 (ARRA) that addresses privacy and security concerns related to the transmission of electronic health information. The HITECH Act broadened the scope of privacy and security measures for personal health records (PHRs) under Health Insurance Portability and Accountability Act (HIPAA), and also increased certain legal liabilities for noncompliance.[35]

HITAC (Health Information Technology Advisory Committee): Group that was established in the 21st Century Cures Act (P.L. 114-255) and is governed by the provisions of the Federal Advisory Committee Act (FACA), P.L. 92-463, as amended, 5 U.S.C. App. 2, which sets forth standards for the formation and use of federal advisory committees. The Health Information Technology Advisory Committee (HITAC) will recommend to the National Coordinator for Health Information Technology, policies, standards, implementation specifications, and certification criteria, relating to the implementation of a health information technology infrastructure, nationally and locally, that advances the electronic access, exchange, and use of health information. HITAC unifies the roles of, and replaces, the Health Information Technology Policy Committee and the Health Information Technology Standards Committee, as in existence before the date of the enactment of the 21st Century Cures Act.[12]

Hospital Availability Exchange: *See* **EDXL-HAVE**.

HL7 V2: A messaging standard for electronic data exchange that is widely implemented in healthcare globally. The standard allows the exchange of clinical data between systems. It is designed to support a central patient care system as well as a more distributed environment where data reside in departmental systems.[9]

Host: For companies or individuals with a web site, a host is a computer with a web server that serves the pages for one or more web sites. A host can also be the company that provides that service, which is known as hosting.[2]

HQMF (Health Quality Measure Format): A standards-based representation of quality measures as electronic documents. It is developed by Health Level Seven International (HL7). HQMF defines the information necessary to compute a quality measure and result value.[88]

HTML (Hypertext markup language): 1. American Standard Code for Information Exchange (ASCII)-based language used for creating files to display documents or web pages to web browsers. **2.** Hypertext markup language is the standard provided by World Wide Web Consortium (W3G) used for web pages on the Internet.[2]

HTTP (Hypertext transfer protocol): 1. Communication link protocol used by web servers and browsers to transfer/exchange HTML documents or files (text, graphic images, sound, video, and other multimedia files) over the Internet. **2.** Protocol with lightness and speed necessary for a distributed collaborative hypermedia information system. It is a generic, stateless, object-oriented protocol, which may be used for many similar tasks, such as name servers and distributed object-oriented systems, by extending the commands or "methods" used.[2,9] *See* **HTTPS**.

HTTPS (HTTP Secure or HTTP over SSL): The use of Secure Socket Layer (SSL) or Transport Layer Security (TLS) as a sublayer of regular HTTP application layering. HTTPS is a web protocol developed by Netscape and built into its and other browsers, which encrypts and decrypts user page requests, as well as the pages that are returned by the web server.[2]

Hub: Electronic network device to which multiple networked computers are attached. Divides a data channel into two or more channels of lower bandwidth. Hubs function at the physical layer (first layer) of the open systems interconnection (OSI) model. These devices have long since been replaced by switches, but it is possible to see variants (e.g., switching hubs/intelligent hubs).[39] *See* **Concentrator.**

HUD (Heads-up display): Any transparent or miniaturized display that presents data without requiring users to look away from their usual viewpoints.[2]

Hybrid network: A communications network comprising public and private transports.[150]

Hybrid smartcard: A card that has two chips: one with a contact interface and one with a contactless interface. The chips are not interconnected.[316]

Hype cycle: Hype Cycle of Emerging Technology (Gartner Group), a five-stage progression concerning "the visibility" of an emerging technology (e.g., in the popular press): 1. technology trigger; 2. peak of inflated expectations; 3. trough of disillusionment; 4. slope of enlightenment; and 5. plateau of productivity. Relative values on a 0–10 scale: 0, 9, 2, 3, 4. Used to convey the sense that new technologies are always oversold at first. Though they eventually are useful, they seldom live up to initial expectations.[142]

Hyperledger: An open source collaborative effort to advance cross-industry blockchain technologies, hosted by the Linux Foundation. Hyperledger offers a number of tools, frameworks, and platforms for developers looking to implement blockchain and distributed ledger technologies.[317]

Hypertext markup language: *See* **HTML.**

Hypertext transfer protocol: *See* **HTTP.**

Hypervisor: A function which abstracts operating systems and applications from the underlying computer hardware. This abstraction allows the underlying host machine hardware to independently operate one or more virtual machines as guests, allowing multiple guest VMs to effectively share the system's physical compute resources, such as processor cycles, memory space, network bandwidth, and so on. A hypervisor is sometimes also called a virtual machine monitor.[2]

Hz (Hertz): One cycle per second. Processing speeds for CPUs are measured in GHz.[73]

I

I/O (Input/output device): A hardware device that has the ability to accept inputted, outputted, or other processed data.[52]

I/O bus: A signal route to which a number of input and output devices can be connected in parallel.[56]

IAM (Identity access management): Set of services to include authentication, user provisioning (UP), password management, role matrix management, enterprise single sign-on, enterprise access management, federation, virtual and meta-directory services, and auditing.[20]

ICC (Integrated circuit chip): A small chip that can function as an amplifier, oscillator, timer, microprocessor, or even computer memory. An ICC is a small wafer, usually made of silicon, that can hold billions of transistors, resistors, and capacitors. These extremely small electronics can perform calculations and store data using either digital or analog technology.[2]

ICD (International Classification of Diseases): The standard diagnostic tool for epidemiology, health management, and clinical purposes, including the analysis of the general health situation of population groups. Also used to monitor the incidence and prevalence of diseases and other health programs and to classify diseases and other health problem records on the many types of health and vital records include death certificates and health records. It may also be used for reimbursement and resource allocation decision-making by countries. It is published by the World Health Organization. The latest edition currently in practice in the United States is ICD-10, endorsed in 1990 by the World Health Assembly but not implemented within the US healthcare system until 2015.[184]

ICIDH (International Classification of Improvements, Disability, and Health): Classification that promotes a common framework and definitions of disability-related issues. The ICIDH was published in 1980 by the World Health Organisation, Geneva. The ICIDH distinguishes three dimensions that can be studied to monitor the situation of people with disability: impairment (organ and body dimension), disability (individual dimension), and handicap (social dimension).

ICMP (Internet control message protocol): An extension to the Internet protocol, or IP, that supports packets containing error, control, and information messages. The PING command uses ICMP to test an Internet connection.[73]

ICO (Initial coin offering): An unregulated means by which funds are raised for a new cryptocurrency venture. An ICO is used by startups to bypass the rigorous and regulated capital-raising process required by venture capitalists or banks. In an ICO campaign, a percentage of the cryptocurrency is sold to early backers of the project in exchange for legal tender or other cryptocurrencies.[18]

Icon: A picture or symbol that graphically represents an object or a concept.[29]

ICON: An informational tool to describe nursing practice and provide data representing nursing practice in comprehensive health information systems. A combinatorial terminology for nursing practice that includes nursing phenomena, nursing actions, and nursing outcomes, and facilitates cross-mapping of local terms and existing vocabularies and classifications.[185]

ICR (Intelligent call routing): Capability that automatically routes each call, based on caller profile, to the best available agent to handle the need, anywhere in the network.[73] *See* **PING.**

ICR (Intelligent character recognition): The computer translation of manually entered text characters into machine-readable characters.[73]

Identification: The ability to identify uniquely a user of a system or an application that is running in the system.[64]

Identification and authentication: **1.** Identification is the ability to identify uniquely a user of a system or an application that is running in the system. Authentication is the ability to prove that a user or application is genuinely who that person or what that application claims to be. Authentication can occur through a variety of mechanisms, including challenge/response, time-based code sequences, biometric comparison, or other techniques. **2.** Use of a password, or some other form of identification, to screen users and to check their authorization.[64]

Identifier: Unique data used to represent a person's identity and associated attributes. A name or a card number are examples of identifiers.[64]

Identity: The set of physical and behavioral characteristics by which an individual is uniquely recognizable.[64]

Identity access management: *See* **IAM.**

Identity digital management: *See* **IDM.**

Identity management system: *See* **IDMS.**

Identity proofing: The process of providing sufficient information (e.g., identity history, credentials, documents) to a personal identity verification (PIV) registrar when attempting to establish an identity.[64]

Identity verification: The process of confirming or denying that a claimed identity is correct by comparing the credentials of a person requesting access with those previously proven and stored in the personal identity verification (PIV) card/system, and associated with the identity being claimed.[64]

IDM (Identity digital management): Composed of the set of business processes, and a supporting infrastructure, for the creation, maintenance, and use of digital identities within a legal and policy context.[20]

IDMS (Identity management system): 1. Composed of one or more systems or applications that manage identity verification, validation, and issuance process. **2.** Software that is used to automate administrative tasks such as resetting user passwords. It enables users to reset their own passwords. There is also identity management "password synchronization" software that enables users to access resources across the system with a single password, or single sign-on. In an enterprise setting, identity management is used to increase security and productivity, while decreasing cost and redundant effort.[10,64]

IDN (Integrated delivery network): A formal system of providers and sites of care that provides both healthcare services and a health insurance plan to patients in a particular geographic area. The functionalities included in an IDN vary but can include acute care, long-term health, specialty clinics, primary care, and home care services—all supporting an owned health plan.[186]

IDR (Intelligent document recognition): 1. Based on intelligent character recognition, the IT system automatically identifies structural features of a document to allow for a more rapid creation of the document text. **2.** Provides the ability to make sense of and help manage the unstructured, untagged information that is coming into the corporation or organization. It can provide the front-end understanding needed to feed business process management (BPM) and business intelligence (BI) applications, as well as traditional accounting and document or records management systems.[187,]

IDS (Integrated delivery system): *See* **IDN.**

IGP (Interior gateway protocol): A protocol for exchanging routing information between gateways (hosts with routers) within an autonomous network.[2]

IHE (Integrating the Healthcare Enterprise): An initiative by healthcare professionals and industry to improve the way computer systems in healthcare share information. IHE promotes the coordinated use of established standards such as DICOM and HL7 to address specific clinical need in support of optimal patient care. Systems developed in accordance with IHE communicate with one another better, are easier to implement, and enable care providers to use information more effectively.[27] *See* **Appendix B.**

IHE profile: Provides a common language for purchasers and vendors to discuss the integration needs of healthcare sites and the integration capabilities of healthcare IT products. IHE profiles offer developers a clear implementation path for communication standards supported by industry partners and are carefully documented, reviewed, and tested. They give purchasers a tool that reduces the complexity, cost, and anxiety of implementing operating systems.[27]

IIF (Information in identifiable form): Any representation of information that permits the identity of an individual to whom the information applies to be reasonably inferred by either direct or indirect means.[64]

IIS (Immunization information systems): Confidential, population-based, computerized databases that record all immunization doses and related information as administered by participating providers to persons residing within a given geopolitical area.[80]

IIS (Internet information systems): A flexible, general-purpose web server from Microsoft that runs on Windows® systems to serve requested HTML pages or files.[2]

IKE (Internet key exchange): A key management protocol standard that is used in conjunction with the IPSec standard. IPSec is an IP security feature that provides robust authentication and encryption of IP packets.[52]

ILD (Injection laser diode): Also known as an injection laser or diode laser, it is a semiconductor device that produces coherent radiation (in which the waves are all at the same frequency and phase) in the visible or infrared (IR) spectrum when current passes through it. Laser diodes are used in optical fiber systems, compact disk (CD) players, laser printers, remote control devices, and intrusion detection systems.[2]

Image compression: The process of encoding or converting an image file in such a way that it consumes less space than the original file.[52]

Imaging: In medicine, the use of a variety of technologies to view the human body in order to diagnose, monitor, or treat medical conditions. Each type of technology gives different information about the area of the body being studied or treated, related to possible disease, injury, or the effectiveness of medical treatment.[41]

Immunization information systems: *See* **IIS**.

Immutable object: In computer science, an object whose state, or data, cannot change after it is constructed. Maximum reliance on immutable objects is widely accepted as a sound strategy for creating simple, reliable code. Immutable objects are particularly useful in concurrent applications. Since they cannot change state, they cannot be corrupted by thread interference or observed in an inconsistent state.[11]

Impact analysis: Process of analyzing all operational functions and the effect that an operational interruption might have upon them.[87]

Implementation: In an IT context, software or hardware implementation refers to the process of installing and maintaining a new system and making sure it operates correctly in its new business environment.[2]

Implementation guide: 1. A document explaining the proper use of a standard for a specific purpose. **2.** Method for standardized installation and maintenance of computer software and hardware. The implementation guidelines include recommended administrative processes and span the devices' lifecycle.[2,113]

Implementation specification: Specific instructions for implementing a standard.[113]

In-band: Communications that occur together in a common communications method or channel. For example, a privacy label that applies to a clinical document will be sent in-band with the document.[113]

Incident: Event that has the capacity to lead to human, intangible, or physical loss, or a disruption of an organization's operations, services, or functions—which, if not managed, can escalate into an emergency, crisis, or disaster.[87]

Independent practice association: *See* **IPA.**

Indicator: A measurable variable (or characteristic) that can be used to determine the degree of adherence to a standard or the level of quality achieved.[2]

Individual: Person who is the subject of information collected, used, or disclosed by the entity holding the information.[20]

Individually identifiable data: Data that are a part of health information, including demographic information collected from an individual that are individually identifying.[318]

Individually identifiable health information: Information that is a subset of health information, including demographic information collected from an individual, and: (1) is created or received by a healthcare provider, health plan, employer, or healthcare clearinghouse; and (2) relates to the past, present, or future physical or mental health or condition of an individual; the provision of healthcare to an individual; or the past, present, or future payment for the provision of healthcare to an individual. Information that (1) identifies the individual; or (2) with respect to which there is a reasonable basis to believe the information can be used to identify the individual.[20]

Individually identifying information: Single item or compilation of information or data that indicate or reveal the identity of an individual, either specifically (such as the individual's name or Social Security number), or that do not specifically identify the individual but from which the individual's identity can reasonably be ascertained.[20]

Infobutton: A simple alerting system that provides information on request. The information may be keyed to topic and/or user. May or may not be linked to decision support system.[189]

Infographics: A representation of information in a graphic format designed to make the data easily understandable at a glance. The ability to package more information in a smaller space makes infographics an attractive tool for instruction and marketing.[2,52]

Informatics: The study of the behavior and structure of any system that generates, stores, processes, and then presents information; it is basically the science of information. The field takes into consideration the interaction between the information systems and the user, as well as the construction of the interfaces between the two, such as the user interface.[52]

Information: Data that have been processed, organized, structured, or presented in a given context to make them meaningful or useful.[319]

Information asset: Refers to any information in any form (e.g., written, verbal, oral, or electronic) upon which the organization places a measurable value. This includes information created by the entity holding the information, gathered for the entity, or stored by the entity for external parties.[20]

Information compromise: An intentional or accidental disclosure or surrender of clinical data to an unauthorized receiver.[73]

Information exchange initiative: Efforts by two or more independent healthcare organizations (HCOs) in a geographic area to collaborate to share common patient information for the improvement in community health status, patient care, or viability of the HCOs.[10]

Information flow model: A diagrammatic representation of the flow and exchange of information within a system. Data flow models are used to graphically represent the flow of data in an information system by describing the processes involved in transferring data from input to file storage and reports generation.[190]

Information infrastructure: **1.** The combination of computers and an information system. **2.** The standards, laws, regulations, business practices, and technologies needed to facilitate unauthorized sharing of comparable data in a safe and secure manner.[43]

Information in identifiable form: *See* **IIF.**

Information interchange: (American Standard Code) A code for information exchange between computers made by different companies; a string of seven binary digits represents each character; used in most microcomputers.[73]

Information model: **1.** A conceptual model of the information needed to support a business function or process. **2.** A representation of concepts, relationships, constraints, rules, and operations to specify data semantics for a chosen domain.[117]

Information modeling: The building of abstract models for the purpose of developing an abstract system.[236]

Information privacy: The ability an organization or individual has to determine what data in a computer system can be shared with third parties.[2]

Information resource department: *See* **IRD.**

Information resource management: *See* **IRM.**

Information security: A set of strategies for managing the processes, tools, and policies necessary to prevent, detect, document, and counter threats to digital and non-digital information. Information security responsibilities include establishing a set of business processes that will protect information assets regardless of how the information is formatted or whether it is in transit, is being processed, or is at rest in storage.[2]

Information system: An integrated set of components for collecting, storing, and processing data and for providing information, knowledge, and digital products.[320]

Information system architecture: A framework from which applications, system software, and hardware can be developed in a coherent manner, and in which every part fits together without containing a mass of design details.[236]

Information technology: The hardware, firmware, and software used as part of the information system to perform information functions. This definition includes computers, telecommunications, automated information systems, and automatic data processing equipment. Information technology (IT) includes any assembly of computer hardware, software, and/or firmware configured to collect, create, communicate, compute, disseminate, process, store, and/or control data or information.[1]

Information Technology Management Reform Act of 1996: *See* **ITMRA.**

Information warfare: The tactical and strategic use of information to gain an advantage.[52]

Infrared Data Association: *See* **IrDA.**

Infrastructure-centric: A security management approach that considers information systems and their computing environment as a single entity.[21]

Inheritance: In object-oriented programming, the concept that when a class of objects is defined, any subclass that is defined can inherit the definitions of one or more general classes. For the programmer this means that an object in a subclass need not carry its own definition of data and methods that are generic to the class (or classes) of which it is a part. This not only speeds up program development; it also ensures an inherent validity to the defined subclass object (what works and is consistent about the class will also work for the subclass).[2]

Initiator: An (authenticated) entity (e.g., human user or computer-based entity) that attempts to access other entities.[24] Also known as claimant or principal.

Injection laser diode: *See* **ILD.**

Inpatient: Patient in the hospital who receives lodging and food as well as treatment.[26]

Inpatient record: Healthcare record of a hospitalized patient.[26]

Inputs: The resources needed to carry out a process or provide a service. Inputs required in healthcare are usually financial, physical structures, such as buildings, supplies and equipment, personnel, and clients.[2]

Integrated care: The systematic coordination of general and behavioral healthcare. Integrating mental health, substance abuse, and primary care services produces the best outcomes and proves the most effective approach to caring for people with multiple healthcare needs.[193]

Integrated circuit chip: *See* **ICC.**

Integrated client: Existing applications in hospitals and other medical facilities that will provide EHR functionality by integrating with the EHR using specified HL7 v3 messages.[57]

Integrated delivery network: *See* **IDN.**

Integrated delivery system: *See* **IDS**.

Integrated device electronics: *See* **IDE**.

Integrated network: A health network working together, using proven protocols and measures, to improve patient care, decrease cost, and demonstrate value to the market. Also known as clinically integrated network.[321]

Integrated service digital network: *See* **ISDN**.

Integrating the Healthcare Enterprise: *See* **IHE**.

Integration: **1.** The process of bringing together related parts into a single system. To make various components function as a connected system. **2.** Combining separately developed parts into a whole, so that they work together. The means of integration may vary, from simply mating the parts together at an interface to radically altering the parts or providing something to mediate between them.[57]

Integration layer: Software component that presents a single, consolidated point of access to several systems and/or services.[57]

Integration profile: A precise description of how standards are to be implemented to address a specific clinical or operational integration need. Each integration profile includes definition of the use case, the information and workflow involved, and the set of actors and transactions that address that need. Integration profiles reference the fully detailed implementation specifications defined in the IHE technical framework in a form that is convenient to use in requests for proposals and product descriptions.[27]

Integration services: This group of services is made up of services that manage the integration, message brokering, and service catalog functions.[2]

Integration testing: A testing event that seeks to uncover errors in the interactions and interfaces among application software components when they are combined to form larger parts of a system.[50]

Integrity: **1.** Quality of an IT system reflecting the logical correctness and reliability of the operating system; the logical completeness of the hardware and software implementing the protection mechanisms; and the consistency of the data structures and occurrence of the stored data. It is composed of data integrity and system integrity. **2.** Knowledge that a message has not been modified while in transit. May be done with digitally signed message digest codes. Data integrity, the accuracy and completeness of the data, program integrity, system integrity, and network integrity are all components of computer and system security.[21]

Intelligent agent: A type of software application that searches, retrieves, and presents information from the Internet. This application automates the process of extracting data from the Internet, such as information selected based on a predefined criterion, keywords, or any specified information/entity to be searched.[52]

Intelligent call routing: *See* **ICR**.

Intelligent character recognition: *See* **ICR**.

Intelligent document recognition: *See* **IDR**.

Intended use/intended purpose: Use for which a product, process, or service is intended according to the specifications, instructions, and information provided by the manufacturer.[194]

Interaction model: Logical diagram or narrative describing the exchange of data and sequence of method invocation between objects to perform a specific task within a use case.[2]

Interactive services detection: A feature for legacy applications that detect if a service is trying to interact with the Windows® desktop.[322]

Interactive voice response: *See* **IVR**.

Interface: Computer hardware or software that is designed to communicate information between devices, between programs, or between a computer and a user.[43]

Interface engine: Tool that translates functions from different systems and protocols into a common format to facilitate information sharing. It is a translator for data or files to pass between systems.[10]

Interface terminology: Support interactions between healthcare providers and computer-based applications. They aid practitioners in converting clinical "free text" thoughts into the structured, formal data representations, used internally by application programs.[115]

Interior gateway protocol: *See* **IGP**.

International standard: Standard that is adopted by an international standardizing/standards organization and made available to the public.[52]

Internet: The global communication network that allows almost all computers worldwide to connect and exchange information.[44]

Internet control message protocol: *See* **ICMP**.

Internet information server: *See* **IIS**.

Internet key exchange: *See* **IKE**.

Internet of things: *See* **IoT**.

Internet Network Information Center: *See* **InterNIC**.

Internet protocol: *See* **IP**.

Internet protocol address: *See* **IP address**.

Internet protocol datagram: *See* **IPsec**.

Internet protocol security: *See* **IPsec**.

Internet relay chat: *See* **IRC**.

Internet service provider: *See* **ISP**.

Internetwork packet exchange/sequence packet exchange: *See* **IPX/SPX**.

Interoperability: Interoperability is the ability of different information systems, devices or applications to connect, in a coordinated manner, within and across organizational boundaries to access, exchange and cooperatively use data amongst stakeholders, with the goal of optimizing the health of the individuals and populations. Health data exchange architectures and standards allow relevant data to be shared effectively and securely across the complete spectrum of care, within all applicable settings, and with relevant stakeholders (including with the person whose information is being shared). Optimally, interoperability facilitates connections and integrations across these systems to occur regardless of the data's origin or destination or the applications employed, and ensures the data are usable and readily available to share without additional intervention by the end user. In the health ecosystem, interoperability furthers the goal of optimizing health by providing seamless access to the right information needed to more comprehensively understand and address the health of individuals and populations.[53] *Definition current as of December 2018. To review any updates to this definition please visit the HIMSS website.*

Interoperability Standards Advisory: *See* **ISA**.

Interpreted language: In programming language, code that is saved in the same format that it is entered. Code that is not compiled.[323]

Interrupt: A signal from a device attached to a computer or from a program within the computer that requires the operating system to stop and figure out next steps.[2]

Interrupt request: *See* **IRQ**.

Intranet: Private computer network that uses Internet protocols and Internet-derived technologies, including web browsers, web servers, and web languages, to facilitate collaborative data sharing within an enterprise.[10]

Intrusion detection: The act of detecting actions that attempt to compromise the confidentiality, integrity, or availability of a resource.[10]

iOS (formerly iPhone OS): A mobile operating system created and developed by Apple Inc. exclusively for its hardware and devices, including the iPhone, iPad, and iPod Touch. The iOS user interface is based upon direct manipulation, using multi-touch gestures. Interface control elements consist of sliders, switches, and buttons. Interaction with the OS includes gestures such as swipe, tap, pinch, and reverse pinch, all of which have specific definitions within the context of the iOS operating system and its multi-touch interface. Internal accelerometers are used by some applications to respond to shaking the device (one common result is the undo command) or rotating it in three dimensions (one common result is switching between portrait and landscape mode).[73]

IoT (Internet of things): 1. The ever-growing network of physical objects that feature an IP address for Internet connectivity, and the communication that occurs between these objects and other Internet-enabled devices and systems. IoT extends Internet connectivity beyond traditional devices like desktop and laptop computers, smartphones and tablets to a diverse range of devices and everyday items with embedded technology to communicate and interact with the external environment via the Internet.[39] **2.** A system of interrelated computing devices, mechanical and digital machines, objects, animals, or people that are provided with unique identifiers and the ability to transfer data over a network without requiring human-to-human or human-to-computer interaction.[2]

IP (Internet protocol): The method or protocol by which data is sent from one computer to another on the Internet. Each computer (known as a host) on the Internet has at least one IP address that uniquely identifies it from all other computers on the Internet.[2]

IP address (Internet protocol address): The equivalent of an Internet mailing address, which identifies the network, the subnet, and the host, such as 168.100.209.246. A specific 32-bit (4 octet) unique address assigned to each networked device.[2]

IP datagram (Internet protocol datagram): Format of data that can be recognized by IP. It consists of two components, namely, the header and data, which need to be transmitted.[324]

IPA (Independent practice association): A business entity organized and owned by a network of *independent physician* practices for the purpose of reducing overhead or pursuing business ventures such as contracts with employers, accountable care organizations (ACO), and/or managed care organizations (MCOs).[196]

iPhone operating system: *See* **iOS.**

IPsec (Internet protocol security): 1. A developing low-level protocol for encrypting the Internet protocol packet layer of a transmission instead of the application layer to provide improved confidentiality, authentication, and integrity. IPsec can be handled without requiring changes to individual user computers. **2.** IPSec virtual private network (VPN) is a compilation of standards created by the Internet Engineering Task Force to help the user filter the encrypted data packet.[10]

IPX/SPX (Internetwork packet exchange/sequence packet exchange): A set of network protocols that provide packet switching and sequencing for small and large networks. IPX works at layer three of the Open Systems Interconnection (OSI) model and SPX works at layer 4.[52]

IPv4 and IPv6 (Internet Protocols versions 4 and 6): Used to identify computers on the Internet.[325]

IRC (Internet relay chat): An application-layer protocol that facilitates real-time communication using a client-server platform.[2]

IrDA (Infrared Data Association): A group of device manufacturers that developed a standard for transmitting data via infrared light waves. Increasingly, computers and other devices (such as printers) come with *IrDA* ports. This enables you to transfer data from one device to another without any cables.[39]

IRM (Information resource management): A philosophical and practical approach to managing information. Information is regarded as a valuable resource that should be managed like other resources and should contribute directly to accomplishing organizational goals and objectives. IRM provides an integrated view for managing the entire life-cycle of information, from generation to dissemination to archiving and/or destruction, for maximizing the overall usefulness of information, and improving service delivery and program management. IRM views information and information technology as an integrating factor in the organization, that is, the various organizational positions that manage information are coordinated and work together toward common ends. Further, IRM looks for ways in which the management of information and the management of information technology are interrelated, and fosters that interrelationship and organizational integration. IRM includes the management of (1) the broad range of information resources, e.g., printed materials, electronic information, and microforms; (2) the various technologies and equipment that manipulate these resources; and (3) the people who generate, organize, and disseminate those resources.[44]

IRQ (Interrupt request line): Hardware lines over which devices can send interrupt signals to the microprocessor.[39]

ISA (Interoperability Standards Advisory): The model by which the Office of the National Coordinator for Health Information Technology (ONC) coordinates the identification, assessment, and determination of "recognized" interoperability standards and implementation specifications for industry use to fulfill specific clinical health IT interoperability needs.[12]

ISBT 128: The global standard for the terminology, identification, coding, and labeling of medical products of human origin (including blood, cell, tissue, milk, and organ products). It is used in more than 77 countries across six continents and disparate healthcare systems. It is widely endorsed by the professional community. The standard has been designed to ensure the highest levels of accuracy, safety, and efficiency for the benefit of donors and patients worldwide. ISBT 128 provides international consistency to support the transfer, traceability, and transfusion/transplantation of blood, cells, tissues, and organs.[198]

ISDN (Integrated service digital network): A data transfer technology that can transfer data significantly faster than a dial-up modem. ISDN enables wider bandwidth digital transmission over the public telephone network, which means more data can be sent at one time.[10]

ISO/IEEE 11073 Standards: Health Informatics and Medical Devices Communication Standards that provide the interconnection and interoperation of medical devices with computerized healthcare information systems in a way that is suitable for a clinical environment. This family of standards provides real-time plug-and-play interoperability and facilitates the efficient exchange of vital signs and medical device data acquired at the point of care.[326]

ISO/TC 215 International Organization for Standardization (ISO) Technical Committee for Health Informatics: Committee that focuses on standardization in the field of information for health, and Health Information and Communications Technology (ICT). Promotes interoperability between independent systems, to enable compatibility and consistency for health information and data, as well as to reduce duplication of effort and redundancies.[36]

Isolation: **1.** A transaction's effect is not visible to other transactions until the transaction is committed. **2.** Transaction isolation levels specify what data are visible to statements within a transaction. These levels directly impact the level of concurrent access by defining what interaction is possible between transactions against the same target data source.[11,89] *See* **ACID.**

ISP (Internet service provider): Company that provides Internet connectivity and Internet-related services, online computer access, web site hosting, and domain name registration.[18]

ITIM Group: Group that administers user access to the Tivoli Identity Manager system. An ITIM group is a generic user group for the Tivoli Identity Manager Server; it is used to grant access to ITIM users through the use of Access Control Information (ACIs). You can structure the system access and administration with ITIM groups. Before a person entity can be assigned to an ITIM group as an ITIM user, the entity must be provisioned with a Tivoli Identity Manager account. ITIM groups have four basic properties: Name, Description, Access option, and User list.[199]

ITMRA (Information Technology Management Reform Act): Division E of the 1996 National Defense Authorization Act (NDAA). It repealed the Brooks Act, defined information technology and National Security Systems (NSS), established the requirement to designate a Chief Information Officer (CIO) for each major federal agency, assigned the responsibility for management of IT to the Director, Office of Management and Budget (OMB), and moved procurement protest authority from the General Services Administration (GSA) to the Government Accountability Office (GAO). Frequently, but erroneously, referred to as the Clinger-Cohen Act (CCA).[200]

IVR (Interactive voice response): Ability to access information over the phone (claim payments, claim status, and a patient's eligibility).[46]

J

JAD (Joint application development): A development methodology that involves continuous interaction with users and designers of the system in development. JAD centers on workshop sessions that are structured and focused to improve the quality of the final product by focusing on the up-front portion of the development lifecycle, thus reducing the likelihood of errors that are expensive to correct later.[39]

JASON: An independent federal scientific advisory group that provides consulting services to the U.S. government on matters of defense, science, and technology. It was established in 1960. In 2014, the group published a Robust Health Data Infrastructure, which focuses on a joint task force of HIT standards and Policy Committees. [268,327,12]

JavaScript Object Notation: *See* **JSON**.

J-codes: A subset of the Healthcare Common Procedure Coding System (HCPCS) level II code set with a high-order value of "J" that has been used to identify certain drugs and other items. The final HIPAA transactions and code sets rule states that these J-codes will be dropped from the HCPCS and that NDC codes will be used to identify the associated pharmaceuticals and supplies.[113]

JCR (Joint Commission Resources): Consulting division of The Joint Commission whose mission is to continuously improve the safety and quality of healthcare in the United States and in the international community through the provision of education, publications, consultation, and evaluation services.[328]

JFS (Journaling file system): A fault-resilient file system in which data integrity is ensured because updates to directories and bitmaps are constantly written to a serial log on disk before the original disk log is updated. In the event of a system failure, a full journaling file system ensures that the data on the disk has been restored to its pre-crash configuration. It also recovers unsaved data and stores it in the location where it would have gone if the computer had not crashed, making it an important feature for mission-critical applications.[2]

JIRA: Issue tracking system used by organizations, including The Office of the National Coordinator for Health Information Technology (ONC). JIRA is a commercial software program developed by Atlassian that is used for issue tracking and project management.[12,329]

Joins: A data query operation performed on data tables in a relational database management system (DBMS), in which the data from two or more tables are combined using common data elements into a single table. Typically performed using Structured Query Language (SQL).[330]

Joint application development: *See* **JAD**.

Joint Commission: An independent, not-for-profit organization, The Joint Commission accredits and certifies nearly 21,000 healthcare organizations and programs in the United States. Joint Commission accreditation and certification is recognized nationwide as a symbol of quality that reflects an organization's commitment to meeting certain performance standards.[229]

Joint Commission Resources: *See* **JCR**.

Joint photographic experts group: *See* **JPEG**.

Journaling file system: *See* **JFS**.

JPEG (Joint photographic experts group): An image file format. It is commonly used by digital cameras to store photos since it supports 16,777,216 colors. The format also supports varying levels of compression, which makes it ideal for web graphics.[2] Also referred to as JPG.

JPEG compression: A process to reduce the size of a JPEG image file.[2]

JPG: *See* **JPEG**.

JSON (JavaScript Object Notation): A lightweight data interchange format that is easy for humans to read and write and easy for machines to parse and generate. It is based on a subject of JavaScript Programming Language, Standard ECMA-262 3rd Edition. JSON is a text format that is completely language independent but uses conventions familiar to programmers of the C-family of languages, including C, C++, C#, Java, JavaScript, Perl, Python, and others. JSON is built on two structures: (1) a collection of name/value pairs, also known as an object; and (2) an ordered list of values, also known as an array.[201]

JTC (Joint Technical Committee): A standards body straddling the International Organization for Standardization (ISO) and International Electrotechnical Commission (IEC).[60]

K

KAS (Clinical Decision Support (CDS) Knowledge Artifact Specification): Provides guidance on how to specify and implement shareable CDS knowledge artifacts using XML. The scope of the specification includes event-condition-action rules, order sets, and documentation templates.[9]

KB (Kilobyte): Equal to 1024 bytes of digital data.[73]

Kbps (Kilobits per second): Transmission of a thousand bits per second.[2]

Kerberos: A protocol for authenticating service requests between trusted hosts across an untrusted network, such as the Internet.[2]

Kernel: The central module of an operating system (OS). It is the part of the operating system that loads first, and it remains in main memory. The kernel is responsible for memory management, process and task management, and disk management. The kernel connects the system hardware to the application software.[39]

Key: 1. A field or combination of fields in a database table used to retrieve and sort rows based on certain requirements. **2.** A value that particularizes the use of a cryptographic system. **3.** An input that controls the transformation of data by an encryption algorithm.[52,64]

Key management services: As data are brought in from various sources, there will be cases where certain primary source identity keys are not unique across source systems. The key management service will generate and manage keys during insert and update operations in the EHR repository.[57]

Keystroke verification: The determination of the accuracy of data entry by the re-entry of the same data through a keyboard.[36]

Keyword: In the context of search engine optimization, a particular word or phrase that describes the contents of a Web page. Keywords are intended to act as shortcuts that sum up an entire page. Keywords form part of a Web page's metadata and help search engines match a page with an appropriate search query.[52]

KHz (Kilohertz): One thousand cycles per second.[2]

Knowledge: The distillation of information that has been collected, classified, organized, integrated, abstracted, and value-added. Knowledge is at the level of abstraction higher than the data and information on which it is based and can be used to deduce new information and new knowledge.[236]

Knowledge acquisition: The process of eliciting, analyzing, transforming, classifying, organizing, and integrating knowledge; representing that knowledge in a form that can be used in a computer system.[236]

Knowledge base: Data tables, databases, and other tools designed to assist the process of care.[43]

Knowledge engineering: Converting knowledge, rules, relationships, heuristics, and decision-making strategies into a form understandable to the artificial software upon which an expert system is built.[50]

Knowledge Management: The process of creating, sharing, using, and managing the knowledge and information of an organization. Typically refers to a multidisciplinary approach to achieving organizational objectives by making the best use of knowledge.[287]

Knowledge representation: The process and results of formalization of knowledge in such a way that the knowledge can be used automatically for problem-solving.[236]

K

L

Lab Results Interface: *See* **LRI**.

Laboratory information management system: *See* **LIS**.

Laboratory information system: *See* **LIS**.

LAN (Learning and Action Network): The U.S. Department of Health and Human Services launched (through CMS) the Health Care Payment Learning and Action Network (LAN) in March 2015 to align with public and private sector stakeholders in shifting away from the current FFS, volume-based payment system to one that pays for high-quality care and improved health. The LAN provides a forum for generating evidence, sharing best practices, developing common approaches to the design and monitoring of APMs, and removing barriers to healthcare transformation across the U.S. healthcare system.[26]

LAN (Local area network): A single network of physically interconnected computers that is localized within a small geographical area. Operates in a span of short distances (office, building, or complex of buildings).[10] *See* **MAN, WAN,** and **WLAN**.

LAN adapter: Allows access to a network, usually wireless network.[202]

LASA (Look alike/Sound alike Drugs): Care providers developed a list of look-alike/sound-alike medications it stores, dispenses, or administers. LASA lists are used to determine which medications require special safeguards to reduce the risk of errors and minimize harm.[229]

Large dialysis organization: *See* **LDO**.

LAT (Local area transport): A proprietary network protocol developed by Digital Equipment Corp. and used in local area networks and terminal server connections. LAT was created to provide connection between terminal servers and host computers via Ethernet cable, and enable communication between these hosts and serial devices such as video terminals and printers.[52]

Latent Dirichlet allocation: *See* **LDA**.

Lattice Security Model: A security model with increasing degrees of security.[45]

Layered defense: Also called overlapping controls; employing more than one control against an attack on the computer or network where one control will compensate for a failure in another.[45]

Layered trust: Concept in design of a secure operating system utilizing a layered design, in which the trustworthiness and access rights of a process can be judged by the process's proximity to the center. The more trusted processes are closer to the center.[45]

Layering networks: Each layer in the OSI model reformats the transmission and exchanges information with its peer layer.[45]

LDA (Latent Dirichlet allocation): In natural language processing, a generative statistical model that allows sets of observations to be explained by unobserved groups that explain why some parts of the data are similar; used as a topic model.[332]

LDAP (Lightweight directory access protocol): An open, vendor-neutral, industry standard application protocol for accessing and maintaining distributed directory information services over an Internet Protocol (IP) network. Covers message standards, interactions and the XML data model for provider registry.[333]

LDO (Large dialysis organization): An ESRD Seamless Care Organization (ESCO) that operates out-patient end-stage renal disease centers and that has at least twenty-five percent (25%) of the market share (measured by number of patients as determined by USRDS or any successor) of dialysis centers in the U.S. and Dialysis Clinic Inc.[26]

LEAP (Lightweight and efficient application protocol): One of several protocols used with the International Electrical and Electronics Engineers (IEEE) 802.1 standard for local area network (LAN) port access control. In the IEEE framework, a LAN station cannot pass traffic through an Ethernet hub or wide local area network (WLAN) access point until it successfully authenticates itself. The station must identify itself and prove that it is an authorized user before it is actually allowed to use the LAN.[10]

Learning and Action Network: *See* **LAN.**

Least privilege: 1. The principle that a security architecture should be designed so that each entity is granted the minimum system resources and authorizations that the entity needs to perform its function. **2.** A security principle that restricts the access privileges of authorized personnel (e.g., program execution privileges, file modification privileges) to the minimum necessary to perform their jobs.[1]

Ledger: A written or computerized record of all the transactions a business has completed.[331]

Left Without Being Seen: *See* **LWBS.**

Legacy systems: 1. Usually refers to computers that have been in use for a long period of time, that contain many years of data, and have been used over many years of software development. **2.** Data that were collected and maintained using a "previous" system, but are now preserved on a "current" system. **3.** May also refer to an unsupported system.[63]

Letter of intent: *See* **LOI.**

Level of effort: *See* **LOE.**

Lexicon: A group of related terms used in a particular profession, subject area, or style.[29]

Lexicon query service: *See* **LQS.**

Licensed Independent Practitioner: *see* **LIP.**

Life Safety Code: *See* **LSC.**

Lifecycle: All phases in the life of a medical device or system, from the initial conception to final decommissioning and disposal.[194]

LIFO (Last in, first out): A queue that executes last-in requests before previously queued requests.[73] Also called a stack.

Lightweight directory access protocol: *See* **LDAP.**

Limited data set: Specifies health information from which identifiers have been removed. Information in a limited data set is protected but may be used for research, healthcare operations, and public health activities without the individual's authorization.[20]

Limited privilege: A program is allowed to access secure data, but the access is minimized and neither the access rights nor the data are passed along the other untrusted programs or back to an untrusted caller.[45]

Link: A connection between two network devices.[1] Also known as anchors, hot-links, and hyperlinks.

LINUX: A newer version of UNIX, a nonproprietary operating system, available free on the web. An operating system that runs many healthcare applications.[45]

LIP (Licensed independent practitioner): An individual, as permitted by law and regulation, and also by the organization, to provide care and services without direction or supervision within the scope of the individual's license and consistent with the privileges granted by the organization. Each state has different laws as to who can practice without supervision.[229]

LIS (Laboratory information system): An application to streamline the process management of the laboratory for basic clinical services, such as hematology and chemistry. This application may provide general functional support for microbiology reporting but does not generally support blood bank functions. Provides an automatic interface to laboratory analytical instruments to transfer verified results to nurse stations, chart carts, and remote physician offices. The module allows the user to receive orders from any designated location, process the order and report results, and maintain technical, statistical, and account information. It eliminates tedious paperwork, calculations, and written documentation, while allowing for easy retrieval of data and statistics.[10] Also known as LIS, laboratory information management system (LIMS), and laboratory management system (LMS).

LISTSERV: A program that automatically redistributes e-mail to names on a mailing list. Users can subscribe to a mailing list by sending an e-mail note to a mailing list they learn about; listserv will automatically add the name and distribute future e-mail postings to every subscriber.[2]

LLC (Logical link control): One of two sublayers that make up the Data Link Layer of the OSI model. The logical link control layer controls frame synchronization, flow control and error checking.[39]

Local area network: *See* **LAN.**

Local area transport: *See* **LAT.**

Local codes: Generic term for code values that are defined for specific payers, providers, or political jurisdictions.[46]

Local name space: Collection of objects to which a process has access. The local name space or domain might include some programs, files, data segments, and I/O devices such as a printer and a terminal.[45]

Lock out/Tag out: *See* **LOTO.**

LOE (Level of effort): Any particular support type activity that customarily does not lend itself to the ultimate establishment via measure of the sum total of discrete accomplishment. The level of effort is typically denoted through and via a uniform set of work performance rates over a period of time (typically a predefined period of time) over which the activities of note took place. Level of effort can be measured via an independent observation or by members of the project group.[334]

Log: Record of event occurring within an organization's systems and networks.[1]

Log analysis: Studying log entries to identify events of interest or suppress log entries for insignificant events.[1]

Log archival: Retaining logs for an extended period of time, typically on removable media, a storage area network (SAN), or a specialized log archival appliance or server.[1]

Log clearing: Removal of all entries from a log that precede a certain date and time.[1]

Log compression: Storing a log file in a way that reduces the amount of storage space needed for the file without altering the meaning of its contents.[1]

Log conversion: The process of parsing a log in one format and storing its entries in a second format.[1]

Log entry: Individual record within a log.[1]

Log management: Process for generating, transmitting, storing, analyzing, and disposing of log data.[1]

Logic bombs: Malicious software that is triggered by a response to an event, such as launching an application or when a specific date/time is reached.[203]

Logical access control: An automated system that controls an individual's ability to access one or more computer system resources, such as a workstation, network, application, or database.[64]

Logical Data Model: Represents the structure of the relationship of data elements and entities within an information system. The logical model is crucial to the proper function of any system within an enterprise. The logical model allows for elegance in system design so that the system is adaptable to the changing information needs of the enterprise.[204]

Logical drive: A part of a physical disk drive that has been partitioned and allocated as an independent unit, and functions as a separate drive altogether. For example, one physical drive can be partitioned into drives F:, G:, and H:, each representing a separate logical drive but all still part of the one physical drive.[39]

Logical link control: *See* **LLC.**

Logical observation identifiers names and codes: *See* **LOINC.**

Logical separation: Users operate under the illusion that no other processes exist, as when an operating system constrains a program's accesses so that the program cannot access objects outside its permitted domain.[45]

Logical system design: Describes the functionality of the system and presents the vision of system performance and its features.[204]

Logical topology: Describes how data are transmitted through the physical devices.[205]

Logical unit number: *See* **LUN.**

Logoff/logout: To formally exit from the computer's environment.[2]

Logon: Process to get access to an operating system or application, often requiring a user ID and password.[2]

LOI (Letter of intent): Used in most major business transactions, a letter of intent (LOI) outlines the terms of a deal and serves as an "agreement to agree" between two parties.[18]

LOINC (Logical observation identifiers names and codes): Universal identifiers for laboratory and clinical observations, measurements, and documents, including such things as vital signs, hemodynamic measures, intake/output, EKG, obstetric ultrasound, cardiac echo, urologic imaging, gastro-endoscopic procedures, pulmonary ventilator management, selected survey instruments, and other clinical observations.[206]

Long-term care: *See* **LTC.**

Long-term care facility: *See* **LTCF.**

Long-term and post-acute care: *See* **LTPAC.**

Long-term services and support: *See* **LTSS.**

Longitudinal patient disease registries: *See* **LPDR.**

Longitudinal health record: A comprehensive clinical summary of a patient-based clinical experience as opposed to encounter-based or provider-based records.[335] *See* **EHR.**

Look alike/Sound alike: *See* **LASA.**

Loop: 1. A repeating structure or process. 2. A collection of segments that can repeat.[59,114]

Loophole: An incompleteness or error in a computer code that can allow a program to be manipulated or exploited; usually referred to in relation to computer or network security.[336]

Loose lipped system: System provides too much information to an unknown user.[45]

Loosely coupled: Describes how multiple computer systems, even those with incompatible technologies, can be joined together for transactions regardless of function components.[39]

Loss reduction: A protection risk management strategy, loss reduction focuses on a single incident or claim and requires immediate response to any adverse occurrence.[204]

Lossless compression: Method of data compression that permits reconstruction of the original data exactly, bit-for-bit. The graphics interchange file (GIF) is an image format used on the web that provides lossless compression.[117]

Lossy compression: Method of data compression that permits reconstruction of the original data approximately, rather than exactly. JPEG is an example of lossy compression.[117]

LOTO (Lock out/Tag out): Addresses the practices and procedures necessary to disable machinery or equipment, thereby preventing the release of hazardous energy while employees perform servicing and maintenance activities. This is generally done by affixing the appropriate lockout or tag out devices to energy-isolating devices and by de-energizing machines and equipment.[337]

Low-Volume Threshold: *See* **LVT.**

LPDR (Longitudinal patient disease registries): A secure informatics system designed to enable enhanced data collection, sharing, management and analysis for conditions identified as part of newborn screening or for conditions that may benefit from newborn screening.[338]

LQS (Lexicon query service): Standardizes a set of read-only interfaces able to access medical terminology system definitions, ranging from sets of codes, to complex hierarchical classification and categorization schemes.[125]

LRI (Lab Results Interface): Support the electronic transmission of clinical results from a Laboratory Information System (LIS) into an Electronic Health Record (EHR). This class of interface is designed to allow the unattended transfer and real-time processing of interface messages from a remotely located trading partner system, or the EHR.[9]

LSC (Life Safety Code): A set of fire protection requirements designed to provide a reasonable degree of safety from fire for healthcare facilities. The code covers construction, protection, and operational features designed to provide safety from fire, smoke, and panic. The Health Care Facilities Code Requirements (HCFC) is a set of requirements intended to provide minimum requirements for the installation, inspection, testing, maintenance, performance, and safe practices for facilities, material, equipment, and appliances. The LSC and HCFC, which is revised periodically, is a publication of the National Fire Protection Association (NFPA), which was founded in 1896 to promote the science and improve the methods of fire protection.[26]

LTC (Long-term care): A continuum of medical and social services designed to support the needs of people living with chronic health problems that affect their ability to perform everyday activities. Services include traditional medical services, social services, and housing.[339]

LTCF (Long-term care facility): Nursing homes, skilled nursing facilities, and assisted living facilities, known as long-term care facilities (LTCFs), provide a variety of services, both medical and personal care, to patients who are unable to manage independently in the community.[80]

LTPAC (Long-term and post-acute care): Segment of the healthcare continuum that works to provide comprehensive longitudinal chronic care over a long period of time. Skilled nursing facilities, home care, hospice, long-term acute care, inpatient rehabilitation, assisted living, medication management, Program of All-Inclusive Care for the Elderly (PACE), and independent care fall within this spectrum of care.[12]

LTSS (Long-term services and support): A wide array of medical and nonmedical services which are provided over a prolonged period of time for people of all ages with impaired mobility, impaired cognitive function, physical or mental disabilities, complex medical needs, or chronic disease. Caregivers provide services and supports to help individuals with daily living activities—such as eating, bathing, and dressing—or other activities such as housekeeping or managing medications that help people live independently.[340]

LU (Logical unit): Portion of the arithmetic logic unit (ALU) within the CPU that coordinates logical operations.[2]

LUN (Logical unit number): A unique identifier for designating an individual or collection of physical or virtual storage devices that execute input/output (I/O) commands with a host computer, as defined by the Small System Computer Interface (SSCI) standard.[2]

Luminance brightness: The amount of light, in lumens, that is emitted by a pixel or an area of the computer screen.[117]

LVT (Low-volume threshold): Part of the Quality Payment Program (QPP) through Medicare for Medicare Part B, established in 1977 to control the cost of payments from Medicare to Physicians, Clinicians, or Health Care Providers must meet the Low-Volume Threshold (LVT) to qualify for the Merit-based Incentive Payment System (MIPS). The LVT is less than or equal to $30,000 in Medicare Part B patients allowed charges or less than or equal to 100 Medicare patients.[26]

LWBS (Left without being seen): Refers the status of a patient who left a healthcare facility without examination or treatment.[123]

M

MAC (Mandatory access control): A security strategy that restricts the ability individual resource owners have to grant or deny access to resource objects in a file system. MAC criteria are defined by the system administrator, strictly enforced by the operating system (OS) or security kernel, and are unable to be altered by end users.[52]

MAC (Message authentication code): A cryptographic checksum that is generated on data using a cryptographic algorithm that is parameterized by a symmetric key. The message authentication code is designed to provide data origin authentication and detect both accidental errors and the intentional modification of the data.[1]

MAC address (Media access control address): A hardware identification number that uniquely identifies each device on a network.[18]

Machine code/machine language: The lowest-level programming language (except for computers that utilize programmable microcode).[39]

Machine learning: A subset of artificial intelligence that permits computers to learn either inductively or deductively. Inductive machine learning is the process of reasoning and making generalizations or extracting patterns and rules from huge data sets; that is, reasoning from a large number of examples to a general rule. Deductive machine learning moves from premises that are assumed to be true to conclusions that must be true if the premises are true.[48]

Machine readable card: A card capable of storing information in a form that can be read by a computer. Information may be written to the card on manufacture, or may be added during the use of the card. If the card contains a processor, the card is known as a smartcard.[341]

MACRA (Medicare Access and CHIP Reauthorization Act 2015): A law that dictates three major changes to how Medicare reimburses those providers delivering care. These changes, which created the Quality Payment Program (QPP) under MACRA include (1) ending the Sustainable Growth Rate (SGR), a formula previously used to determine Medicare payment for provider services, (2) creating a framework to reward providers for delivering better care instead of more care, and (3) aligning existing quality programs into one single program to measure provider care quality and reduce duplicative reporting. Eligible Clinicians (ECs) have two paths within QPP; (1) the Merit-Based Incentive Payment System (MIPS), which includes the merging of existing quality programs or (2) Advanced Alternative Payment Models (Advanced APMs), which allow providers to explore new models to deliver outcomes-focused care.[26] *See* **MIPS, ECs,** and **Advanced APMs**.

Macro: Small program that automates a function for an application program. Although many of these are supplied with the purchase of a program, in many applications, users can create their own by either recording keystrokes or writing the commands using the language that the application program provides. (This process is usually very similar to the BASIC language.)[66]

Mail merge: The connecting of a single form template with a data source that contains information about the recipient's name, address, or other information. Mail merge enables the automation of sending bulk mail.[52]

Mailing list: A list of people who subscribe to a periodic mailing distribution. On the Internet, these lists include each person's email address instead of postal address.[2]

Mailslots: Connection-oriented interprocess communications (IPC) interface between clients and servers in a Windows® environment. Mailslots are a simple way for a process to broadcast messages to multiple processes.[68]

Malicious code: Software that includes spyware, viruses, worms, and Trojan horses with the intent of destroying or overtaking computer processing.[48]

Malware: Malicious software, which is designed to damage or do other unwanted actions to another unsuspecting computer.[12]

MAN (Metropolitan-area network): Similar to a local area network (LAN) but spans an entire city or campus. MANs are formed by connecting multiple LANs. A MAN mostly works on the data link layer, Layer 2, of the OSI model. An IEEE 802.6 standard. *See* **LAN**, **WAN**, and **WLAN**.

Manage consent directives: Ensure that protected health information is only accessed with a consumer's consent.[20]

Managed care: Use of a planned and coordinated approach to providing healthcare with the goal of quality care at a lower cost. Usually emphasizes preventive care, and often associated with a health management organization.[50]

Management information system (service): *See* **MIS**.

Management service organization: *See* **MSO**.

Mandatory access control: *See* **MAC**.

MAO (Maximum acceptable/allowable outage): The timeframe during which a recovery must become effective before an outage compromises the ability of an organization to achieve its business objectives or its survival.[342]

Map: A relationship between a concept in a terminology and a concept in the same or another terminology, according to a mapping scheme or rules.[75]

Mapping: 1. Assigning an element in one set to an element in another set through semantic correspondence. **2.** A rule of correspondence established between data sets that associates each element of a set with an element in the same or another set.[29,76] *See* **Data mapping** and **Crosswalk**.

Marketing: A communication about a product or service that encourages recipients of the communication to purchase or use the product or service.[20]

Mask: Method that a proxy server uses to protect the identity of a corporation's employees while they are surfing the Internet. The proxy server keeps track of which employees are using which masks and directs the traffic appropriately.[48]

Masquerading: A type of attack where the attacker pretends to be an authorized user in order to gain access or gain greater privileges.[2]

Massively parallel processing: *See* **MPP.**

Master browser: Computer that collects and maintains a list of available servers that have shared network resources in its domain.[343]

Master data: 1. Core data that are essential to operations in a specific business or business unit and varies by industry and company. **2.** Often refers to data units that are nontransactional that an organization may reuse across a variety of software programs and technologies.[2,52] Also known as reference data.

Master data management: *See* **MDM.**

Master patient index: *See* **MPI.**

Master services agreement: *See* **MSA.**

Match/matching: The process of comparing biometric information against a previously stored biometric data, and scoring the level of similarity.[64]

Math coprocessor: A mathematical circuit that performs high-speed floating point operations. Also called a "floating point unit" (FPU), the math coprocessor may be a stand-alone chip or circuits built into the CPU. Floating point capability is very important to computation-intensive work such as computer-aided design (CAD), and many CAD programs will not operate without it.[150]

MAU (Media access unit): A network hub or switch.[150] *See* **MSAU.**

Maximum acceptable/allowable outage: *See* **MAO.**

Maximum defined data set: All of the required data elements for a particular standard based on a specific implementation specification. An entity creating a transaction is free to include whatever data any receiver might want or need. The recipient is free to ignore any portion of the data that is not needed to conduct his or her part of the associated business transaction, unless the inessential data is needed for coordination of benefits.[113]

Maximum tolerable period of disruption or MTPOD: *See* **MAO.**

Mb (Megabit): 1,048,576 bits or 1024kb.[2]

MBDS (Minimum basic data set): A set of data that is the minimum required for a healthcare record to conform to a given standard.[34]

Mbps (Megabits per second): Transmission of a million bits per second.[2]

MDA (Model-driven architecture): A platform independent model providing for separate business and application functionality from the technology specific code, while enabling interoperability within and across platform boundaries.[164]

MDI (Medical device interface): Includes all points of interaction between the user and the device, including all elements of the device with which the user interacts. A device user interface might be used while the user sets up the device (e.g., unpacking, set up, calibration), uses the device, or performs maintenance on the device (e.g., cleaning, replacing a battery, repairing parts).[41]

MDI-X port (Medium Dependent Interface Crossover): An MDI port or uplink port is a port on a switch, router, or network hub connecting to another switch or hub using a straight-through cable rather than an Ethernet crossover cable. Generally there are one to two ports on a switch or hub with an uplink switch, which can be used to alter between an MDI and MDIX interface. The "X" or crossover is in reference to the transmitting wires (MDI), which must be connected to the receiving (MDIX) wires to "crossover" signals.[52]

MDM (Master data management): A comprehensive method of enabling an enterprise to link all of its critical data to one file, called a master file, which provides a common point of reference. MDM can help streamline data sharing among departments and can facilitate computing in multiple system architectures, platforms, and applications. MDM tools are used in healthcare by health information organizations to maintain a high degree of confidence that patient identity information is consistent, disambiguated, and de-duplicated across multiple disparate systems.[2,12]

MDM (Medical document management message): The HL7 MDM message helps manage medical records by transmitting new or updated documents, or by transmitting important status information and/or updates for the record. Trigger events and messages can be one of two categories: they can either describe the status of the document, or they can describe the status of the document AND contain the document contents. MDM messages can be created in relation to an order or independently of them.[208]

MDM (Mobile device management): Software dealing with deploying, securing, monitoring, integrating, and managing mobile devices, such as smartphones, laptops, and tablets, in the workplace. The intent is to optimize the functionality and security of devices within the enterprise while protecting the corporate network.[2]

MDS (Minimum data set): A core of elements to use in performing comprehensive assessments in long-term care facilities.[26]

Mean time between failure: *See* **MTBF.**

Mean time to diagnose: *See* **MTTD.**

Mean time to repair: *See* **MTTR.**

Meaningful use: *See* **MU.**

Measure: A number or quantity that records a directly observable value or performance. All measures have a unit attached to them and can be expressed as counts (45 visits), rates (10 visits/day), proportions (45 primary healthcare visits/380 total visits = .118), percentages (12 percent of the visits made), or ratios (45 visits four health workers = 11.25).[4]

MedDRA (Medical Dictionary for Regulatory Activities): 1. Used by regulatory agencies and drug manufacturers. **2.** A terminology developed under the auspices of the International Conference on Harmonization of Technical Requirements for Registration of Pharmaceuticals for Human Use. MedDRA is a standard international terminology for regulatory communication in the registration, documentation, and safety monitoring of medical products throughout all phases of their regulatory cycle. As a standard, MedDRA is expected to promote the harmonization of regulatory requirements and documentation for medical products in the United States, Japan, and the European Union.[43,94]

Media access control: Lower portion of the second layer, the data link layer, of the open systems interconnection (OSI) model. Responsible for the transmission of data packets to and from the network interface card, and to and from another remotely shared channel.[52] *See* **MAC address.**

Media access control address: *See* **MAC address.**

Media access unit: *See* **MAU.**

Medicaid information technology architecture: *See* **MITA.**

Medicaid management information system: *See* **MMIS.**

Medical code sets: Codes that characterize a medical condition to treatment. These code sets are usually maintained by professional societies and public health organizations.[113]

Medical device: Any instrument, apparatus, implement, machine, appliance, implant, in vitro reagent or calibrator, software, material, or other similar or related article, intended by the manufacturer to be used, alone or in combination, for human beings for one or more of the specific purposes of diagnosis, prevention, monitoring, treatment, or alleviation of disease; diagnosis, monitoring, treatment, alleviation of, or compensation for an injury; investigation, replacement, modification, or support of the anatomy or of a physiological process; supporting or sustaining life; control of conception; disinfection of medical devices; providing information for medical purposes by means of in vitro examination of specimens derived from the human body; and which does not achieve its primary intended action in or on the human body by pharmacological, immunological, or metabolic means, but which may be assisted in its function by such means.[194]

Medical error: 1. The failure of a planned action to be completed as intended, or the use of a wrong plan to achieve an aim in the healthcare delivery process. **2.** A mistake that harms a patient. Adverse drug events, hospital-acquired infections and wrong-site surgeries are examples of preventable medical errors.[344,13]

Medical home: 1. A model of delivering primary care that is accessible, continuous, comprehensive, family-centered, coordinated, compassionate, and culturally effective. **2.** In a medical home model, primary care clinicians and allied professionals provide conventional diagnostic and therapeutic services, as well as coordination of care for patients who require services not available in primary care settings. The goal is to provide a patient with a broad spectrum of care, both preventive and curative, over a period of time and to coordinate all of the care the patient receives.[209,210]

Medical informatics: Scientific discipline concerned with the cognitive, information processing, and communication task of healthcare practice, education, and research, including the information science and technology to support healthcare tasks.[34]

Medical information BUS: *See* **MIB**.

Medical record: *See* **EHR**, **EMR**.

Medical subject heading: *See* **MeSH**.

Medical terminology: A system of words that are used to describe specific medical aspects and diseases.[56]

Medication error: Mishaps that occur during prescribing, transcribing, dispensing, administering, adherence, or monitoring a drug.[31]

MEDIX: A terminology developed for use in monitoring medical products throughout all phases of their regulatory cycle.[164]

Megabyte: One million bytes of data used as a measure of computer processor storage and real and virtual memory. A megabyte is actually 2 to the 20th power or 1,048,576 bytes.[2]

Memorandum of understanding: *See* **MOU**.

Memory: 1. Any medium of data storage, but usually refers to random access memory, RAM. **2.** Any information or data, often in binary format, that a technology can recall or use.[73,52] *See* **RAM** and **ROM**.

Memory ballooning: A management technique that allows a physical host to take advantage of unused memory on its guest virtual machines (VMs).[2]

Menu: A list of options listed on the screen from which to choose. Usually labeled, and the customer is asked to press the key corresponding to a choice.[34]

Merit-based incentive payment system: *See* **MIPS**.

MeSH (Medical subject heading): A thesaurus of concepts and terms used for the indexing of biomedical literature.[34]

Message: An organized set of data exchanged between people or computer processes.[34]

Message authentication: Ensuring that a message is genuine, has arrived exactly as was sent, and comes from the stated source.[34]

Message authentication code: *See* **MAC**.

Message format standards: Protocols that make communication between disparate systems possible. These message format standards should be universal enough that they do not require negotiation of an interface agreement between the two systems in order to make the two systems communicate.[43]

Message syntax: System of rules and definitions specifying the basic component types of messages, interrelationships, and arrangement.[34]

Message type: An identified, named, and structured set of functionally related information that fulfills a specific business purpose.[34]

Message, instant: A package of information communicated from one application to another.[57]

Messaging: Creating, storing, exchanging, and managing data messages across a communications network. The two main messaging architectures are publish-subscribe and point-to-point.[117]

Messaging services: A group of services that handles messages. Services in this group include parsing, serialization, encryption and decryption, encoding and decoding, transformation, and routing.[345]

Meta tag: An HTML coding statement that provides information about a web page. The information in a meta tag is used by search engines to index a page.[2]

Metadata: Structured information that describes other data to help make such data easier to retrieve, use, or manage as an information resource. There are three main types of metadata: (1) descriptive metadata describe a resource for purposes of discovery and identification; (2) structural metadata indicate how compound objects are put together; and (3) administrative metadata provide information to help manage a resource, such as when or how it was created, file type, and other technical information.[152]

Metadata registry: A system that contains information that describes the origin, structure, format, and definitions of data. These registries provide an integrating resource for legacy data, acts as a lookup tool for designers of new databases, and documents each data element.[152]

Metadata stewards: Organizations that have the responsibility for the ongoing maintenance of a metadata item.[2]

Metathesaurus: The National Library of Medicine's Unified Medical Language System (UMLS) Metathesaurus cross-references national and international medical vocabularies.[43] *See* **UMLS**.

Metropolitan-area network: *See* **MAN**.

mHealth (Mobile health): General term for the use of mobile phones and other wireless technology in medical care. Examples of use include patient education, remote monitoring, treatment support, epidemic outbreak tracking, and chronic disease management.[2]

MHz (Megahertz): One million times, cycles, occurrences, alterations, or pulses per second. Used to describe a measurement of CPU or processor speed.[2]

MIB (Medical information BUS): 1. A hardware and software standard (IEEE P1073) that enables standardized connections between medical monitoring devices and clinical information systems. **2.** Institute of Electrical and Electronics Engineers (IEEE) P1073 (standard designation) standard for data exchange in a medical environment.[16,211]

Microcomputer: A computer with a central processing unit (CPU) as a microprocessor. Designed for individual use.[52]

Microprocessor: Central processing unit. A microprocessor is a computer processor on a microchip. It is the "engine" that goes into motion when you turn your computer on. Designed to perform arithmetic and logic operations that make use of small number-holding areas called *remote monitoring.*[2] *See* **CPU.**

Middleware: Software systems that function as a conversion or translation layer. Middleware is also a consolidator and integrator. Custom-programmed middleware solutions have been developed for decades to enable one application to interface with another, which either runs on a different platform or comes from a different vendor.[150]

MIME (Multipurpose Internet mail extensions): A method for transmitting non-text files via Internet email, which was originally designed for only ASCII text. Defined by IETF RFC 2822, MIME encodes the files using one of two encoding methods and decodes it back to its original format at the receiving end. A MIME header is added to the file which includes the type of data contained and the encoding method used. The MIME "type" (renamed "Internet media type") has become the de facto standard for describing files on the Internet.[150]

Minimum basic data set: *See* **MBDS.**

Minimum necessary: Minimum amount of protected health information necessary to accomplish permitted use or disclosure for payment or healthcare operations.[20]

Minimum scope of disclosure: The principle that, to the extent practical, individually identifiable health information should only be disclosed to the extent needed to support the purpose of the disclosure.[113]

MIPS (Merit-based incentive payment system): A program created as a result of MACRA enacted in 2015 that combines the components of existing quality and incentive programs such as the Physician Quality Reporting System (PQRS), the Value-based Payment Modifier (VM), and the Medicare Electronic Health Record Incentive Program (also known as Medicare's version of Meaningful Use). Under MIPS, eligible clinicians (ECs) are measured on quality, cost, improvement activities, and the Promoting Interoperability Program.[26] *See* **Promoting Interoperability Program, MACRA, QPP.**

Mirror site: A website that is a replica of an already existing site, used to reduce network traffic (hits on a server) or improve the availability of the original site. Mirror sites are useful when the original site generates too much traffic for a single server to support.[39]

MIS (Management information system): A set of systems and procedures that gather data from a range of sources, compile them, and present them in a readable format. An MIS is used to create reports with an overview of all information needed to make management decisions.[346]

Mission critical: Activities, processing, etc., which are deemed vital to the organization's business success, and possibly, its very existence.[20]

MITA (Medicaid information technology architecture): A national framework to support improved systems development and healthcare management for the Medicaid enterprise.[26]

MMIS (Medicaid management information system): An integrated group of procedures and computer processing operations (subsystems) developed at the general design level to meet the principal objectives of a state-directed program.[26]

Mobile app: A software application developed specifically for use on small, wireless computing devices, such as smartphones and tablets, rather than desktop or laptop computers. Mobile apps are sometimes categorized by whether they are web-based or native apps created specifically for a given platform. A third category, hybrid apps, combines elements of both web-based and native apps.[2]

Mobile computing: The use of portable computing devices, such as laptop or handheld computers, in conjunction with mobile communication technologies to enable users to access the Internet and data on their home or work computer from any location. Also known as nomadic computing.[2]

Mobile device management: *See* **MDM**.

Mobile device: A portable device that uses wireless technologies to transmit and exchange data and has a capacity for general computing[2]

Mobile health: *See* **mHealth**.

Model: A very detailed description or scaled representation of one component of a larger system that can be created, operated, and analyzed to predict actual operational characteristics of the final produced component.[64]

Model-driven architecture: *See* **MDA**.

Modeling: The process of defining concepts to reflect their unique definition and meaning.[77] *See* **Data modeling**.

Modified frequency modulation: *See* **MFM**.

Modularity: The characteristic of a system that has been divided into small subsystems which interact with each other.[150]

MOLAP (Multidimensional online analytical processing [OLAP]): A technical OLAP approach that uses a multidimensional data model to analyze data. MOLAP requires that information first be processed before it is indexed directly into a multidimensional database.[52]

Moore's Law: The empirical observation that at our rate of technological development, the complexity of an integrated circuit, with respect to minimum component cost, will double in about 18 months. It is attributed to Gordon E. Moore, a cofounder of Intel, and published in 1965.[18]

Motion picture experts group: *See* **MPEG**.

MOU (Memorandum of understanding): A nonbinding agreement between two or more parties outlining the terms and details of an understanding, including each parties' requirements and responsibilities. An MOU is often the first stage in the formation of a formal contract.[18]

MPEG (Motion picture experts group): International standards for compression, decompression, processing, and coded representation of moving pictures, audio, and their combination.[347]

MPI (Master patient index): Facilitates the identification and linkage of patients' clinical information within a particular institution. The term "enterprise master patient index" (EMPI) is sometimes used to distinguish between an index that serves a single institution (i.e., MPI) and one that contains data from multiple institutions (EMPI). MPIs are not themselves patient identity management strategies, but rather informational infrastructures within which those strategies are applied. Most MPIs use a patient matching algorithm to identify matches and then assign a unique patient identifier that is associated with that patient record going forward.[348] *See* **EMPI**.

MPP (Massively parallel processing): The coordinated processing of a program by multiple processors that work on different parts of the program, with each processor using its own operating system and memory.[2]

MSA (Master services agreement): An agreement between two or more parties that sets forth terms and conditions relevant to one or more services and transactions between parties. Additional terms, conditions, and other information may be incorporated by reference.[212]

MSAU (Multiple station access unit): A central device/hub used in computer networking to connect network nodes, computers, or devices with local area networks. MSAU provides a means of data sharing between different computing devices in an organization. The working mechanism of MSAU is based on token-ring network topology in which all computers and computing devices are connected with each other in a logical circle. In this system, connectivity with other computers remains stable and users continue to communicate with each other when one computer or computing device fails. Also known as a media access unit (MAU), which is often called an Ethernet transceiver. MSAU is a standalone device or connector that is used to connect devices attached to a network over a token-ring network.[52]

MSO (Management service organizations): These are entities designed to help with the administrative, or non medical, work involved in running a practice. These organizations may be owned by non-healthcare provider investors, hospitals, groups of physicians, be a joint venture between a hospital and physicians, or even owned by health plans. MSOs can assist practices with operational issues, financial management, human resources, staff training, coding, billing and collection services, office space needs, discounts on EHRs and medical equipment, regulatory compliance, contract management, credentialing, group purchasing, and risk management.[213]

MTBF (Mean time between failures): Measure of how reliable a hardware product is, indicating the amount of time before a product fails to function properly.[2] *See* **Risk tolerance.**

MTTD (Mean time to diagnose): The difference in time between the onset of an undesired event and its actual detection by the technician[349]. *See* **Risk tolerance.**

MTTR (Mean time to repair): The time it takes to restore a device to service from a failure.[2] *See* **Risk tolerance.**

MU (Meaningful use): The set of standards defined by the Centers for Medicare & Medicaid Services (CMS) Incentive Programs that governs the use of electronic health records and allows eligible providers and hospitals to earn incentive payments by meeting specific criteria. MU Stage 1. Data capture and sharing. MU Stage 2. Advance clinical processes. MU Stage 3. Improved outcomes.[12]

Multicast network transmission: Sends IP packets to a group of hosts on a network, allowing for data to be streamed at multiple concurrent locations.[350]

Multidimensional online analytical processing: *See* **MOLAP.**

Multi-homed host: Computer that is physically connected to multiple data links on the same or different networks. Has two IP addresses assigned to it, one for each network interface.[2]

Multimedia: Applications and technologies that manipulate text, data, images, sound, and full-motion-video objects. Given the usage of multiple formats, multimedia is capable of delivering a stronger and more engaging message than standard text. Multimedia files are typically larger than text-based information and are therefore usually stored on CD-ROMs. Games and educational software commonly use multimedia.[142]

Multiple station access unit: *See* **MSAU.**

Multiplexing: Technique that involves taking multiple signals and combining them into one signal for transmission over a single medium, such as a telephone line. The input signals can be either analog or digital. The purpose of multiplexing is to enable signals to be transmitted more efficiently over a given communication channel, thereby decreasing transmission costs.[52]

Multiplexer, multipleXer, or multipleXor: *See* **MUX.**

Multipurpose Internet mail extensions: *See* **MIME.**

Multisite testing: A testing event that determines the ability of the application or its subsystems to function in multiple geographical settings.[50]

Mutual authentication: Occurs when parties at both ends of a communication activity authenticate each other.[20]

MUX (Multiplexer, multipleXer, or multipleXor): A network device allowing one or more low-speed analog or digital input signals to be selected, combined and transmitted at a higher speed on a single shared medium or within a single shared device.[52]

M

Mware vSphere Metro Storage Cluster (VMware vMSC): A configuration option that allows clustered servers to be spread across geographical locations. This configuration, which is referred to as stretched clustering or distributed clustering, allows an organization to perform load balancing and nondisruptive live migrations between active data centers.[2]

MyHealthEData: An initiative to empower patients by ensuring that they control their healthcare data and can decide how their data are going to be used, all while keeping the information safe and secure. The initiative is led by the U.S. Centers for Medicare and Medicaid Services (CMS), the Office of the National Coordinator for Health Information Technology (ONC), the National Institutes of Health (NIH), and the Department of Veterans Affairs (VA).[26]

M

N

NAC (Network access control/network admission control): A method of bolstering the security of a proprietary network by restricting the availability of network resources to endpoint devices that comply with a defined security policy.[2]

Name: Designation of an object by a linguistic expression.[34]

Name resolution: *See* **ARP.**

Named pipes: Allows data to be exchanged from one application to another either over a network or running within the same computer.[150]

NANDA taxonomy II: A taxonomy of nursing diagnostic concepts that identify and code a patient's responses to health problems or life processes.[5]

Narrowband: A telecommunications medium that uses (relatively) low-frequency signals, exceeding 1.544 Mbps.[167]

NAS (Network attached storage): A file server that connects to the network. An NAS contains the file sharing components of a server and generally does not run applications like a general-purpose computer. However, it is often designed to run NAS-related programs such as backup, cloud synchronization, streaming, surveillance, and other services.[150]

NAT (Network address translation): The technology that maintains the privacy of the addresses of the computers in a home or business network when accessing the Internet. It converts the private addresses that are assigned to the internal computers to one or more public addresses that are visible on the Internet. NAT is an IETF standard that is implemented in a router or firewall as well as in any user's machine that is configured to share its Internet connection.[150]

National Drug Code: *See* **NDC.**

National Emergency Medical System (EMS) Information System: *See* **NEMSIS.**

National employer ID: A system for uniquely identifying all sponsors of healthcare benefits.[121]

National Health Information Infrastructure: *See* **NHII.**

National Health-Related Items Code: *See* **NHRIC.**

National member body: *See* **NMB.**

National patient identifier (ID): A system for uniquely identifying all recipients of healthcare services.[113] Sometimes referred to as the National Individual Identifier, or as the healthcare ID.

National payer ID: A system for uniquely identifying all organizations that pay for healthcare services.[113]

National provider file: *See* **NPF.**

National provider identifier: *See* **NPI.**

National standard format: *See* **NSF.**

National standardization: Standardization that takes place at the level of a specific country.[34]

National standards body: Standards body recognized at the national level that is eligible to be the national member of the corresponding international and regional standards organization.[34]

National standards system network: *See* **NSSN.**

Native format: Default file format that an application uses to create or save files.[52]

Natural language: Spoken or written human language in contrast to a computer language.[39]

Natural language processing: *See* **NLP.**

Navigation tools: Allows users to find their way around a website or multimedia presentation. They can be hypertext links, clickable buttons, icons, or image maps.[351]

NCPDP batch standard: 1. A National Council for Prescription Drug Programs (NCPDP) standard designed for use by low-volume dispensers of pharmaceuticals, such as nursing homes. Use of Version 1 of this standard has been mandated under the Health Insurance Portability and Accountability Act (HIPAA). **2.** Created to use the functionality of the NCPDP Telecommunication Standard. Uses the same syntax, formatting, data set, and rules as the Telecommunication Standard. The Batch Standard wraps the Telecommunication Standard around a detail record; then adds a batch header and trailer. This allows implementers to code one. It was intended that once an NCPDP Data Record (containing the Telecommunication Standard transaction) was built, it could then be wrapped with the Detail Data Record. Then, the Transmission Header Record and the Transmission Trailer Record are created. The Batch consisting of Header, Detail Data Records, and Trailer are formed into a batch file.[113,214]

NCPDP Telecommunication Standard: 1. A National Council for Prescription Drug Programs (NCPDP) standard designed for use by high-volume dispensers of pharmaceuticals, such as retail pharmacies. Use of Version 5.1 of this standard has been mandated under HIPAA. **2.** Developed to provide a standard format for the electronic submission of third-party drug claims. The development of the standard was to accommodate the eligibility verification process at the point-of-sale and to provide a consistent format for electronic claims processing.[113,214]

NDC (National Drug Code): The Drug Listing Act of 1972 requires registered drug establishments to provide the Food and Drug Administration (FDA) with a current list of all drugs manufactured, prepared, propagated, compounded, or processed by it for commercial distribution. (*See* Section 510 of the Federal Food, Drug, and Cosmetic Act [Act] [21 U.S.C. § 360]). Drug products are identified and reported using a unique, three-segment number, called the National Drug Code (NDC), which is a universal product identifier for human drugs.[41]

NDIS (Network driver interface specification): A Windows® specification for how communication protocol programs and network device drivers should communicate with each other. It is an application programming interface (API) standard for network devices.[2,52]

NEDSS (National Electronic Disease Surveillance System): An initiative that promotes the use of data and information system standards to advance the development of efficient, integrated, and interoperable surveillance systems at federal, state, and local levels. It is a major component of the Public Health Information Network (PHIN).[20]

Needs assessment: The identification, definition, and description of the problems to be addressed for a selected system.[50]

NEMSIS (National EMS Information System): Framework for collecting, storing, and sharing standardized emergency medical system (EMS) data from states nationwide.[215]

Nesting: Embedding one object in another object of the same type. Nesting is common in programming, where different logic structures are combined.[39]

Net-centric: Depending on the internet to sell products, manage services or get information.[135]

Network: A group of two or more devices, such as computers, printers, modems, servers, etc., that can communicate. Networks allow computers and/or individuals to share information and resources.[52]

Network access control: *See* **NAC.**

Network adapter: Component of a computer's internal hardware that is used for communicating over a network with another computer.[52]

Network address translation: *See* **NAT.**

Network administration: The process of managing all components of network operations. This may include WANs as well as LANs. Network administration includes the design, installation and evaluation of the network, execution of backups, creation of technical documentation, provision for authentication to access resources, troubleshooting assistance, and administration of network security.[52]

Network architecture: Specifies the function and data transmission needed to convey information across a network.[34]

Network attached storage: *See* **NAS.**

Network drive: A disk drive that contains files and applications that is accessible by users in the network.[150].

Network driver interface specification: *See* **NDIS.**

Network file system: *See* **NFS.**

Network information center: *See* **NIC.**

Network layer: Third layer of the OSI model. Provides routing path for network communication. Data is transferred in the form of packets via logical network paths in an ordered format controlled by the network layer.[52]

N

Network operating system: *See* **NOS**.

Network operation center: *See* **NOC**.

Network printer: Shared printer available to network users. Can be connected to a print server, directly connected to the network, or shared from a workstation.[203]

Network protocol services: The network protocol service will provide communication capabilities over the physical network. The primary network protocol that will be supported is TCP/IP.[57]

Network redirector: Software components installed on a client computer that are used for accessing files and other resources. The network redirector sends or redirects requests for file operations from local client applications to a remote server where the request are processed.[30]

Network server: A computer designed to act as a central repository and help in providing various resources like hardware access, disk space, printer access to other computers in the network.[52]

Network service provider: *See* **NSP**.

Network topology: The arrangement of a network including its nodes and connecting lines. The physical topology is the actual geometric layout of workstations. Logical topology refers to the nature of the paths the signals follow between nodes.[2]

Network traffic: The amount of data moving across a network at a given point of time.[52]

Network weaving: A penetration technique in which different communication networks are used to gain access to a data processing system to avoid detection and trace back.[36]

New work item proposal: *See* **NWIP**.

NFS (Network file system): A client/server application that allows a computer user to view and optionally store and update files on a remote computer as if they were on its local disks.[2]

NHRIC (National Health-Related Items Code): A system for identification and numbering of marketed device packages that is compatible with other numbering systems such as the National Drug Code (NDC) or Universal Product Code (UPC). In the early 1970s, the Drug Listing Branch of the FDA set aside a block of numbers that could be assigned to medical device manufacturers and distributors. Those manufacturers who desire to use the NHRIC number for unique product identification may apply to the FDA for a labeler code.[41]

NIC (Network interface card): A computer hardware component that allows one to access a network.[52] *See* **LAN adapter**.

NIC (Nursing intervention classification): A comprehensive, research-based, standardized classification of interventions that nurses perform. NIC is useful for standardizing clinical documentation, communication of care across settings, integration of data across systems and settings, effectiveness research, productivity measurement, competency evaluation, reimbursement, and curricular design.[216]

NLP (Natural language processing): A subfield of artificial intelligence that helps computers understand, interpret and manipulate human language. NLP draws from many disciplines, including computer science and computational linguistics in its pursuit to fill the gap between human communication and computer understanding.[116]

NMB (National member body): The standards institute in each country that is a member of the International Organization for Standardization (ISO).[36]

NMDS (Nursing minimum data set): 1. The foundation for nursing languages development that identified nursing diagnosis, nursing intervention, nursing outcomes, and intensity of nursing care as unique nursing components of the Uniform Hospital Discharge Data Set (UHDDS). **2.** Essential set of information items that has uniform definitions and categories concerned with nursing. It is designed to be an abstraction tool or system for collecting uniform, standard, compatible, minimum nursing data.[5,50]

NMMDS (Nursing management minimum data set): A data set used to describe the environment at unit level of service related to nursing delivery (unit/service, patient/client population, care delivery method), as well as nursing care resources and financial resources.[5]

NOC (Network operation center): A location from which the operation of a network or Internet is monitored. Additionally, this center usually serves as a clearinghouse for connectivity problems and efforts to resolve those problems.[2]

NOC (Nursing outcome classification): A comprehensive, standardized classification of patient/client outcomes developed to evaluate the effects of nursing interventions. Standardized outcomes are necessary for documentation in electronic records, for use in clinical information systems, for the development of nursing knowledge, and the education of professional nurses.[216]

Node: 1. A connection point that can receive, create, store or send data along distributed network routes. **2.** Computer or device connected to a network. Also known as a host.[2,39]

NOI (Notice of intent): A document that describes a subject area for which the federal government is considering developing regulations. It may describe the presumably relevant considerations and invite comments from interested parties. These comments can then be used in developing a notice of proposed rulemaking (NPRM) or a final regulation.[113]

Nomenclature: A consistent method for assigning names to elements of a system.[50]

Nonconformity: Deviation from a specification, a standard, or an expectation.[4]

Non-overwriting virus: A computer virus that appends the virus code to the physical end of a program, or moves the original code to another location.[1]

Nonrepudiation: Cryptographic receipts created so that an author of a message cannot falsely deny sending a message. Proof to a third party that only the signer could have created a signature.[1]

Nonuniform memory architecture: *See* **NUMA.**

Nonvolatile data: Data that persist even when power is removed.[1]

Normalization: 1. The process of creating a uniform and agreed-upon set of standards, policies, definitions, and technical procedures to allow for interoperability. **2.** The process of organizing the fields and tables of a relational database to minimize redundancy.[352,108]

Normalization services: This service will take various data from different sources, normalize, and store them in the EHR's internal form. This service could be extended to include normal values based on incoming and outgoing profiles.[345]

Normative document: Document that provides rules, guidelines, or characteristics for activities or results.[34]

NOS (Network operating system): Operating system that includes special functions for connecting computers and devices into a LAN. The term *network operating system* is generally reserved for software that enhances a basic operating system by adding networking features.[39]

NoSQL: Originally referring to not SQL or non-relational data models, an approach to databases that shifts away from traditional relational database management systems (RDBMS). NoSQL databases do not rely on the traditional structures in RDBMS (tables, columns, rows, and schemas) and use more flexible data models. It is useful for storing unstructured data, including user and session data, chat, messaging, log data, time series data, Internet of Things (IoT), and device data, etc. Unlike SQL, many NoSQL databases can be scaled horizontally across thousands of servers.[353,354] *See* **RDBMS, SQL.**

Notice of intent: *See* **NOI.**

NPF (National provider file): The database envisioned for use in maintaining a national provider registry.[113]

NPI (National provider identifier): 1. A system for uniquely identifying all providers of healthcare services, supplies, and equipment. **2.** A Health Insurance Portability and Accountability Act (HIPAA) Administrative Simplification Standard. The NPI is a unique identification number for covered healthcare providers. Covered healthcare providers and all health plans and healthcare clearinghouses must use the NPIs in the administrative and financial transactions adopted under HIPAA. The NPI is a 10-position, intelligence-free numeric identifier (10-digit number). This means that the numbers do not carry other information about healthcare providers, such as the state in which they live or their medical specialty. The NPI must be used in lieu of legacy provider identifiers in the HIPAA standards transactions.[26,113]

NSF (National standard format): Generically, this applies to any nationally standardized data format, but it is often used in a more limited way to designate the professional flat file record format used to submit professional claims.[113]

NSP (Network service provider): A company providing consolidated service such as network access and bandwidth by allowing access into its backbone infrastructure or access to its network access points.[52]

NSSN (National standards system network): A National Resource for Global Standards is a search engine that provides users with standards-related information from a wide range of developers, including organizations accredited by the American National Standards Institute (ANSI), other U.S. private sector standards bodies, government agencies, and international organizations.[19]

NUMA (Nonuniform memory architecture): A method of configuring a cluster of microprocessors in a multiprocessing system so they can share memory locally, improving performance and the ability of the system to be expanded. NUMA is used in a SMP system.[2] *See* **SMP** and **MPP.**

Nursing informatics: The specialty that integrates nursing science with multiple information and analytical sciences to identify, define, manage, and communicate data, information, knowledge, and wisdom in nursing practice.[5]

Nursing information system: Part of the healthcare information system that deals with nursing documentation, particularly the maintenance of the nursing record.[34]

Nursing intervention classification: *See* **NIC.**

Nursing management minimum data set: *See* **NMMDS.**

Nursing minimum data set: *See* **NMDS.**

Nursing outcome classification: *See* **NOC.**

Nutrition informatics: The effective retrieval, organization, storage and optimum use of information, data and knowledge for food and nutrition related problem-solving and decision-making. Informatics is supported by the use of information standards, processes and technology.[355]

NwHIN Direct: *See* **Direct Project.**

NWIP (New work item proposal): First balloting phase for draft standards and draft technical specifications. During this phase, at least five experts from five participating ISO/TC 215 countries are chosen to work on the document.[36]

O

OASIS (Outcome and Assessment Information Set): A group of data elements that represent core items of a comprehensive assessment for an adult home care patient, and form the basis for measuring patient outcomes for purposes of outcome-based quality improvement. This assessment is performed on every patient receiving services of home health agencies that are approved to participate in the Medicare and/or Medicaid programs.[26]

OAuth (Open Authorization): An open standard for token-based authentication and authorization on the Internet. OAuth allows an end user's account information to be used by third-party services without exposing the user's password.[2]

Object: Any item that can be individually selected and manipulated. In object-oriented programming, an object is a self-contained entity that consists of both data and procedures to manipulate the data.[39]

Object identifier: *See* **OID**.

Object linking and embedding: *See* **OLE**.

Object model: Conceptual representation, typically in the form of a diagram, which describes a set of objects and their relationship.[57]

Object-oriented: A programming language, system or software methodology that is built on the concept of logical objects. It works through the creation, utilization, and manipulation of reusable objects to perform a specific task, process, or objective. While conventional programming focuses on functions/behaviors, object-oriented works on the interactions of one or more objects.[52]

Object-oriented programming: *See* **OOP**.

Object request broker: *See* **ORB**.

Object reuse: Reassignment and reuse of a storage medium containing one or more objects after ensuring no residual data remains on the storage medium.[1]

Objective evidence: Data supporting the existence or verity of something.[102]

OC (Optical carrier): Used to specify the speed of fiber optic networks conforming to the Synchronous Optical Networking (SONET) standard.[10]

OCR (Optical character recognition): Recognition of printed or written text characters by a computer, using a technology that involves photo-scanning of the text, analysis of the image, and translation of the character image into character codes.[2]

OCSP (Online certificate status protocol): An Internet protocol used for obtaining the revocation status of an SSL certificate.[356]

Octal: Base eight numbering system where three bits are used to represent each digit. Uses the 0–7 digits for representations.[2]

Octet: Eight-bit or 1-byte unit of data. Four octets are used in an IP address.[2]

ODA (Open document architecture): An internationally standardized electronic representation for document content and structure. ODA has been ratified by the International Organization of Standardization as ISO 8613. ODA is a critical standard for anyone who wants to share documents without sacrificing control over content, structure and layout of those documents. It is designed to solve difficulties created by the variety of document formats that exist. An ODA document can be opened, changed, exchanged, stored, and reproduced by any ODA-compliant program.[357]

ODBC (Open Database Connectivity): A standard application programming interface (API) for accessing database management systems (DBMS).[30]

ODS (Operational data store): A type of database that serves as an interim area for a data warehouse in order to store time-sensitive operational data that can be accessed quickly and efficiently. In contrast to a data warehouse, which contains large amounts of static data, an ODS contains small amounts of information that is updated through the course of business transactions. The general purpose of an ODS is to integrate data from disparate source systems in a single structure, using data integration technologies like data virtualization, data federation, or extract, transform, and load. This will allow operational access to the data for operational reporting, master data or reference data management.[39,10]

OEID (Other entity identifier): Data element adopted by the Department of Health and Human Services (HHS) and intended to function as a voluntary identifier for entities that are not health plans, healthcare providers, or individuals.[358]

Offline: Condition of being capable of but not currently connected to a network or other device.[2]

OID (Object identifier): A string, usually of numbers, used to uniquely name an object that is registered with the International Organization for Standardization (ISO).[1]

OLAP (Online analytical processing): A high-level concept that describes a category of tools that aid in the analysis of multidimensional queries.[52]

OLE (Object linking and embedding): 1. A document standard developed by Microsoft® that allows for the creation of objects within one application, and links them into a second application. **2.** OLE is used for compound document management, as well as application data transfer via drag-and-drop and clipboard operations.[52]

OLTP (Online transaction processing): A class of systems that supports or facilitates high transaction-oriented applications. OLTP's primary system features are immediate client feedback and high individual transaction volume.[52]

OM (Outbreak management): The capture and management of information associated with the investigation and containment of a disease outbreak or public health emergency.[80]

Omaha nursing diagnosis/intervention: *See* **Omaha system**.

Omaha system (Omaha nursing diagnosis/intervention): A research-based, comprehensive, and standardized taxonomy designed to enhance practice, documentation, and information management. It consists of three relational, reliable, and valid components: The Problem Classification Scheme, the Intervention Scheme, and the Problem Rating Scale for Outcomes. The components provide a structure to document client needs and strengths, describe multidisciplinary practitioner interventions, and measure client outcomes in a simple, yet comprehensive, manner.[217]

Ombudsman: An official appointed to investigate individuals' complaints of maladministration.[4]

On-chip applications: Applications that reside on the integrated circuit chip.[150]

Online: Condition of being connected to a network of computers or other devices.[2]

Online analytical processing: *See* **OLAP**.

Online certificate status protocol: *See* **OCSP**.

Online service provider: Any company, organization or group that provides an online service. These types of services may include web sites, discussion forums, chat rooms, or web mail. OSPs may also refer to a company that provides dial-up access to the Internet.[39]

Online transaction processing: *See* **OLTP**.

Ontology: 1. A specification of a conceptualization of a knowledge domain. An ontology is a controlled vocabulary that describes objects and the relations between them in a formal way, and has a grammar for using the vocabulary terms to express something meaningful within a specified domain of interest. The vocabulary is used to make queries and assertions. Ontological commitments are agreements to use the vocabulary in a consistent way for knowledge sharing. Ontologies can include glossaries, taxonomies, and thesauri, but normally have greater expressivity and stricter rules than these tools. A formal ontology is a controlled vocabulary expressed in an ontology representation language. **2.** An information model of entities and interactions in some particular domain of knowledge and practices. It serves as a set of concepts, such as things, events, and relations, which are specified in some way in order to create an agreed-upon vocabulary for exchanging information.[359,2]

OOA (Out of area): Not within the market geographic bounds.[46]

OON (Out of network): In healthcare, refers to physicians, hospitals, or other providers who do not participate in an insurer's provider network.[360]

OOP (Object-oriented programming): 1. A style of programming characterized by the identification of classes of objects closely linked with the methods (functions) with which they are associated. It also includes ideas of inheritance of attributes and methods. It is a technique based on a mathematical discipline, called "abstract data types," for storing data with the procedures needed to process that data. OOP offers the potential to evolve programming to a higher level of abstraction.[142] *See* **SOA**.

OOP (Out of pocket): Expenses for medical care that aren't reimbursed by insurance. Out of pocket costs include deductibles, coinsurance, and copayments for covered services plus all costs for services that aren't covered.[218]

Open access: The free, immediate, online availability of research outputs with the rights to use these articles fully in the digital environment, though there may be some restrictions on use in terms of licensing and copyrights.[220]

Open Authorization: *See* **OAuth**.

Open source: Software in which the source code is available free to users, who can read and modify the code.[82]

Open systems architecture: In telecommunications, the layered hierarchical structure, configuration, or model of a communications or distributed data processing system that (1) enables system description, design, development, installation, operation, improvement, and maintenance to be performed at a given layer or layers in the hierarchical structure; (2) allows each layer to provide a set of accessible functions that can be controlled and used by the functions in the layer above it; (3) enables each layer to be implemented without affecting the implementation of other layers; and (4) allows the alteration of system performance by the modification of one or more layers without altering the existing equipment, procedures, and protocols at the remaining layers.[7]

Open systems: A computer system that combines portability and interoperability, and makes use of open software standards. It typically refers to a computer system that is interoperable between different vendors and standards, allowing for modularity so that hardware and software need not be attached to a single vendor or platform.[52]

Open systems interconnection: *See* **OSI**.

Operating system: *See* **OS**.

Operating system (O/S) interface layer: The software layer that allows the user to interact directly with the operating system. There are two distinct types: the text-based Command Line Interface (CLI) and icon-based Graphical User Interface (GUI). Also known as user interface.[361]

Operational data store: *See* **ODS**.

Operator: A symbol that tells the compiler or interpreter to perform specific mathematical, relational, or logical operation and produce the final result.[52]

Optical card: A form of optical storage in which the medium is in credit-card form, intended for uses similar to those of a magnetic-stripe card with higher capacity.[56]

Optical carrier: *See* **OC**.

Optical character recognition: *See* **OCR**.

Optical disk: 1. An electronic data storage medium that is read or recorded using a low-powered laser beam. There has been a constant succession of optical disk formats, first in CD formats, followed by a number of DVD formats. Optical disk offers a number of advantages over magnetic storage media.

An optical disk holds much more data. **2.** A disk read or written by light, generally laser light; such a disk may store video, audio, or digital data.[10,142]

Optical resolution: The built-in resolution of a scanning device. Contrast with "interpolated resolution" or "digital resolution" which enhances an image by software. Both resolutions are given as dots per inch (dpi), thus a 2400 dpi scanner can be the true resolution of the machine or a computed resolution.[150]

Optimization: An act, process, or methodology of making something (such as a design, system, or decision) as fully perfect, functional, or effective as possible.[29]

Opt-in: Mechanism that states data collection and/or use methods, and provides user choice to accept such collection and/or use.[2]

Opt-out: Mechanism that states data collection and/or use methods, and provides user choice to decline such collection and/or use.[2]

ORB (Object request broker): A middleware application component that uses the common object request broker architecture (CORBA) specification, enabling developers to make application calls within a computer network. ORB is an agent that transmits client/server operation invocations in a distributed environment and ensures transparent object communication.[52]

Order: Request for a certain procedure or activity to be performed.[9]

Order entry system: *See* **CPOE.**

Organized healthcare arrangement: Arrangement in which participants need to share protected health information about their patients to manage and benefit the common enterprise. A key component of any organized healthcare arrangement is that the individual who obtains services from the arrangement has an expectation that the arrangement is integrated and that the participants jointly manage their operations.[362]

Organizational interoperability: Encompasses the technical components as well as clear policy, social and organizational components. These components facilitate the secure, seamless and timely communication and use of data within and between organizations and individuals. Inclusion of these non-technical considerations enables interoperability that is integrated into end-user processes and workflows in a manner that supports efficiencies, relationships and overall health and wellness through cooperative use of shared data both across and within organizational boundaries.[53,440] *Definition current as of December 2018. To review any updates to this definition please visit the HIMSS website. See* **Interoperability.**

OS (Operating system): Software that manages the computer's memory and processes, as well as all of its software and hardware.[223]

OSI (Open systems interconnection): A reference model to the protocols in the seven-layer data communications networking standards model and services performed at each level. It is used by systems open to interconnection and communication with other systems. Each layer makes up a conceptual collection of services provides to the layers above and below it. The OSI standard is defined by the International Organization for Standardization (ISO). The seven layers from the bottom are physical, data link, network, transport, session, presentation, and application.[2]

Out of area: *See* **OOA.**

Out of network: *See* **OON.**

Out of pocket: *See* **OOP.**

Outbreak management: *See* **OM.**

Outcome and Assessment Information Set: *See* **OASIS.**

Outcome measure: A parameter for evaluating the results of an activity, program, system, treatment, or process and their comparison with the intended or projected results.[4]

Out-of-band: Activity that occurs outside of a telecommunications frequency band or channel.[2]

Outpatient: Patient who is not hospitalized overnight but who visits a hospital, clinic, or associated facility for diagnosis or treatment.[29]

Output: The direct result of the interaction of inputs and processes in the system; the types and qualities of goods and services produced by an activity, project, or program.[363]

OWL (Web ontology language): Designed for use by applications that need to process the content of information instead of just presenting information to humans. OWL facilitates greater machine interpretability of web content than that supported by extensible markup language (XML), resource description framework (RDF), and RDF Schema (RDF-S) by providing additional vocabulary along with formal semantics.[61]

O

P

P2P (Peer-to-peer): A network structure in which the computers share processing and storage tasks as equivalent members of the network.[2]

Packet: The unit of data that is routed between an origin and a destination on the Internet or any other packet-switched network. Packets have no set size.[166]

Packet-filtering firewall: A technique used to control network access by monitoring outgoing and incoming packets and allowing them to pass or halt based on the source and destination Internet Protocol (IP) addresses, protocols, and ports.[52]

Packet header: A group of fields in a network packet that describes its content, all required destination addresses to reach its target, and all source information necessary to allow a response to come back.[150]

Packet Internet Groper: *See* **PING.**

Packet sniffing: The inspecting of packets being transmitted in a network.[150]

Packet switched: The type of network in which relatively small units of data called packets are routed through a network based on the destination address contained within each packet. Breaking communication down into packets allows the same data path to be shared among many users in the network.[2]

Packet switching: A digital network transmission process in which data are broken into suitably sized pieces or blocks for fast and efficient transfer via different network devices. When a computer attempts to send a file to another computer, the file is broken into packets so that it can be sent across the network in the most efficient way. These packets are then routed by network devices to the destination.[52]

PACS (Picture archiving and communication system): Medical imaging technology used for storing, retrieving, presenting, and sharing images produced by various medical hardware modalities, such as x-ray, CT scan, MRI, and ultrasound machines. The DICOM standard is commonly used to enable the sharing of images and other medical information within PACS technologies and other information systems.[2] *See* **RIS.**

PAN (Personal-area network): Personal wireless devices, such as mobile phones, headsets, and notebook PCs, connected together wirelessly via protocol such as Bluetooth.[142]

PAP (Password authentication protocol): User authentication protocol that does not encrypt the data and sends the password and username to the authentication server as plain text. PAP is very vulnerable to being read from the Point-to-Point Protocol (PPP) data packets exchanged between the authentication server and the user's machine.

Parallel branching: Specifies that two or more tasks are executed independently of each other.[164] *See* **Exclusive branching.**

Parallel split: The divergence of a branch into two or more parallel branches, each of which execute concurrently.[165]

Parameter: A value that is used to control the operation of a function or that is used by a function to compute one or more outputs.[1]

Parameter RAM: *See* **PRAM**.

Parser: 1. A function that recognizes valid sentences of a language by analyzing the syntax structure of a set of tokens passed to it from a lexical analyzer. **2.** A routine that analyzes a continuous flow of text-based input and breaks it into its constituent pats.[364,150]

Parser services: This service will parse the messages that come in through the protocol layer. The parser will provide support for input formats such as XML, flat files positional, flat file fixed field length, etc.[345]

Partitioning code: Applications can be broken into three logical parts: presentation, logic, and data. These are areas in which the program can be separated to facilitate execution of each logical piece on a different machine. Each segment is known as a partition. For example, the thin-client web model requires that interface presentation be handled by the browser, application logic by the web server and other application servers, and data by a database server. Developers are responsible for determining where the separation occurs.[142]

PAS (Publicly available specification): Standards from the International Organization for Standardization (ISO) which are freely available for standardization purposes. PAS is protected by ISO copyright.[36]

Passive attack: An attack against an authentication protocol where the attacker intercepts data traveling along the network but does not alter the data.[1]

Password: A string of characters used to authenticate an identity or to verify access authorization.[1]

Password authentication protocol: *See* **PAP**.

Password cracking: A process of recovering passwords stored in a computer system or transmitted over a network.[1]

Patch: An update to an operating system, application, or other software or hardware issued specifically to correct particular problems with the software or hardware.[13]

Patent Internet groper: *See* **PING**.

Patient administration system: Information system or subsystem used for patient administration, billing, and reimbursement purposes.[34]

Patient care data set: *See* **PCDS**.

Patient Centered Data Home: *See* **PCDH**.

Patient-centered medical home: *See* **PCMH**.

Patient-centric: 1. Putting the patient first in an open and sustained engagement of the patient to respectfully and compassionately achieve the best experience and outcome for that person and their family. **2.** Technology that puts the patient at the center of the digital experience to drive patient empowerment and engagement.[365,366]

Patient classification: A classification of patients based on specific criteria or data elements.[34]

Patient identifier domain: A single system or a set of interconnected systems that all share a common identification scheme for patients. Such a scheme includes (1) a single identifier-issuing authority; (2) an assignment process of an identifier to a patient; (3) a permanent record of issued patient identifiers with associated traits; and (4) a maintenance process over time. The goal of patient identification is to reduce errors.[27]

Patient portal: A secure online website that gives patients convenient, 24-hour access to personal health information from anywhere with an Internet connection. Using a secure username and password, patients can view health information such as: recent doctor visits, discharge summaries, medications, immunizations, allergies and lab results. Some patient portals also allow you to securely message your doctor, request prescription refills, schedule non-urgent appointments, check benefits and coverage, update contact information, make payments, download and complete forms, and view educational materials.[12]

Patient Protection and Affordable Care Act: *See* **PPACA** and **ACA**.

Patient record: Systematic record of the history of the health of a patient kept by a physician, nurse, or other healthcare practitioner.[34]

Patient registry: 1. A database maintained by a hospital, provider's office, or health plan that allows the identification of patients according to a condition, diagnosis, demographic characteristics, and other factors. Patient registries can help providers better coordinate care for their patients, monitor treatment and progress, and improve overall quality of care. **2.** Patient registries are also maintained by local and state governments (e.g., immunization registry), specialty societies (cardiovascular disease registry of American College of Cardiology), and some patient support organizations.[111,225]

Patient-specific data: All data captured and stored in the system pertaining to a patient, such as clinical assessments, medications, insurance information, etc.[50]

Patient synchronized applications: *See* **PSA**.

Patient Unified Lookup System for Emergencies: *See* **PULSE**.

Payer: A third-party entity that pays for or underwrites coverage for healthcare expenses. A payer may be an insurance company, a health maintenance organization (HMO), a preferred provider organization (PPO), an accountable care organization (ACO), a government agency, or an agency such as a third-party administrator (TPA).[9]

PC (Personal computer): A small computer designed for an individual user. All personal computers are based on the microprocessor technology that enables manufacturers to put an entire CPU on one chip.[39]

PCB (Printed circuit board): The board base for physically supporting and wiring the surface-mounted and socketed components in most electronics. PCBs can be single-layer for simple electronic devices. Printed circuit boards for complex hardware, such as computer graphics cards and motherboards, may have up to twelve layers.[2] Also known as a printed wiring board (PWB) or electronic wiring board.

PCDH (Patient Centered Data Home): A cost-effective, scalable method of exchanging patient data among health information exchanges (HIEs). A PCDH is based on triggering episode alerts, which notify providers a care event has occurred outside of the patient's "home" HIE, and confirms the availability and the specific location of the clinical data, enabling providers to initiate a simple query to access real-time information across state and regional lines and the care continuum. PCDH is an initiative of the Strategic Health Information Exchange Collaborative (SHIEC).[367]

PCDS (Patient care data set): A compilation of pre-coordinated terms used in patient records to record patients' problems, therapeutic goals, and care actions.[43]

PCMH (Patient-centered medical home): A model of the organization of primary care facilities that delivers the core functions of primary healthcare. The medical home encompasses five functions: 1) comprehensive care, 2) patient-centered, 3) coordinated care, 4) accessible services, and 5) quality and safety.[368]

PDC (Primary domain controller): A service in a Windows® server that manages security for its local domain. Every domain has one PDC, which contains a database of usernames, passwords, and permissions. The PDC also provides a time service for the network and typically obtains the time from an edge router, which gets its time from the Internet.[150]

PDF (Portable document format): A file format used to present and exchange documents reliably, independent of software, hardware, or operating system.[369]

PDF 417 (Portable data file 417): A 2-dimensional bar code symbology, enabling error-free transmission of larger blocks of data than is feasible with a 1-dimensional bar code.[7]

PDMP (Prescription drug monitoring program): An electronic database that tracks controlled substance prescriptions, generally at the state level. PDMPs can provide practitioners and health authorities timely information about prescribing and patient behaviors.[80]

PDP (Policy decision point): The system entity that evaluates applicable policy and renders an authorization decision.[24] *See* **ACS**.

Peer-to-peer network: *See* **P2P**.

Penetration: A successful unauthorized breach of a security perimeter.[150]

PEP (Policy enforcement point): The system entity that performs access control, by making decision requests and enforcing authorization decisions.[24] *See* **ACS**.

Per seat license: A software license based on the number of users who have access to the software. The fee is paid per user or "per seat," or per concurrent user, through negotiations with a vendor to allow a fixed number of copies of copyrighted software.[150] *See* **Site license**.

Perioperative nursing data set: *See* **PNDS**.

Peripheral: Any input, output, or storage device connected externally or internally to the computer's CPU, such as a monitor, keyboard, mouse, printer, hard disk, graphics tablet, scanner, joystick, or paddle.[150]

Permanent virtual circuit: *See* **PVC**.

Persistent data: Data that are stored on a permanent basis.[63]

Person identification service: *See* **PIDS**.

Personal computer: *See* **PC**.

Personal connected health: Relates to elements including, but not limited to, an individual's unique characteristics and needs as well as the ability to engage with health-related information and services. It encompasses individuals taking ownership of their own health through wellness and prevention. An important aspect of personal connected health is the enabling nature of technology to empower the person to make sustainable health behavior change by gaining visibility and insights into personal health information.[370]

Personal health management tool: *See* **PHMT**.

Personal health record: *See* **PHR** and **ePHR**.

Personal identification number: *See* **PIN**.

Personal identification verification: *See* **PIV**.

Personal-area network: *See* **PAN**.

Pervasive computing: The use of computing devices in everyday life, not only at a desk. It includes laptops, tablets, smartphones, wearable devices, appliances, and sensors. Pervasive computing implies that people are not necessarily aware of every information-gathering unit surrounding them.[150] *See* **Ubiquitous computing**.

Pharmacy informatics: The scientific field that focuses on medication-related data and knowledge within the continuum of healthcare systems, including its acquisition, storage, analysis, use, and dissemination, in the delivery of optimal medication-related patient care and health outcomes.[53]

Pharmacy information system: Health information system that deals with the pharmacy. Such systems can be linked to prescribing system for electronic processing of requests for medications and can provide inventory control.[34]

Pharmacy management system: An application that provides support to the pharmacy department from an operational, clinical, and management perspective, helping to optimize patient safety, streamline workflow, and reduce operational costs.[10]

PHI (Protected health information): Any individually identifiable health information, whether oral or recorded in any form or medium that is created or received by a healthcare provider, health plan, public health authority, employer, life insurer, school or university, or healthcare clearinghouse; and relates to the past, present, or future physical or mental health or condition of an individual; the provision of healthcare to an individual;

or the past, present, or future payment for the provision of healthcare to an individual. Any data transmitted or maintained in any other form or medium by covered entities, including paper records, fax documents, and all oral communications, or any other form (i.e., screen prints of eligibility information, printed e-mails that have identified individual's health information, claim, or billing information, hard copy birth or death certificate). Protected health information excludes school records that are subject to the Family Educational Rights and Privacy Act, and employment records held in the Department of Homeland Security's role as an employer.[13] *See* **Individually IdentifiableHealth Information.**

PHIN (Public health information network): The Centers for Disease Control and Prevention (CDC) vision for advancing fully capable and interoperable information systems in the many organizations that participate in public health. PHIN is a national initiative to implement a multi-organizational business and technical architecture for public health information systems.[80]

PHIN-MS (Public health information network-messaging system): A protocol for secure transmission of data, based on the ebXML model. Developed and supported by the Centers for Disease Control and Prevention (CDC), the protocol allows for rapid and secure messages to send sensitive health information over the Internet to other local, state, and federal organizations, as well as the CDC.[80]

Phishing: Deceptive computer-based means to trick individuals into disclosing sensitive personal information.[1]

PHMT (Personal health management tool): A set of functions that assist a consumer in managing his or her health status or healthcare.[142]

PHR (Personal health record): 1. An electronic personal health record ("ePHR") is a universally accessible, layperson comprehensible, lifelong tool for managing relevant health information, promoting health maintenance, and assisting with chronic disease management via an interactive, common data set of electronic health information and e-health tools. The PHR is owned, managed, and shared by the individual or his or her legal proxy(s) and must be secure to protect the privacy and confidentiality of the health information it contains. It is not a legal record unless so defined and is subject to various legal limitations. **2.** Usually used when referring to the version of the health/medical record owned by the consumer/patient. **3.** An electronic record of health-related information on an individual that conforms to nationally recognized interoperability standards and that can be drawn from multiple sources while being managed, shared, and controlled by the individual.[12,46,53]

Physical access control: An automated system that controls an individual's ability to access a physical location, such as a building, parking lot, office, or other designated physical space. A physical access control system requires validation of an individual's identity through some mechanism, such as a personal identification number (PIN), card, biometric, or other token prior to providing access. It has the capability to assign different access privileges to different persons, depending on their roles and responsibilities in an organization.[64]

Physical layer: First layer in the OSI model. Defines the physical characteristics of a link between communicating devices, such as wireless transmission, cabling, cabling standards and types, connectors and types, network interface cards and more.[52]

Physical safeguards: The physical measures, policies, and procedures to protect a covered entity's or business associate's electronic information system and related buildings and equipment from natural and environmental hazards and unauthorized intrusion.[13]

Physical security: The protection of personnel, hardware, software, networks and data from physical actions and events that could cause serious loss or damage to an enterprise, agency or institution. This includes protection from fire, flood, natural disasters, burglary, theft, vandalism, and terrorism.[2]

Picosecond: One trillionth of a second.[2]

Picture archiving and communication system: *See* **PACS**.

PIDS (Person identification service): Specification defined by Object Management Group that organizes person ID management functionality to meet healthcare needs. PIDS is designed to support the assignment of IDs within a particular ID domain and the correlation of IDs among multiple ID domains. It supports the searching and matching of people, independent of a matching algorithm.[118]

Piggybacking: Unauthorized access of a wireless LAN. The usual purpose of piggybacking is to gain free network access, but can slow down data transfer for legitimate network users.[2]

PIM (Platform independent model): A model of a software or business system that is independent of the specific technological platform used to implement it. For example, HTML defines a model for hypertext that includes concepts such as title, headings, paragraphs, etc. This model is not linked to a specific operating system or web browser and is, therefore, being successfully implemented on a variety of different computing systems. The term is most frequently used in the context of model-driven architectures.[7]

PIN (Personal identification number): Code used to authenticate or identify a user.[52]

PING (Packet Internet Groper): Utility used to test destination reachability. Sends an Internet control message protocol (ICMP) echo request to the destination and waits for a reply. Used to test and debug a network as well as to see if a user is online.[150]

PIP (Policy information point): Point that can provide external information to a policy decision point.[24] *See* **ACS**.

PIV (Personal identification verification): A physical artifact (e.g., identity card, "smart" card) issued to an individual that contains stored identity credentials (e.g., photograph, cryptographic keys, digitized fingerprint representation) so that the claimed identity of the cardholder can be verified against the stored credentials by another person (human readable and verifiable) or an automated process (computer readable and verifiable).[16]

PIX (Patient identifier cross-referencing): Provides cross-referencing of patient identifiers from multiple patient identifier domains. These patient identifiers can then be used by identity consumer systems to correlate information about a single patient from sources that know the patient by different identifiers.[27] *See* **Profile**. NOTE: PIX is an Integrating the Healthcare Enterprise (IHE) Profile.

Pixel (Picture Element): The fundamental display element of an electronic screen or bitmapped image. Screen resolution is rated by the number of horizontal and vertical pixels.[150]

PKC (Public key certificate): X.509 public key certificates (PKCs), which bind an identity and a public key; the identity may be used to support identity-based access control decisions after the client proves that it has access to the private key that corresponds to the public key contained in the PKC.[72]

PKI (Public key infrastructure): 1. Technology, facilities, people, operational procedures, and policy to support public key-based security mechanisms. It is an enabler for these encryption and digital signatures. **2.** Infrastructure used in the relation between a key holder and a relying party that allows a relying party to use a certificate relating to the key holder for at least one application using a public key dependent security service, and that includes a certification authority, a certificate data structure, means for the relying party to obtain current information on the revocation status of the certificate, a certification policy, and methods to validate the certification practice.[72]

Plain text: Any string (i.e., finite sequence of characters) that consists entirely of printable characters (i.e., human-readable characters) and, optionally, a very few specific types of control characters (e.g., characters indicating a tab or the start of a new line). Plain text usually refers to text that consists entirely of the ASCII printable characters and a few of its control characters. ASCII, an acronym for American standard code for information interchange, is based on the characters used to write the English language as it is used in the United States. It is the de facto standard for the character encoding (i.e., representing characters by numbers) that is utilized by computers and communications equipment to represent text, and it (or some compatible extension of it) is used on most computers, including nearly all personal computers and workstations.[228]

Plan of care (Also interdisciplinary plan of care): A plan, based on data gathered during patient assessment, that identifies the participant's care needs, describes the strategy for providing services to meet those needs, documents treatment goals and objectives, outlines the criteria for terminating specified interventions, and documents the participant's progress in meeting goals and objectives. Patient-specific policies and procedures, protocols, clinical practice guidelines, clinical paths, care maps, or a combination thereof, may guide the format of the plan in some organizations. The care plan may include care, treatment, habilitation, and rehabilitation.[229]

Platform independent model: *See* **PIM.**

Plenum cable: Fire-resistant cable that is installed in false ceilings. Uses a coating that will not emit toxic fumes in the event of a fire.[150]

Plotter: A printer that interprets commands from a computer to make line drawings on paper with one or more automated pens. Unlike a regular printer, the plotter can draw continuous point-to-point lines directly from vector graphics files or commands.[2]

Plug-and-play: Software that can be plugged into the operating system, or other software, and used immediately, without any adaptation or reconfiguration on the part of the user.[150]

Plug-in: Software that is installed into an existing application in order to enhance its capability.[150]

(PMP) Point-to-multipoint communication: A communications architecture that is accomplished through a distinct and specific form of one-to-many connections, offering several paths from one single location to various locations. PMP communication is commonly used in telecommunications. It is often used for establishing private enterprise connectivity to offices in remote locations, long-range wireless backhaul solutions for sites, and last-mile broadband access. Point-to-multipoint is generally abbreviated as PTMP, P2MP or PMP.[52]

PNDS (Perioperative nursing data set): A standardized nursing vocabulary of nursing diagnoses, nursing interventions, and nurse-sensitive patient outcomes, which addresses the perioperative patient experience from pre-admission to discharge.[5]

PNG (Portable network graphics): A file format for image compression that, in time, is expected to replace the Graphics Interchange Format (GIF) that is widely used on today's Internet. Unlike GIF, which involves licensing or other legal considerations for its usage, the PNG format was developed by an Internet committee expressly to be patent-free.[2]

Point-of-care system: Hospital information system that includes bedside workstations or other devices for capturing and entering data at the locations where patients receive care.[34]

Point-of-presence: *See* **POP.**

Point-to-multipoint communication: *See* **PMP.**

Point-to-point protocol: *See* **PPP.**

Point-to-point tunneling protocol: *See* **PPTP.**

Policy: Overall intention and direction as formally expressed by management.[125]

Policy decision point: *See* **PDP.**

Policy enforcement point: *See* **PEP.**

Policy information point: *See* **PIP.**

POP3 (Post office protocol): A programming interface (API) that enables a user's email program to access the mail server (RFC 1939 standard). Email clients such as Outlook, Mail, Eudora, and Thunderbird are typically configured to retrieve mail either via POP3 or IMAP4, the other popular standard.[150]

Pop-down list box: Common type of menu used with a graphical user interface (GUI). Clicking a menu title causes the menu items to appear to drop down from that position and be displayed.[150]

POP (Point-of-presence): A point at which two or more different networks or communication devices build a connection with each other. POP mainly refers to an access point, location, or facility that connects to and helps other devices establish a connection with the Internet.[52] *See* **ISP.**

Portability: 1. The capability of a program to be executed on various types of data processing systems with little or no modification, and without converting the program to a different language. **2.** The ability of a program to run on systems with different architectures.[371,34]

Portable document format: *See* **PDF.**

Portable network graphics: *See* **PNG.**

Portable open systems interface: *See* **POSIX.**

Portal: *See* **Web portal.**

Porting: Moving software and data files to other computer systems.[34]

POSIX (Portable open systems interface): IEEE standard for operating system interface and environment, including a command interpreter (or "shell"), and common utility programs to support applications portability at the source code level. It is intended to be used by both application developers and system implementers.[372]

Post office protocol: *See* **POP3.**

Post-coordination: 1. Describes representation of a concept using a combination of two or more codes. **2.** Using more than one concept from one or many formal systems, combined using mechanisms within or outside the formal systems.[77,114]

Postproduction: Part of the lifecycle of the product after the design has been completed and the medical device has been manufactured and released.[194]

PowerPC: Microprocessor developed by IBM, Apple and Motorola that employs a reduced instruction set computing (RISC). The architecture is open standard.[2]

PPACA (Patient Protection and Affordable Care Act) (Public Law 111-148): Legislation that focuses on provisions to expand healthcare coverage, control healthcare costs, and improve the healthcare delivery system.[230] *See* **ACA.**

PPP (Point-to-point protocol): Method for transporting IP packets over a serial link between the user and the ISP. PPP establishes the session between the user's computer and the ISP using its own Link Control Protocol (LCP).[150]

PPTP (Point-to-point tunneling protocol): A protocol used to create a virtual private network (VPN) over the Internet. Remote users can access their corporate networks via any ISP that supports PPTP on its servers.[150]

Practice management system: Term used to reference a management system used to automate particular aspects of practice activities related to transactions and workflows, such as capturing patient demographics, scheduling and registration, and revenue cycle management.[3]

PRAM (Parameter RAM): A battery-powered form of RAM where vital system information such as the date and time are stored. It also contains computer configuration information. Because PRAM is powered by an internal battery, the information isn't lost when the computer powers off.[2]

Precision medicine: An emerging approach for disease treatment and prevention that takes into account individual variability in genes, environment, and lifestyle in striving to deliver the right treatment at the right time to the right person. The National Institutes of Health lead the All of Us Research Program, which is working to build a 1 million person research cohort to pioneer research on this approach. The research phases emphasize engaged research participants, responsible data sharing, and privacy protections.[231]

Predicate migration: Steps taken to enable preexisting data retrieval predicates (including queries, standard reports, and decision support protocols) to be converted or utilized in a system using a mappable vocabulary.[77]

Predictive modeling: A statistical technique to predict future outcomes. Predictive modeling solutions are a form of data-mining technology that works by analyzing historical and current data and generating a model to help predict future outcomes.[142]

Preferred term: The term that is deemed to be the most clinically appropriate way of expressing a concept in a clinical record. Preferred term is one of the three types of terms that can be indicated by the description type field.[77]

Preparedness: Activities, programs, and systems developed and implemented prior to an incident that may be used to support and enhance mitigation of, response to, and recovery from disruptions, disasters, or emergencies.[87] Also known as readiness.

Prescribing system: An information system used in healthcare for processing the prescription of medication by a provider; such a system links the provider with pharmacies and others engaged in prescription of medication.[34] *See* **e-Prescribing**.

Prescription drug monitoring program: *See* **PDMP**.

Presentation layer: Sixth layer of the open systems interconnection (OSI) model. It is used to present data to the application layer (layer 7) in an accurate, well-defined and standardized format.[52]

Prevention: Measures that enable an organization to avoid, preclude, or limit the impact of a disruption.[87]

Preventive action: Action to eliminate the cause of a potential nonconformity.[87]

PRG (Procedure-related group): A classification system that groups patients based on the procedure rather than the diagnosis. This classification is based on the main procedures performed in the course of a patient's treatment. A potential benefit from this classification system includes incentives for the use of advanced technology. A drawback that currently exists in current models is that non-interventional procedures are still reimbursed on a per diem basis.[232]

Primary domain controller: *See* **PDC**.

Primary key: A key in a relational database that is unique for each record. It is a unique identifier. Primary keys typically appear as columns in relational database tables.[2]

Print server: A software application, network device, or computer that manages print requests from many different users by holding them in a queue until they can be printed. Print servers are used in both large enterprise and small office networks.[2]

Printed circuit board: *See* **PCB**.

Privacy: *See* **Health information privacy**.

Privacy consent policy: One of the acceptable use privacy consent policies that are agreed to and understood in the affinity domain.[27]

Privacy consent policy identifier: An affinity domain assigned object identifier (OID) that uniquely identifies the affinity domain, privacy consent policy. There is one unique OID for each privacy consent policy within the affinity domain.[27]

Privacy impact assessment: Tells the "story" of a project or policy initiative from a privacy perspective, and helps to manage privacy impacts.[233]

Privacy officer: Appointed by a covered entity to be responsible for developing and implementing policies and procedures for complying with the health information privacy requirements of the Health Insurance Portability and Accountability Act.[20]

Privacy rights: Specific actions that an individual can take, or request to be taken, with regard to the uses and disclosures of their information.[20]

Private key: A bit of code that is paired with a public key to set off algorithms for text encryption and decryption. It is created as part of public key cryptography during asymmetric-key encryption and used to decrypt and transform a message to a readable format.[52]

Privilege: The rights granted to a single user or group of users who operate a computer. Administrative privileges allow a user the right to make any and all changes in the computer, including setting up accounts for other users. User-level privileges are more restricted.[150]

Privileged information: Alternative term for confidential information.[4]

Problem-oriented medical record: Healthcare record in which all data may be linked to a list of health problems of an individual patient.[34]

Procedure-related group: *See* **PRG**.

Process: Set of interrelated or interacting activities which transform inputs into outputs.[194]

Process model: A number of tasks that have to be carried out, and a set of conditions that determine the order of the tasks.[164]

Process standard: Standard that specifies requirements to be fulfilled by a process, to establish fitness for purpose.[34]

Processor: The term *processor* has generally replaced the term central processing unit. *See* **CPU**[150]

Product standard: Standard that specifies requirements to be fulfilled by a product or groups of products to establish fitness for purpose.[34]

Profile: A set of selected parameters that describes a particular implementation of a standard or standards.[34]

Program: A set of instructions that can be recognized by a computer system and used to carry out a set of processes.[34]

Program manager: The person ultimately responsible for the overall procurement, development, integration, modification, operation and maintenance of an IT system.[1]

Programmable read-only memory: *See* **PROM**.

Project Gemini: A joint initiative of HL7 and IHE to align efforts to achieve interoperability by leveraging the HL7 FHIR® standard and capitalizing on the individual strengths of the two standards development organizations. The initiative aims to create new robust, jointly-owned specifications.[9]

Project management: A set of principles, methods, tools, and techniques for effective planning of work, thereby establishing a sound basis for effective scheduling, controlling, and preplanning in the implementation and management of programs and products.[50]

PROM (Programmable read-only memory): A permanent memory chip in which the content is created (programmed) by the customer rather than by the chip manufacturer. It differs from a ROM chip, which is created at the time of manufacture.[150]

Promoting Interoperability Performance Category for Merit-based Incentive Payment System (MIPS) Eligible Clinicians: Performance category defined under the Medicare Access and CHIP Reauthorization Act of 2015 (MACRA) as part of the Quality Payment Program's (QPP) MIPS. This performance category focuses on interoperability, improving reporting flexibility, relieving burden, and placing an emphasis on measures that require the electronic exchange of health information between providers and patients. This may include sharing test results, visit summaries, and therapeutic plans with the patient and other facilities to coordinate care. This program replaces the Medicare EHR Incentive Program for eligible clinicians, commonly known as Meaningful Use.[373] *See* **QPP, MACRA, MIPS**.

Prompt: A message displayed on the monitor screen, which asks the customer to perform some action and shows that the computer is ready to accept a command or instruction.[34]

Proof of concept: A demonstration, the purpose of which is to verify that certain concepts or theories have the potential for real-world application.[52]

Proof of elapsed time: A blockchain network consensus mechanism algorithm that prevents high resource utilization and high energy consumption, and keeps the process more efficient by following a fair lottery system. Each participating node in the network is required to wait for a randomly chosen time period, and the first one to complete the designated waiting time wins the new block. Each node in the blockchain network generates a random wait time and goes to sleep for that specified duration. The one to wake up first—that is, the one with the shortest wait time—commits a new block to the blockchain, broadcasting the necessary information to the whole peer network. The same process then repeats for the discovery of the next block.[18]

Proof of stake: In distributed ledger technology and cryptocurrency, the concept that a person can mine or validate block transactions according to how many coins he or she holds.[18]

Proof of work: A puzzle that is designed to take time to complete. In order to impede spammers, a proof of work algorithm has been suggested as a mandatory technique when sending email. For example, if every email message required just 30 seconds more to process, a compromised computer could never quickly unleash millions of messages. Cryptocurrency mining also uses a proof of work algorithm.[150]

Properties: Attributes that are associated with something. Windows® uses the term extensively to refer to the current settings of hardware, software and data.[150]

Protected health information: *See* **PHI**.

Protocol: A special set of rules using end points in a telecommunication connection for communication. Protocols exist at several levels.[94]

Protocol stack: A group of protocols that are running concurrently that are employed for the implementation of network protocol suite.[52]

Proximity: Refers to a technology used to provide physical access control. This technology uses a contactless interface with a card reader.[64]

Proxy server: Hardware security tool to help protect an organization against security breaches.[48]

Psychotherapy notes: Recorded in any medium by a healthcare provider who is a mental health professional, documenting or analyzing the contents of conversation during a private counseling session, or a group, joint, or family counseling session, when notes are separated from the rest of the individual's record.[20]

Public health agency: An agency that performs or conducts one or more of the following essential functions that characterize public health programs, services, or activities: (a) monitor health status to identify community health problems; (b) diagnose and investigate health problems and health hazards in the community; (c) inform, educate, and empower people about health issues; (d) mobilize community partnerships to identify and solve health problems; (e) develop policies and plans that support individual and community health efforts; (f) enforce laws and regulations that protect health and ensure safety; (g) link people to needed personal health services and ensure the provision of healthcare when otherwise unavailable; (h) ensure a competent public health and personal healthcare workforce; (i) evaluate effectiveness, accessibility, and quality of personal and population-based health services; and (j) research for new insights and innovation solutions to health problems.[13]

Public health information network: *See* **PHIN**.

Public information: Any information, regardless of form or format, that an agency discloses, disseminates, or makes available to the public.[161]

Public key: An encryption key that can be made public or sent by ordinary means such as an email message.[150]

Public key certificate: *See* **PKC**.

Public key cryptography: An encryption method that uses a two-part key: one private; the other public. To send an encrypted message to someone, the recipient's public key is used, which can be published anywhere or sent openly via email. When the message arrives, the recipient uses his or her private key, which is always kept secret. Public key cryptography differs from "secret key cryptography," which uses the same key to encrypt and decrypt.[150]

Public key infrastructure: *See* **PKI**.

Publicly available specification: *See* **PAS**.

PULSE (Patient Unified Lookup System for Emergencies): A nationwide health IT disaster response platform that can be deployed at the city, county, or state level to authenticate disaster healthcare volunteer providers. It allows disaster workers to query and view patient documents from all connected healthcare organizations.[437]

Push: Delivery of information on the web that is initiated by the information server rather than by the information user. The opposite of query.[2]

PVC (Permanent virtual circuit): A point-to-point connection that is established ahead of time. A group of PVCs defined at the time of subscription to a particular service is known as a "virtual private network" (VPN).[150] *See* **SVC, VPN**.

Q

QA (Quality assurance): An ongoing planned and systematic effort to ensure confidence that processes and products meet established goals.[234]

QAPI (Quality assessment performance improvement): The coordinated application of two mutually reinforcing aspects of a quality management system: quality assurance (QA) and performance improvement (PI). QAPI takes a systematic, comprehensive, and data-driven approach to maintaining and improving safety and quality in nursing homes while involving all nursing home caregivers in practical and creative problem-solving.[26]

QASP (Quality assurance surveillance plan): The key government-developed surveillance process document, and applied to Performance-Based Service Contracting (PBSC). The QASP is used for managing contractor performance assessment by ensuring that systematic quality assurance methods validate that contractor quality control efforts are timely, effective, and are delivering the results specified in the contract or task order. The QASP directly corresponds to the performance objectives and standards (i.e., quality, quantity, timeliness) specified in the Performance Work Statement (PWS).[374]

QC (Quality control): A procedure or set of procedures intended to ensure that a manufactured product or performed service adheres to a defined set of quality criteria or meets the requirements of the client or customer.[2]

QCDR (Qualified clinical data registry): An entity that collects clinical data from MIPS clinicians (both individual and groups) and submits it to CMS on their behalf for purposes of MIPS. The QCDR reporting option is different from a qualified registry because it is not limited to measures within the Quality Payment Program.[26]

QDM (Quality data model): An information model that defines concepts used in quality care and is intended to enable automation of EHR use.[182]

QE (Quality entity): The CMS Qualified Entity (QE) Program (also known as the Medicare Data Sharing for Performance Measurement Program) enables organizations to receive Medicare claims data under Parts A, B, and D for use in evaluating provider performance. Organizations approved as QEs are required to use the Medicare data to produce and publicly disseminate CMS-approved reports on provider performance.[26]

QHP (Qualified health plan): An insurance plan that's certified by the Health Insurance Marketplace, provides essential health benefits, follows established limits on cost-sharing (like deductibles, copayments, and out of pocket maximum amounts), and meets other requirements under the Affordable Care Act. All qualified health plans meet the Affordable

Care Act requirement for having health coverage, known as "minimum essential coverage." [218]

QI (Quality improvement): A systematic, formal approach to the analysis of practice performance and efforts to improve performance.[375]

QIDAM (Quality improvement domain analysis model): Also known as HL7 Domain Analysis Model: Health Quality Improvement; A conceptual model for health data for use in the health quality domain. It harmonizes the requirements for patient data use in quality measurement and clinical decision support enabling a single model to be used in both aspects of quality improvement. This model will facilitate the development of unified knowledge representation standards such as structured formats for quality measures and clinical decision support knowledge artifacts.[9]

QIN/QIO (Quality innovation network – Quality improvement organizations): Assist patients and families, providers, and communities to: make care safer, support active engagement and self-management of chronic conditions, eliminate health disparities, promote best practices for healthy living, improve access to care, and make care affordable.[26]

QIO (Quality improvement organization): A group of health quality experts, clinicians, and consumers organized to improve the quality of care delivered to people.[26]

QMF (Query management facility): Ad hoc query tool to extract data from some mainframe systems.[46]

QMR (Quick medical reference): Search system for the U.S. National Library of Medicine.[235]

QMS (Quality management system): A collection of business processes focused on consistently meeting customer requirements and enhancing their satisfaction. The QMS is aligned with an organization's purpose and strategic direction.[376]

QoS (Quality of service): 1. A negotiated contract between a user and a network provider that renders some degree of reliable capacity in the shared network. **2.** A network's ability to achieve maximum bandwidth and deal with other network performance elements like latency, error rate, and uptime. Quality of service also involves controlling and managing network resources by setting priorities for specific types of data (video, audio, files) on the network.[142,52]

QP (Qualified professional): One who, by possession of a recognized degree, certificate, or professional standing, or who by extensive knowledge, training, and experience, has successfully demonstrated his ability to solve or resolve problems relating to the subject matter, the work, or the project.[377]

QP (Qualifying APM participant): Clinicians who participate in an Advanced Alternative Payment Model (APM) as a part of the Quality Payment Program (QPP) are considered Qualifying APM Participants.[26]

QPP (Quality Payment Program): A quality incentive payment program implemented by the Centers for Medicare and Medicaid Services (CMS) as part of the Medicare Access and CHIP Reauthorization Act of 2015 (MACRA). QPP replaced the Sustainable Growth Rate (SGR) previously used to define payment for Medicare services. Clinicians have two tracks to choose from: the Merit-based Incentive Payment System (MIPS) or the Advanced Alternative Payment Models track. QPP started on January 1, 2017.[26] *See* **MACRA, MIPS, ACI.**

QPS (Quality positioning system): A web-based tool developed by the National Quality Forum (NQF) to help people select and use NQF-endorsed measures. It allows a user to search for NQF-endorsed measures in a number of ways: export search results; and view types of measures. Using QPS, a user can find NQF-endorsed measures on particular topics, track and get reminders about measures that are important to them, provide feedback on measures, and see which measures others are using.[182]

QR codes (Quick response codes): High-density, two-dimensional bar codes that are readable by mobile phones and computer cameras with the correct software.[142] *See* **Bar Code.**

QRDA (Quality reporting data architecture): The data submission standard used for a variety of quality measurement and reporting initiatives. QRDA creates a standard method to report quality measure results in a structured, consistent format and can be used to exchange eCQM data between systems.[88]

QRUR (Quality and resource use report): Report that shows how payments under Medicare Part B fee-for-service (FFS) will be adjusted based on quality and cost.[26]

Qualified certificate: In public key infrastructure security information technology, a qualified certificate is used to describe a certificate with a certain qualified status within applicable governing law.[72]

Qualified Clinical Data Registry: *See* **QCDR.**

Qualified Health Plan: *See* **QHP.**

Qualified Professional: *See* **QP.**

Qualifying Participant: *See* **QP.**

Quality: The totality of features and other characteristics of a product or service that bear on its ability to satisfy stated or implied needs.[123]

Quality and Resource Use Report: *See* **QRUR.**

Quality Assessment Performance Improvement: *See* **QAPI.**

Quality Assurance Surveillance Plan: *See* **QASP.**

Quality control: *See* **QC.**

Quality data model: *See* **QDM.**

Quality design: Systematic approach to service design that identifies the key features needed or desired by both external and internal clients, creates design options for the desired features, and then selects the combination of options that will maximize satisfaction within available resources.[378]

Quality entity: *see* **QE.**

Quality Improvement: *see* **QI.**

Quality Improvement Domain Analysis Model: *See* **QIDAM.**

Quality Improvement Organization: *See* **QIO.**

Quality indicator: An agreed-upon process for outcome measurement that is used to determine the level of quality achieved. A measurable variable, or characteristic, that can be used to determine the degree of adherence to a standard or achievement of quality goals.[53]

Quality information and clinical knowledge: *See* **QUICK.**

Quality Innovation Network – Quality Improvement Organizations: *See* **QIN/QIO.**

Quality management: An ongoing effort to provide services that meet or exceed customer expectations through a structured, systematic process for creating organizational participation in planning and implementing quality improvements.[379]

Quality Management System: *See* **QMS.**

Quality measures: Mechanisms used to assign a quantity to quality of care by comparison to a criterion.[108]

Quality Measures Reporting Tool: *See* **QMRT.**

Quality monitoring: The collection and analysis of data for selected indicators that enable managers to determine whether key standards are being achieved as planned, and are having the expected effect on the target population.[91]

Quality of care: Degrees to which healthcare services for individuals and populations increase the likelihood of desired health outcomes and are consistent with current professional knowledge. The National Academy of Medicine (formerly the Institute of Medicine) defines quality as having the following domains: effectiveness, efficiency, equity, patient centeredness, safety, and timeliness.[91]

Quality of Service: *See* **QoS.**

Quality Payment Program: *See* **QPP.**

Quality Positioning System: *See* **QPS.**

Quality Reporting Data Architecture: *See* **QRDA.**

Quantity: The extent, size or sum of countable or measurable discrete events, objects, phenomenon, expressed as a numerical value.[4]

Query: 1. The process by which a web client requests specific information from a web server, based on a character string that is passed along. **2.** A request for information that results in the aggregation and retrieval of data.[39]

Query management facility: *See* **QMF.**

Queue: A storage concept in which data are ordered in such a manner that the next data item to be retrieved is the one stored first. This concept is also characterized as "first in, first out" (FIFO).[57]

Queuing services: This service provides store-and-forward capabilities. It can use message queues, as well as other persistence mechanisms, to store information. This service can be used for asynchronous types of operations.[57]

QUICK (Quality information and clinical knowledge): The QICore model defines a set of HL7 FHIR® profiles that provide a physical implementation of the Quality Information and Clinical Knowledge (QUICK) logical model. The goal is to have a single logical data model (QUICK), as well as a single logical processing language (CQL), for CDS and clinical quality measurement (CQM).[9]

Quick response codes: *See* **QR codes**.

Q

R

RA (Registration authority): **1.** Body responsible for assigning healthcare coding scheme designators and for maintaining the Register of Health Care Coding Schemes as described in a standard. **2.** Entity that is responsible for identification and authentication of certificate subjects, but that does not sign or issue certificates (i.e., an RA is delegated certain tasks on behalf of a CA).[34,72] *See* **CA**.

RAD (Rapid application development): An application development (AD) approach that includes small teams—typically two to six people, but never more than 10—using joint application development (JAD) and iterative-prototyping techniques to construct interactive systems of low to medium complexity within a timeframe of 60 to 120 days.[142]

Radio frequency identification: *See* **RFID**.

Radio frequency interference: Disruption of the normal functionality of a satellite due to the interference of radio astronomy. Radio frequency interference can disrupt and disturb the normal functioning of electronic and electrical devices, a subset of electromagnetic interference.[52] *See* **EMI**.

Radiology information system: *See* **RIS**.

RAID (Redundant array of independent disks): A method of storing data on multiple hard disks. When disks are arranged in a RAID configuration, the computer sees them all as one large disk. However, they operate much more efficiently than a single hard drive. Since the data are spread out over multiple disks, the reading and writing operations can take place on multiple disks at once, which can speed up hard-drive access time significantly.[73]

RAM (Random access memory): 1. Primary storage of data or program instructions that can directly access any randomly chosen location in the same amount of time. **2.** The data in RAM stay there only as long as your computer is running. When you turn the computer off, RAM loses its data.[2]

Random access memory: *See* **RAM**.

Ransomware: A type of malware that encrypts, or locks, valuable digital files and demands a ransom to release them.[83]

Rapid application development: *See* **RAD**.

RAS (Remote access server): Server dedicated to handling users that are not on a LAN but need remote access to the network.[39]

RBAC (Role-based access control): A method of regulating access to computer or network resources based on the roles of individual users within an enterprise. Roles are defined according to job competency, authority, and responsibility within the enterprise.[2]

RDBMS (Relational database management system): A collection of programs and capabilities that enable IT teams and others to create, update, administer, and interact with a relational database. A type of DBMS with a row-based table structure that connects related data elements and includes functions that maintain the security, accuracy, integrity, and consistency of the data. *See* **DBMS.**

RDF (Resource description framework): A standard model for data interchange on the web. It has features that facilitate data merging even if the underlying schemas differ, and it specifically supports the evolution of schemas over time without requiring all the data consumers to be changed.[61]

Read codes: A coded thesaurus of clinical terms. There are two versions: version 2 (v2) and version 3 (CTV3 or v3).[380]

Readiness: *See* **Preparedness.**

Read-only memory: *See* **ROM.**

Realm: A sphere of authority, expertise, or preference that influences the range of components required, or the frequency with which they are used. A realm may be a nation, an organization, a professional discipline, a specialty, or an individual user.[77]

Real-time location system: *See* **RTLS.**

Real-time operating system: Operating system that guarantees a certain capability within a specific time constraint.[2]

REC (Regional extension center): Organizations previously established by the Office of the National Coordinator (ONC) though the Health Information Technology for Economic and Clinical Health (HITECH) Act (enacted as part of the American Recovery and Reinvestment Act of 2009) to serve local communities by providing technical assistance, guidance, and information on best practices to support and accelerate healthcare providers' efforts to become meaningful users of certified electronic health records (EHRs).[12]

Record: 1. A database entry that may contain one or more variables. **2.** A collection of data items arranged for processing by a program. **3.** Document stating results achieved or providing evidence of activities performed.[73,2,87]

Records management: *See* **RM.**

Recovery point objective: *See* **RPO.**

Recovery time objective: *See* **RTO.**

Redaction tools: Software used to edit content, and thereby, selectively and reliably remove information from documents or websites before sharing the remaining content with someone who is not authorized to see the entire original document.[142]

Reduced instruction set computer: *See* **RISC.**

Redundant array of independent disks: *See* **RAID.**

Reference architecture: Generalized architecture of several end systems that share one or more common domains. The reference architecture defines the infrastructure common to the end systems and the interfaces of components that will be included in the end systems. The reference architecture is then instantiated to create a software architecture of a specific system.[57]

Reference information model: *See* **RIM.**

Reference model: An abstract framework for understanding significant relationships among the entities of some environments, and for the development of consistent standards or specifications supporting that environment. It is based on a small number of unifying concepts and may be used as a basis for education and explaining standards to a non-specialist.[157]

Reference model for open distributed processing: *See* **RM-ODP.**

Reference terminology: A terminology in which each term has a formal computer processable definition that supports meaning based retrieval and aggregation. SNOMED–CT is a reference terminology.[77]

Reference terminology model: *See* **RTM.**

Regional extension center: *See* **REC.**

Regional health information organization: *See* **RHIO.** *See* **HIE.**

Registration authority: *See* **RA.**

Registry: Directory-like system that focuses on managing data pertaining to one conceptual entity. In an EHR, registries store, maintain, and provide access to peripheral information not categorized as clinical in nature, but required to operationalize an EHR. The primary purpose of a registry is to respond to searches using one or more predefined parameters in order to find and retrieve a unique occurrence of an entity.[57] *See* **Disease registry.**

Regression model: Models used to predict the value of one variable from one or more other variables. Regression models provide the scientist with a powerful tool, allowing predictions about past, present, or future events to be made with information about past or present events.[237]

Regression testing: 1. The process of testing changes to computer programs to make sure that the older programming still works with the new changes. Regression testing is a normal part of the program development process. **2.** Repeated testing of an already tested program, after modification, to discover any defects introduced or uncovered as a result of the changes in the software being tested or in another related or unrelated software components.[2,381]

Relational database: A collection of data items organized as a set of formally described tables from which data can be accessed or reassembled in many different ways without having to reorganize the database tables.[2]

Relational database management system: *See* **RDBMS.**

Relational online analytical processing: *See* **ROLAP.**

Relational model: A method of structuring data using relations, grid-like mathematical structures consisting of columns and rows. In this model, all data must be stored in relations with keys to order data or relate data to other relations.[2]

Relationship: A connection, association or involvement between two or more items or concepts. An association between a source concept and a destination concept. The type of association is indicated by a reference to an attribute concept.[44,77]

Relative value unit: *See* **RVU**.

Release of information: *See* **ROI**.

Reliability: A measure of consistency of data items based on the reproducibility of the results under the same conditions.[382]

Relying party: Recipient of a certificate who acts in reliance on that certificate and/or digital signature verified using that certificate.[72]

Remote access: The ability to gain access to a network or system that is not in the same physical location.[34]

Remote access server: *See* **RAS**.

Remote access software: A type of software that enables a local user to connect to and access a remote computer, server, or network. It enables connectivity of two or more computers/network nodes that are on separate networks and/or in different geographical locations.[52]

Remote hosting: A computer that resides in some distant location from which data are retrieved. It typically refers to a server in a private network or the public Internet. However, it can also refer to a user's PC in another location that is accessed over the Internet for file transfer or remote control operation.[150]

Remote method invocation: *See* **RMI**.

Remote network monitor: *See* **RMON**.

Remote patient monitoring: The use of digital technologies to collect medical and other forms of health data from individuals in one location and electronically transmit that information securely to healthcare providers in a different location for assessment and recommendations.[383]

Removable media: *See* **Electronic media**.

Rendering: The process of generating a final digital product from a specific type of input. The term usually applies to graphics and video, but it can refer to audio as well.[73]

Repeater: A network device that retransmits a received signal with more power and to an extended geographical or topological network boundary than what would be capable with the original signal. Also known as a signal booster.[52]

Repetition separator: Used in some data fields to separate multiple occurrences of a field. It is used only where specifically authorized in the descriptions of the relevant data fields.[9]

Replication: The process of copying data from one location to another.[2]

Reporting workflow: *See* **RWF**.

Repository: 1. An implementation of a collection of information along with data access and control mechanisms, such as search, indexing, storage,

R

retrieval, and security. **2.** A generic term for a storehouse of data. **3.** A database of information about application software that includes author, data elements, inputs, processes, outputs, and interrelationships. **4.** A database of digital certificate information. The repository is maintained by the certificate authority (CA) and is queried to find out if a certificate is valid, has expired or has been revoked.[57,150] *See* **CA.**

Representational state transfer: *See* **REST.**

Repudiation: Act, intention, or threat of disowning or rejection of an agreement already accepted or agreed to.[4]

Request for information: *See* **RFI.**

Request for proposal: *See* **RFP.**

Request to send: *See* **RTS.**

Requirements: A set of needs, functions, and demands that need to be satisfied by a particular software implementation or specification.[384]

Resident virus: A type of computer virus that hides and stores itself within the computer memory, which then allows it to infect any file that is run by the computer, depending on the virus' programming.[52]

Residual risk: 1. Risk remaining after risk treatment. **2.** The threat that remains after all efforts to identify and eliminate risk have been made.[87,2]

Resolution: The number of pixels (individual points of color) contained on a display monitor, expressed in terms of the number of pixels on the horizontal axis and the number on the vertical axis. The sharpness of the image on a display depends on the resolution and the size of the monitor. The higher the density, the sharper the display.[2]

Resource description framework: *See* **RDF.**

Response plan (or incident response plan): The documented collection of procedures and information developed, compiled, and maintained in readiness for use in an emergency.[87]

Response team (or incident response team): Group of individuals responsible for developing, executing, rehearsing, and maintaining the response plan, including the processes and procedures.[87] *See* **CERT.**

Response time: The time period between a terminal operator's completion of an inquiry and the receipt of a response. Response time includes the time taken to transmit the inquiry, process it by the computer, and transmit the response back to the terminal. Response time is frequently used as a measure of the performance of an interactive system.[142]

REST (Representational state transfer): 1. A style of software architecture for distributed systems such as the World Wide Web. REST has emerged as a predominant web service design model. REST facilitates the transaction between web servers by allowing loose coupling between different services. REST is less strongly typed than its counterpart, SOAP. The REST language is based on the use of nouns and verbs, and has an emphasis on readability. Unlike SOAP, REST does not require XML parsing and does not require a message header to and from a service provider. This ultimately uses less bandwidth. **2.** Architectural style for developing web services. REST is popular due to its simplicity and the fact that it builds upon existing systems and features of the Internet's HTTP in order to achieve its objectives, as opposed to creating new standards, frameworks, and technologies. [2,64]

Retention: The continued storage of an organization's data for compliance, business, legal, or other reasons.[2]

Retrieve information for display: *See* **RID.**

Return on investment: *See* **ROI.**

Revocation: The process of permanently ending the operational period of a certificate from a specified time forward. Generally, revocation is performed when a private key has been compromised. Revocation most often refers to the revocation of a digital security certificate.[52]

RFI (Request for information): A standard business process whose purpose is to collect written information about the capabilities of various suppliers.[7]

RFID (Radio frequency identification): Refers to technologies that use wireless communication between an object (or tag) and interrogating device (or reader) to automatically track and identify such objects. The tag transmission range is limited to several meters from the reader. A clear line of sight between the reader and tag is not necessarily required.[52]

RFP (Request for proposal): Document that solicits proposal, often made through a bidding process, by an agency or company interested in procurement of a commodity, service, or valuable asset, to potential suppliers to submit business proposals.[7]

RHIO (Regional health information organization): Formerly referenced a group of organizations within a specific area that share healthcare-related information electronically according to accepted healthcare information technology (HIT) standards. A RHIO typically oversaw the means of information exchange among various provider settings, payers, and government agencies. Now more commonly referred to as a Health Information Exchange (HIE).[2] *See* **HIE.**

Rich text format: *See* **RTF.**

RIM (Reference information model): A static model of health and healthcare information as viewed within the scope of HL7 standards development activities. It is the combined consensus view of information from the perspective of the HL7 working group and the HL7 international affiliates. The RIM is the ultimate source from which all HL7 Version 3.0 protocol specification standards draw their information-related content.[9]

Ring network: A local area network (LAN) in which the nodes (workstations or other devices) are connected in a closed loop configuration.[2]

RIS (Radiology information system): 1. A networked software system for managing medical imagery and associated data. A RIS is especially useful for tracking radiology imaging orders and billing information, and is often used in conjunction with PACS and VNAs to manage image archives, record-keeping, and billing. **2.** A type of information system that is used to create, store and manage radiological data and images of patients.[2,52] *See* **PACS**.

RISC (Reduced instruction set computer): A type of microprocessor architecture that utilizes a small, highly optimized set of instructions, rather than a more specialized set of instructions often found in other types of architectures.[238]

Risk: 1. Combination of the probability of an event and its consequences. **2.** An activity or factor that may increase the likelihood of disease or harm **3.** Effect of uncertainty on objectives. A deviation from the expected— positive and/or negative **4.** The expectation of loss. It is a function of the probability and the consequences of harm.[125,34,87,150] *See* **Residual risk**.

Risk analysis: Process to comprehend the nature of risk and to determine the level of risk.[87]

Risk assessment: 1. Overall process of risk identification, risk analysis, and risk evaluation **2.** A report that shows an organization's vulnerabilities and the estimated cost of recovery in the event of damage. It also summarizes defensive measures and associated costs based on the amount of risk the organization is willing to accept (the risk tolerance).[87,150]

Risk control: Process in which decisions are made and measures implemented by which risks are reduced to, or maintained within, specified levels.[18]

Risk estimation: 1. Expressing duration, intensity, magnitude, and reach of the potential consequences of a risk in quantifiable or dollar value (monetary) terms. **2.** Description of the probability that an organism exposed to a specific dose of substance will develop an adverse effect.[4]

Risk evaluation: Determination of risk management priorities through establishment of qualitative and/or quantitative relationships between benefits and associated risks.[4]

Risk management: 1. The culture, processes, and structures that are directed toward the effective management of potential opportunities for adverse events **2.** Coordinated activities to direct and control an organization with regard to risk **3.** The optimal allocation of resources to arrive at a cost-effective investment in defensive measures within an organization. Risk management minimizes both risk and costs. [34,87,150]

Risk tolerance: Organization's readiness to bear the risk after risk treatments in order to achieve its objectives.[87] *See* **MTBF, MTTD, MTTR**.

Risk treatment: Process of selection and implementation of measures to modify risk.[125]

RM (Records management): Technologies that enable organizations to enforce policies and rules for the retention and disposition of content required for documenting business transaction, in addition to automating the management of their record-retention policies. These technologies, implemented with well-formulated and consistently enforced RM strategies and policies, form an essential part of the organization-wide lifecycle management of records. RM principles and technologies apply to both physical and electronic content.[142]

RMI (Remote method invocation): A distributed object technology developed by Sun® for the Java programming language. It is available as part of the core Java application programming interface (API) where the object interfaces are defined as Java interfaces and use object serialization.[52]

RM-ODP (Reference model for open distributed processing): 1. A reference model in computer science, which provides a co-coordinating framework for the standardization of open distributed processing (ODP). It supports distribution, interworking, platform and technology independence, and portability, together with an enterprise architecture framework for the specification of ODP systems. RM-ODP, also named ITU-T Rec. X.901-X.904 and ISO/IEC 10746, is a joint effort by the International Organization for Standardization (ISO), the International Electrotechnical Commission (IEC), and the Telecommunication Standardization Sector (ITU-T). **2. A**n object modeling approach to describe distributed systems. Two structuring approaches are used to simplify the problems of design in large complex systems: five "viewpoints" provide different ways of describing the system. Each viewpoint is associated with a language, which can be used to describe systems from that viewpoint.[9]

RMON (Remote network monitor): A standard specification that facilitates the monitoring of network operational activities through the use of remote devices known as monitors or probes. RMON assists network administrators with efficient network infrastructure control and management.[52]

Roadmap: A flexible technique that is widely used within industry to support strategic and long-range planning. The approach provides a structured (and often graphical) means for exploring and communicating the relationships between evolving and developing markets, products, and technologies over time. It is proposed that the roadmapping technique can help companies survive in turbulent environments by providing a focus for scanning the environment and a means of tracking the performance of individual, including potentially disruptive, technologies. Technology roadmaps are deceptively simple in terms of format, but their development poses significant challenges. In particular the scope is generally broad, covering a number of complex conceptual and human interactions.[385] *See* **Transition plan**.

Robotics: A branch of engineering that involves the conception, design, manufacture, and operation of robots. This field overlaps with electronics, computer science, artificial intelligence, mechatronics, nanotechnology, and bioengineering.[2]

R

ROI (Release of information): Formal process to request to release health information to other healthcare providers and authorized users, ensuring that the information is timely, accurate, complete, and confidential.[28]

ROI (Return on investment): A mathematical formula that investors can use to evaluate their investments and judge how well a particular investment has performed compared to others.[2]

ROLAP (Relational online analytical processing [OLAP]): A technical OLAP approach that analyzes data using multidimensional data models. The difference between ROLAP and other OLAPs is that it accesses data that are stored in a relational database rather than from a multidimensional database, which is the one most commonly used in other OLAPs. It can also generate SQL queries to perform calculations when an end-user wishes to do so.[52] *See* **OLAP.**

Role: 1. Attributes. **2.** Set of behaviors associated with a task.[72,77]

Role-based access control: *See* **RBAC.**

ROM (Read-only memory): Computer memory on which data have been prerecorded. Once data have been written onto a ROM chip, they cannot be removed and can only be read. Unlike main memory (RAM), ROM retains its contents even when the computer is turned off. ROM is referred to as being nonvolatile, whereas RAM is volatile.[39]

Root directory: The top-level directory of a file system. All other directories and files are found under the root directory.[73] *See* **Directory.**

Router: 1. A router connects networks. Based on its current understanding of the state of the network it is connected to, a router acts as a dispatcher as it decides which way to send each information packet. A router is located at any gateway (where one network meets another), including each point-of-presence on the Internet. **2.** A device that combines the functions of a switch, which forwards data by looking at a physical device address, and a router, which forwards packets by locating a next hop address. **3.** A device that provides connectivity between networks (e.g. between your internal network and the Internet). A router forwards data from one network to the other and vice versa. Many routers also have built-in firewall capabilities.[2] *See* **Routing switch.**

Routing switch: Device that combines the functions of a switch, which forwards data by looking at a physical device address, and a router, which forwards packets by locating a next hop address.[2]

RPO (Recovery point objective): The age of files that must be recovered from backup storage for normal operations to resume if a computer, system, or network goes down as a result of a hardware, program, or communications failure. It is an important consideration in disaster recovery planning.[2]

RSA: A public key encryption technology developed by RSA Data Security.[2]

RTF (Rich text format): A text file format used by Microsoft® products, such as Word and Office. The format was developed by Microsoft for use in their products and for cross-platform document interchange. RTF is readable by most word processors. RTF files support text style formatting, as well as images within the text. RTF files can be converted into a different format by changing the formatting selection when saving the word document.[2]

RTLS (Real-time location system): Provides actionable information regarding the location, status, and movement of equipment and people. Advanced RTLS search capabilities allow searching by specific location (floor, area, room) or unique asset identifiers (department owner, type, manufacturer, model number, asset control number, or employee ID number). The detailed asset information and reporting capabilities of RTLS allow further analysis to support a variety of uses including equipment utilization data to identify inefficiencies that have required excess equipment inventory purchases, specific asset searches by manufacturer or model number for retrieval of equipment subject.[10]

RTM (Reference terminology model): A framework of categories or attributes of terms and the relationships among these attributes that provide a structure for the organization of terms to represent concepts. Includes not only the sets of terms to describe relevant concepts, but also specifies the way in which individual concepts may be linked to create compositional expressions.[239]

RTO (Recovery time objective): Time goal for the restoration and recovery of functions or resources based on the acceptable down time and acceptable level of performance in case of a disruption of operations.[87] *See* **MTTD.**

Rule: A formal way of specifying a recommendation, directive, or strategy, expressed as "IF premise THEN conclusion" or "IF condition THEN action."[386]

Run chart: Used to study observed data for trends or patterns over a specified period of time and focus attention on vital changes in the process. The run chart is useful for tracking information and predicting trends or patterns. It can determine if a process has common cause or special cause variation.[148]

RVU (Relative value unit): A comparable service measure used by hospitals to permit comparison of the amount of resource required to perform various services within a single department or between departments. It is determined by assigning weight to such factors as personnel time, level of skill, and sophistication of equipment required to render patient services. RVUs are a common method of physician bonus plans based partially on productivity.[123]

R

S

S/MIME (Secure Multipurpose Internet Mail Extensions): A secure, encrypted method of sending email.[2] *See* **MIME.**

SaaS (Software as a service): Software that is delivered and managed remotely by one or more providers.[142] Also known as on-demand software.

Safeguard: An approved security measure taken to protect computational resources by eliminating or reducing the risk to a system, which may include hardware and software mechanisms, policies, procedures, and physical controls.[1]

SAML (Security assertion markup language): An XML standard for exchanging security information about identity, authentication and authorization data between security domains; that is, between an identity provider and a service provider.[2]

Sample: One or more parts taken, or to be taken from a system, and intended to provide information on that system or a subsystem, or to provide a basis for decision on either.[34]

SAN (Storage area network): A high-speed special-purpose network (or sub-network) that interconnects different kinds of data storage devices with associated data servers on behalf of a larger network of users. Typically, a storage area network is part of the overall network of computing resources for an enterprise.[2]

Sanitization: Process to remove information from media such that recovery is not possible or feasible.[1]

SATA (Serial advanced technology attachment [ATA]): De facto standard for internal PC storage, SATA is the evolutionary replacement for the Parallel ATA storage interface. A serial interface that can operate at speeds up to 6 Gb/s.[240]

SATAN (Security administrator tool for analyzing networks): A tool to help systems administrators. It recognizes several common networking-related security problems, and reports the problems without actually exploiting them.[387]

SBAR (Situation–background–assessment–recommendation): Institute for Healthcare Improvement (IHI) technique that provides a framework for communication between members of the healthcare team about a patient's condition.[388]

Scalability: The ability to support the required quality of service as load increases.[2]

Scanner: An electronic device which can capture images from physical items and convert them into digital formats that can be stored in a computer and viewed or modified with software applications.[52]

Scatter plot: A graphic display of data plotted along two dimensions that uses dots to represent the values obtained for two different variables.[389]

Scenario: Formal description of a class of business activities, including the semantics of business agreements, conventions, and information content.[34]

Scheduler: Software product that allows an enterprise to schedule and track computer batch tasks.[52]

Schema: An abstract representation of an object's characteristics and relationship to other objects. An XML schema represents the interrelationship between the attributes and elements of an XML object (e.g., a document or a portion of a document). To create a schema for a document, one would analyze its structure, defining each structural element as it is encountered (e.g., within a schema for a document describing a website, one would define a website element, a web page element, and other elements that describe possible content divisions within any page on that site). Just as in XML and HTML, elements are defined within a set of tags.[2,61]

Science of clinical informatics: The transformation of clinical data into information, then knowledge, which supports clinical decision-making. This transformation requires an understanding of how clinicians structure decision-making and what data are required to support this process.[50]

SCOS (Smartcard operating system): Organizes data on the integrated circuit chip into files and protects them from unauthorized access.[390]

Screen saver: An animated image that is displayed on the screen when no activity takes place for a specified period of time.[2]

Script: A type of code or program that consists of a set of instructions for another application or utility to use.[52]

SCRIPT standard: A standard published by NCPDP to facilitate the transfer of prescription data between pharmacies, prescribers, intermediaries, facilities and payers. It supports transactions for new prescriptions, prescription changes, refill requests, prescription fill status notifications, cancellations, medication history, long term care transactions and prior authorization exchanges.[214]

SCSI (Small computer system interface): Set of standards for physically connecting and transferring data between computers, storage and peripheral devices. It is not common among consumer hardware devices but still found in some business and enterprise servers.[203]

SCUI (Smartcard user interface): A single common dialog box that lets the user specify or search for a smart card to connect to and use in an application.[30]

SDLC (Systems development lifecycle): Model used in project management to describe the stages and tasks involved in each step of a project to write and deploy software. The process used by a systems analyst to develop an information system, including requirements, validation, training, and user ownership through investigation, analysis, design, implementation, and maintenance.[2]

SDO (Standards development organization): An organization dedicated to standardization in the field of information for health, and health information and communications technology, to achieve compatibility and interoperability between independent systems. Also, to ensure compatibility of data for comparative statistical purposes (e.g., classifications) and to reduce duplication of effort and redundancies.[36]

SDoH (Social determinants of health): Economic and social conditions and their distribution among the population that influence individual and group differences in health status. SDoH are health promoting factors found in one's living and working conditions (such as the distribution of income, wealth, influence, and power), rather than individual risk factors (such as behavioral risk factors or genetics) that influence the risk for a disease, or vulnerability to disease or injury.[10]

SDXC (Secure digital extended capacity): A flash memory card that resembles a secure digital (SD) card with greater storage capacity. SD and SDXC cards make storage portable among devices such as smartphones, eBooks, digital cameras, camcorders, music players, and computers.[2]

Searchable identifiers: Characteristics that uniquely identify an information object, support persistent access to that object, and support access to information about the object (i.e., metadata).[158]

Secondary data use: Use of data for additional purposes than the primary reason for their collection, adding value to this data.[104]

Secret key: Piece of information used to encrypt and decrypt messages.[52]

Secure channel: Protected communication path that is designed to prevent third party interception or corruption of signals flowing through it.[4]

Secure digital extended capacity: *See* **SDXC.**

Secure electronic transmission: *See* **SET.**

Secure file transport protocol: *See* **SFTP.**

Secure MIME: *See* **S/MIME.**

Secure shell: *See* **SSH.**

Secure socket layer: *See* **SSL.**

Secure web server: A program that supports certain security protocols, typically SSL, to prevent eavesdropping on information transferred between a web server and a web browser. A server resistant to a determined attack over the Internet or from corporate insiders.[150]

Security: Measures and controls that ensure confidentiality, integrity, availability, and accountability of the information processed and stored by a computer.[1]

Security administrator: A member of the data system management team trained in data security matters, who manages, monitors, and administers security over one or more computer networks. This person is authorized to enforce the data security measures, and to create a confidentiality/privacy-conscious working environment.[52]

Security and control testing: A testing event that examines the presence and appropriate functioning of the application's security and controls to ensure integrity and confidentiality of data.[50]

Security architecture: A plan and set of principles for an administrative domain and its security domains that describe the security services that a system is required to provide to meet the needs of its users, the system elements required to implement the services, and the performance levels required in the elements to deal with the threat environment.[391]

Security assertion markup language: *See* **SAML**.

Security audit: A systematic evaluation of the security of a company's information system by measuring how well it conforms to a set of established criteria. A thorough audit typically assesses the security of the system's physical configuration and environment, software, information handling processes, and user practices. Security audits are often used to determine regulatory compliance, in the wake of legislation (such as HIPAA, the Sarbanes-Oxley Act, and the California Security Breach Information Act) that specifies how organizations must deal with information.[2] *See* **Audit**.

Security clearance: An authorization that allows access to information that would otherwise be forbidden. Security clearances are commonly used in industry and government. When a security clearance is required for access to specific information, the information is said to be classified. Security clearances can be issued for individuals or for groups.[2]

Security compromise: An event that has resulted in an unauthorized person obtaining classified information.[392] *See* **Breach of security**.

Security incident: The attempted or successful unauthorized access, use, disclosure, modification, or destruction of information or interference with system operations in an information system.[13] *See* **Incident**.

Security process: The series of activities that monitor, evaluate, test, certify, accredit, and maintain the system accreditation throughout the system lifecycle.[1]

Security requirements: Types and levels of protection necessary for equipment, data, information, applications, and facilities to meet security policy.[1]

Security service: A processing or communication service that is provided by a system to give a specific kind of protection to resources, where said resources may reside with said system or reside with other systems (e.g., an authentication service, or a public key infrastructure-based document attribution and authentication service).[391]

Segment: A logical grouping of data fields. Segments of a message may be required or optional. They may occur only once in a message or they may be allowed to repeat. Each segment is identified by a unique character code known as the segment identifier.[9]

Semantic: Pertains to the meaning or interpretation of a word, sign, or other representation.[43]

Semantic correspondence: Measure of similarity between concepts.[76]

Semantic interoperability: The ability of two or more systems to exchange information and to interpret and use that information. Semantic interoperability takes advantage of both the structuring of the data exchange and the codification of the data, including standard, publicly available vocabulary, so that the receiving information management systems can interpret the data. Semantic interoperability supports the electronic exchange of patient data and information among authorized parties via potentially disparate health information and technology systems and products to improve quality, costs, safety, efficiency, experience, and efficacy of healthcare delivery.[53,440] *Definition current as of December 2018. To review any updates to this definition please visit the HIMSS website. See* **Interoperability**.

Semantic link: Formal representation of a directed associative relation or partitive relation between two concepts.[76]

Semantic network: A formalism (often expressed graphically) for representing relational information, the arcs of the network representing the relationships, and the nodes of objects in the network.[34]

Semantic web: A project that intends to create a universal medium for information exchange by giving meaning, in a manner understandable by machines, to the content of documents on the web. The semantic web extends the ability of the web through the use of standards, markup languages, and related processing tools.[393]

Semantics: Refers to the ways that data and commands are presented. A linguistic concept separate from the concept of syntax, which is also often related to attributes of computer programming languages.[52]

Sensitivity label: A security level associated with the content of the information. Society has historically considered as sensitive that information which has a heightened potential for causing harm to the patient or data subject, or to others, such as the subject's spouse, children, friends, or sexual partners.[394]

Sequence: A task in a process is enabled after the completion of a preceding task in the same process.[165]

Serial ATA: *See* **SATA**.

Serial line Internet protocol: *See* **SLIP**.

Serial transmission: Sequential transmission of the signal elements of a group representing a character or other entity of data. The characters are transmitted in a sequence over a single line, rather than simultaneously over two or more lines, as in parallel transmission.[117]

Server: Centralized network computer that provides an array of resources and services to network users. Also, a program that responds to a request from a client.[395]

Service: Discrete units of application logic that expose loosely coupled message based interfaces suitable for being accessed across a network.[396]

Service event: The act of providing a health-related service.[396]

Service-oriented architecture: *See* **SOA**.

Session: A period of interaction. **1.** In computer science, a lasting connection using the session layer of a network protocol or a lasting connection between a user (or user agent) and a peer, typically a server. **2.** In healthcare, a period of treatment; e.g., a "therapy session." **3.** Government: legislative, judicial, or executive session.[123,52,44]

Session layer: Fifth layer of the open systems interconnection (OSI) model. Provides file management needed to support intersystem communication through the use of synchronization and data stream checkpoints. Also responsible for the establishment, management, and termination of sessions.[395]

Session management: The process of securing multiple requests to a service from the same user or entity. A session is often initialized by authenticating a user or entity with factors such as a password. Once the user is authenticated, subsequent requests authenticate the session as opposed to the user themself.[397]

SET (Secure electronic transmission): A cryptographic protocol designed for ensuring the security of financial transactions over the Internet.[2]

Severity system: Expected likelihood of disease progression independent of treatment. Systems attempting to measure severity may use diagnostic codes, such as ICD, and/or additional clinical information.[241]

SFTP (Secure file transfer protocol): Network protocol for accessing, transferring and managing files on remote systems.[2]

SGML (Standard generalized markup language): A metalanguage in which one can define markup languages for documents. SGML should not be confused with the Geography Markup Language (GML) developed by the Open Geographic Information System (Open GIS) Consortium, CFML, or the Game Maker scripting language, GML. SGML provides a variety of markup syntaxes that can be used for many applications.[36]

Shared service: A dedicated unit of people, processes, and technologies that is structured as a centralized point of service and is focused on defined business functions.[142]

Shared space: A mechanism that provides storage of, and access to, data for users with bounded network space. Enterprise-shared space refers to a store of data that are accessible within or across security domains on the global information grid. A shared space provides virtual access to any number of data assets (catalogs, websites, registries, document storage database). Any user, system, or application that posts data uses shared space.[242]

Shareware: Software that can be tried before purchase. It is distributed through online services and user groups.[73]

Shielded twisted pair: *See* **STP**.

Short Message Service: *See* **SMS**.

SIMM (Single in-line memory module): A module containing one or several random access memory (RAM) chips on a small circuit board with pins that connect to the computer motherboard.[2]

S

Simple mail transfer protocol: *See* **SMTP.**

Simple merge: The convergence of two or more branches into a single subsequent branch, such that each enablement of an incoming branch results in the thread of control being passed to the subsequent branch.[165]

Simple network monitoring protocol: *See* **SNMP.**

Simplex: Communication channel/circuit that allows data transmission in one direction only.[39]

Simulation: Resembles a real-life situation that the learner might encounter; learners can engage in safe decision-making.[50]

Simulation exercise: Test performed under conditions as close as practicable to real-world conditions.[398]

Simultaneous peripheral operation online: *See* **SPOOL.**

Single in-line memory module: *See* **SIMM.**

Single sign-on: *See* **SSO.**

Site license: A fee for the usage of purchased, rights-protected work used by multiple users at a single location.[52] *See* **Per seat license.**

Situation–background–assessment–recommendation: *See* **SBAR.**

SLIP (Serial line Internet protocol): A TCP/IP protocol used for communication between two machines that are previously configured for communication with each other.[2]

Slow-scan video: A device that transmits and receives still pictures over a narrow telecommunications channel.[167]

Smart contract: Computer code running on top of a blockchain that contains a set of rules under which participating parties agree to interact with each other. When the pre-defined rules are met, the agreement is automatically enforced. The smart contract facilitates, verifies, and enforces the negotiation or performance of an agreement or transaction. It is the simplest form of decentralized automation.[438]

Smartcard: An integrated circuit card that incorporates a processor unit. The processor may be used for security algorithms, data access, or for other functions according to the nature and purpose of the card.[34]

Smartcard operating system: *See* **SCOS.**

Smartcard user interface: *See* **SCUI.**

Smartphone: A mobile telephone with an integrated computer and other features not originally associated with telephones, such as an operating system, web browsing, and the ability to run software applications.[2]

SMP (Symmetric multiprocessing): A computing platform technology in which a single server uses multiple CPUs in a parallel fashion managed by a single operating system.[399]

SMS (Short message service): Originally part of the Global System for Mobile Communications (GSM) standard developed by the European Telecommunications Standards Institute that enables a mobile device to send, receive, and display messages of up to 160 characters in Roman text and variations for non-Roman character sets. Messages received are stored in the network if the subscriber device is inactive and are relayed when it becomes active. Commonly known as text messaging on mobile devices.[142]

SMTP (Simple mail transfer protocol): Communication protocol used to transfer email between systems and from one computer to another. Email software most commonly uses SMTP for sending mail and Post Office Protocol 3 (POP3) or Internet Message Access Protocol (IMAP) for receiving mail.[203]

SNA (Systems network architecture): Data communication architecture developed by IBM® to specify common conventions for communication among IBM hardware and software products and platforms.[89]

Sniffer: Network tool that intercepts data flowing in a network. If computers are connected to a LAN that is not filtered or switched, the traffic can be broadcast to all computers contained in the same segment.[52]

SNMP (Simple network monitoring protocol): An application-layer protocol used to manage and monitor network devices and their functions. SNMP provides a common language for network devices to relay management information within single- and multivendor environments in a local area network (LAN) or wide area network (WAN).[2]

SNMP (System network management protocol): An application-layer protocol used to manage and monitor network devices and their functions. Provides a common language for network devices to relay management information within single and multivendor environments in a local area network (LAN) or wide area network (WAN).[2]

SNOMED–CT (Systematized nomenclature of medicine–clinical terms): A controlled healthcare terminology developed by the College of American Pathologists in collaboration with the United Kingdom's National Health Service that is used for the purposes of health information exchange. SNOMED–CT includes comprehensive coverage of diseases, clinical findings, therapies, procedures, and outcomes.[77]

SOA (Service-oriented architecture): A software development model for distributed application components that incorporates discovery, access control, data mapping, and security features. Its major functions include creating a broad architectural model that defines the goals of applications and the approaches that will help meet those goals. The second function is to define specific implementation specifications, usually linked to the formal Web Services Description Language (WSDL) and Simple Object Access Protocol (SOAP) specifications.[2]

SOAP (Simple object access protocol): A protocol that allows a program running in one kind of operating system to communicate with a program in the same or different kind of operating system by using HTTP and XML as the mechanisms for information exchange.[2]

Social determinants of health: *See* **SDoH.**

S

Social engineering: An attack vector that relies heavily on human interaction and often involves manipulating people into breaking normal security procedures in order to gain access to systems, networks, or physical locations.[2]

Social network: 1. A chain of individuals and their personal connections. Applications are used to make associations between individuals to further facilitate connections with other people. **2.** A website or platform that allows people with similar interests to come together and share information, photos, and videos.[52,2]

Socket: One endpoint of a two-way communication link between two programs running on the network. It is bound to a port number so the TCP layer can identify the application that data is destined to be sent to.[11]

Soft copy: File maintained on disk in electronic storage format.[2]

Software: A set of instructions or programs instructing a computer to do specific tasks. Software is a generic term used to describe computer programs. Scripts, applications, programs, and a set of instructions are all terms often used to describe software.[52]

Software architecture: The structure or structures of the system, which comprise software components, the externally visible properties of those components, and the relationships among them.[400] *See* **Architecture**.

Software as a service: *See* **SaaS**.

Software asset management: A management process for making software acquisition and disposal decisions. It includes strategies that identify and eliminate unused or infrequently used software, consolidating software licenses, or moving toward new licensing models.[142]

SONET (Synchronous optical network): American National Standard Institute (ANSI) standard for connecting high-speed, high-quality, digital fiber optic transmission systems. The international equivalent of SONET is synchronous digital hierarchy (SDH).[2] *See* **ATM** and **Frame relay**.

SOP (Standard operating procedure): Established or prescribed methods to be followed for the performance of operations or situations.[30]

Source systems: Application systems where service encounter data are collected (e.g., laboratory information systems, pharmaceutical information systems, immunization systems). These clinical data are extracted from the source system and transformed prior to being used in the electronic health record.[57] *See* **Feeder systems**.

SOW (Statement of work): A document describing the scope and other relevant elements associated with the work to be done. It may be incorporated by reference in a contract or other instrument.[113]

Spam: Junk email, unsolicited email, or irrelevant social media or postings to a group, individual, or message board.[73]

SPD (Summary plan description): Document that explains the product and services a subscriber purchased.[46]

Specification: An explicit statement of the required characteristics for an input used in the healthcare system. The requirements are usually related to supplies, equipment, systems, and physical structures used in the delivery of health services.[401]

Spider: *See* **Web crawler.**[7]

SPOOL (Simultaneous peripheral operation online): To read and store a computer document or task list, usually on a hard disk or larger storage medium so that it can be printed or otherwise processed at a more convenient time (for example, when a printer is finished printing its current document).[2]

Spooler: Service that buffers data for low-speed output devices.[2]

Spreadsheet: A software application that enables a user to save, sort, and manage data in an arranged form of rows and columns. A spreadsheet stores data in a tabular format as an electronic document. An electronic spreadsheet is based on and is similar to the paper-based accounting worksheet. A spreadsheet may also be called a worksheet.[52]

SQL (Structured query language): A standard computer language for relational database management and data manipulation. SQL is used to query, insert, update, and modify data. The current standard SQL version is voluntary, vendor-compliant, and monitored by the American National Standards Institute (ANSI).[52]

SRAM (Static random access memory): A type of memory that holds data in static form as long as the memory has power. Unlike dynamic RAM (DRAM), it does not need to be refreshed.[52]

SSH (Secure shell): Network protocol that provides administrators with a secure way to access a remote computer. It also refers to the suite of utilities that implement the protocol.[2]

SSL (Secure socket layer): The standard security technology for establishing an encrypted link between a web server and a browser. This link ensures that all data passed between the web server and browsers remain private and integral. SSL is an industry standard and is used by millions of websites in the protection of their online transactions with their customers.[402] *See* **Socket** and **API.**

SSO (Single sign-on): A session and user authentication service that permits a user to use one set of login credentials (e.g., name and password) to access multiple applications.[2]

Standard: 1. A prescribed set of rules, conditions, or requirements established by consensus and approved by a recognized body that provides, for common and repeated use, rules, guidelines, or characteristics for activities or their results, aimed at the achievement of the optimum degree of order in a given context. **2.** A definition or format that has been approved by a recognized standards organization, or is accepted as a de facto standard by the industry. Standards exist for programming languages, operating systems, data formats, communications protocols, and electrical interfaces.[403,43]

Standard operating procedure: *See* **SOP.**

Standards body: Entity that is recognized at national, regional, or international level that has as a principle function, by virtue of statutes, for the preparation, approval, consensus, and adoption of standards that are made generally available.[34]

Standards development organization: *See* **SDO.**

Standardization: Activity of establishing, with regard to actual or potential problems, provisions for common and repeated use, aimed at the achievement of the optimum degree of order in a given content.[34]

Standardization of terminology: Official recognition of a terminology by an authoritative body.[34]

Standardized generalized markup language: *See* **SGML.**

Standardized taxonomy: Use of common standardized definitions, criteria, terminology, and data elements for treatment processes, outcomes, data collection, and electronic transmission, with the goal of saving much time, effort, and misunderstanding in communicating these elements.[404]

Standing orders: Physicians' orders or protocols that allow patient care to be delivered by members of the care team, like medical assistants, therapists and nurses. Orders are often based on national clinical guidelines but may be customized based on patient population or care environment.[405]

Star schema: The simplest form of a dimensional model in which data are organized into facts and dimensions. It is diagrammed by surrounding each fact with its associated dimensions.[2] *See* **OLTP.**

Start of care: *See* **Admission date.**

Statement of work: *See* **SOW.**

Static audit tool: System scanner that looks for and reports weaknesses.[406]

Static random access memory: *See* **SRAM.**

Stealth virus: A type of resident virus that attempts to evade detection by concealing its presence in infected files. To achieve this, the virus intercepts system calls, which examine the contents and attributes of infected files.[2]

Storage: The function of storing records for future retrieval and use.[244]

Storage area network: *See* **SAN.**

Store-and-forward: Transmission of static images or audio-video clips to a remote data storage device, from which they can be retrieved by a medical practitioner for review and consultation at any time, obviating the need for the simultaneous availability of the consulting parties and reducing transmission costs due to low bandwidth requirements.[167]

Storyboard: A panel or series of panels on which a set of sketches is arranged depicting consecutively the important aspects of scene and action.[29]

STP (Shielded twisted pair): Type of wiring used in some business installations. An out covering or shield is added to the ordinary twisted pair wires, functioning as a ground.[2]

S

Streaming: A technique for delivering data used with audio and video in which the recipient is able to hear or see part of the file before the entire file is delivered. Involves a method for the recipient computer to be able to do a smooth delivery, despite the uneven arrival of data.[66]

Stress testing: A type of performance testing focused on determining an application's robustness, availability, and reliability under extreme conditions. The goal of stress testing is to identify application issues that arise or become apparent only under extreme conditions. These conditions can include heavy loads, high concurrency, or limited computational resources.[68]

Structured data: Coded, semantically interoperable data that are based on a reference information model. The consent directive may be captured as a scanned image, which is not semantically interoperable and would preclude the ability of the consent repository to analyze the data for conflicts with previously persisted consent directives.[20]

Structural interoperability: The structure or format of data exchange (i.e., the message format standards) where there is uniform movement of healthcare data from one system to another such that the clinical or operational purpose and meaning of the data is preserved and unaltered. Structural interoperability defines the syntax of the data exchange. It ensures that data exchanges between information technology systems can be interpreted at the data field level.[53] *Definition current as of December 2018. To review any updates to this definition please visit the HIMSS website. See* **Interoperability**.

Subject field: Domain field of special knowledge.[75]

Subject matter expert: *See* **SME**.

Subject of care identifier: A unique number or code issued for the purpose of identifying a subject of healthcare.[244]

Subset: Represents groups of components that share specified characteristics that affect the way they are displayed or otherwise accessible within a particular realm, specialty, application, or context.[77]

Substitution: A method of cryptography based on the principle of replacing each letter in the message with another one. A cipher that replaces the characters of the original plain text. The characters retain their original position, but are altered.[320]

SVC (Switched virtual circuit): A temporary virtual circuit that is set up and used only as long as data are being transmitted. Once the communication between the two hosts is complete, the SVC disappears. In contrast, a permanent virtual circuit (PVC) remains available at all times.[2]

Symmetric-key cryptography: An encryption system in which the sender and receiver of a message share a single, common key that is used to encrypt and decrypt the message. Symmetric-key systems are simpler and faster, but their main drawback is that both parties must exchange the key in a secure way.[39]

S

System: The combination of hardware and software which processes information for the customer.[34]

System administrator: A person who is responsible for managing a multi-user computing environment, such as a local area network. The responsibilities typically include installing and configuring system hardware and software, establishing and managing user accounts, upgrading software, and backup and recovery tasks.[2] Also known as sysadmin or systems administrator.

System analysis: The process of determining how a set of interconnected components whose individual characteristics are known will behave in response to a given input of a set of inputs. Closely related to requirements analysis and operations research.[84]

System design: A specification of human factors, and hardware and software requirements, for an information system.[50]

System integration: 1. The composition of a capability by assembling elements in a way that allows them to work together to achieve an intended purpose. **2.** The process of creating a complex information system that may include designing or building a customized architecture or application, integrating it with new or existing hardware, packaged and custom software, and communications.[142,245] *See* **EAI**.

Systems integrator: An individual or business that builds computing systems for clients by combining hardware, software, networking, and storage products from multiple vendors.[2]

System network management protocol: *See* **SNMP**.

System security: The result of all safeguards, including hardware, software, personnel policies, information practice policies, disaster preparedness, and oversight of these components.[52]

System of Record: The authoritative data source for a given data element or piece of information.[10]

System testing: A multifaceted testing event that evaluates the functionality, performance, and fit of the whole application. System testing encompasses usability, final requirements, volume and stress, security and controls, recovery, documentation and procedures, and multisite testing.[50]

Systematized nomenclature of medicine–clinical terms: *See* **SNOMED–CT**.

T

Table: Database object with a unique name, and structured in columns and rows.[20]

TCO (Total cost of ownership): A document that describes the cost of a project or initiative that usually includes hardware, software, development, and ongoing expenses.[20]

TCP/IP (Transmission control protocol/Internet protocol): 1. Routable protocol required for Internet access. TCP portion is associated with data. IP is associated with source to destination packet delivery. **2.** A set of communication protocols encompassing media access, packet transport, session communications, file transfer, electronic mail, and terminal emulation. It is supported by a large number of hardware and software vendors and is the basis for Internet transactions.[20]

TDR (Time-domain reflectometer): Identifies and measures errors related to aerial and underground cable and fiber optic wiring through the analysis of pulse reflection polarity. The TDR technique accurately detects errors and bugs in amplitude, frequencies, and other electrical signatures.[52]

Technical specification: International Organization for Standardization (ISO) deliverable that addresses work still under technical development, or where it is believed that there will be a future, but not immediate, possibility of agreement on an International Standard. A Technical Specification is published for immediate use, but it also provides a means to obtain feedback. The aim is that it will eventually be transformed and republished as an International Standard.

TEFCA (Trusted Exchange Framework and Common Agreement): In the 21st Century Cures Act (Cures Act), Congress identified the importance of interoperability and set out a path for the interoperable exchange of Electronic Health Information. Specifically, Congress directed ONC to "develop or support a trusted exchange framework, including a common agreement among health information networks nationally." The framework aims to outline a common set of principles for trusted exchange and the minimum terms and conditions for trusted exchange. This is designed to bridge the gap between providers' and patients' information systems and enable interoperability across disparate health information networks (HINs). A draft framework was released in January 2018.[12]

Telehealth: A broad variety of technologies and tactics to deliver virtual medical, health, and education services. A collection of means to enhance care and education delivery. This term encompasses the concept of "telemedicine," which refers to traditional clinical diagnosis and monitoring delivered by technology. The term "telehealth" covers a wide range of diagnosis, management, education, and other related healthcare fields including but not limited to dentistry, counseling, physical and occupational therapy, home health, chronic disease monitoring and management, and consumer and professional education.[246]

Telemedicine: *See* **Telehealth.**

TELNET (TELecommunications NETwork): A protocol used on the Internet or local area network to provide a bidirectional interactive text-oriented communication facility using a virtual terminal connection.[7]

Terabyte: Approximately one trillion bytes; unit of computer storage capacity.[2]

Terminal: 1. A device that enables you to communicate with a computer. Generally, a combination of keyboard and display screen. Terminals are sometimes divided into three classes based on how much processing power they contain: intelligent terminal: a stand-alone device that contains main memory and a CPU; smart terminal: contains some processing power, but not as much as an intelligent terminal; dumb terminal: has no processing capabilities. It relies entirely on the computer's processor. **2.** In networking, a terminal is a personal computer or workstation connected to a mainframe.[39] *See* **Workstation.**

Terminal server: A hardware device or server that provides terminals (PCs, printers, and other devices) with a common connection point to a local or wide area network.[2]

Terminal window: For local or remote execution of a program, it is a window in a graphical interface that is used to display a command line.[150]

Terminology: A system of words used to name things in a particular discipline.[29]

TFTP (Trivial file transfer protocol): An Internet software utility for transferring files that is simpler to use than the File Transfer Protocol (FTP). TFTP uses the User Datagram Protocol (UDP) rather than the Transmission Control Protocol (TCP).[2]

TGE (Token generation event): *See* **ICO.**

Thesaurus: The vocabulary of a controlled indexing language, formally organized so that the a priori relationships between concepts (e.g., broader and narrower) are made explicit.[407]

Thin client/dumb terminal: A computer or computer program that depends heavily on some other computer (such as an application or network server) to fulfill its traditional computational roles. A thin client is used to access data; does not process data.[150]

Third-party administrator: *See* **TPA.**

Third-party vendor: *See* **TPV.**

Thread: A collection of any number of online posts defined by a title. A thread is a component of an Internet forum.[20]

Threat: 1. Any circumstance or event with the potential to adversely impact organizational operations (including mission, functions, image, or reputation), organizational assets, or individuals through an information system via unauthorized access, destruction, disclosure, modification of information, and/or denial of service. Also, the potential for a threat-source to successfully exploit a particular information system vulnerability.[1]

Threshold: Minimum or maximum value (established for an attribute, characteristic, or parameter) that serves as a benchmark for comparison or guidance and any breach of which may call for a complete review of the situation or the redesign of a system.[4]

TIFF (Tagged image file format): A standard file format that is largely used in the publishing and printing industry. The extensible feature of this format allows storage of multiple bitmap images having different pixel depths, which makes it advantageous for image storage needs.[52]

Tightly coupling: A coupling technique in which hardware and software components are highly dependent on each other. It is used to refer to the state/intent of interconnectivity between two or more computing instances in an integrated system.[52]

Time bomb: A malicious program that is programmed to "detonate" at a specific time and release a virus onto the computer system or network.[39] *See* **Logic bomb**.

Time-domain reflectometer: *See* **TDR**.

Time to live: *See* **TTL**.

TKIP (Temporal key integrity protocol): A wireless network security protocol of the Institute of Electrical and Electronics Engineers (IEEE) 802.11. TKIP encryption is more robust than Wired Equivalent Privacy (WEP), which was the first Wi-Fi security protocol, or WPA2 protocol.[52]

TLS (Transport layer security): A protocol that provides privacy and data integrity between two communicating applications. It is used for Web browsers and other applications that require data to be securely exchanged over a network, such as file transfers, VPN connections, instant messaging, and voice over IP.[2]

TOC: *See* **Transitions of care**.

Token: An object that represents something else, such as another object (either physical or virtual), or an abstract concept. In computer science, there are a number of types of tokens. A programming token is the basic component of source code. Characters are categorized as one of five classes of tokens that describe their functions (constants, identifiers, operators, reserved words, and separators) in accordance with the rules of the programming language. A security token is a physical device, such as a special smart card, that together with something that a user knows, such as a PIN, will enable authorized access to a computer system or network.[2]

Top-level concept: A concept that is directly related to the Root Concept by a single relationship of the Relationship Type.[408]

T

Topology: The arrangement of a network, including its nodes and connecting lines. There are two ways of defining network geometry: the physical topology and the logical (or signal) topology.[2]

Total cost of ownership: *See* **TCO.**

Touch screen: A computer display screen that is also an input device. The screens are sensitive to pressure; a user interacts with the computer by touching pictures or words on the screen.[2]

TPA (Third-party administrator): An organization that administers group insurance policies for an employer. This organization works with the employer as well as the insurer to communicate information between the two, as well as processing claims and determining eligibility.[4]

Traceroute: A network diagnostic tool used to track the pathway taken by a packet on an IP network from source to destination. Traceroute also records the time taken for each hop the packet makes during its route to the destination. Traceroute uses Internet Control Message Protocol (ICMP) echo packets with variable time to live (TTL) values.[52]

Trading partner agreement: 1. An agreement that may include various terms of trade, such as duties, responsibilities, liabilities, including delivery and receipt of goods and services. This is meant to provide additional security for each party to prevent disputes, since the terms of trade have been outlined and agreed upon. **2.** As defined in HIPAA, an agreement related to the exchange of information in electronic transactions, whether the agreement is distinct or part of a larger agreement, between each party to the agreement.[4,55]

Train the trainer: A model used to describe, much as the name would imply, training potential instructors or less experienced instructors, on the best ways to deliver training materials to others.[409]

Transaction: 1. Under HIPAA, the exchange of information between two parties to carry out clinical, financial, and administrative activities related to healthcare. **2.** An exchange of information between actors. For each transaction, the technical framework describes how to use an established standard, such as HL7, DICOM, or W3C.[113,27]

Transaction standard: A standard specifying the format of messages being sent from or received by a system, rather than for how the information is stored in the system.[113]

Transactional data: Information recorded from transactions. A transaction, in this context, is a sequence of information exchange and related work (such as database updating) that is treated as a unit for the purposes of satisfying a request. Transactional data can be financial, logistical, or work-related, involving everything from a purchase order to shipping status to employee hours worked to insurance costs and claims.[2]

Transition plan: A set of techniques to address all aspects of transitioning to a new environment. The key aspects of change that must be addressed are managerial (M), operational (O), social (S), and technical (T).[428]

Transitions of care: The movement of a patient from one setting of care (hospital, ambulatory primary care practice, ambulatory specialty care practice, long-term care, home health, rehabilitation facility) to another.[26]

Transmission: The exchange of data between person and system, or system and system, when the sender and receiver are remote from each other.[410]

Transmission confidentiality: Process to ensure that information in transit is not disclosed to unauthorized individuals, entities, or processes.[410] *See* **Confidentiality.**

Transmission control protocol/Internet protocol: See **TCP/IP.**

Transmission integrity: Process to guard against improper information modification or destruction while in transit.[410] *See* **Integrity.**

Transparent background: An image file that has one color assigned to be "transparent" so that the assigned color will be replaced by the browser's background color, whatever it may be.[2] *See* **GIF.**

Transport layer: Fourth layer of the open system interconnection (OSI) model responsible for end-to-end communication over a network. It provides logical communication between application processes running on different hosts within a layered architecture of protocols and other network components. The transport layer is also responsible for the management of error correction, providing quality, and reliability to the end user. This layer enables the host to send and receive error corrected data, packets or messages over a network, and is the network component that allows multiplexing.[52]

Transport layer security: *See* **TLS.**

Trap doors: Provides an undocumented method of gaining access to an application, operating system, or online service. Programmers write trapdoors into programs for a variety of reasons. Left in place, trapdoors can facilitate a range of activities from benign troubleshooting to illegal access.[411] *See* **Back-door.**

Trial implementation supplement: A specification candidate for addition to an IHE Domain Technical Framework (e.g., a new profile) that is issued for early implementation by any interested party. The authoring technical committee expects developers' feedback.[124]

Trigger event: An event that causes the system to initiate a response.[1]

Trivial file transfer protocol: *See* **TFTP.**

Trojan horse: A computer program that appears to have a useful function, but also has a hidden and potentially malicious function that evades security mechanisms, sometimes by exploiting legitimate authorizations of a system entity that invokes the program.[1] *See* **Malware.**

Trunk: A communications line or link designed to carry multiple signals simultaneously to provide network access between two points. Trunks typically connect switching centers in a communications system.[2]

T

Trust anchor: Acts as an intermediary between users and certificate authorities, reviewing and approving certificate requests.[9]

Trusted Exchange Framework and Common Agreement: *See* **TEFCA.**

Tunneling: *See* **Virtual private network.**[57]

Tutorial: A program that provides step-by-step information in presenting a concept or learning unit.[4]

Twisted pair cable: A type of cable made by putting two separate insulated wires together in a twisted pattern and running them parallel to each other. This type of cable is widely used in different kinds of data and voice infrastructures.[52]

U

UART (Universal asynchronous receiver transmitter): The microchip with programming that controls a computer's interface to its attached serial devices.[2]

Ubiquitous computing: The growing trend toward embedding microprocessors in everyday objects so they can communicate information. The words pervasive and ubiquitous mean "existing everywhere." Ubiquitous computing devices are completely connected and constantly available. *See* **Pervasive computing.**[2]

UDDI (Universal description, discover, and integration): A web-based distributed directory that enables businesses to list themselves on the Internet and discover each other, similar to a traditional phone book's yellow and white pages.[39]

UDI (Unique device identifier): A unique numeric or alphanumeric code that consists of two parts: a device identifier (DI), a mandatory, fixed portion of a UDI that identifies the labeler and the specific version or model of a device, and a production identifier (PI), a conditional, variable portion of a UDI that identifies one or more of the following when included on the label of a device: the lot or batch number within which a device was manufactured; the serial number of a specific device; the expiration date of a specific device; the date a specific device was manufactured; the distinct identification code required by §1271.290(c) for a human cell, tissue, or cellular and tissue-based product (HCT/P) regulated as a device.[41]

UDP (User datagram protocol): Part of the Internet Protocol suite used by programs running on different computers on a network. UDP is used to send short messages called datagrams but overall, it is an unreliable, connectionless protocol. An OSI transport layer protocol. This protocol contrasts with TCP.[52]

UI (User interface): Term to describe everything designed into an information device with which a person may interact. This can include display screens, keyboards, a mouse, and the appearance of a desktop. It is also the way through which a user interacts with an application or a website.[2]

UID (Unique Identifier): A numeric or alphanumeric string that is associated with a single entity within a given system, making it possible to access and interact with that entity.[2]

UM (Utilization management): The evaluation of the necessity, appropriateness, and efficiency of the use of healthcare services, procedures, and facilities.[412]

UMDNS (Universal medical device nomenclature system): The purpose of UMDNS is to facilitate identifying, processing, filing, storing, retrieving, transferring, and communicating data about medical devices. The nomenclature is used in applications ranging from hospital inventory and work order controls to national agency medical device regulatory systems, and from eCommerce and procurement to medical device databases.[248]

UML (Unified modeling language): A language for specifying, visualizing, constructing, and documenting the artifacts of software systems. UML is a standard notation for the modeling of real-world objects.[293]

UMLS (Unified medical language system): The National Library of Medicine (NLM) produces the Unified Medical Language System® (UMLS®) to facilitate the development of computer systems that behave as if they "understand" the meaning of the language of biomedicine and health. As part of the UMLS, NLM produces and distributes the UMLS Knowledge Sources (databases) and associated software tools (programs) for use by system developers in building or enhancing electronic information systems that create, process, retrieve, integrate, and/or aggregate biomedical and health data and information, as well as in informatics research.[269]

UMS (Unified messaging system): The handling of voice, fax, and regular text messages as objects in a single mailbox that a user can access either with a regular e-mail client or by telephone.[2]

UNC (Universal naming convention): Text-based method to identify the path to a remote device, server, directory, or file. Implemented as: \\computername \sharename\directoryname\filename.[2]

Underuse: Refers to the failure to provide a healthcare service when it would have produced a favorable outcome for a patient. Standard examples include failures to provide appropriate preventive services to eligible patients (e.g., Pap smears, flu shots for elderly patients, screening for hypertension) and proven medications for chronic illnesses (e.g., steroid inhalers for asthmatics, aspirin, beta-blockers, and lipid-lowering agents for patients who have suffered a recent myocardial infarction).[413]

Unicode: A standard character set that represents most of the characters used in the world using a 16-bit encoding. Unicode can be encoded in using UTF-8 (USC Transformation Format) to more efficiently store the most common ASCII characters.[414]

Unified messaging system: *See* **UMS.**
Unified modeling language: *See* **UML.**
Uniform data standards: Methods, protocols, or terminologies agreed to by an industry to allow disparate information systems to operate successfully with one another.[43]
Uniform resource locator: *See* **URL.**
Uninterruptible power supply: *See* **UPS.**
Unique device identifier: *See* **UDI.**
Unique health plan identifier: *See* **HPID.**
Unique identifier: *See* **UID.**

Unique patient identifier: *See* **UPI.**

Unit testing: A software development process in which the smallest testable parts of an application, called units, are individually and independently scrutinized for proper operation. Unit testing is often automated but it can also be done manually.[2]

Universal asynchronous receiver transmitter: *See* **UART.**

Universal identifier: *See* **UPI.**

Universal medical device nomenclature system: *See* **UMDNS.**

Universal naming convention: *See* **UNC.**

Universal product number: *See* **UPN.**

Universal serial bus: *See* **USB.**

Unstructured data: Represents any data that do not have a recognizable structure. These data are unorganized and raw and can be non-textual or textual. Unstructured data also may be identified as loosely structured data, wherein the data sources include a structure, but not all data in a data set follow the same structure.[52]

UPI (Unique patient identifier): 1. The identity of an individual consists of a set of personal characters by which that individual can be recognized. Identification is the proof of one's identity. Identifier verifies the sameness of one's identity. Patient identifier is the value assigned to an individual to facilitate positive identification of that individual for healthcare purposes. Unique patient identifier is the value permanently assigned to an individual for identification purposes and is unique across the entire national healthcare system. Unique patient identifier is not shared with any other individual. **2.** A form of identification and access control that identifies humans by their characteristics or traits. Biometric identifiers (or biometric authentication) are the distinctive, measurable characteristics used to label and describe individuals. Two categories of biometric identifiers include physiological and behavioral characteristics.[7]

UPS (Uninterruptible power supply): Device that keeps a computer running by protecting against power outages, power surges, and power sags by maintaining constant power via battery. Provides the opportunity for a graceful shutdown in a commercial power-out condition.[2]

URI (Uniform resource identifier): A sequence of characters that identifies a logical or physical resource. URL is an example of a type of URI.[2]

URL (Uniform resource locator): The method to locate a resource on the web. It contains the name of the protocol to be used to access the resource and the resource name.[2]

Usability: The effectiveness, efficiency, and satisfaction with which specified users achieve specified goals in particular environments. Effectiveness refers to the accuracy and completeness with which specified users can achieve specified goals in particular environments.[90]

U

Usability testing: Evaluating a product or service by testing it with representative users. Typically, during a test, participants will try to complete typical tasks while observers watch, listen, and takes notes. The goal is to identify any usability problems, collect qualitative and quantitative data, and determine the participant's satisfaction with the product.[251]

USB (Universal serial bus): A plug-and-play interface between a computer and peripheral devices, such as media players, keyboards, digital cameras, printers, etc. It can also support electrical power. It enables the operating system to spontaneously configure and discover a new peripheral device without having to restart the computer.[2,52]

USCDI (U.S. Core Data for Interoperability): Outlined by the Office of the National Coordinator for Health Information Technology (ONC), as part of the effort to establish the Trusted Exchange Framework and Common Agreement (TEFCA), USCDI is a common set of data classes that are required for interoperable exchange. USCDI lists data classes and associated standards, and outlines a process to review and update these data classes with additional data classes for future versions of the document. This document incorporates and expands on the Common Clinical Data Set (CCDS). *See* **TEFCA, CCDS**.[12]

U.S. Core Data for Interoperability: *See* **USCDI**.

Use: With respect to individually identifiable health information, the sharing, employment, application, utilization, examination, or analysis of information within the entity that maintains such information.[261]

Use case: A methodology used in system analysis to identify, clarify, and organize system requirements. The use case is made up of a set of possible sequences of interactions between systems and users in a particular environment and related to a particular goal. It consists of a group of elements (for example, classes and interfaces) that can be used together in a way that will have an effect larger than the sum of the separate elements combined. The use case should contain all system activities that have significance to the users. A use case can be thought of as a collection of possible scenarios related to a particular goal, indeed, the use case and goal are sometimes considered to be synonymous.[2]

User authentication: *See* **Authentication**.

User datagram protocol: *See* **UDP**.

User-friendly: Refers to anything that makes it easier for individuals to use a computer.[39]

User interface: *See* **UI**.

User experience: A person's perceptions and responses that result from the use and/or anticipated use of a product, system, or service. User experience includes all the users' emotions, beliefs, preferences, perceptions, physical and psychological responses, behaviors, and accomplishments that occur before, during, and after use. User experience is a consequence of: brand image, presentation, functionality, system performance, interactive behavior, and assistive capabilities of the interactive system, the user's internal and physical state resulting from prior experiences, attitudes, skills, and personality, and the context of use. Usability, when interpreted from the perspective of the users' personal goals, can include the kind of perceptual and emotional aspects typically associated with user experience. Usability criteria can be used to assess aspects of user experience.[90]

User permissions: The authorization given to users that enables them to access specific resources on the network, such as data files, applications, printers, and scanners. Permissions also designate the type of access, such as read only or read/write privileges.[150]

User profile: 1. Information about an individual user. **2.** The preferences and current desktop configuration of a user's machine.[150]

USHIK (United States Health Information Knowledgebase): A metadata registry of healthcare-related data elements from Standard Development Organizations supported by the Agency for Healthcare Research and Quality (AHRQ).[252]

Utilization management: *See* **UM.**

UTP (Unshielded twisted pair): A popular type of cable that consists of two unshielded wires twisted around each other. Due to its low cost, UTP cabling is used extensively for local area networks (LANs) and telephone connections. UTP cabling does not offer as high bandwidth or as good protection from interference as coaxial or fiber optic cables, but it is less expensive and easier to work with.[39]

U

V

Validation: Process of demonstrating that a system under consideration meets the specifications of that system. Confirmation that requirements for a specific intended use or application have been fulfilled.[1]

Value-added network: *See* **VAN**.

Value-based payment: *See* **VBC**.

Value stream: The specific activities within a supply chain required to design, order, and provide a specific product or service.[142]

Value stream mapping: *See* **VSM**.

VAN (Value-added network): A network that provides services in addition to a standard telephone system, such as fax, data transmission, or e-mail.[107]

Vanilla: In information technology, an adjective meaning plain or basic. The original, uncustomized version of a product is sometimes referred to as the vanilla version.[2]

Variance analysis: Process aimed at computing differences between actual and budgeted or targeted levels of performance, and identification of their causes.[4]

VAX (Virtual address extension): An established line of mid-range server computers from the Digital Equipment Corporation (DEC, now a part of Hewlett-Packard).[2]

VBC (Value-based care): A healthcare delivery model in which providers, including hospitals and physicians, are paid based on patient health outcomes. Under value-based care agreements, providers are rewarded for helping patients improve their health, reduce the effects and incidence of chronic disease, and live healthier lives in an evidence-based way. Value-based care differs from a fee-for-service approach, in which providers are paid based on the amount of healthcare services they deliver. The "value" in value-based healthcare is derived from measuring health outcomes against the cost of delivering those outcomes.[415]

VBID (Value-based insurance design): Promotes patients' use of high-value care options by changing the cost-sharing consumers must pay for different care options. Under a VBID approach, treatments that provide high clinical value have reduced or no cost-sharing (out of pocket costs like copays), to make sure they are affordable for patients. In some situations, health plans may have higher cost-sharing for services that offer little or no added clinical benefit, compared to their added cost.[416]

VBP (Value-based payment): *See* **VM**.

VDT (View, download, transmit): Activity previously listed as part of the CMS Meaningful Use Stage 2 core measures. View refers to the patient (or authorized representative) accessing their health information online. Download refs to ambulatory or inpatient summaries (as applicable to the EHR technology setting for which certification is requested) in human-readable format or formatted according to the standard adopted with minimum information requirements. Transmit refers to third party access to the downloaded ambulatory and inpatient summaries.[26]

Vendor: A company/consortium that provides products and/or services.[135]

Verification confirmation: Process used to determine whether the product or functionality fulfills the intended use and user requirements.[194]

Veterans Health Information Systems Technology Architecture: *See* **VistA.**

Video RAM or video random access memory: *See* **VRAM.**

Virtual address extension: *See* **VAX.**

Virtual appliance: A virtual machine image file consisting of a preconfigured operating system environment and a single application.[2]

Virtual community: A community of people sharing common interests, ideas, and feelings over the Internet of collaborative networks.[2]

Virtual CPU: A physical central processing unit that is assigned to a virtual machine. Also known as a virtual processor.[2]

Virtual hospital: 1. A format for providing healthcare in a central location that relies on the components of telemedicine and high-tech communications devices to connect it to a regional hospital, where a greater range of expertise is available. **2.** Model in which caregivers are able to provide care to patients, regardless of where the patient is located.[123,417]

Virtual machine: *See* **VM.**

Virtual machine monitor: *See* **Hypervisor.**

Virtual private network: *See* **VPN.**

Virtual reality: The computer-generated simulation of a three-dimensional image or environment that can be interacted with in a seemingly real or physical way by a person using special electronic equipment, such as a helmet with a screen inside or gloves fitted with sensors.[107]

Virtual reality modeling language: *See* **VRML.**

Virtual SAN appliance: *See* **VSA.**

Virtual server farm: A networking environment that employs multiple application and infrastructure servers running on two or more physical servers using a server virtualization program such as VMware or Microsoft Virtual Server®.[2]

Virtual to virtual (V2V): A term that refers to the migration of an operating system (OS), application programs, and data from a virtual machine or disk partition to another virtual machine or disk partition. The target can be a single system or multiple systems. To streamline the operation, part or all of the migration can be carried out automatically by means of specialized programs known as migration tools.[2]

Virtualization: The creation of a virtual (rather than actual) version of something, such as an operating system, a server, a storage device, or network

V

resources. Virtualization can be viewed as part of an overall trend in enterprise IT that includes autonomic computing, a scenario in which the IT environment will be able to manage itself based on perceived activity, and utility computing, in which computer processing power is seen as a utility that clients can pay for only as needed. The usual goal of virtualization is to centralize administrative tasks while improving scalability and workloads.[2]

Virtualization software: Virtualization software acts as a layer between a computer's primary OS and the virtual OS. It allows the virtual system to access the computer's hardware, such as the RAM, CPU, and video card, just like the primary OS. This is different than emulation, which actually translates each command into a form that the system's processor can understand. Since Apple and Windows® computers now both use the "x86" processor architecture, it is possible to run both OSes on the same machine via virtualization, rather than emulation.[73]

Virus: Software used to infect a computer. After the virus code is written, it is buried within an existing program. Once that program is executed, the virus code is activated and attaches copies of itself to other programs in the computer and other computers in the network. Infected programs continue to propagate the virus, which is how it spreads. A virus cannot run by itself; it requires that its host program be run to make the virus active.[150,1]

Vishing (voice or VoIP phishing): An electronic fraud tactic in which individuals are tricked into revealing critical financial or personal information to unauthorized entities. Vishing works like phishing but does not always occur over the Internet and is carried out using voice technology. A vishing attack can be conducted by voice email, VoIP (voice over IP), or landline or cellular telephone.[2] *See* **Social engineering**.

VISN (Veterans Integrated Service Network): VA's Veterans Health Administration is divided into 21 areas called VISNs. VISNs are regional systems of care working together to better meet local healthcare needs and provides greater access to care.[418,419]

VistA (Veterans Health Information Systems Technology Architecture): A Health Information Technology (HIT) system created and used by the Veterans Health Administration (VHA) of the U.S. Department of Veterans Affairs (VA) in serving America's veterans through the provision of exceptional-quality healthcare that enhances our veterans' health and well-being.[255]

VM (Value Modifier): Before the enactment of the Quality Payment Program, the Value Modifier previously measured the quality and cost of care provided to people with Medicare under the Medicare Physician Fee Schedule (PFS). The Value Modifier is an adjustment made on a per claim basis to Medicare payments for items and services under the Medicare PFS. It's applied at the Taxpayer Identification Number (TIN) level to doctors billing under the TIN. It determines the amount of Medicare payments to physicians based on their performance on specified quality and cost measures. The program rewards quality performance and lower costs.[26]

VM (Virtual machine): 1. The name given to various programming language interpreters. **2.** One instance of an operating system along with one or more applications running in an isolated partition within the computer. It enables different operating systems to run in the same computer at the same time. Virtual machines (VMs) are also widely used to run multiple instances of the same operating system, each running the same set or a different set of applications. Each virtual machine functions as if it owned the entire computer. The operating systems in each VM partition are called "guest operating systems," and they communicate with the hardware via the hypervisor control program. *See* **Hypervisor**.[150]

VMR (Virtual Medical Record): A data model for representing the data that are analyzed and/or produced by clinical decision support (CDS) engines. The term VMR has historically been used in the CDS community to refer to a simplified representation of the clinical record that is suitable and safe for a CDS knowledge engineer to directly manipulate in order to derive patient-specific assessments and recommendations. Historically, the challenge has been that different organizations used different VMRs. The purpose of the VMR effort is to define a standard VMR that can be used across CDS implementations. Moreover, due to the intended use of the VMR, a primary goal is simple and intuitive representation of data that is easy and safe for a typical CDS knowledge engineer to understand, use, and implement.[9]

Voice ID (voice authentication): A type of user authentication that uses voice print biometrics. It relies on the fact that vocal characteristics, like fingerprints and the patterns of people's irises, are unique for each individual.[2]

Voice over Internet protocol: *See* **VoIP**.

Voice recognition: Computer analysis of the human voice, especially for the purposes of interpreting words and phrases or identifying an individual voice.[107]

Voice response system: *See* **VRS**.

Voice response unit: *See* **VRU**.

VoIP (Voice over Internet protocol): 1. A technology that allows telephone calls using an Internet connection instead of a regular (or analog) phone line. Some services using VoIP may only allow you to call other people using the same service, but others may allow you to call anyone who has a telephone number—including local, long distance, mobile, and international numbers. **2.** Refers to the use of the Internet protocol (IP) to transfer voice communications in much the same way that web pages and e-mail are transferred. Each piece of voice data is digitized into chunks and then sent across the Internet (in the case of public VoIP) to a destination server where the chunks are reassembled. This process happens in real time so that two or more people can carry on a conversation.[257,258]

Volume testing: Also known as load testing, evaluates system performance with predefined load levels. Load testing measures how long it takes a system to perform various program tasks and functions under normal or predetermined conditions.[259]

VPN (Virtual private network): A network that is constructed using public wires—usually the Internet—to connect remote users or regional offices to a company's private, internal network. A VPN secures the private network, using encryption and other security mechanisms to ensure that only authorized users can access the network and that the data cannot be intercepted. This type of network is designed to provide a secure, encrypted tunnel in which to transmit the data between the remote user and the company network.[39]

VRAM (Video RAM or video random access memory): Refers to any type of random access memory used to store image data for computer display. VRAM is a type of buffer between a computer processor and the display.[2]

VRML (Virtual reality modeling language): An open-standard programming language created to design three-dimensional (3-D) and web-based models, textures, and illusions. VRML is used to illustrate 3-D objects, buildings, landscapes, or other items requiring 3-D structure and is very similar to Hypertext Markup Language (HTML). VRML also uses textual representation to define 3-D illusion presentation methods.[52]

VRS (Voice response system): Specialized technologies designed for providing callers with verbal and faxed answers to inquiries without assistance from a person. They provide account information, fulfill requests for mailable items, prescreen callers for script customization, interact with host systems (read and write), and produce reports.[142]

VRU (Voice response unit): An automated telephone answering system consisting of hardware and software that allows the caller to navigate through a series of prerecorded messages and use a menu of options through the buttons on a touch-tone telephone or through voice recognition.[142]

VSA (Virtual SAN appliance): Also called a virtual storage appliance (VSA), is a software bundle that allows a storage manager to turn the unused storage capacity in his or her network's virtual servers into a storage area network (SAN). The SAN provides a pool of shared storage that can be accessed by the virtual servers as needed.[2]

VSM (Value stream mapping): A lean manufacturing or lean enterprise technique used to document, analyze, and improve the flow of information or materials required to produce a product or service.[148]

Vulnerability: A cybersecurity term that refers to a flaw in a system that can leave it open to attack. A vulnerability may also refer to any type of weakness in a computer system itself, in a set of procedures, or in anything that leaves information security exposed to a threat.[52]

Vulnerability assessment: 1. Systematic examination of an information system or product to determine the adequacy of security measures, identify security deficiencies, provide data from which to predict the effectiveness of proposed security measures, and confirm the adequacy of such measures after implementation. **2.** The process of identifying and quantifying vulnerabilities and prioritizing (or ranking) the vulnerabilities in a system.[1,87]

V

W

WAN (Wide area network): A computer network that spans a relatively large geographical area and consists of two or more local area networks. Often connected through public networks, such as phone systems, but can also be connected through lease lines or satellites.[39] *See* **LAN**, **MAN**, and **WLAN**.

WAP (Wireless application protocol): A secure specification that allows users to access information instantly via handheld wireless devices such as mobile phones, pagers, two-way radios, smartphones, and communicators.[39]

WASP (Wireless application service provider): Provides the same service of a regular application service provider but to wireless clients. WASPs are typically used in enterprises to connect a mobile workforce to company data, including e-mail, Internet access, CRM, ERP, and company financials.[39]

WAV or WAVE (Waveform audio format [.wav]): An audio file format standard for storing an audio bitstream.[39]

Waveform audio format (.wav): *See* **WAV** or **WAVE**.

Wavelet: A mathematical function useful in digital signal processing and image compression. Wavelet compression works by analyzing an image and converting it into a set of mathematical expressions that can then be decoded by the receiver.[2]

WCF (Windows Communication Foundation): A technology for developing applications based on service-oriented architecture (SOA). WCF is implemented using a set of classes placed on top of the .NET Common Language Runtime (CLR). It addresses the problem of interoperability using .NET for distributed applications.[52]

Wearable technology: Technology, worn in clothing or accessories, which records and reports information about behaviors such as physical activity or sleep patterns. This technology aims to educate and motivate individuals toward better habits and better health. Also known as Wearables.[260]

Web Analytics: The process of analyzing the behavior of visitors to a website. The use of web analytics is said to enable a business to attract more visitors, retain or attract new customers for goods or services, or to increase the dollar volume each customer spends.[2]

Web crawler: An Internet bot that helps in web indexing. They "crawl" one page at a time through a website until all pages have been indexed. Web crawlers help in collecting information about a website and the links related to them, and also help in validating the HTML code and hyperlinks. A web crawler is also known as a web spider, automatic indexer, or simply crawler.[52]

Web portal: 1. A website or service that offers a broad array of resources and services, such as e-mail, forums, search engines, and online shopping malls. The first web portals were online services, such as AOL, which provided access to the web. **2.** An enterprise portal is a web-based interface for users of enterprise applications. Enterprise portals also provide access to enterprise information such as corporate databases, applications (including web applications), and systems. **3.** Web portals come in two types—internal and external. Internal portals are designed to provide services within an organization, while external portals serve as a starting point for browsing the web.[39,73]

Webmaster: An individual who manages and ensures that a website effectively and efficiently meets its deliverables.[39]

Web server: 1. A program that uses HTTP (Hypertext Transfer Protocol) to serve the files that form web pages to users, in response to their requests, which are forwarded by their computers' HTTP clients. Dedicated computers and appliances may be referred to as web servers as well. The process is an example of the client/server model. All computers that host websites must have web server programs.[2] See **HTTP** and **HTTPS**.

Web services: A standardized way of integrating Web-based applications using the XML, SOAP, WSDL, and UDDI open standards over an Internet protocol backbone.[39] Services that are made available from a business's web server for web users or other web-connected programs. Web services range from such major services as storage management and customer relationship management (CRM) down to more limited services.[2]

Web services description language: See **WSDL**.

Web stack: The collection of software required for web development. At a minimum, a web stack contains an operating system (OS), a programming language, database software, and a web server.[2]

WEP (Wired equivalent privacy): A security protocol for wireless local area networks (WLANs) defined in the 802.11b standard. WEP is designed to provide the same level of security as that of a wired LAN. LANs are inherently more secure than WLANs because LANs are somewhat protected by the physicalities of their structure, having some or all part of the network inside a building that can be protected from unauthorized access. This has been replaced by WPA.[39]

Wet signature: Created when a person physically marks a document. Ink on paper signature.[262]

WHOIS: A query and response protocol that is widely used for querying databases that store the registered users or assignees of an Internet resource, such as a domain name, an IP address block, or an autonomous system, but is also used for a wider range of other information.[7]

WI (Web interface): 1. The interaction between a user and software running on a web server. The user interface is the web browser and the web page it

W

downloaded and rendered. *See* **Web server. 2.** A programming connection to the web. *See* **Web services and API**.[150]

Wide area information server: *See* **WAIS**.

Wide area network: *See* **WAN**.

Wide SCSI (Wide small computer system interface): 20–40 Mbps high-speed interface for connecting devices to the computer bus.[52]

Wide small computer system interface: *See* **Wide SCSI**.

Wi-Fi: A wireless networking technology that uses radio waves to provide high-speed network and Internet connections. The Wi-Fi Alliance, the organization that owns the Wi-Fi (registered trademark) term specifically defines Wi-Fi as "wireless local area network (WLAN) products that are based on the Institute of Electrical and Electronics Engineers' (IEEE) 802.11 standards." Initially, Wi-Fi was used in place of only the 2.4GHz 802.11b standard, but the Wi-Fi Alliance has expanded the generic use of the Wi-Fi term to include any type of network or WLAN product based on any of the 802.11 standards, including 802.11b, 802.11a, dual-band, and others, in an attempt to stop confusion about wireless LAN interoperability.[39]

Wi-Fi protected access: *See* **WPA**.

Wiki: Piece of server software that allows users to freely create and edit web page content using any web browser.[29]

Wildcard: A character (usually * or ?) that can stand for one or more unknown characters during a search, and cause the search results to yield all files within a general description or type of software.[2]

Window: A separate viewing area on a computer display screen in a system that allows multiple viewing areas as part of a graphical user interface (GUI).[2]

Windows Communication Foundation: *See* **WCF**.

Wiper: Malware whose goal is to completely destroy or erase all data from the targeted computer or network.[420]

Wired equivalent privacy: *See* **WEP**.

Wireless application protocol: *See* **WAP**.

Wireless application service provider: *See* **WASP**.

Wireless local area network: *See* **WLAN**.

Wireless technology: An encompassing term that describes numerous communication technologies that rely on a wireless signal to send data rather than using a physical medium (often a wire). In wireless transmission, the medium used is the air, through electromagnetic, radio, and microwave signals. The term communication here not only means communication between people but between devices and other technologies as well.[52]

WLAN (Wireless local area network): Also referred to as LAWN. A type of local area network that uses high-frequency radio waves rather than wires to communicate between nodes. *See* **Wi-Fi**.[39]

Workflow: Progression of steps (tasks, events, interactions) that comprise a work process, involve two or more persons, and create or add value to the organization's activities. In a sequential workflow, each step is dependent on occurrence of the previous step; in a parallel workflow, two or more steps can occur concurrently.[4]

Workflow management: 1. An approach that allows for the definition and control of business processes that span applications. **2.** Automated events or processes—a workflow approach that enables automated tasks (e.g., the automation of steps in a marketing campaign or a sales process) to be performed.[142]

Workstation: 1. A computer (and often the surrounding area) that has been configured to perform a certain set of tasks, such as processing orders, recording notes, audio recording, or video production. **2.** Workstations generally come with a large, high-resolution graphics screen, large amounts of RAM, accesses shared network resources, and runs local applications. Most workstations also have a mass storage device such as a disk drive, but a special type of workstation, called a diskless workstation, comes without a disk drive. The most common operating systems for workstations are UNIX and Windows® NT.[52,39]

Workstation on wheels: *See* **WOW**. *See also* **COW**.

World Wide Web: *See* **WWW**.

WORM (Write once, read many times): 1. An optical disk technology that allows you to write data onto a disk just once. After that, the data are permanent and can be read any number of times. **2.** A program or algorithm that replicates itself over a computer network and usually performs malicious actions, such as using up the computer's resources and possibly shutting the system down.[39] *See* **Virus**.

WOW (Workstation on wheels): Mobile computer stations that can easily be transported between patients and around the hospital. Also known as mobile workstations.[421]

WPA (Wi-Fi protected access): A security scheme for wireless networks, developed by the networking industry in response to the shortcomings of Wired Equivalent Privacy (WEP). WPA uses Temporal Key Integrity Protocol (TKIP) encryption and provides built-in authentication, giving security comparable to VPN tunneling with WEP, with the benefit of easier administration and use. The current version of these protocols is WPA3.[8,150]

Write back: A storage method in which data are written into the cache every time a change occurs, but is written into the corresponding location in main memory only at specified intervals or under certain conditions.[2]

Write once, read many times: *See* **WORM**.

WSDL (Web services description language): An XML-formatted language used to describe a web service's capabilities as collections of communication end points capable of exchanging messages. WSDL is an integral part of

W

UDDI, an XML-based worldwide business registry. WSDL is the language that UDDI uses. WSDL was developed jointly by Microsoft and IBM.[39]

WWW (World Wide Web): The web, or World Wide Web, is basically a system of Internet servers that support specially formatted documents. The documents are formatted in a markup language called HTML (HyperText Markup Language) that supports links to other documents, as well as graphics, audio, and video files.[39]

WYSIWYG (What you see is what you get): Some early systems yielded a screen image that was unlike a printed document or file. This term is used to confirm that the system presents a screen image that matches what prints on paper. Pronounced "wizzy-wig."[2]

WYSIWYP (What you see is what you print): Pronounced wizzy-whip, refers to the ability of a computer system to print colors exactly as they appear on a monitor. WYSIWYP printing requires a special program, called a color management system (CMS), to calibrate the monitor and printer.[39] Interactive whiteboard display in which multiple computer users in different geographical locations can write or draw while others watch. They are often used in teleconferencing.[2]

X

X.25: 1. Standard protocol for packet-switched wide area network (WAN) communication developed by the International Telecommunication Union-Telecommunication (ITU-T) Standard Sector. **2.** Interface between Data Terminal Equipment (DTE) and Data Circuit-terminating Equipment (DCE) for terminals operating in the packet mode and connected to public data networks by dedicated circuit.[263]

X12 standard (ASC X12): Chartered by the American National Standards Institute (ANSI), ASC X12 develops and maintains EDI (Electronic Data Interchange) and CICA (Context Inspired Component Architecture) standards along with XML schemas which drive business processes globally. The ASC X12 organization develops and maintains EDI standards that facilitate electronic interchange relating to business transactions such as order placement and processing, shipping and receiving information, invoicing, payment and cash application data, and data to and from entities involved in finance, insurance, transportation, supply chains, and state and federal governments. Committee members jointly develop and promote EDI standards that streamline business transactions, using a common, uniform business language.[264] *See* **EDI**.

XDS (Cross-enterprise document sharing): Focused on providing a standards-based specification for managing the sharing of documents that healthcare enterprises (anywhere from a private physician, to a clinic, to health information exchange (HIE), to an acute care inpatient facility) have decided to explicitly share. This contributes to the foundation of a shared electronic health record.[27] *See* **Profile**. NOTE: XDS is an Integrating the Healthcare Enterprise (IHE) Profile.

XML (Extensible markup language): 1. General-purpose markup language for creating special-purpose markup languages. It is a simplified subset of standard generalized markup language, capable of describing many different kinds of data. Its primary purpose is to facilitate the sharing of data across different systems, particularly systems connected via the Internet. **2.** Describes a class of data objects, called XML documents, and partially describes the behavior of computer programs that process them. XML is an application profile or restricted form of SGML, the Standard Generalized Markup Language (ISO 8879). By construction, XML documents are conforming SGML documents.[7] Extensible Markup Language, a specification developed by the W3C. XML is a pared-down version of SGML (Standard Generalized Markup Language) (ISO 8879), designed especially for web documents. It allows designers to create their own customized tags, enabling the definition, transmission, validation, and interpretation of data between applications and between organizations.[39]

XSL (Extensible Stylesheet Language): A standard developed by the World Wide Web Consortium defining a language for transforming and formatting XML (eXtensible Markup Language) documents. An XSL stylesheet is written in XML and consists of instructions for tree transformation and formatting. The tree transformations describe how each XML tag relates to other data and the formatting instructions describe how to output the various types of data.[2]

Z

Zero day attack: Exploitation by a malicious actor of a vulnerability that is unknown to the manufacturer.[48]

Zero latency enterprise: *See* **ZLE**.

Zigbee: A specification for a suite of high-level communication protocols using small, low-power digital radios based on an IEEE 802 standard for personal-area networks.[265]

Zip or zipping: A popular data compression format. Files that have been compressed with the ZIP format are called ZIP files and usually end with a .ZIP extension.[39]

ZLE (Zero latency enterprise): The immediate exchange of information across geographical, technical, and organizational boundaries so that all departments, customers, and related parties can work together in real time.[142]

Zombie process: A process in its terminated state. Usually occurring in a program with parent-child functions, the process occurs after a child function has finished execution and it sends an exit status to its parent function. Until the parent function receives and acknowledges the message, the child function is in zombie state, meaning it has executed but not exited.[39]

Appendix A: Healthcare and Information Technology Organizations

Academy of Nutrition and Dietetics
> Organization representing food and nutrition professionals with over 75,000 members. The Academy is committed to improving the nation's health and advancing the profession of dietetics through research, education, and advocacy.
> *120 South Riverside Plaza, Suite 2000*
> *Chicago, IL 60606-6995*
> *Tel: 800-877-1600*
> *www.eatrightpro.org*

AAAAI (American Academy of Allergy, Asthma & Immunology)
> Physician membership organization focused on advancing the knowledge and practice of allergies, asthma, and immunology.
> *555 East Wells Street*
> *Suite 1100*
> *Milwaukee, WI 53202-3823*
> *Tel: 414-272-6071*
> *www.aaaai.org*

AAACN (American Association of Ambulatory Care Nursing)
> The association of professional nurses and associates who identify ambulatory care practice as essential to the continuum of high-quality, cost-effective healthcare.
> *East Holly Avenue*
> *Box 56*
> *Pitman, NJ 08071-0056*
> *Tel: 800-262-6877*
> *www.aaacn.org*

AACN (American Association of Colleges of Nursing)
The national voice for America's baccalaureate and higher-degree nursing education programs.
655 K Street, NW
Suite 750
Washington, DC 20001
Tel: 202-463-6930
www.aacn.nche.edu

AACN (American Association of Critical-Care Nurses)
Acute and critical care nurses rely on AACN for expert knowledge and the influence to fulfill their promise to patients and their families.
101 Columbia
Aliso Viejo, CA 92656-4109
Toll free: 800-899-2226
www.aacn.org

AAD (American Academy of Dermatology)
Physician membership organization for dermatologists inside or outside the United States.
P.O. Box 1968
Des Plaines, IL 60017
Toll free: 866-462-DERM (3376)
International: 847-240-1280
www.aad.org

AADE (American Association of Diabetic Educators)
A professional association dedicated to promoting the expertise of the diabetes educator.
200 W. Madison Street
Suite 800
Chicago, IL 60606
Toll free: 800-338-3633
www.diabeteseducator.org

AAFP (American Academy of Family Physicians)
Membership organization for physicians and physicians in training engaged in family medicine, the teaching of family medicine, or medical administration inside or outside the United States.
P.O. Box 11210
Shawnee Mission, KS 66207-1210
Tel: 913-906-6000
Toll free: 800-274-2237
www.aafp.org

AAHAM (American Association of Healthcare Administrative Management)
National membership association that represents a broad-based constituency of healthcare professionals.
11240 Waples Mill Road
Suite 200
Fairfax, VA 22030
Tel: 703-281-4043
www.aaham.org

AAHC (Association of Academic Health Centers)
Nonprofit organization to improve the healthcare system by mobilizing and enhancing the strengths and resources of the academic health centers.
1400 Sixteenth Street, NW
Suite 720
Washington, DC 20036
Tel: 202-265-9600
www.aahcdc.org

AAHN (American Association for the History of Nursing)
Membership network to advance historical scholarship in nursing and healthcare.
P.O. Box 7
Mullica Hill, NJ
Tel: 609-519-9689
www.aahn.org

AAHomecare (American Association for Homecare)
Membership association of companies in the homecare community.
241 18th Street, South
Suite 500
Arlington, VA 22202
Tel: 202-372-0107
Toll free: 866-289-0492
www.aahomecare.org

AAIHDS (American Association of Integrated Healthcare Delivery Systems)
A nonprofit dedicated to the educational advancement of provider-based managed care professionals involved in integrated healthcare delivery.
4435 Waterfront Drive
Suite 101
Glen Allen, VA 23060
Tel: 804-747-5823
www.aaihds.org

AALNA (American Assisted Living Nurses Association)
Nationwide network of assisted living nurses.
P.O. Box 10469
Napa, CA 94581
Tel: 707-622-5628
www.alnursing.org

AALNC (American Association Legal Nurse Consultants)
A not-for-profit membership organization dedicated to the professional
enhancement and growth of registered nurses practicing in the specialty area
of legal nurse consulting and to advancing this nursing specialty.
330 N. Wabash Avenue
Suite 2000
Chicago, IL 60611
Tel: 877-402-2562
www.aalnc.org

AAMA (American Association of Medical Assistants)
Membership organization for medical assistants.
20 N. Wacker Drive
Suite 1575
Chicago, IL 60606
Tel: 312-899-1500
www.aama-ntl.org

AAMC (Association of American Medical Colleges)
Membership association of medical schools accredited by the Liaison Committee
on Medical Education (LCME), not-for-profit teaching hospitals and academic
society 501(c)3 organizations with primary missions that include advancing
medical education and/or biomedical research in the United States and Canada.
655 K Street NW
Suite 100
Washington, DC 20001-2399
Tel: 202-828-0400
www.aamc.org

AAMCN (American Association of Managed Care Nurses)
Membership community of nurses working in managed care throughout the
country.
4435 Waterfront Drive
Suite 101
Glen Allen, VA 23060
Tel: 804-707-9698
www.aamcn.org

AAMEDA (American Academy of Medical Administrators)
Membership association of multispecialty healthcare administrators in federal and public and private sectors.
www.aameda.org

AAMI (Association for Advancement of Medical Instrumentation)
A unique alliance of over 6000 members united by the common goal of increasing the understanding and beneficial use of medical instrumentation.
4301 N. Fairfax Drive
Suite 301
Arlington, VA 22203-1633
Tel: 703-525-4890
www.aami.org

AAN (American Academy of Neurology)
Membership academy for physicians, medical students, and nonphysician neurology professionals.
201 Chicago Avenue South
Minneapolis, MN 55415
Tel: 612-928-6000
Toll free: 800-879-1960
www.aan.com

AAN (American Academy of Nursing)
Membership academy for nurse fellows. The American Academy of Nursing serves the public and the nursing profession by advancing health policy and practice through the generation, synthesis, and dissemination of nursing knowledge.
1000 Vermont Avenue, NW
Suite 910
Washington, DC 20005
Tel: 202-777-1170
www.aannet.org

AANA (American Association of Nurse Anesthetists)
Membership association of national and international nurse anesthetists.
222 S. Prospect Avenue
Park Ridge, IL 60068
Tel: 847-692-7050
www.aana.com

AANN (American Association of Neuroscience Nurses)
Membership organization of nurses passionate about neuroscience.
8735 W. Higgins Road
Suite 300
Chicago, IL 60631
Tel: 847-375-4733
Toll free: 888-557-2266 (US only)
www.aann.org

AANP (American Academy of Nurse Practitioners)
Membership-focused organization for nurse practitioners and others interested in fostering the objectives of the NP profession.
P.O. Box 12846
Austin, TX 78711
Tel: 512-442-4262
www.aanp.org

AAOHN (American Association of Occupational Health Nurses)
Membership association of nurses engaged in occupational and environmental health nursing.
330 N. Wabash Avenue
Suite 2000
Chicago, IL 60611
Tel: 312-321-5173
www.aaohn.org

AAOS (American Academy of Orthopedic Surgeons/American Association of Orthopedic Surgeons)
Physician membership organization for physicians in the exclusive practice of orthopedic surgery in the United States and physicians enrolled in approved orthopedic residency programs inside and outside the United States.
9400 W. Higgins Road
Rosemont, IL 60018
Tel: 847-823-7186
www.aaos.org

AAP (American Academy of Pediatrics)
Physician membership organization for pediatricians, pediatric medical subspecialists, pediatric surgical specialists, and physicians in approved pediatric residency programs inside or outside the United States.
345 Park Boulevard
Itasca, IL 60143
Toll free: 800-433-9016
www.aap.org

AAPA (American Academy of Physician Assistants)
Membership organization for ARC-PA or NCCPA-certified physician assistants, PA affiliates, physicians, and related businesses.
2318 Mill Road
Suite 1300
Alexandria, VA 22314
Tel: 703-836-2272
www.aapa.org

AAPL (American Association for Physician Leadership)
U.S. organization for physician leaders. Members of the association include chief executive officers, chief medical officers, vice presidents of medical affairs, medical directors, and other physician leaders inside or outside the United States.
400 North Ashley Drive
Suite 400
Tampa, FL 33602
Toll free: 800-562-8088
www.physicianleaders.org/

AAPAN (American Association of Payers, Administrators and Networks)
National association providing a unified, integrated voice for payers, third-party administrators, networks and care management in the group/government health, and workers' compensation markets.
3774 LaVista Road
Suite 101
Tucker, GA 30084
Tel: 502-403-1122
www.aapan.org/

AAPM&R (American Academy of Physical Medicine and Rehabilitation)
Physician membership organization for Diplomats of the American Board of Physical Medicine and Rehabilitation and physicians in an approved PM&R residency program inside or outside the United States.
9700 W. Bryn Mawr Avenue
Suite 200
Rosemont, IL 60018
Tel: 847-737-6000
www.aapmr.org

AARC (American Association for Respiratory Care)
Membership association for credentialed respiratory care professionals, individuals with a position related to respiratory care, and students in a respiratory care program.
9425 N. MacArthur Boulevard
Suite 100
Irving, TX 75063-4706
Tel: 972-243-2272
www.aarc.org

ABA (American Board of Anesthesiology)
Physician certification organization to qualify and examine anesthesiology candidates who have successfully completed an accredited program of anesthesiology training in the United States.
4208 Six Forks Road
Suite 1500
Raleigh, NC 27609-5765
Tel: 866-999-7501
www.theABA.org

ABAI (American Board of Allergy and Immunology)
Physician certification organization to qualify and examine allergists/immunologists who have successfully completed an accredited educational program.
1835 Market Street
Suite 1210
Philadelphia, PA 19103
Tel: 215-592-9466
Toll free: 866-264-5568
www.abai.org

ABCGN (American Board of Certification for Gastroenterology Nurses)
A volunteer nonprofit organization to maintain and improve the knowledge, understanding, and skill of nurses in the fields of gastroenterology and gastroenterology endoscopy by developing and administering a certification program.
330 N. Wabash Avenue
Suite 2000
Chicago, IL 60611
Tel: 855-25-ABCGN and 855-252-2246
www.abcgn.org

ABCRS (American Board of Colon and Rectal Surgery)
   Physician certification organization to qualify and examine colon and rectal surgery candidates who have successfully completed an accredited educational program.
   20600 Eureka Road
   Suite 600
   Taylor, MI 48180
   Tel: 734-282-9400
   www.abcrs.org

ABD (American Board of Dermatology)
   Physician certification organization to qualify and examine dermatologist and dermatology subspecialist candidates who have successfully completed an accredited educational program.
   2 Wells Avenue
   Newton, MA 02459
   Tel: 617-910-6400
   www.abderm.org

ABEM (American Board of Emergency Medicine)
   Physician certification organization to qualify and examine emergency medicine and seven subspecialty candidates who successfully meet certification requirements.
   3000 Coolidge Road
   East Lansing, MI 48823-6319
   Tel: 517-332-4800
   www.abem.org

ABFM (American Board of Family Medicine)
   Physician certification organization to qualify and examine family medicine and subspecialty candidates who have successfully completed an accredited program and meet certification requirements.
   1648 McGrathiana Parkway
   Suite 550
   Lexington, KY 40511-1247
   Tel: 859-269-5626
   Toll free: 888-995-5700
   www.theabfm.org

ABIM (American Board of Internal Medicine)
A nonprofit independent evaluation organization for physicians in internal medicine and its 19 subspecialties.
510 Walnut Street
Suite 1700
Philadelphia, PA 19106-3699
Toll free: 800-441-2246
www.abim.org

ABMGG (American Board of Medical Genetics and Genomics)
Physician/PhD certification organization to qualify and examine medical genetic and subspecialty candidates who successfully meet certification requirements.
9650 Rockville Pike
Bethesda, MD 20814-3998
Tel: 301-634-7315
www.abmgg.org

ABNM (American Board of Nuclear Medicine)
The primary certifying organization for nuclear medicine physicians in the United States.
4555 Forest Park Boulevard
Suite 119
St. Louis, MO 63108-2173
Tel: 314-367-2225
www.abnm.org

ABNS (American Board of Neurological Surgery)
Physician certification organization to qualify and examine neurological surgery candidates who have successfully completed an accredited educational program.
245 Amity Road
Suite 208
Woodbridge, CT 06525
Tel: 203-397-2267
www.abns.org

ABOG (American Board of Obstetrics and Gynecology)
Independent, nonprofit organization that certifies obstetricians and gynecologists in the United States.
2915 Vine Street
Dallas, TX 75204
Tel: 214-871-1619
www.abog.org

ABOHN (American Board for Occupational Health Nurses)
Nursing certification organization to qualify and examine occupational health and subspecialty candidates who successfully meet certification requirements.
201 East Ogden Avenue
Suite 114
Hinsdale, IL 60521-3652
Tel: 630-789-5799
Toll free: 888-842-2646
www.abohn.org

ABOP (American Board of Ophthalmology)
Physician certification organization to qualify and examine ophthalmologist candidates who have successfully completed an accredited educational program and meet certification requirements.
111 Presidential Boulevard
Suite 241
Bala Cynwyd, PA 19004-1075
Tel: 610-664-1175
www.abop.org

ABOS (American Board of Orthopaedic Surgery)
Physician certification organization to qualify and examine orthopedic surgery candidates who have successfully completed an accredited educational program and meet certification requirements.
400 Silver Cedar Court
Chapel Hill, NC 27514
Tel: 919-929-7103
www.abos.org

ABOHNS (American Board of Otolaryngology – Head and Neck Surgery)
Physician certification organization to qualify and examine otolaryngology candidates who have successfully completed an accredited educational program and meet certification requirements.
5615 Kirby Drive
Suite 600
Houston, TX 77005
Tel: 713-850-0399
www.aboto.org

ABP (American Board of Pathology)

Physician certification organization to qualify and examine anatomic pathology, clinical pathology, and subspecialties candidates who have successfully completed an accredited educational program and meet certification requirements.

4830 W Kennedy Boulevard
Suite 690
Tampa, FL 33609
Tel: 813-286-2444
www.abpath.org

ABP (American Board of Pediatrics)

Physician certification organization to qualify and examine pediatric and pediatric subspecialty candidates who have successfully completed an accredited educational program and meet certification requirements.

111 Silver Cedar Court
Chapel Hill, NC 27514
Tel: 919-929-0461
www.abp.org

ABPM (American Board of Preventive Medicine)

Physician certification organization to qualify and examine physicians in aerospace medicine, occupational medicine, public health, and general preventive medicine to candidates who have successfully completed an accredited program and meet certification requirements.

111 West Jackson Boulevard
Suite 1340
Chicago, IL
Tel: 312-939-2276
www.theabpm.org

ABPMR (American Board of Physical Medicine and Rehabilitation)

Physician certification organization to qualify and examine physical medicine and rehabilitation candidates who have successfully completed an accredited educational program and meet certification requirements.

3015 Allegro Park Lane SW
Rochester, MN 55902-4139
Tel: 507-282-1776
www.abpmr.org

ABPN (American Board of Psychiatry and Neurology)
Physician certification organization to qualify and examine psychiatry and neurology candidates who have successfully completed an accredited program and meet certification requirements.
7 Parkway North
Deerfield, IL 60015
Tel: 847-229-6500
www.abpn.com

ABPS (American Board of Plastic Surgery)
Physician certification organization to qualify and examine plastic surgery specialists and subspecialty candidates who have successfully completed an accredited program and meet certification requirements.
Seven Penn Center
1635 Market Street
Suite 400
Philadelphia, PA 19103-2204
Tel: 215-587-9322
www.abplasticsurgery.org

ABR (American Board of Radiology)
Physician certification organization to qualify and examine diagnostic radiology, radiation oncology, and medical physics candidates who have successfully completed an accredited program and meet certification requirements.
5441 E. Williams Circle
Tucson, AZ 85711-7412
Tel: 520-790-2900
www.theabr.org

ABS (American Board of Surgery)
An independent, nonprofit organization certifying surgeons who have met a defined standard of education, training, and knowledge.
1617 John F. Kennedy Boulevard
Suite 860
Philadelphia, PA 19103
Tel: 215-568-4000
www.absurgery.org

ABTS (American Board of Thoracic Surgery)
Physician certification organization to qualify and examine thoracic candidates who have successfully met certification requirements.
633 North St. Clair Street
Suite 2150
Chicago, IL 60611
Tel: 312-202-5900
www.abts.org

ABU (American Board of Urology)
Physician certification organization to examine urology candidates who meet certification requirements.
600 Peter Jefferson Parkway
Suite 150
Charlottesville, VA 22911
Tel: 434-979-0059
www.abu.org

ABUCM (American Board for Urgent Care Medicine)
An independent certifying body for urgent care medicine.
2813 S. Hiawassee Road
Suite 206
Orlando, FL 32835
Tel: 407-521-5789
www.abucm.org

ACAAI (American College of Allergy, Asthma & Immunology)
Membership organization for allergists/immunologists, and allied health professionals inside or outside the United States who meet eligibility requirements.
85 West Algonquin Road
Suite 550
Arlington Heights, IL 60005
Tel: 847-427-1200
www.acaai.org

AcademyHealth
National organization serving the fields of health services and policy research and the professionals who produce and use this important work.
1666 K Street NW
Suite 1100
Washington, DC 20006
Tel: 202-292-6700
www.academyhealth.org

ACAP (Alliance of Claims Assistance Professionals)
A national, nonprofit organization dedicated to the growth and development of the claims assistance industry.
1127 High Ridge Road, #216
Stamford, CT 06905
or
9600 Escarpment, Suite 745-65
Austin, TX 78749
Toll free: 888-394-5163
www.claims.org

ACC (American College of Cardiology)
Membership organization for physicians, nurses, nurse practitioners, physician assistants, pharmacists, and practice managers inside and outside the United States.
Heart House
2400 N Street, NW
Washington, DC 20037
Tel: 202-375-6000, ext. 5603
Toll free: 800-253-4636, ext. 5603
www.acc.org

ACCE (American College of Clinical Engineering)
Membership organization for engineers in a clinical environment.
5200 Butler Pike
Plymouth Meeting, PA 19462
Tel: 610-825-6067
www.accenet.org

ACCP (American College of Chest Physicians)
Physician education and board review organization for chest physicians and subspecialty candidates.
2595 Patriot Boulevard
Glenview, IL 60026
Tel: 224-521-9800
Toll free: 800-343-2227
www.chestnet.org

ACEP (American College of Emergency Physicians)
Physician membership organization for emergency physician specialists.
4950 W. Royal Lane
Irving, TX 75038
Mailing:
P.O. Box 619911
Dallas, TX 75261-9911
Tel: 972-550-0911
Toll free: 800-798-1822
www.acep.org

ACGME (Accreditation Council for Graduate Medical Education)
A private professional organization responsible for the accreditation of residency education programs.
401 North Michigan Avenue
Suite 2000
Chicago, IL 60611
Tel: 312-755-5000
www.acgme.org

ACHA (American College of Healthcare Architects)
Professional education and board review organization for architects in the field of healthcare architecture.
4400 College Boulevard
Suite 220
Overland Park, KS 66211
Tel: 913-222-8653
www.healtharchitects.org

ACHCA (American College of Health Care Administrators)
Membership organization for administrators, those with substantial interest in health/residential care administration, allied health professionals, and individual providers of healthcare products/services.
1101 Connecticut Avenue NW
Suite 450
Washington, DC 20036
Toll free: 800-561-3148
www.achca.org

ACHE (American College of Healthcare Executives)
Membership organization for healthcare executives who lead hospitals, healthcare systems, and other healthcare organizations.
300 S. Riverside Plaza
Suite 1900
Chicago, IL 60606
Tel: 312-424-2800
www.ache.org

ACHP (Alliance of Community Health Plans)
National membership advocacy organization for health plans and provider groups.
1825 Eye Street, NW
Suite 401
Washington, DC 20006
Tel: 202-785-2247
www.achp.org

ACL (Administration for Community Living)
Department of Health and Human Services administration that funds services and supports provided by community-based organizations to help older adults and people with disabilities of all ages be able to live where they chose.
330 C St SW
Washington, DC 20201
Tel: 202-401-4634
www.acl.gov

ACM (Association for Computing Machinery)
Professional organization of computing professionals. The special interest group (SIGHIT) emphasizes the computing and information science-related aspects of health informatics.
2 Penn Plaza
Suite 701
New York, NY 10121-0701
Tel: 212-869-7440
Toll free: 800-342-6626
www.acm.org

ACMA (American Case Management Association)
Certification organization to qualify and examine hospital/health system case management professionals who successfully meet certification requirements.
11701 W. 36th Street
Little Rock, AR 72211
Tel: 501-907-ACMA (2262)
www.acmaweb.org

ACNM (American College of Nurse-Midwives)
Membership organization for certified nurse-midwives and certified midwives who meet eligibility requirements in the United States.
8403 Colesville Road
Suite 1550
Silver Spring, MD 20910
Tel: 240-485-1800
www.midwife.org

ACOG (American Congress of Obstetricians and Gynecologists)
Physician certification organization for obstetrics and/or gynecology candidates.
P.O. Box 70620
Washington, DC 20024-9998
409 12th Street, SW
Washington, DC 20024-2188
Tel: 202-638-5577
Toll free: 800-673-8444
www.acog.org

ACP (American College of Physicians)
Physician membership organization for internists, internal medicine subspecialists, medical students, residents, and fellows and physicians in an approved pediatric residency program inside or outside the United States.
190 North Independence Mall West
Philadelphia, PA 19106-1572
Tel: 215-351-2600
Toll free: 800-523-1546
www.acponline.org

ACPeds (American College of Pediatricians)
National organization of pediatricians and other healthcare professionals dedicated to the health and well-being of children.
P.O. Box 357190
Gainesville, FL 32635
Tel: 352-376-1877
www.acpeds.org

ACR (American College of Radiology)
Physician membership organization for radiologists, radiation specialists, and physicians in an approved residency program who meet eligibility requirements.
1891 Preston White Drive
Reston, VA 20191
Tel: 703-648-8900
www.acr.org

ACS (American College of Surgeons)
Physician membership organization for surgeons, subspecialists, physicians in approved residency programs, and members of the surgical team inside or outside the United States who meet eligibility requirements.
633 North St. Clair Street
Chicago, IL 60611
Tel: 312-202-5000
Toll free: 800-621-4111
www.facs.org

ACT | The App Association
Advocacy organization for small and mid-size application developers and information technology firms.
1401 K Street NW
Suite 501
Washington, DC 20005
Tel: 202-331-2130
www.actonline.org

ACU (Association of Clinicians for the Underserved)
Transdisciplinary organization of clinicians, advocates, and healthcare organizations that provide healthcare for the underserved.
1420 Spring Hill Road
Suite 600
Tysons Corner, VA 22102
Tel: 844-422-8247
www.clinicians.org

ADA (American Dental Association)
Membership organization for dentists, students, or charitable practitioners inside or outside the United States.
211 E. Chicago Avenue
Chicago, IL 60611-2678
Tel: 312-440-2500
www.ada.org

ADA (American Diabetes Association)
General membership organization designed for people with diabetes, their families, friends, and caregivers.
2451 Crystal Drive
Suite 900
Arlington, VA 22202
Toll free: 800-342-2383
www.diabetes.org

AdvaMed (Advanced Medical Technology Association)
Membership organization open to medical technology firms worldwide.
701 Pennsylvania Ave, NW
Suite 800
Washington, DC 20004-2654
Tel: 202-783-8700
www.advamed.org

AEHIA (Association for Executives in Healthcare Information Applications)
An association within CHIME launched to provide an education and networking platform to healthcare's senior IT applications leaders.
710 Avis Drive
Suite 200
Ann Arbor, MI 48108
Tel: 734-665-0000
http://aehia.org/

AEHIS (Association for Executives in Healthcare Information Security)
An association within CHIME launched to provide an education and networking platform to healthcare's senior IT security leaders.
710 Avis Drive
Suite 200
Ann Arbor, MI 48108
Tel: 734-665-0000
http://aehis.org/

AEHIT (Association for Executives in Healthcare Information Technology)
An association within CHIME launched to provide an education and networking platform to healthcare's senior IT technology leaders.
710 Avis Drive
Suite 200
Ann Arbor, MI 48108
Tel: 734-665-0000
http://aehit.org/

AfPP (Association for Perioperative Practice)
Membership organization for all who work in or around the perioperative environment.
Daisy Ayris House
42 Freemans Way
Harrogate, North Yorkshire, HG3 1DH
Tel: 01423 881300
www.afpp.org.uk

AHA (American Heart Association)
  Volunteer organization dedicated to building healthier lives free of cardiovascular (heart) diseases and stroke.
  7272 Greenville Avenue
  Dallas, TX 75231
  Toll free: 800-AHA-USA-1 (8721)
  www.heart.org

AHA (American Hospital Association)
  Membership organization for hospitals, healthcare systems, pre-acute/post-acute patient care facilities, and hospital-affiliated educational programs (e.g., hospital school of nursing, program in health administration).
  155 N. Wacker Drive
  Chicago, IL 60606
  Tel: 312-422-3000
  800 10th Street, N.W.
  Two City Center, Suite 400
  Washington, DC 20001-4956
  Tel: 202-638-1100
  Toll free: 800-424-4301
  www.aha.org

AHCA (American Health Care Association)
  Nonprofit federation of affiliate state health organizations, together representing more than 11,000 nonprofit and for-profit nursing facility, assisted living, developmentally disabled, and subacute care providers that care for approximately one million elderly and disabled individuals each day.
  1201 L Street NW
  Washington, DC 20005
  Tel: 202-842-4444
  www.ahcancal.org

AHCJ (Association of Health Care Journalists)
  An independent, nonprofit organization dedicated to advancing public understanding of healthcare issues. Its mission is to improve the quality, accuracy, and visibility of healthcare reporting, writing, and editing.
  Missouri School of Journalism
  10 Neff Hall
  Columbia, MO 65211
  Tel: 573-884-5606
  www.healthjournalism.org

AHDI (Association for Healthcare Documentation Integrity)
Membership organization for individuals enrolled in a medical transcription program, individual professionals working or involved in healthcare documentation and data capture, healthcare delivery facilities, companies or manufacturers that employ healthcare documentation specialists or provide services or products to the profession, and educational facilities that train medical transcriptionists.
4120 Dale Road
Suite J8-233
Modesto, CA 95356
Tel: 209-527-9620
Toll free: 800-982-2182
www.ahdionline.org

AHIMA (American Health Information Management Association)
Membership organization for health information management (HIM) professionals interested in promoting the business and clinical uses of electronic and paper-based medical information.
233 N. Michigan Avenue
21st Floor
Chicago, IL 60601-5809
Tel: 312-233-1100
Toll free: 800-335-5535
www.ahima.org

AHIP (America's Health Insurance Plans)
National trade association for the health insurance industry.
601 Pennsylvania Avenue, NW
South Building
Suite 500
Washington, DC 20004
Tel: 202-778-3200
www.ahip.org

AHLA (American Health Lawyers Association)
Nonpartisan, 501(c)(3) educational organization devoted to legal issues in the healthcare field.
1620 Eye Street NW
6th Floor
Washington, DC 20006-4010
Tel: 202-833-1100
www.healthlawyers.org

AHNA (American Holistic Nurses Association)
Membership organization open to everyone (nurses, other healthcare professionals, and the public) interested in all aspects of holistic caring and healing.
2900 SW Plass Court
Topeka, KS 66611-1980
Tel: 785-234-1712
Toll free: 800-278-2462
www.ahna.org

AHQA (American Health Quality Association)
Membership organization of State Health Care Quality Associations.
7918 Jones Branch Drive
Suite 300
McLean, VA 22102
Tel: 202-331-5790
www.ahqa.org

AHRMM (Association for Healthcare Resource & Materials Management)
Membership organization within the American Hospital Association, representing supply chain provider and suppliers for professionals, students, and retirees.
155 N. Wacker Drive
Suite 400
Chicago, IL 60606
Tel: 312-422-3840
www.ahrmm.org

AHRQ (Agency for Healthcare Research and Quality)
Federal agency within the Department of Health and Human Services focused on the national mission to improve the quality, safety, efficiency, and effectiveness of healthcare for Americans.
5600 Fishers Lane
7th Floor
Rockville, MD 20857
Tel: 301-427-1364
www.ahrq.gov

AIM (Association for Automatic Identification and Mobility)
An international trade association representing automatic identification and mobility technology solution providers.
20399 Route 19
Suite 203
Cranberry Township, PA 16066
Tel: 724-742-4470
www.aimglobal.org

ALA (American Lung Association)
Volunteer organization to prevent lung disease and promote lung health.
55 W. Wacker Drive
Suite 1150
Chicago, IL 60601
Toll free: 1-800-LUNGUSA (1-800-548-8252)
www.lung.org

Alliance HPSR (Alliance for Health Policy and Systems Research)
International partnership hosted by the World Health Organization to promote health policy and systems research in developing countries.
20 Avenue Appia
1211 Geneva
Switzerland
Tel: +41 22 791 2973
Fax: +41 22 791 4817
www.who.int/alliance-hpsr

AMA (American Medical Association)
Association of physicians and physicians in training committed to ethics in medicine.
330 N. Wabash Avenue
Suite 39300
Chicago, IL 60611-5885
Tel: 800-621-8335
www.ama-assn.org

AMCP (Academy of Managed Care Pharmacy)
National professional association of pharmacists and other healthcare practitioners organizations.
675 North Washington Street
Suite 220
Alexandria, VA 22314
Tel: 703-684-2600
www.amcp.org

AMDA (American Medical Directors Association—The Society for Post-Acute and Long-Term Care Medicine)
Professional association of medical directors and physicians practicing in the long-term care continuum.
10500 Little Patuxent Parkway
Suite 210
Columbia, MD 21044
Tel: 410-740-9743
Toll free: 800-876-2632
www.paltc.org

AMDIS (Association of Medical Directors of Information Systems)
Membership organization for medical directors of information systems.
682 Peninsula Drive
Lake Almanor, CA 96137
Tel: 719-548-9360
www.amdis.org

America's Physician Groups (formerly CAPG)
Organization representing physician organizations practicing capitated, coordinated care. Members provide comprehensive healthcare through coordinated and accountable physician group practices.
915 Wilshire Boulevard
Suite 1620
Los Angeles, CA 90017
www.apg.org

AMGA (American Medical Group Association)
Physician membership organization for group practices, independent practice associations, academic/faculty practices, integrated delivery systems, and other organized systems of care including groups with three or more licensed physicians organized to deliver healthcare services.
One Prince Street
Alexandria, VA 22314-3318
Tel: 703-838-0033
www.amga.org

AMIA (American Medical Informatics Association)
Membership organization open to individuals interested in biomedical and health informatics. AMIA focuses on transforming healthcare through trusted science, education, and the practice of informatics.
4720 Montgomery Lane
Suite 500
Bethesda, MD 20814
Tel: 301-657-1291
www.amia.org

AMP (Applied Measurement Professionals, Inc.)
Certification organization for psychometric consultation, testing, and measurement services.
18000 W. 105th Street
Olathe, KS 66061
Tel: 913-895-4600
www.goamp.com

AMSA (American Medical Student Association)
Student-governed, national organization committed to representing the concerns of physicians in training. AMSA members are medical students, premedical students, interns, residents, and practicing physicians.
45610 Woodland Road
Sterling, VA 20166
Tel: 703-620-6600
www.amsa.org

AMSN (Academy of Medical-Surgical Nurses)
Membership organization for nurses and licensed healthcare professionals interested in the care of adults.
200 East Holly Avenue
Sewell, NJ 08080
Toll free: 866-877-2676
www.amsn.org

ANA (American Nurses Association)
Professional membership organization representing the interests of registered nurses through its constituent and state nurses associations and organizational affiliates.
8515 Georgia Avenue
Suite 400
Silver Spring, MD 20910-3492
Toll free: 800-284-2378
www.nursingworld.org

ANCC (American Nurses Credentialing Center)
Nursing certification organization to qualify and examine nurse candidates who have successfully completed an accredited program and meet certification requirements.
8515 Georgia Avenue
Suite 400
Silver Spring, MD 20910-3492
Toll free: 800-284-2378
www.nursingworld.org/ancc

ANI (Alliance for Nursing Informatics)
Membership organization of nursing informatics associations and groups.
33 West Monroe Street
Suite 1700
Chicago, IL 60603-5616
www.allianceni.org

ANIA (American Nursing Informatics Association)
Membership organization to advance the field of nursing informatics.
200 East Holly Avenue
Sewell, NJ 08080
Toll free: 866-552-6404
www.ania.org

ANNA (American Nephrology Nurses Association)
Membership organization for nurses, allied health professionals, and others inside and outside the United States involved in the care of nephrology patients.
East Holly Avenue
Box 56
Pitman, NJ 08071
Tel: 856-256-2320
Toll free: 888-600-2662
www.annanurse.org

ANSI (American National Standards Institute)
National voice of the U.S. standards and conformity assessment system, the American National Standards Institute is a membership organization for government agencies, organizations, companies, academic and international bodies, and individuals.
1899 L Street, NW
11th Floor
Washington, DC 20036
Tel: 202-293-8020
www.ansi.org

AOA (American Osteopathic Association)
Membership organization for osteopathic physicians, associates, and allied healthcare providers inside and outside the United States.
142 E. Ontario Street
Chicago, IL 60611-2864
Toll free: 888-62-MYAOA
www.osteopathic.org

AONE (American Organization of Nurse Executives)
Membership organization within the American Hospital Association for nurses in leadership positions, students, and individuals interested in supporting the AONE mission and vision.
200 10th Street, NW
Two City Center
Suite 400
Washington, DC 20001-4956
Tel: 202-626-2240
www.aone.org

AORN (Association of periOperative Registered Nurses)
Membership organization of perioperative nurses, nursing students, and industry professionals who provide direct or indirect perioperative services.
2170 South Parker Road
Suite 400
Denver, CO 80231
Tel: 303-755-6304
Toll free: 800-755-2676
www.aorn.org

APhA (American Pharmacists Association)
Membership organization for pharmacists, students, spouses, technicians, and retirees inside or outside the United States.
2215 Constitution Avenue, NW
Washington, DC 20037
Tel: 202-628-4410
Toll free: 800-237-APhA (2742)
www.pharmacist.com

APHA (American Public Health Association)
Membership organization open to health professionals, other career workers in the health field, and persons interested in public health.
800 I Street, NW
Washington, DC 20001
Tel: 202-777-2742
www.apha.org

API (Association for Pathology Informatics)
Membership organization for individuals, trainees (e.g., residents, fellows, students, and post-docs), teaching institutions, commercial entities, and other organizations interested in pathology informatics.
P.O. ox 90319
Pittsburgh, PA 15224
Tel: 412-648-9552
www.pathologyinformatics.org

APNA (American Psychiatric Nurses Association)
Membership organization for nurses and affiliated mental health profession-als inside and outside the United States who are committed to the specialty practice of psychiatric-mental health (PMH) nursing, wellness promotion, prevention of mental health problems, and the care and treatment of persons with psychiatric disorders.
3141 Fairview Park Drive
Suite 625
Falls Church, VA 22042
Tel: 571-533-1919
Toll free: 855-863-2762
www.apna.org

APTA (American Physical Therapy Association)
Membership organization for physical therapists (PT) and assistants (PTA) inside and outside the United States.
1111 North Fairfax Street
Alexandria, VA 22314-1488
Tel: 703-684-APTA (2782)
Toll free: 800-999-2782
www.apta.org

AQIPS (Alliance for Quality Improvement and Patient Safety)
Professional association for patient safety organizations and their healthcare provider members.
5114 Cherokee Avenue
Alexandria, Virginia 22312
Tel: 703-581-9285
www.allianceforqualityimprovement.org

ARN (Association of Rehabilitation Nurses)
To promote and advance professional rehabilitation nursing practice through education, advocacy, collaboration, and research to enhance the quality of life for those affected by disability and chronic illness.
8735 W. Higgins Road
Suite 300
Chicago, IL 60631-2738
Toll free: 800-229-7530
www.rehabnurse.org

ASA (American Society of Anesthesiologists)
An educational, research, and scientific association of physicians organized to raise and maintain the standards of the medical practice of anesthesiology and improve the care of the patient.
1061 American LaneSchaumburg, IL 60173-4973
Tel: (847) 825-5586
www.asahq.org

ASAE (American Society of Association Executives)
Membership organization for professional staff, students, consultants, executives of a nonprofit association or association management companies.
1575 I Street, NW
Washington, DC 20005
Tel: 202-626-2723
Toll free: 888-950-2723
www.asaecenter.org

ASC X12 (Accredited Standards Committee X12)
Membership organization chartered by American National Standards Institute (ANSI) to support business and technical professionals in a cross-industry forum to enhance business processes.
8300 Greensboro Drive
Suite 800
McLean, VA 22102
Tel: 703-970-4480
www.x12.org

ASCIP (Academy of Spinal Cord Injury Professionals)
Membership association of physicians, nurses, psychologists, social workers, counselors, therapists, and researchers engaged in education, research, advocacy, and policy for spinal cord injuries inside and outside the United States.
206 South Sixth Street
Springfield, IL 62701
Tel: 217-321-2488
www.academyscipro.org

ASCO (American Society of Clinical Oncology)
  Membership organization for oncology professionals.
  2318 Mill Road
  Suite 800
  Alexandria, VA 22314
  Tel: 571-483-1300
  www.asco.org

ASCP (American Society for Clinical Pathology)
  Membership organization for pathologists and laboratory professionals.
  33 West Monroe Street
  Suite 1600
  Chicago, IL 60603
  Toll free: 800-267-2727
  www.ascp.org

ASHE (American Society for Healthcare Engineering)
  Membership organization within the American Hospital Association for individuals devoted to optimizing the healthcare physical environment in a healthcare facility, company, or organization other than healthcare, educators, and students.
  155 N. Wacker Drive
  Suite 400
  Chicago, Illinois 60606
  Tel: 312-422-3800
  www.ashe.org

ASHP (American Society of Health-System Pharmacists)
  Membership organization for pharmacists, students, spouses, technicians, and retirees inside or outside the United States.
  4500 East-West Highway
  Suite 900
  Bethesda, MD 20814
  Toll free: 866-279-0681
  www.ashp.org

ASHRM (American Society for Health Care Risk Management)
  Membership organization with the American Hospital Association for anyone who is actively involved or interested in healthcare risk management or whose primary job responsibility includes healthcare risk management.
  155 N. Wacker Drive
  Suite 400
  Chicago, IL 60606
  Tel: 312-422-3980
  www.ashrm.org

ASN (American Society of Nephrology)
Organization working to fight against kidney disease by educating health professionals, advancing research, and advocating the highest quality care for patients.
1510 H Street, NW
Suite 800
Washington, DC 20005
Tel: 202-640-4660
www.asn-online.org

ASNC (American Society of Nuclear Cardiology)
Membership organization for physicians, scientists, technologists, biomedical engineers, computer specialists, and other healthcare personnel involved in nuclear cardiology as well as industry representatives who actively work in this field of medicine.
4340 East-West Highway
Suite 1120
Bethesda, MD 20814
Tel: 301-215-7575
www.asnc.org

ASPAN (American Society of PeriAnesthesia Nurses)
Membership organization for nurses involved in all phases of preanesthesia and postanesthesia care, ambulatory surgery, and pain management or in the management, teaching, or research of the same, students, and licensed healthcare professionals interested in perianesthesia inside or outside the United States.
90 Frontage Road
Cherry Hill, NJ 08034-1424
Toll free: 877-737-9696
www.aspan.org

ASQ (American Society for Quality)
Global membership community of people passionate about quality who use the tools, their ideas and expertise to make our world work better.
P.O. Box 3005
Milwaukee, WI 53201-3005
600 North Plankinton Avenue
Milwaukee, WI 53203
Tel: 800-248-1946
www.asq.org

ASSP (American Society of Safety Professionals)
Membership organization for the safety, health, and environmental (SH&E) profession with an interest in the healthcare practice specialty.
520 N. Northwest Highway
Park Ridge, IL 60068
Tel: 847-699-2929
www.assp.org

ASTHO (Association of State and Territorial Health Officials)
All state and territorial health agency staff members are eligible to participate in open meetings.
2231 Crystal Drive
Suite 450
Arlington, VA 22202
Tel: 202-371-9090
www.astho.org

ASTM International (American Society for Testing and Materials)
Membership organization chartered by ASTM under the American National Standards Institute (ANSI) to support the development of test methods, specifications, guides, and practice standards that support industries and governments worldwide.
100 Barr Harbor Drive
P.O. Box C700
West Conshohocken, PA 19428-2959
Toll free: 877-909-2786
International: 610-832-9585
www.astm.org

ATA (American Telemedicine Association)
Membership is open to all individuals and organizations interested in providing distance healthcare through technology.
901 N Glebe Road
Suite 850
Arlington, VA 22203
Tel: 703-373-9600
www.americantelemed.org

AUPHA (Association of University Programs in Health Administration)
Membership organization of healthcare management/administration education programs in North America includes non-academic institutions and individuals inside and outside the United States.
1730 M St, NW
Suite 407
Washington, DC 20036
Tel: 202-763-7283
www.aupha.org

Australian Digital Health Agency
Managed by the Australian Department of Health, the Agency is responsible for national
digital health services and systems with a focus on engagement, innovation, and clinical quality and safety.
Level 25, 56 Pitt Street
Sydney NSW 2000 Australia
Tel: (02) 8298 2600

AWHONN (Association of Women's Health, Obstetric and Neonatal Nurses)
Membership organization for nurses and other healthcare professionals interested in improving the health of women and newborns.
1800 M Street
Suite 740S
Washington, DC 20036
Tel: 202-261-2400
Toll free US: 800-673-8499
Toll free Canada: 800-245-0231
www.awhonn.org

BACCN (British Association of Critical Care Nurses)
Membership organization open to any professional with an interest in critical care.
The Grainger Suite
Dobson House, Regent Centre
Newcastle Upon Tyne
NE3 3PF
Tel: 0844 800 8843
www.baccn.org

BCI (Business Continuity Institute)

Membership organization open to business continuity management practitioners at all levels of experience worldwide.
10-11 Southview Park, Marsack Street
Caversham, Berkshire, RG4 5AF
United Kingdom
Tel: +44 (0) 118-947-8215
www.thebci.org

Beryl Institute

The Beryl Institute is the global community of practice dedicated to improving the patient experience through collaboration and shared knowledge.
550 Reserve Street
Suite 190 #26
Southlake, TX 76092
Tel: 866-488-2379
www.theberylinstitute.org

BioEnterprise

BioEnterprise partners with people who have a passion for improving health and wellbeing. They are scientists, entrepreneurs, innovators and company founders with creativity and drive woven into their very DNA.
11000 Cedar Avenue
Cleveland, OH 44106
Tel: 216-658-3999
www.bioenterprise.com

BRI (Blockchain Research Institute)

Conducts studies on the impact of blockchain technology on business, government, and society.
180 John Street
5th Floor
Toronto, ON
M5T 1X5 Canada
Tel: 416-863-8809
www.blockchainresearchinstitute.org

CAC (Citizen Advocacy Center)

Membership organization for state health professional licensing boards and other interested organizations and individuals.
1601 18th Street NW
Suite 4
Washington, DC 20009
Tel: 202-462-1174
www.cacenter.org

CACCN (Canadian Association of Critical Care Nurses)
Canadian nursing membership organization for any registered nurse with an interest in critical care who possesses a current and valid license or certificate.
P.O. Box 25322
London, Ontario
N6B 6B1 Canada
Tel: 519-649-5284
Toll free: 866-477-9077
www.caccn.ca

CADTH (Canadian Agency for Drugs and Technologies)
An independent, not-for-profit agency funded by Canadian federal, provincial, and territorial governments to provide credible, impartial advice and evidence-based information about the effectiveness of drugs and other health technologies to Canadian healthcare decision makers.
865 Carling Avenue
Suite 600
Ottawa, Ontario
K1S 5S8 Canada
Tel: 613-226-2553
Toll free: 866-988-1444
www.cadth.ca

CAHME (Commission on Accreditation of Healthcare Management Education)
Any interested healthcare organization or corporation may become a corporate member.
6110 Executive Boulevard
Suite 614
Rockville, MD 20852
Tel: 301-298-1820
www.cahme.org

CAP (College of American Pathologists)
Membership organization exclusively for pathology residents.
325 Waukegan Road
Northfield, IL 60093-2750
Toll free: 800-323-4040
www.cap.org

CAQH (Council for Affordable Quality Healthcare)
Membership alliance of nonprofit health plans and trade associations.
1900 K Street, NW
Suite 650
Washington, DC 20006
www.caqh.org

Carequality
A public-private, multi-stakeholder collaborative from across the healthcare ecosystem that uses a consensus-based process to enable seamless connectivity across all participating networks. Carequality is a collaborative under the Sequoia Project.
8300 Boone Boulevard
Suite 500
Vienna, VA 22182
Tel: 571-327-3640
www.sequoiaproject.org/carequality

CARIN Alliance (Creating Access to Real-time Information Now through Consumer-Directed Exchange)
A bi-partisan, multi-sector alliance convened to unite industry leaders in advancing the adoption of consumer-directed exchange across the U.S.
www.carinalliance.com

CCC (Computing Community Consortium)
Cooperative consortium formed by the Computing Research Association (CRA) and the U.S. National Science Foundation, CCC is broadly inclusive, and is open to any computing researcher who wishes to become involved.
1828 L Street, NW
Suite 800
Washington, DC 20036-4632
Tel: 202-234-2111
www.cra.org/ccc

CCHIIM (Commission on Certification for Health Informatics and Information Management)
Certification organization focused on establishing, implementing and enforcing standards and procedures for certification and recertification of health informatics and information management (HIIM) professionals.
233 N. Michigan Avenue
21st Floor
Chicago, IL 60601-5800
Tel: 312-233-1100
www.ahima.org/certification

CDC (Centers for Disease Control and Prevention)
Federal agency within the Department of Health and Human Services focused on the national mission to improve the quality, safety, efficiency, and effectiveness of healthcare for Americans.
1600 Clifton Road
Atlanta, GA 30333-4027
Toll free: 800-CDC-INFO (800-232-4636)
www.cdc.gov

CDISC (Clinical Data Interchange Standards Consortium)
Membership organization open to any organization of any size interested in information system interoperability to improve medical research and related areas of healthcare.
401 West 15th Street
Suite 975
Austin, TX 78701
www.cdisc.org

CEN (European Committee for Standardization)
Membership is the 27 European Union National Standards Bodies (NSBs), Croatia, the Former Yugoslav Republic of Macedonia, Turkey, and three countries of the European Free Trade Association (Iceland, Norway, and Switzerland).
CEN-CENELEC Management Centre
Rue de la Science 23
B-1040 Brussels, Belgium
Tel: +32 2 550 08 11
www.cen.eu

Center for Medical Interoperability
A 501(c)(3) cooperative research and development lab founded by health systems to simplify and advance data sharing among medical technologies and systems.
8 City Boulevard
Suite 203
Nashville, TN 37209
Tel: 615-257-6400
www.medicalinteroperability.org

CHA (Children's Hospital Association)
CHA advances child health through innovation in the quality, cost, and delivery of care with our children's hospitals.
16011 College Boulevard
Suite 250
Lenexa, KS 66219
Tel: (913) 262-1436
600 13th Street, NW Suite 500
Washington, DC 20005
Tel: (202) 753-5500
www.childrenshospitals.org

Chamber of Digital Commerce
Our mission is to promote the acceptance and use of digital assets and block-chain technologies. Through education, advocacy and working closely with policymakers, regulatory agencies and industry, our goal is to develop an environment that fosters innovation, jobs and investment.
https://digitalchamber.org

CHI (Canada Health Infoway)
Organization accountable to Canada's 14 federal, provincial, and territorial governments represented by their Deputy Ministers of Health to foster development and adoption of information technology to transform healthcare in Canada.
150 King Street West
Suite 1300
Toronto, Ontario M5H 1J9
Tel: 416-979-4606
Toll free: 888-733-6462
www.infoway-inforoute.ca

CHI (Center for Healthcare Innovation)
Organization encouraging and enabling meaningful and executable innovation that aims to address existing and ensuing healthcare dynamics through communication, education, training, symposia, reports, and research.
706 S. Ada Street
Chicago, IL 60607
Tel: 773-330-2416
www.chisite.org

CHIME (College of Healthcare Information Management Executives)
Membership open to CIOs and senior IT leaders at healthcare-related organizations.
710 Avis Drive
Suite 200
Ann Arbor, MI 48108
Tel: 734-665-0000
www.chimecentral.org

CHT (Center for Health and Technology)
Private, academic research organization working to advance innovation in telehealth and connected healthcare.
Center for Health and Technology Building
4610 X Street
Suite 2301
Sacramento, CA 95817
Tel: 916-734-5675
www.ucdmc.ucdavis.edu/cht/

CIAQ (Center for Innovation Access & Quality)
Organization promoting the creation and implementation of innovative approaches to improving quality care at safety net systems.
1001 Potrero Ave
San Francisco, CA 94110
Tel: 415-206-4523
www.ciaqsf.org

CIHI (Canadian Institute for Health Information)
An independent, not-for-profit organization that provides essential data and analysis on Canada's health system and the health of Canadians.
495 Richmond Road
Suite 600
Ottawa, Ontario
K2A 4H6 Canada
Tel: 613-241-7860
www.cihi.ca

CIHR (Canadian Institutes of Health Research)
Agency responsible for funding health research in Canada.
160 Elgin Street
9th Floor
Address Locator 4809A
Ottawa, Ontario
K19 0W9 Canada
Tel: 613-954-1968
Toll free: 888-603-4178
www.cihr-irsc.gc.ca

CITPH (Center for Innovation and Technology in Public Health)
A research group engaged in public policy development, public health (PH) practices, and the direct provision of services related to enabling technologies. *See* **Public Health Institute**.
www.citph.org

Clinical Research Forum
Provide leadership to the national clinical and translational research enterprise and promote understanding and support for clinical research and its impact on health and healthcare.
2025 M Street NW
Suite 800
Washington, DC 20036
Tel: 202-367-1176
www.clinicalresearchforum.org

CLMA (Clinical Laboratory Management Association)
Membership organization for individuals who hold, have held, or aspire to hold an administrative, managerial, or supervisory position in the clinical laboratory or whose administrative responsibilities include diagnostic services.
330 N. Wabash Avenue
Suite 2000
Chicago, IL 60611
Tel: 312-321-5111
www.clma.org

CLSI (Clinical and Laboratory Standards Institute)
Membership organization for IVD manufacturers and suppliers, LIS/HIS companies, pharmaceutical and biotechnology companies, consulting firms, professional societies, trade associations, and government agencies.
950 West Valley Road
Suite 2500
Wayne, PA 19087
Tel: 610-688-0100
www.clsi.org

CMS (Centers for Medicare & Medicaid Services)
Federal agency within the Department of Health and Human Services focused on the national mission to improve the quality, safety, efficiency, and effectiveness of healthcare for Americans.
7500 Security Boulevard
Baltimore, MD 21244
Tel: 410-786-3000
Toll free: 877-267-2323
www.cms.gov

CMSA (Case Management Society of America)
Membership organization for individuals engaged in the field of case management inside and outside the United States.
6301 Ranch Drive
Little Rock, AR 72223
Tel: 501-225-2229
Toll free: 800-216-2672
www.cmsa.org

CMSS (Council of Medical Specialty Societies)
An independent forum for the discussion by medical specialists of issues of national interest and mutual concern representing thirty-eight societies.
35 E. Wacker Drive
Chicago, IL 60601
Tel: 312-224-2585
www.cmss.org

CNA (Canadian Nurses Association)
National professional membership organization for registered nurses in Canada.
50 Driveway
Ottawa, Ontario
K2P 1E2 Canada
Tel: 613-237-2133
Toll free: 800-361-8404
www.cna-aiic.ca

CNC (Center for Nursing Classification and Clinical Effectiveness)
Academia research center at the University of Iowa School of Nursing that facilitates the development of Nursing Interventions Classification (NIC) and Nursing Outcomes Classification (NOC).
101 College of Nursing Building
50 Newton Road
Iowa City, IA 52242-1121
Tel: 319-335-7018
www.nursing.uiowa.edu/center-for-nursing-classification-and-clinical-effectiveness

CommonWell Health Alliance
Membership is open to all organizations that share CommonWell's vision that health IT must be inherently interoperable, including health IT suppliers, healthcare providers, and other health-focused organizations such as nonprofit and for-profit institutes.
http://www.commonwellalliance.org/

CompTIA (The Computing Technology Industry Association Trade Association)
Nonprofit trade association for IT professionals and companies inside and outside the United States.
3500 Lacey Road
Suite 100
Downers Grove, IL 60515
Tel: 630-678-8300
Toll free: 866-835-8020
www.comptia.org

Csweetener
A 501c3 non-profit organization with a mission to advance women in healthcare into the C-Suite.
www.csweetener.org

CVAA (Canadian Vascular Access Association)
Membership organization open to corporations and all nurses registered with their provincial governing body, extended to the United States and Bermuda, engaged in the field of intravenous or vascular access therapy.
753 Main Street East
P.O. Box 68030
Hamilton, Ontario
L8M 3M7 Canada
Toll Free Telephone and Fax: 888-243-9307
www.cvaa.info

DAHTA (German Agency for Health Technology Assessment)
German Institute of Medical Documentation and Information (DIMDI) agency responsible for granting research assignments for the assessment of procedures and technology relevant to health in the form of health technology assessment reports and for the maintenance of a database-supported information system for the assessment of the effectiveness and cost of medical procedures and technologies.
Tel: +49 221 4724-1
www.dimdi.de

DAMA (Data Management Association International)
Chapter-based, as well as global, membership organization for those who engage in information and data management.
364 E. Main Street
Suite 157
Middletown, DE 19709
www.dama.org

Danish Health Authority
Government agency for the regulation of health and medicines in Denmark.
Islands Brygge 67
2300 København S
Denmark
Tel: +45 72 22 74 00
www.sst.dk

DARPA (Defense Advanced Research Projects Agency)
U.S. Military research agency that invests in breakthrough technologies for national security.
675 North Randolph Street
Arlington, VA 22203-2114
Tel: 703-526-6630
www.darpa.mil

DHHS (Department of Health and Human Services)
The U.S. government's principal agency for protecting the health of all Americans and providing essential human services, especially for those who are least able to help themselves.
200 Independence Avenue, SW
Washington, DC 20201
Toll free: 877-696-6775
www.hhs.gov

DICOM (Digital Imaging and Communications in Medicine)
Membership organization chartered by Digital Imaging and Communications in Medicine (DICOM) under the American National Standards Institute (ANSI) to develop health information standards.
NEMA
1300 N. 17th Street
Rosslyn, VA 22209
Tel: 703-475-9217
http://dicom.nema.org/

Digital Bridge
Partnership that establishes effective bidirectional data exchange between healthcare and
public health. It creates a forum for key stakeholders in healthcare, public health, and health IT to address information sharing challenges.
www.digitalbridge.us

Digital Health Canada
Connects, inspires, and educates digital health professionals creating the future of health in Canada.
https://digitalhealthcanada.com

DirectTrust
DirectTrust is a collaborative non-profit association of health IT and health-care provider organizations to support secure, interoperable health information exchange via the Direct message protocols.
1101 Pennsylvania Ave NW
3rd Floor
Washington, DC 20004
www.directtrust.org

DISA (Data Interchange Standards Association)
See **ASCX12**

DNA (Dermatology Nurses' Association)
Professional membership organization for nurses, individuals in related healthcare fields, and corporations interested in or involved in the care of dermatology patients.
435 N. Bennett Street
Southern Pines, NC 28387
Tel: 800-454-4362
www.dnanurse.org

DoD (Department of Defense) (Health Affairs)
U.S. Military department responsible for the health benefits and healthcare operations of those entrusted to our care.
http://prhome.defense.gov/HA

ECRI Institute
A nonprofit organization dedicated to bringing the discipline of applied scientific research to discover which medical procedures, devices, drugs, and processes are best, all to enable you to improve patient care.
5200 Butler Pike
Plymouth Meeting, PA 19462-1298
Tel: 610-825-6000
www.ecri.org

eHealth Exchange
A network of exchange partners who securely share clinical information over the Internet across the US, using a standardized approach. eHealth Exchange is part of the Sequoia Project.
8300 Boone Boulevard
Suite 500
Vienna, VA 22182
Tel: 571-327-3640
www.sequoiaproject.org/ehealth-exchange/

eHI (eHealth Initiative)
Independent, non-profit organization whose mission is to drive improvements in the quality, safety, and efficiency of healthcare through information technology.
One Thomas Circle, NW
Suite 300
Washington, DC 20005
Tel: 202-624-3270
www.ehidc.org

EHNAC (Electronic Healthcare Network Accreditation Commission)

A voluntary, self-governing standards development organization established to develop standard criteria and accredit organizations that electronically exchange healthcare data.

Tel: 860-408-1620
www.ehnac.org

EHRA (Electronic Health Record Association)

A trade association of Electronic Health Record (EHR) companies within HIMSS addressing national efforts to create interoperable EHRs in hospital and ambulatory care settings. The EHR Association operates on the premise that the rapid, widespread adoption of EHRs will help improve the quality of patient care, as well as the productivity and sustainability of the healthcare system.

33 West Monroe Street
Suite 1700
Chicago, IL 60603-5616
Tel: 312-664-4467
www.ehra.org

EMEA (European Medicines Agency)

Decentralized agency of the European Union responsible for the scientific evaluation of medicines developed by pharmaceutical companies for use in the European Union.

30 Churchill Place
Canary Wharf
London E14 5EU
United Kingdom
Tel: +44 (0) 20 3660 600
www.ema.europa.eu/ema

ENA (Emergency Nurses Association)

Membership organization for nurses in emergency nursing practice.

915 Lee Street
Des Plaines, IL 60016-6569
Tel: 800-900-9659
www.ena.org

ESQH (European Society for Quality in Healthcare)
A not-for-profit organization dedicated to the improvement of quality in European healthcare.
St. Camillus Hospital
Shelbourne Road
Limerick
Ireland
Tel: 00353 61 483315
www.esqh.net

Ethereum Foundation
Promotes and supports the Ehtereum platform and base layer research, development, and education to bring decentralized protocols and tools to the world that empower developers to produce next generation decentralized applications and build a more globally accessible, more free, and trustworthy Internet.
www.ethereum.org/foundation

ETSI (European Telecommunications Standards Institute)
Membership organization for individuals, nonprofit associations, universities, public research bodies, governmental organizations, and observers interested in globally applicable standards for Information and Communications Technologies (ICT), including fixed, mobile, radio, converged, broadcast, and Internet technologies.
06921 Sophia-Antipolis Cedex
France
Tel: +33 (0)4 92 94 42 00
www.etsi.org

EUnetHTA (European Network for Health Technology Assessment)
Organization supporting collaboration between European Health Technology Applications.
Hosted by Danish Health and Medicines Authority
Axel Heides Gade 1
2300 Copenhagen S
Denmark
Tel: +45 7222 7727
www.eunethta.eu

FAH (Federation of American Hospitals)
Membership organization for investor-owned community hospitals and health systems including institutions, associations (hospital associations, medical societies, law firms and foundations, suppliers of services and products to the healthcare industry, management companies) and individual student members enrolled in a course in hospital administration or other career study in the healthcare industry.
750 9th Street, NW
Suite 600
Washington, DC 20001-4524
Tel: 202-624-1500
www.fah.org

FCC (Federal Communications Commission)
An independent U.S. government agency directly responsible to Congress charged with regulating interstate and international communications by radio, television, wire, satellite, and cable.
445 12th Street SW
Washington, DC 20554
Toll free: 888-225-5322
www.fcc.gov

FDA (U.S. Food and Drug Administration)
Federal agency responsible for protecting the public health by assuring the safety, efficacy, and security of human and veterinary drugs, biological products, medical devices, our nation's food supply, cosmetics, and products that emit radiation.
10903 New Hampshire Avenue
Silver Spring, MD 20993
Tel: 888-463-6332
www.fda.gov

George Institute for Global Health
Global research and health policy center.
Level 5, 1 King Street
Newtown, NSW
Australia 2042
Tel: +61 2 8052 4300
www.thegeorgeinstitute.org

GBA (Government Blockchain Association)
An International Professional Association and a US-based non-profit, membership organization that consists of individuals and organizations that are interested in promoting blockchain related solutions to government requirements.
www.gbaglobal.org

GHC (Global Health Care, LLC)
GHC seeks to illuminate complex issues of healthcare practice and policy by bringing together leading-edge doers and thinkers. Since 1997, it has offered conferences and symposia sponsored by over 250 healthcare associations, organizations, and publications and attended by approximately 25,000 registrants.
37 Tatoosh Key
Bellevue, WA 98006
Tel: (206) 757-8053
www.globalhealthcarellc.com/

GS1 (U.S. Global Standards-1)
Authorized provider of globally unique GS1 company prefixes for businesses and the design and implementation of supply chain standards and solutions.
Local GS1 offices by country: USA
Princeton Pike Corporate Center
1009 Lenox Drive
Suite 202
Lawrenceville, NJ 08648
Tel: 609-620-0200
www.gs1.org

HBMA (Healthcare Business Management Association)
A non-profit professional trade association focused on the revenue cycle management industry in the United States.
2025 M Street NW
Suite 800
Washington, DC 20036
Toll free: 877-640-HBMA (4262)
www.hbma.org

HC3 (Health Care Cloud Coalition)
Not-for-profit group of stakeholders representing cloud computing, telecommunication, digital health, and healthcare companies in the healthcare sector.
1919 Pennsylvania Ave NW, Ste 800
Washington DC, DC 20006
www.hcccoalition.org

HCCA (Health Care Compliance Association)
Membership organization for all compliance professionals, corporations, and students.
6500 Barrie Road
Suite 250
Minneapolis, MN 55435
Tel: 952-988-0141
Toll free: 888-580-8373
www.hcca-info.org

HCEA (Healthcare Convention and Exhibitors Association)
Trade association for healthcare organizations involved as exhibitors at healthcare conventions and exhibitions. Membership includes healthcare associations and companies that provide products and services to the healthcare convention and exhibition industry.
7918 Jones Branch Drive
Suite 300
McLean, VA 22102
Tel: 703.935.1961
www.hcea.org

HCTAA (Home Care Technology Association of America)
Association representing home care and hospice providers and technology companies that support health information technology, health information exchange, and telehealth in the home.
228 7th Street SE
Washington, DC 20003
Tel: 202-547-2871
www.hctaa.org

HDAA (Healthcare Data and Analytics Association)
Forum where healthcare organizations planning or engaged in data warehousing and analytics can share ideas and lessons learned.
www.hdwa.org

Health 2.0
Health 2.0 promotes, showcases and catalyzes new technologies in healthcare. Through a worldwide series of conferences, code-a-thons, and prize challenges, we bring together the best minds, resources and technology for compelling panels, discussions and product demonstrations, and more.
https://health2con.com/

Healthbox
A HIMSS Innovation Company, Healthbox is a healthcare advisory firm that leading organizations trust with innovation and digital strategy development and execution.
1000 West Fulton Market
Suite 213
Chicago, IL 60607
Tel: 312-228-4669
https://healthbox.com/

HealthCare*CAN*
The national voice of healthcare organizations and hospitals across Canada with the goal to improve the health of Canadians through an evidence-based and innovative healthcare system.
17 York Street
Suite 100
Ottawa, Ontario K15 5S7
Canada
Tel: 613-241-8005
www.healthcarecan.ca

#HealthITchicks
#HealthITchicks is a grassroots, high-energy networking group of women (and men) focused on raising awareness of gender-related issues in healthcare technology and the workplace at large.
https://healthitchicks.org/

Healthwise
Nonprofit organization with a mission to help people make better health decisions.
2601 N. Bogus Baisin Road
Boise, ID 83702
Tel: 1-800-706-9646
www.healthwise.org

HEN World Health Organization (Health Evidence Network)
Network of organizations and institutions promoting the use of evidence in health policy or health technology assessment.
WHO Regional Office for Europe
UN City
Marmorvej 51DK-2100 Copenhagen Ø Denmark
Tel: +45 45 33 70 00
http://www.euro.who.int/en/data-and-evidence/evidence-informed-policy-making/health-evidence-network-hen

HFES (Human Factors and Ergonomics Society)
Association representing human factors/ergonomics professionals. Members include psychologists and other scientists, designers, and engineers, all of whom have a common interest in designing systems and equipment to be safe and effective for the people who operate and maintain them.
1124 Montana Avenue, Suite B
Santa Monica, CA 90403-1617
Tel: 310-394-1811
www.hfes.org

HFMA (Healthcare Financial Management Association)
Membership organization for healthcare financial management executives and leaders.
3 Westbrook Corporate Center
Suite 600
Westchester, IL 60154
Tel: 708-531-9600
Toll free: 800-252-4362
www.hfma.org

HHS (Department of Health and Human Services)
See **DHHS**.

HIBCC (Health Industry Business Communications Council)
An industry-sponsored and supported nonprofit organization. As an ANSI-accredited organization, its primary function is to facilitate electronic communications by developing appropriate standards for information exchange among all healthcare trading partners.
2525 E. Arizona Biltmore Circle
Suite 127
Phoenix, AZ 85016
Tel: 602-381-1091
www.hibcc.org

HIMA (Health Industry Manufacturers Association)
See **AdvaMed**.

HIMSS (Healthcare Information and Management Systems Society)
HIMSS is a global advisor and thought leader supporting the transformation of health through the application of information and technology.
33 West Monroe Street
Suite 1700
Chicago, IL 60603-5616
Tel: 312-664-4467
www.himss.org

HL7 (Health Level Seven)
A not-for-profit, ANSI-accredited standards developing organization dedicated to providing a comprehensive framework and related standards for the exchange, integration, sharing, and retrieval of electronic health information that supports clinical practice and the management, delivery, and evaluation of health services.
3300 Washtenaw Avenue
Suite 227
Ann Arbor, MI 48104
Tel: 734-677-7777
www.hl7.org

HLC (Healthcare Leadership Council)
A coalition of chief executives from all disciplines within the healthcare system.
750 9th Street, NW
Suite 500
Washington, DC 20001
Tel: 202-452-8700
www.hlc.org

HMD (Health and Medicine Division of the National Academies)
A division of the National Academies of Sciences, Engineering and Medicine, whose aim is to help those in government and the private sector make informed health decisions by providing evidence. Previously referred to as the Institute of Medicine of the National Academies (IOM).
Tel: 202-334-2352
www.nationalacademies.org/hmd

HPNA (Hospice and Palliative Nurses Association)
Membership organization for all members of the nursing team—nurses, nursing assistants, students, and non-nurses—engaged in hospice and palliative end-of-life care.
One Penn Center West
Suite 425
Pittsburgh, PA 15276
Tel: 412-787-9301
www.hpna.org

HSPC (Healthcare Service Platform Consortium)
A provider-led consortium working to improve health by creating a vibrant, open ecosystem of interoperable applications, knowledge, content and services.
www.hspconsortium.org

(HTA) Health Technology Alliance
> The HTA provides a forum for the productive exchange of ideas and the identification of challenges and solutions common to the use and support of medical and information technologies in all care delivery settings.
> *33 West Monroe Street*
> *Suite 1700*
> *Chicago, IL 60606*
> *Tel: (312) 664-4467*
> *www.healthtechnologyalliance.org*

HTAi (Health Technology Assessment International)
> Membership organization embracing all stakeholders, including researchers, agencies, policymakers, industry, academia, health service providers, and patients/consumers interested in the field of scientific research to inform policy and clinical decision-making around the introduction and diffusion of health technologies.
> *HTAi Secretariat*
> *1200, 10405 Jasper Avenue*
> *Edmonton, Alberta*
> *T5J 3N4 Canada*
> *Tel: 780-448-4881*
> *www.htai.org*

IAPP (International Association of Privacy Professionals)
> Membership organization for privacy professionals, corporations, government agencies, and nonprofit groups from around the world.
> *Pease International Tradeport*
> *75 Rochester Avenue*
> *Suite 4*
> *Portsmouth, NH 03801 USA*
> *Tel: +1 603-427-9200*
> *Toll free: 800-266-6501*
> *https://iapp.org/*

IBIA (International Biometrics and Identity Association)
> The leading international trade group representing the identification technology industry. IBIA advances the adoption and responsible use of technologies for managing human identity to enhance security, privacy, productivity, and convenience for individuals, organizations, and governments. To effectively carry out its mission, IBIA focuses on three core activities: Advocacy, Connections, and Education.
> *1090 Vermont Avenue, NW*
> *6th Floor*
> *Washington, DC 20005*
> *www.ibia.org*

ICCBBA (International Council for Commonality in Blood Bank Automation)
Registration and licensing organization for the ISBT 128 global standard
for the identification, labeling, and information processing of human blood,
cell, tissue, and organ products across international borders and disparate
healthcare systems.
P.O. Box 11309
San Bernardino, CA 92423-1309
Tel: 909-793-6516
www.iccbba.org

ICE (Institute for Credentialing Excellence)
Developer of standards for certification and certificate programs. Organizations
may join at any time whether the organization has any programs accredited by
the National Commission for Certifying Agencies (NCCA).
2025 M Street, NW
Suite 800
Washington, DC 20036
Tel: 202-367-1165
www.credentialingexcellence.org

ICN (International Council of Nurses)
A federation of more than 130 national nurses associations representing 20
million nurses worldwide.
3, Place Jean Marteau
1201 - Geneva
Switzerland
Tel: +41-22-908-01-00
www.icn.ch

ICOR (International Consortium of Organizational Resilience)
Membership organization for professionals from a wide variety of public and
private sectors including international organizations, government, consul-
tant, or vendor with demonstrated experience in organizational resilience.
P.O. Box 1171
Lombard, IL 60148
Tel: 630-705-0910
Toll free: 866-765-8321
www.build-resilience.org

IDESG (Identity Ecosystem Steering Group)
A voluntary, public-private partnership dedicated to redefining how people and organizations identify themselves online by fostering the creation of privacy-enhancing trusted digital identities.
2400 Camino Ramon, #375
San Ramon, CA 94583
Tel: 925-275-6608
www.idesg.org

IDF (Immune Deficiency Foundation)
Patient organization dedicated to improving the diagnosis, treatment, and quality of life of persons with primary immunodeficiency diseases (PI) through advocacy, education, and research.
110 West Road
Suite 300
Towson, MD 21204
Toll free: 800-296-4433
www.primaryimmune.org

IEC (International Electrotechnical Commission)
A not-for-profit, nongovernmental organization. Members are national committees and their appointed experts and delegates coming from industry, government bodies, associations, and academia to participate in technical and conformity assessments.
3, rue de Varembé, 1st Floor
P.O. Box 131
CH - 1211 Geneva 20 Switzerland
Tel: +41 22 919 02 11
www.iec.ch

IEEE (Institute of Electrical and Electronics Engineers)
Membership organization for individuals and students who are contributing or working in a technology or engineering field.
3 Park Avenue
17ᵗʰ Floor
New York, NY 10016
Tel: 212-419-7900
Toll free: 800-678-4333 (USA and Canada)
Toll free: 732-981-0060 (Worldwide)
www.ieee.org

IEFT (Internet Engineering Task Force)
An open international community of network designers, operators, vendors, and researchers concerned with the evolution of the Internet architecture and the smooth operation of the Internet. Membership is open to any interested individual.
c/o Association Management Solutions, LLC (AMS)
177 Brandin Court
Fremont, California 94538
Tel: 510-492-4080
www.ietf.org

IHA (Intelligent Health Association)
Nonprofit organization with the mission to raise the level of awareness through educational programs, empower the health community with vendor-neutral information, and encourage the adoption and implementation of technology.
www.ihassociation.org

IHE International (Integrating the Healthcare Enterprise)
A nonprofit organization that promotes the coordinated use of established standards such as DICOM and HL7 to address specific clinical needs in support of optimal patient care.
820 Jorie Boulevard
Oak Brook, IL 60523
www.ihe.net

IHF (International Hospital Federation)
Global association of healthcare organizations, which includes in particular, but not exclusively, hospital associations and representative bodies, as well as their members and other healthcare-related organizations.
P.A. Hôpital de Loëx
Route de Loëx 151
1233 Bernex
Switzerland
Tel: +41 (0) 22 850 94 20
www.ihf-fih.org

IHI (Institute for Healthcare Improvement)
An independent, not-for-profit organization, serving as a leading innovator, convener, partner and driver of results in health and healthcare improvement worldwide.
53 State Street
19th Floor
Boston, MA 02109
Tel: 617-301-4800
Toll Free: 866-787-0831
www.ihi.org

IIE (International Institute of Education)
An international education and training organization providing global fellowships and scholarships in applied research and policy analysis.
Tel: 212-883-8200
www.iie.org

IMDMC (Indiana Medical Device Manufacturers Council)
IMDMC serves the interests of its member companies in the delivery of innovative, life-changing technologies to patients by increasing public awareness of the economic and health benefits, providing training and educational opportunities to industry employees and advocating on behalf of the medical device industry at both the state and federal level.
P.O. Box 441385
Indianapolis, IN 46244
Tel: 833-245-8828
www.imdmc.org

IMIA (International Medical Informatics Association)
Membership is limited to organizations, societies, and corporations interested in promoting informatics in healthcare.
c/o Health On the Net
Chemin du Petit-Bel-Air 2
CH-1225 Chêne-Bourg, Geneva
Switzerland
Tel: +41-22-3727249
www.imia.org

INAHTA (International Network of Agencies for Health Technology Assessment)
An organization of nonprofit making organizations producing health technology assessments and linked to regional or national governments.
NAHTA Secretariat
c/o Institute of Health Economics
#1200, 10405 Jasper Avenue
Edmonton, Alberta
Canada T5J 3N4
Tel: 780 401 1770
www.inahta.org

INS (International Neuropsychological Society)
Membership organization for persons with a significant proportion of activities devoted to neuropsychology or related fields.
2319 South Foothill Drive
Suite 260
Salt Lake City, Utah 84109
Tel: 801-487-0475
www.the-ins.org

INS (Infusion Nurses Society)
Membership is open to healthcare professionals from all practice settings who are involved in or interested in the specialty practice of infusion therapy.
315 Norwood Park South
Norwood, MA 02062
Tel: 781-440-9408
www.ins1.org

Institute for e-Health Policy
Nonprofit organization providing research and educational opportunities for public and private sector stakeholders—two key constituents that make and are most directly impacted by e-health policy decisions.
4300 Wilson Boulevard
Arlington, VA 22203
www.e-healthpolicy.org

INCITS (InterNational Committee for Information Technology Standards)
Membership is open to organizations directly and materially affected by standardization in the field of Information and Communications Technologies (ICT), encompassing storage, processing, transfer, display, management, organization, and retrieval of information.
1101 K Street, NW
Suite 610
Washington, DC 20005
Tel: 202-737-8888
www.incits.org

IOM (Institute of Medicine of the National Academies)
(On March 15, 2016, the IOM program unit of the National Academies was renamed HMD (Health and Medicine Division) to emphasize its increased focus on a wider range of health matters.)

IOMSN (International Organization for Multiple Sclerosis Nurses)
Membership organization for licensed nursing professional whose professional interest and activities are devoted to the care of patients with multiple sclerosis either through direct practice, research, or education who reside throughout the world.
3 University Plaza Drive
Suite 116
Hackensack, NJ 07601
Tel: 201-487-1050
www.iomsn.org

ISACA (previously known as the Information Systems Audit and Control Association)
Nonprofit, global association engaging in the development, adoption, and use of globally accepted, industry-leading knowledge and practices for information systems. ISACA now goes by its acronym only.
1700 E. Golf Road, Suite 400
Schaumburg, Illinois 60173, USA
Phone: +1.847.253.1545
www.isaca.org

(ISC)² (International Information Systems Security Certification Consortium)
An international, nonprofit membership association for information security leaders.
311 Park Place Boulevard
Suite 400 Clearwater, Florida 33759
+1.866.331.ISC2(4722)
www.isc2.org

ISNCC (International Society of Nurses in Cancer Care)
Membership is open to cancer nursing associations, institutions, and individual cancer nursing professionals worldwide.
1201 West Pender Street
Suite 300
Vancouver, British Columbia
V6E 2V2 Canada
Tel: +1-647-323-2152
www.isncc.org

ISO (International Organization for Standardization)
A network of national standards bodies that develop and publish International Standards. The national standards bodies represent ISO in their country.
ISO Central Secretariat
BIBC II
Chemin de Blandonnet 8
CP 401
1214 Vernier, Geneva Switzerland
Tel: +41 22 749 01 11
www.iso.org

ISPN (International Society of Psychiatric-Mental Health Nurses)
An international membership organization for all advanced practice psychiatric nurses.
2424 American Lane
Madison, WI 53704-3102
Tel: 608-443-2463
www.ispn-psych.org

ISQua (International Society for Quality in Health Care)
Membership organization with individual, institutional, and affiliated categories for those engaged in quality improvement.
4th Floor, Huguenot House
35-38 St Stephens Green
Dublin 2
D02 Y729 Ireland
Tel: +353 (0)1 6706750
www.isqua.org

ISSA (Information Systems Security Association)
Volunteer organization for information security professionals and practitioners.
1964 Gallows Road
Suite 310
Vienna, VA 22182
Tel: 703-495-2973
www.issa.org

ITAC (Information Technology Association of Canada)
A membership organization of for-profit companies with a presence in Canada, for whom the provision of information technology products or services is a significant component of revenue and of strategic importance, or one which increases the efficiency of electronic markets by facilitating the meeting and interaction of buyers and sellers over the Internet.
220 Laurier Avenue West
Suite 1120
Ottawa, Ontario
Canada K1P 5Z9
Tel: 613-238-4822
www.itac.ca

ITIF (Information Technology and Innovation Foundation)
An independent, nonpartisan research and educational institute focusing on the intersection of technological innovation and public policy.
1101 K Street NW
Suite 610
Washington, DC 20005
Tel: 202-449-1351
www.itif.org

ITU (International Telecommunication Union)
Membership organization representing a cross-section of the global Information and Communication Technologies (ICT) sector along with leading research and development (R&D) institutions and academia. ITU is the United Nations specialized agency for ICT.
Place des Nations
1211 Geneva 20
Switzerland
Tel: +41 22 730 5111
www.itu.int

JCAHO (The Joint Commission on Accreditation of Healthcare Organizations)
See **Joint Commission**. (JCAHO is now The Joint Commission.)

JCR (Joint Commission Resources)
Publication subsidiary of The Joint Commission offering products, publications, educational conferences, consulting, and distance learning services.
1515 W. 22nd Street
Suite 1300W
Oak Brook, IL 60523
Tel: 630-268-7400
www.jcrinc.com

The Joint Commission
Accreditation organization to support performance improvement in healthcare organizations.
1 Renaissance Blvd
Oakbrook Terrace, IL 60181
Tel: 630-792-5800
www.jointcommission.org

JPHIT (Joint Public Health Informatics Taskforce)
Coalition of nine national associations that help U.S. governmental agencies build modern information systems across a spectrum of public health programs.
www.jphit.org

JumpStart
JumpStart's mission is to unlock the full potential of diverse and ambitious entrepreneurs to economically transform entire communities.
6701 Carnegie Ave
Suite 100
Cleveland, OH 44103
Tel: 216-363-3400
www.jumpstartinc.org

Kantara Initiative
Organization providing strategic vision and real-world innovation for the digital identity transformation. Developing initiatives including: Identity Relationship Management, User Managed Access, Identities of Things, and Minimum Viable Consent Receipt, Kantara Initiative connects a global, open, and transparent leadership community.
401 Edgewater Place
Wakefield, MA 01880
www.kantarainitiative.org

Leapfrog Group
  Voluntary program aimed at mobilizing employer purchasing power to alert America's health industry that big leaps in healthcare safety, quality, and customer value will be recognized and rewarded.
  1660 L Street, NW
  Suite 308
  Washington, DC 20036
  Tel: 202-292-6713
  www.leapfroggroup.org

Linux Foundation
  Supports the creation of sustainable open source ecosystems by providing financial and intellectual resources, infrastructure, services, events, and training.
  1 Letterman Drive
  Building D, Suite D4700
  San Francisco, CA 94129
  Tel: 415-723-9709
  www.linuxfoundation.org

LOINC (Logical Observation Identifiers Names and Codes)
  LOINC is a database and universal standard for identifying medical laboratory observations developed and maintained by the Regenstrief Institute, an international nonprofit medical research organization, associated with Indiana University. The scope of the LOINC effort includes laboratory and other clinical observations.
  LOINC c/o Regenstrief Center for Biomedical Informatics
  410 W. 10th Street
  Suite 2000
  Indianapolis, IN 46202-3012
  www.loinc.org

MassChallenge HealthTech
  MassChallenge strengthens the global innovation ecosystem by accelerating high-potential startups across all industries, from anywhere in the world.
  https://masschallenge.org/programs-healthtech

MATTER

> MATTER is a community of healthcare innovators, an incubator of ideas, and a catalyst for change. They are boots-on-the-ground entrepreneurs pushing against the status quo and established institutions dedicated to improving patients' lives.
> *222 Merchandise Mart Plaza*
> *Suite 1230*
> *Chicago, IL 60654*
> *Tel: 312-374-8423*
> *https://matter.health/*

MDISS (Medical Device Innovation, Safety and Security Consortium)

> Nonprofit professional organization committed to advancing quality healthcare with a focus on the safety and security of medical devices. Serves providers, payers, manufacturers, universities, government agencies, technology companies, individuals, patients, patient advocates, and associations.
> *3620 Oxford Avenue*
> *Suite 3A*
> *Bronx, NY 10463*
> *www.mdiss.org*

MGMA (Medical Group Management Association)

> Membership organization for individuals, teaching faculty, students, and uniformed services interested in practice management.
> *104 Inverness Terrace East*
> *Englewood, CO 80112-5306*
> *Tel: 303-799-1111*
> *Toll free: 877-275-6462*
> *www.mgma.com*

MITA (Medical Imaging and Technology Alliance)

> The leading organization and collective voice of medical imaging equipment manufacturers, innovators, and product developers, a division of the National Electrical Manufacturers Association (NEMA).
> *1300 North 17th Street*
> *Suite 900*
> *Arlington, VA 22209*
> *Tel: 703-841-3200*
> *www.medicalimaging.org*

MLA (Medical Library Association)
Membership organization for individuals with an interest in the health sciences information field.
65 East Wacker Place
Suite 1900
Chicago, IL 60601-7246
Tel: 312-419-9094
www.mlanet.org

MSIG (MEMS & Sensors Industry Group)
Nonprofit organization linking the MEMS and sensors supply chain to diverse markets, MSIG helps companies in and around the MEMS and sensors industry to make meaningful business connections and informed decisions.
1620 Murray Avenue
Pittsburgh, PA 15217
Tel: 412-390-1644
http://www.semi.org/en/msig-information-hub

MTPPI (Medical Technology & Practice Patterns Institute)
A nonprofit organization conducting research on the clinical and economic implications of healthcare technologies. MTPPI research is directed toward the formulation and implementation of local and national healthcare policies.
5272 River Road
Suite 365
Bethesda, MD 20816
Tel: 301-652-4005
www.mtppi.org

NACCHO (National Association of County and City Health Officials)
Organization dedicated to serving every local health department in the nation. NACCHO comprises nearly 3,000 local health departments across the United States forming an organization focused on being a leader, partner, catalyst, and voice for change for local health departments around the nation.
1201 Eye Street, NW
4th Floor
Washington, DC 20005
Tel: 202-783-5550
www.naccho.org

NACHC (National Association of Community Health Centers)
Serves as the national healthcare advocacy organization for America's medi-
cally underserved and uninsured and the community health centers that
serve as their healthcare home.
7501 Wisconsin Ave
Suite 1100W
Bethesda, MD 20814
Tel: 301-347-0400
www.nachc.org/

NAEMT (National Association of Emergency Medical Technicians)
National association representing the professional interests of all emergency
and mobile healthcare practitioners. NAEMT members work in all sectors
of EMS, including government agencies, fire departments, hospital-based
ambulance services, private companies, industrial and special operations settings, and in the military.
P.O. Box 1400
Clinton, MS 39060
Tel: 601-924-7744
www.naemt.org

NAHC (National Association for Home Care & Hospice)
A membership organization for agencies delivering hands-on care to patients
at home, corporate (multi-entity) providers delivering care at home, businesses that provide products or services to home care agencies, state home
care and hospice associations that are organized into the National Association
for Home Care's Forum of State Associations, and nonprofit groups, universities, libraries, schools of nursing, and international groups with an interest in
home care and/or hospice.
228 Seventh Street, SE
Washington, DC 20003
Tel: 202-547-7424
www.nahc.org

NAHDO (National Association of Health Data Organizations)
A national, not-for-profit membership organization dedicated to improving
healthcare through the collection, analysis, dissemination, public availability,
and use of health data.
124 South 400 East
Suite 220
Salt Lake City, UT 84111-5312
Tel: 801-532-2299
www.nahdo.org

NAHHE (National Association of Hispanic Healthcare Executives)
Membership organization for individuals in healthcare administration or persons on a career path to healthcare management, including healthcare consultants and full-time academicians who support AHHE's mission and objectives.
153 West 78th Street
Suite 1
New York, NY 10024
Tel: 917-974-8164
www.ahhe.org

NAHQ (National Association for Healthcare Quality)
Membership organization open to anyone involved in the healthcare quality field and any healthcare organization with four or more individuals is eligible for membership.
8600 W. Bryn Mawr Avenue
Suite 710
Chicago, IL 60631
Tel: 847-375-4720
www.nahq.org

NAHSE (National Association of Health Services Executives)
Nonprofit association of black healthcare executives for the purpose of promoting the advancement and development of black healthcare leaders, and elevating the quality of healthcare services rendered to minority and underserved communities.
1050 Connecticut Avenue NW
5ᵗʰ Floor
Washington, DC 20036
Tel: 202-772-1030
www.nahse.org

NANDA International
NANDA International is an organization focused on the development and use of nursing's standardized terminology to ensure patient safety through evidence-based care, thereby improving the healthcare of all people.
P.O. Box 72
Mountain, WI 54149
Tel: 617-552-3547
www.nanda.org

NAPHSIS (National Association for Public Health Statistics and Information Systems)
Membership association of state vital records and public health statistics offices in the United States.
P.O. Box 79489
Baltimore, MD 21279
Tel: 301-563-6001
www.naphsis.org

NASCIO (National Association of State Chief Information Officers)
Membership organization of state chief information and information technology executives from the states, territories, and the District of Columbia. Leading advocate for technology policy at all levels of government. Other public sector and nonprofit organizations may join.
c/o AMR Management Services
201 East Main Street
Suite 1405
Lexington, KY 40507
Tel: 859-514-9156
www.nascio.org

NASEMSO (National Association of State EMS Officials)
Membership organization for individuals in state Emergency Medical Service (EMS) office, federal agencies, and individuals with an interest in emergency care, education, professional standards, trauma systems, and data systems.
201 Park Washington Court
Falls Church, VA 22046-4527
Tel: 703-538-1799
www.nasemso.org

NASL (National Association for the Support of Long Term Care)
A consortium of ancillary services and products for providers serving the long-term and post-acute care (LTPAC) sector.
1444 Eye Street, NW
Suite 301
Washington, DC 20005
Tel: 202-803-2385
www.nasl.org

NASN (National Association of School Nurses)
Membership organization for registered professional nurses having as their primary assignment the administration, education, or the provision of school health services.
1100 Wayne Avenue
Suite 925
Silver Spring, MD 20910
Tel: 240-821-1130
www.nasn.org

NASPA (National Alliance of State Pharmacy Associations)
Association dedicated to enhancing the success of state pharmacy associations in their efforts to advance the profession of pharmacy. NASPA's membership is comprised of state pharmacy associations and over 70 other stakeholder organizations. NASPA promotes leadership, sharing, learning, and policy exchange among its members and pharmacy leaders nationwide.
2530 Professional Road
Suite 202
North Chesterfield, VA 23235
Tel: 804-285-4431
www.naspa.us

NATE (National Association for Trusted Exchange)
Nonprofit association bringing the expertise of its membership and other stakeholders together to find common solutions that optimize the appropriate exchange of health information for greater gains in adoption and outcomes.
www.nate-trust.org

National Partnership for Women and Families
A nonprofit, nonpartisan 501(c)(3) organization promoting fairness in the workplace, reproductive health and rights, access to quality, affordable healthcare, and policies that help women and men meet the dual demands of work and family.
1875 Connecticut Avenue NW
Suite 650
Washington, DC 20009
Tel: 202-986-2600
www.nationalpartnership.org

NBDHMT (National Board of Diving & Hyperbaric Medical Technology)
Certification organization for hyperbaric technologists, nurses, and diving medical technicians to ensure that the fields of hyperbaric medicine, hyperbaric chamber operation, and diving medicine are filled with highly qualified personnel.
9 Medical Park
Suite 330
Columbia, SC 29203
Tel: 803-434-7802
www.nbdhmt.org

NCCLS (National Committee for Clinical Laboratory Standards)
See **CLSI.**

NCHN (National Cooperative of Health Networks)
National association of health networks and strategic partners.
400 S Main Street
Hardinsburg, KY 40143
www.nchn.org

NCHS (National Center for Health Statistics)
Centers for Disease Control and Prevention (CDC) center for statistical information.
1600 Clifton Road
Atlanta, GA 30333
Toll free: 800-232-4636
www.cdc.gov/nchs

NCPDP (National Council for Prescription Drug Programs)
A not-for-profit, multi-stakeholder forum for developing and promoting industry standards and business solutions that improve patient safety and health outcomes, while also decreasing costs.
9240 East Raintree Drive
Scottsdale, AZ 85260-7518
Tel: 480-477-1000
www.ncpdp.org

NCQA (National Committee for Quality Assurance)
Certification organization to improve the quality of healthcare.
1100 13th Street, NW
3rd Floor
Washington, DC 20005
Tel: 202-955-3500
www.ncqa.org

NCSA (National Cyber Security Alliance)
Organization building strong public/private partnerships to create and implement broad-reaching education and awareness efforts to empower users at home, work, and school with the information they need to keep themselves, their organizations, their systems, and their sensitive information safe and secure online and encourage a culture of cybersecurity.
www.staysafeonline.org

NCSBN (National Council of State Boards of Nursing)
Nursing examination organization to qualify and examine nurses who have successfully completed an accredited program and meet examination requirements for the National Council Licensure Examination for Registered Nurses (NCLEX-RN) and the National Council Licensure Examination for Practical Nurses (NCLEX-PN) that are used by boards of nursing to assist in making state licensure decisions.
111 East Wacker Drive
Suite 2900
Chicago, IL 60601-4277
Tel: 312-525-3600
International Tel: 001 1 312 525 3600
www.ncsbn.org

NCSL (National Conference of State Legislatures)
The strength of NCSL is bipartisanship and commitment to serving both Republicans and Democrats. It is recognized in their comprehensive, unbiased research. NCSL serves both legislators and staff.
444 North Capitol Street, N.W., Suite 515
Washington, DC 20001
Tel: 202-624-5400
www.ncsl.org

NCTRC (National Consortium of Telehealth Resources Centers)
Consortium of federally funded Telehealth Resource Centers (TRCs) expanding the availability of healthcare to underserved populations.
www.telehealthresourcecenter.org

NCVHS (National Committee on Vital and Health Statistics)
Established by Congress to serve as an advisory body to the Department of Health and Human Services on health data, statistics, and national health information policy.
3311 Toledo Road
Hyattsville, MD 20782
Tel: 301-458-4715
www.ncvhs.hhs.gov

NEHI (Network for Excellence in Health Innovation)
Dedicated to identifying innovations that improve the quality and lower the costs of healthcare. NEHI's network of nearly 100 healthcare organizations is a hotbed for consensus solutions that cut across traditional silos and drive policy change.
133 Federal Street
9ᵗʰ Floor
Boston, MA 02110
Tel: 617-225-0857
www.NEHI.net

NEHTA (National E-Health Transition Authority)
(In 2015, NEHTA transitioned to a new entity called the Australian Digital Health Agency).

NHCAA (National Health Care Anti-Fraud Association)
Member organization open to private for-profit and not-for-profit healthcare reimbursement organizations (health insurers, managed care organizations, self-insured/self-administered organizations, third-party administrators, Medicare Program Safeguard Contractors [PSC]) interested in fighting against healthcare fraud.
1200 L Street, NW
Suite 600
Washington, DC 20005
Tel: 202-659-5955
www.nhcaa.org

NHIC (National Health Information Center)
A health information referral service sponsored by the Office of Disease Prevention and Health Promotion, Office of Public Health and Science, Office of the Secretary, and U.S. Department of Health and Human Services (HHS). NHIC links people to organizations that provide reliable health information.
U.S. Department of Health and Human Services
1101 Wootton Parkway, Suite LL100
Rockville, MD 20852
www.health.gov/nhic

NH-ISAC (National Health Information Sharing and Analysis Center)
A trusted community of critical infrastructure owners and operators within the Health Care and Public Health sector (HPH).
226 North Nova Road, Suite 391
Ormond Beach, Florida 32174
www.nhisac.org

NHIT (National Health IT Collaborative for the Underserved)
Nonprofit organization working to ensure that underserved populations are not left behind as health information technologies are developed and employed.
1629 K Street
Washington, DC 20006
www.nhitunderserved.org

NHLBI (National Heart, Lung, and Blood Institute)
The Institute, part of the National Institutes of Health, promotes the prevention and treatment of diseases of the heart, lungs, and blood.
Building 31, Room 5A52
31 Center Drive MSC 2486
Bethesda, MD 20892
Tel: 301-592-8573
www.nhlbi.nih.gov

NHS England (National Health Service)
Sets the priorities and direction of the national health services and encourage and inform the national debate to improve health and care.
P.O. Box 16738
Redditch, B97 9PT
Tel: 0300 311 22 33
www.england.nhs.uk

NIC (National Interoperability Collaborative)
An initiative with Stewards of Change Institute (SOCI) and AcademyHealth to increase collaboration among sectors that impact health and well-being by improving information sharing, interoperability, and use of technology.
www.nic-us.org

NIH (National Institutes of Health)
A part of the U.S. Department of Health & Human Services, NIH is the nation's medical research agency.
9000 Rockville Pike
Bethesda, MD 20892
www.nih.gov

NIHR (National Institute of Health Research)
An independent research center producing information about the effectiveness, costs, and broader impact of healthcare treatments and tests for those who plan, provide, or receive care in the National Health Service, U.K.
National Institute for Health Research
Room 132
Richmond House
79 Whitehall
London SW1A 2NS
www.nihr.ac.uk

NINR (National Institute of Nursing Research)
Institute, part of the National Institutes of Health, supports and conducts nursing and clinical research and research training on health and illness across the lifespan.
31 Center Drive
Room 5B03
Bethesda, MD 20892-2178
Tel: 301-496-0207
www.ninr.nih.gov

NIST (National Institute of Standards and Technology)
Federal agency responsible for advancing measurement science, standards, and technology to improve quality of life.
100 Bureau Drive
Gaithersburg, MD 20899-1070
Tel: 301-975-6478
TTY: 800-877-8339
www.nist.gov

NITRD (Networking and Information Technology Research and Development Program)
National program that provides a framework in which many federal agencies coordinate networking and information technology research and development efforts. Operates under the aegis of the NITRD Subcommittee of the National Science and Technology Council's (NSTC) Committee on Technology.
2415 Eisenhower Avenue
Alexandria, VA 22314
Tel: 202-459-9674
www.nitrd.gov

NKF (National Kidney Foundation)
A major health organization. NKF seeks to prevent kidney and urinary tract diseases, improve the health and well-being of individuals and families affected by these diseases, and increase the availability of all organs for transplantation.
30 East 33rd Street
New York, NY 10016
Toll free: 800-622-9010
www.kidney.org

NLM (National Library of Medicine)
NLM is the world's largest medical library. The library collects materials in all areas of biomedicine and healthcare, as well as works on biomedical aspects of technology, the humanities, and the physical, life, and social sciences. The collections stand at more than 9 million items—books, journals, technical reports, manuscripts, microfilms, photographs, and images. NLM is a national resource for all U.S. health science libraries through a National Network of Libraries of Medicine®.
8600 Rockville Pike
Bethesda, MD 20894
Tel: 301-594-5983
TTD: 800-735-2258
www.nlm.nih.gov

NLN (National League for Nursing)
A membership organization for nurse faculty and leaders in nursing education dedicated to excellence in nursing. Members include nurse educators, healthcare agencies, and interested members of the public.
2600 Virginia Avenue, NW
8th Floor
Washington, DC 20037
Toll free: 800-669-1656
www.nln.org

NOA (Nursing Organizations Alliance)
Membership is open to any nursing organization whose focus is to address current and emerging nursing and healthcare issues. Structural nursing components of a multidisciplinary organization are also welcome.
Tel: 859-514-9157
www.nursing-alliance.org

NOKC (Norwegian Knowledge Centre for Health Services)
Organized under the Norwegian Directorate of Health, product and services include systematic reviews, health economic evaluations, patient and user experience surveys, and other quality measurements to support the development of quality in the health services by summarizing research, promoting the use of research results, measuring the quality of health services, and working to improve patient safety.
Norwegian Institute of Public Health
P.O. Box 4404 Nydalen
0403 Oslo
N-0130 Oslo, Norway
Tel: +47 21 07 70 00
Fax: +47 22 35 36 05
https://www.fhi.no/sys/ks/

NPSF (National Patient Safety Foundation)
(In May 2017, the NPSF began working with IHI as one organization.)

NQF (National Quality Forum)
Private sector standard setting organization whose efforts center on the evaluation and endorsement of standardized performance measurement.
1030 15th Street, NW
Suite 800
Washington, DC 20005
Tel: 202-783-1300
www.qualityforum.org

NRHA (National Rural Health Association)
National nonprofit membership organization with the mission to provide leadership on rural health issues through advocacy, education, and research. NRHA membership consists of a diverse collection of individuals and organizations, all of whom share the common bond of an interest in rural health.
4501 College Boulevard
Leawood, KS 66211
Tel: 816-756-3140
www.ruralhealthweb.org

NRHRC (National Rural Health Resource Center)
Nonprofit organization that provides technical assistance, information, tools, and resources for the improvement of rural healthcare. It serves as a national rural health knowledge center and strives to build state and local capacity.
525 S. Lake Avenue
Suite 320
Duluth, MN 55802
Tel: 800-997-6685
www.ruralcenter.org

NSF (National Science Foundation)
An independent federal agency funding approximately 20 percent of all federally supported basic research conducted by America's colleges and universities. In many fields, such as mathematics, computer science, and the social sciences, NSF is the major source of federal backing.
2415 Eisenhower Avenue
Alexandria, VA 22314
Tel: 703-292-5111
www.nsf.gov

NTCA – The Rural Broadband Association
Association representing independent, community-based telecommunications companies that are leading innovation in rural and small-town America.
4121 Wilson Boulevard, Suite 1000
Arlington, VA 22203
www.ntca.org

NUBC (National Uniform Billing Committee)
Goal is to achieve administrative simplification as outlined in HIPAA. Membership includes national provider and payer organizations. Recently, the NUBC increased its membership to include the public health sector as well as the electronic standard development organization. NUBC maintains the integrity of the UB-92 data set.
c/o American Hospital Association
155 North Wacker Drive, Suite 400
Chicago, IL 60606
Tel: 312-422-3000
www.nubc.org

NUCC (National Uniform Claim Committee)
A voluntary organization comprised of key parties affected by healthcare electronic data interchange (EDI), generally payers and providers. Criteria for membership include a national scope and representation of a unique constituency affected by healthcare EDI, with an emphasis on maintaining or enhancing the provider/payer balance.
www.nucc.org

OASIS (Advancing Open Standards for the Information Society)
Open membership to ensure that all those affected by open standards have a voice in their creation.
35 Corporate Drive Suite 150
Burlington, MA 01803-4238
Tel: 781-425-5073
www.oasis-open.org

OMG (Object Management Group)
An international, open membership, not-for-profit computer industry consortium of government agencies, small and large information technology users, vendors, and research institutions. Any organization may join OMG and participate in the standards-setting process. OMG Task Forces develop enterprise integration standards for a wide range of technologies.
109 Highland Avenue
Needham, MA 02494
Tel: 781-444 0404
www.omg.org

ONC (Office of the National Coordinator for Health Information Technology)
The Office of the National Coordinator for Health Information Technology is the principal federal entity charged with coordination of nationwide efforts to implement and use the most advanced health information technology and the electronic exchange of health information. ONC is organizationally located within the Office of the Secretary for the U.S. Department of Health & Human Services.
U.S. Department of Health and Human Services
330 C Street SW
Floor 7
Washington, DC 20024
Tel: 202-690-7151
www.healthit.gov

ONS (Oncology Nursing Society)
A professional membership organization for registered nurses and other healthcare providers dedicated to excellence in patient care, education, research, and administration in oncology nursing.
125 Enterprise Drive
Pittsburgh, PA 15275
Tel: 412-859-6100
Toll free: 866-257-4ONS
www.ons.org

OSHA (Occupational Safety & Health Administration)
Part of the U.S. Department of Labor with responsibility to assure the safety and health of America's workers by setting and enforcing standards; providing training, outreach, and education; establishing partnerships; and encouraging continual improvement in workplace safety and health.
200 Constitution Avenue, NW
Washington, DC 20210
Toll free: 800-321-6742
TTY: 877-889-5627
www.osha.gov

Patient Safety Movement

Nonprofit organization working to confront the large-scale problem of more than 200,000 preventable patient deaths in U.S. hospitals each year by providing actionable ideas and innovations that can transform the process of care, dramatically improve patient safety, and help eliminate patient preventable deaths.

15776 Laguna Canyon Road
Irvine, CA 92618
Toll free: 877-236-0279
www.patientsafetymovement.org

Patientory Association

The Patientory Association is a global nonprofit healthcare member organization that connects healthcare industry adopters of disruptive healthcare technologies.

https://ptoy.org/

PCH Alliance (Personal Connected Health Alliance)

A non-profit organization formed by HIMSS that believes that health is personal and extends beyond healthcare. The Alliance mobilizes a coalition of stakeholders to realize the full potential of personal connected health.

www.pchalliance.org

PCORI (Patient-Centered Outcomes Research Institute)

An independent nonprofit, nongovernmental organization located in Washington, DC, authorized by Congress in 2010, focused on improving the quality and relevance of evidence available to help patients, caregivers, clinicians, employers, insurers, and policy makers make informed health decisions.

1828 L Street, NW, Suite 900
Washington, DC 20036
Tel: (202) 827-7700
www.pcori.org

PCPCC (Patient-Centered Primary Care Collaborative)

Organization dedicated to advancing primary care and the patient-centered medical home (PCMH) though activities to ensure innovations in care delivery, payment reform, benefit design, and patient engagement.

601 Thirteenth Street, NW
Suite 430 North
Washington, DC 20005
Tel: 202-417-2081
www.pcpcc.net

PEHRC (Physicians' EHR Coalition)
A coalition comprised of more than 20 medical societies representing more than 600,000 physicians, who share information to support the use of health information technology.
www.pehrc.org

Perio (American Academy of Peridontology)
Membership organization of periodontists and general dentists inside the United States and around the world.
737 N. Michigan Avenue
Suite 800
Chicago, IL 60611-6660
Tel: 312-787-5518
www.perio.org

Pharmacy HIT (Health Information Technology) Collaborative
Formed by 9 pharmacy professional associations representing over 250,000 members, the Pharmacy HIT Collaborative's vision and mission is for the U.S. healthcare system to be supported by the integration of pharmacists for the provision of quality patient care.
www.pharmacyhit.org

PHDSC (Public Health Data Standards Consortium)
A nonprofit membership-based organization representing stakeholders including federal, state, and local health agencies; professional associations; academia; public and private sector organizations; international members; and individuals with an interest in health information technology and population health.
111 South Calvert Street
Suite 2700
Baltimore, MD 21202
Tel: 410-385-5272
www.phdsc.org

PHI (Public Health Institute)
An independent, nonprofit organization that partners with foundations, federal and state agencies, and other nonprofit organizations to support a diverse array of research products and public health interventions.
555 12th Street
10th Floor
Oakland, CA 946075
Tel: 510-285-5500
www.phi.org

PHII (Public Health Informatics Institute)
A program of the Task Force for Global Health at the Centers for Disease Control and Prevention that works to improve health outcomes worldwide by transforming health practitioners' ability to apply information effectively. The Institute works with public health organizations, both domestically and internationally, through a variety of projects funded by government agencies and private foundations.
325 Swanton Way
Decatur, Georgia 30030
Toll free: 866-815-9704
www.phii.org

PhRMA (Pharmaceutical Research and Manufacturers Association)
Represents the country's leading biopharmaceutical research companies and supports the search for new treatments and cures.
950 F Street, NW
Suite 300
Washington, DC 20004
Tel: 202-835-3400
www.phrma.org

PMI (Project Management Institute)
Individual membership is open to anyone interested in project management.
14 Campus Boulevard
Newtown Square, PA 19073-3299
Tel: 610-356-4600
www.pmi.org

RCN (Royal College of Nursing)
Professional nursing body and union for nurses in the United Kingdom (UK).
20 Cavendish Square
London W1G 0RN
United Kingdom
Tel: +020 7409 3333
www.rcn.org.uk

Regenstrief Institute
An internationally recognized informatics and healthcare research organization. It is closely affiliated with the Indiana University School of Medicine, Roudebush VA Medical Center, and Wishard Health Services to improve health through research that enhances the quality and cost-effectiveness of healthcare.
1101 West 10th Street
Indianapolis, IN 46202
Tel: 317-270-9000
www.regenstrief.org

RSNA (Radiological Society of North America)
International physician membership organization of radiologists, medical physicists, and other medical professionals.
820 Jorie Boulevard
Oak Brook, IL 60523-2251
Tel: 630-571-2670
www.rsna.org

Savvy Cooperative
An organization that works to provide patients direct ways to share their experiences with health innovators, and advocates that they be fairly compensated for their contributions.
https://www.savvy.coop/

SBU (Swedish Agency for Health Technology Assessment and Assessment of Social Services)
Mandated by the Swedish government to comprehensively assess healthcare technology from medical, economic, ethical, and social standpoints.
P.O. Box 6183,
SE-102 33 Stockholm, Sweden
S:t Eriksgatan 117
Tel: +46 8 412 32 00
www.sbu.se/en

Scottsdale Institute
A not-for-profit membership organization of prominent healthcare systems whose goal is to support members as they move forward to achieve clinical integration and transformation through information technology.
7767 Elm Creek Boulevard North
Suite 208
Maple Grove, MN 55369
Tel: 763-710-7089
www.scottsdaleinstitute.org

The Sequoia Project
A non-profit, 501c3, public-private collaborative chartered to advance implementation of secure, interoperable nationwide health information exchange.
8300 Boone Boulevard, Suite 500
Vienna, VA, 22182
Tel: 571.327.3640
www.sequoiaproject.org

SGNA (Society of Gastroenterology Nurses and Associates)
A professional organization of nurses and associates dedicated to the safe and effective practice of gastroenterology and endoscopy nursing. SGNA carries out its mission by advancing the science and practice of gastroenterology and endoscopy nursing through education, research, advocacy, and collaboration, and by promoting the professional development of its members in an atmosphere of mutual support.
330 North Wabash Avenue
Suite 200
Chicago, IL 60611-7621
Tel: 312-321-5165
Toll free: 800-245-7462
Fax: 312-673-6694
www.sgna.org

SHIEC (Strategic Health Information Exchange Collaborative)
A national collaborative representing health information exchanges (HIEs) representing 60 HIEs, which collectively cover more than 200 million people across the U.S.
744 Horizon Court
Suite 210
Grand Junction, CO 81506
Toll free: 877-MY-SHIEC
www.strategichie.com

SHS (Society for Health Systems)
Membership association for productivity and efficiency professionals specializing in industrial engineering, healthcare, ergonomics, and other related professions.
3577 Parkway Lane
Suite 200
Norcross, GA 30092
Tel: 770-449-0460
Toll free: 800-494-0460
www.iise.org/shs/

SIIM (Society for Imaging Informatics in Medicine)
Membership open to anyone with an interest in the vital and growing field of medical imaging informatics and image management.
19440 Golf Vista Plaza
Suite 330
Leesburg, VA 20176-8264
Tel: 703-723-0432
www.siim.org

SIMGHOSTS
Nonprofit organization dedicated to supporting individuals and institutions operating medical simulation technology and spaces through hands-on training events, online resources, and professional development.
3870 E Flamingo Road
Las Vegas, NV 89121
Tel: 702-763-3457
www.simghosts.org

SIR (Society of Interventional Radiology)
Membership organization for individuals who have a special interest in interventional radiology inside and outside the United States.
3975 Fair Ridge Drive
Suite 400 North
Fairfax, VA 22033
Tel: 703-691-1805
Toll free: 800-488-7284
www.sirweb.org

SNOMED International
A not-for-profit organization that owns, administers, and develops SNOMED–CT, a clinical terminology created by a range of healthcare specialists to support clinical decision-making and analytics in software programs.
One Kingdom Street, Paddington Central
London W2 6BD, United Kingdom
Tel: +44 (0) 203 755 0974
www.snomed.org

SNRS (Southern Nursing Research Society)
Membership organization for registered professional nurses, non-nurses, corporations, and institutions interested in promoting nursing research.
10200 W. 44th Avenue
Suite 304
Wheat Ridge, CO 80033
Tel: 303-327-7548
Toll free: 877-314-SNRS
www.snrs.org

SOCI (Stewards of Change Institute)
A national nonprofit organization that provides catalytic leadership to inspire and initiate transformational change in health and human services.
100 Centershore Road
Centerport, NY 11721
Tel: 631-385-9246
www.stewardsofchange.org

Society for Participatory Medicine
Not-for-profit organization devoted to promoting the concept of participatory medicine, a movement in which patients shift from being mere passengers to responsible drivers of their health, and in which providers encourage and value them as full partners.
P.O. Box 1183
Newburyport, MA 01950-1183
www.participatorymedicine.org

Springboard Enterprises
Nonprofit network of innovators, investors and influencers who are dedicated to building high-growth technology-oriented companies led by women.
2100 Foxhall Road NW
Washington, DC 20007
www.sb.co

TAANA (The American Association of Nurse Attorneys)
Membership association of nurse attorneys.
3416 Primm Lane
Birmingham, AL 35216
Tel: 205-824-7615,
Toll free: 877-538-2262
www.taana.org

TIGER Initiative (Technology Informatics Guiding Education Reform)
An initiative focused on education reform and interprofessional community
development to maximize the integration of technology and informatics into
seamless practice, education, and research resource development.
33 West Monroe Street
Suite 1700
Chicago, IL 60603-5616
Tel: 312-664-4467
www.himss.org/professional-development/tiger-initiative

TNA (Transplant Nurses' Association)
Membership organization to advance the education of nurses and allied
health professionals involved in the transplant process.
P.O. Box M94
Missenden Road
NSW 2050
Australia
Tel: 08 9336 3178
www.tna.asn.au

UNECE (United Nations Economic Commission for Europe)
Aims to promote pan-European economic integration with 56 member states
in Europe, North America, and Asia.
Palais des Nations, Office 363
CH - 1211
Geneva 10
Switzerland
Tel: +41 (0) 22 917 12 34
http://www.unece.org/

VA (Department of Veterans Affairs); Veterans Health Administration
Comprehensive system of assistance to serve our nation's veterans and their
families.
810 Vermont Avenue, NW
Washington, DC 20420
Toll free: 800-827-1000
www.va.gov

VNAA (Visiting Nurse Associations of America)
Membership organization for nonprofit, free-standing home health and/or hospice providers, organizations that provide or promote home healthcare and/or hospice-related services, and individuals who wish to stay connected and advance nonprofit home healthcare and hospice.
1800 Diagonal Road
Suite 600
Alexandria, VA 22314
Tel: 571-527-1520
Toll free: 888-866-8773
www.vnaa.org

W3C (World Wide Web Consortium)
An international community where member organizations, a full-time staff, and the public work together to develop Web standards. The W3C mission is to lead the World Wide Web to its full potential by developing protocols and guidelines that ensure the long-term growth of the Web.
W3C/MIT
32 Vassar Street
Room 32-G515
Cambridge, MA 02139 USA
Contact Information for non-US locations on website
www.w3.org

WEDI (Workgroup for Electronic Data Interchange)
Membership organization actively seeking membership of all key parties in healthcare to ensure broad representation from throughout the healthcare community including individuals, providers, health plans, hybrid organizations (formerly mixed provider/health plan), government organizations, standards organizations, vendors, not-for-profit, and affiliates/regional entities.
4401A Connecticut Ave, NW
Suite 205
Washington, DC 20008
Tel: 202-480-2909
www.wedi.org

WHO (World Health Organization)
The directing and coordinating authority for health within the United Nations system. It is responsible for providing leadership on global health matters, shaping the health research agenda, setting norms and standards, articulating evidence-based policy options, providing technical support to countries, and monitoring and assessing health trends.
Avenue Appia 20
1211 Geneva 27
Switzerland
Tel: +41 22 791 21 11
www.who.int

WEGO Health
A mission-driven company connecting healthcare with the experience, skills and insights of Patient Leaders. WEGO Health is the world's largest network of over 100,000 Patient Leaders, working across virtually all health conditions and topics. The network collaborates with pharmaceutical and life sciences companies, agencies, consultancies, startups and all types of organizations across healthcare.
50 Milk Street
16th Floor
Boston, MA 02109
https://www.wegohealth.com/

Appendix B: Healthcare IT Related Credentials

Certifications, Degrees, Professional Fellowships, Honors Designations

I. Certifications

Credential	Full Name	Organization Acronym	Organization Full Name
ACNP-BC	Acute Care Nurse Practitioner	ANCC	American Nurses Credentialing Center
ACNPC	(Adult) Acute Care Nurse Practitioner	AACN	American Association of Critical-Care Nurses Certification Corporation
ACNPC-AG	(Adult-Gerontology) Acute Care Nurse Practitioner	AACN	American Association of Critical-Care Nurses Certification Corporation
ACNS-BC	Adult Health Clinical Nurse Specialist	ANCC	American Nurses Credentialing Center
AGACNP	Adult-Gerontology Acute Care Nurse Practitioner	ANCC	American Nurses Credentialing Center
AGCNS-BC	Adult-Gerontology Clinical Nurse Specialist	ANCC	American Nurses Credentialing Center

Credential	Full Name	Organization Acronym	Organization Full Name
A-GNP	Adult-Gerontology Primary Care Nurse Practitioner	AANPCP	American Academy of Nurse Practitioners Certification Program
AGPCNP-BC	Adult-Gerontology Primary Care Nurse Practitioner	ANCC	American Nurses Credentialing Center
ANP-C	Adult Nurse Practitioner Certified	AANP	American Academy of Nurse Practitioners
ANP-BC	Adult Nurse Practitioner, Board Certified	ANCC	American Nurses Credentialing Center
AOCN	Advanced Oncology Certified Nurse	ONCC	Oncology Nursing Certification Corporation
AOCNP	Advanced Oncology Certified Nurse Practitioner	ONCC	Oncology Nursing Certification Corporation
AOCNS	Advanced Oncology Certified Clinical Nurse Specialist	ONCC	Oncology Nursing Certification Corporation
APHN-BC	Advanced Practice Holistic Nurse, Board Certified	AHNCC	American Holistic Nurses Credentialing Corporation
BB	Technologist in Blood Banking	ASCP BOC	American Society for Clinical Pathology Board of Certification
BC	Board Certified	ANCC	American Nurses Credentialing Center
BC-ADM	Board Certified Advanced Diabetes Management	AADE	American Association of Diabetes Educators
CAHIMS	Certified Associate in Healthcare Information and Management Systems	HIMSS	Healthcare Information and Management Systems Society

Credential	Full Name	Organization Acronym	Organization Full Name
CAP	Certification and Accreditation Professional	(ISC)^2	International Information Systems Security Certification Consortium
CAPM	Certified Associate in Project Management	PMI	Project Management Institute
CCA	Certified Coding Associate	AHIMA	American Health Information Management Association
CCC-A	Certificate of Clinical Competence, Audiology	ASHA	American Speech-Language-Hearing Association
CCC-SLP	Certificate of Clinical Competence, Speech-Language Pathology	ASHA	American Speech-Language-Hearing Association
CCHT	Certified Clinical Hemodialysis Technician	NNCC	Nephrology Nursing Certification Commission
CCHT-A	Certified Clinical Hemodialysis Technician, Advanced	NNCC	Nephrology Nursing Certification Commission
CCM	Certified Case Manager	CCMC	Commission for Case Manager Certification
CCMHC	Certified Clinical Mental Health Counselor	NBCC	National Board for Certified Counselors
CCRA	Certified Clinical Research Associate	ACRP	Association of Clinical Research Professionals
CCRC	Certified Clinical Research Coordinator	ACRP	Association of Clinical Research Professionals

Credential	Full Name	Organization Acronym	Organization Full Name
CCRN	Critical Care Registered Nurse	AACN	American Association of Critical-Care Nurses
CCS	Certified Coding Specialist	AHIMA	American Health Information Management Association
CCS-P	Certified Coding Specialist, Physician-Based	AHIMA	American Health Information Management Association
CDE	Certified Diabetes Educator	NCBDE	National Certification Board for Diabetes Educators
CDIP	Certified Documentation Improvement Practitioner	AHIMA	American Health Information Management Association
CDIP	Certified DICOM Integration Professional	PARCA	PACS Administrators Registry and Certification Association
CERT	Community Emergency Response Team	FEMA	Federal Emergency Management Agency
CGRN	Certified Gastroenterology Registered Nurse	ABCGN	American Board of Certification for Gastroenterology Nurses
CHCIO	Certified Healthcare CIO	CHIME	College of Healthcare Information Management Executives
CHDA	Certified Health Data Analyst	AHIMA	American Health Information Management Association

Credential	Full Name	Organization Acronym	Organization Full Name
CHFM	Certified Healthcare Facility Manager	AHA-CC	American Hospital Association Credentialing Center
CHFP	Certified Healthcare Financial Professional	HFMA	Healthcare Financial Management Association
CHPCA	Certified Hospice and Palliative Care Administrator	HPCC	Hospice and Palliative Credentialing Center
CHPS	Certified in Healthcare Privacy and Security	AHIMA	American Health Information Management Association
CHTS	Certified Healthcare Technology Specialist	AHIMA	American Health Information Management Association
CIC	Certification in Infection Control	CBIC	Certification Board of Infection Control and Epidemiology
CIIP	Certified Imaging Informatics Professional	SIIM	Society for Imaging Informatics in Medicine
CISA	Certified Information Systems Auditor	ISACA	Information Systems Audit and Control Association
CISM	Certified Information Security Manager	ISACA	Information Systems Audit and Control Association
CISSP	Certified Information Systems Security Professional	(ISC)^2	International Information Systems Security Certification Consortium
CSSBB	Certified Lean Six Sigma Black Belt	ASQ	American Society for Quality or other certified credentialing body

Credential	Full Name	Organization Acronym	Organization Full Name
CSSGB	Certified Lean Six Sigma Green Belt	ASQ	American Society for Quality or other certified credentialing body
CM	Certified Midwife	AMCB	American Midwifery Certification Board
CMA	Certified Management Accountant	IMA	Institute of Management Accountants
CMAS	Certification of Medical Auditors	CCMA	Council for Certification of Medical Auditors, Inc.
CNM	Certified Nurse Midwife	AMCB	American Midwifery Certification Board
CNS	Clinical Nurse Specialist	AACN	American Association of Critical-Care Nurses Certification Corporation
COTA	Certified Occupational Therapy Assistant	NBCOT	National Board for Certification in Occupational Therapy
CPA	Certified Public Accountant	AICPA	American Institute of Certified Public Accountants
CPAS	Certified PACS Associate	PARCA	PACS Administrators Registry and Certification Association
CPC	Certified Professional Coder	AAPC	American Academy of Professional Coders
CPEHR*	Certified Professional in Electronic Health Records	HITC	Health IT Certification

Credential	Full Name	Organization Acronym	Organization Full Name
CPHI	Certified Professional in Health Informatics	AHIMA	American Health Information Management Association
CPHIMS	Certified Professional in Healthcare Information and Management Systems	HIMSS	Healthcare Information and Management Systems Society
CPHIMS-CA	Certified Professional in Healthcare Information and Management Systems, Canada	HIMSS	Healthcare Information and Management Systems Society
CPHIT*	Certified Professional in Health Information Technology	HITC	Health IT Certification
CPHQ	Certified Professional in Healthcare Quality	NAHQ	National Association for Healthcare Quality
CPhT	Certified Pharmacy Technician	PTCB	Pharmacy Technician Certification Board
CPNP-PC	Certified Pediatric Nurse Practitioner, Primary Care	PNCB	Pediatric Nurse Certification Board
CPNP-AC	Certified Pediatric Nurse Practitioner, Acute Care	PNCB	Pediatric Nursing Certification Board
CPSA	Certified PACS System Analyst	PARCA	PACS Administrators Registry and Certification Association
CRNA	Certified Registered Nurse Anesthetist	AANA	American Association of Nurse Anesthetists

Credential	*Full Name*	*Organization Acronym*	*Organization Full Name*
CRNFA	Certified Registered Nurse First Assistant	CCI	Competency and Credentialing Institute of the Association of Perioperative Nurses
CRT	Certified Respiratory Therapist	NBRC	National Board for Respiratory Care
CSP	Certified Specialty Pharmacist	SPCB	Specialty Pharmacy Certification Board
CT	Cytotechnologist	ASCP BOC	American Society for Clinical Pathology Board of Certification
FACHE	Fellow of the American College of Healthcare Executives	ACHE	American College of Healthcare Executives
FNP	Family Nurse Practitioner	ANCC AANPCP	American Nurses Credentialing Center, American Academy of Nurse Practitioners Certification Program
GCNS	Gerontological Nurse Practitioner	ANCC	American Nurses Credentialing Center
GNP	Gerontological Clinical Nurse Specialist	ANCC	American Nurses Credentialing Center
HCISPP	Healthcare Certified Information Security Privacy Practitioner	(ISC)^2	International Information Systems Security Certification Consortium
ISSAP	Information Systems Security Architecture Professional	(ISC)^2	International Information Systems Security Certification Consortium

Credential	Full Name	Organization Acronym	Organization Full Name
ISSEP	Information Systems Security Engineering Professional	(ISC)²	International Information Systems Security Certification Consortium
ISSMP	Information Systems Security Management Professional	(ISC)²	International Information Systems Security Certification Consortium
MT (ASCP)	Certified Medical Technologist	ASCP, ABOR	American Society for Clinical Pathology, American Association of Bioanalysts Board of Registry
NNP-BC	Neonatal Nurse Practitioner, Board Certified	NCC	National Certification Corporation
NP-C	Nurse Practitioner, Certified	AANPCP	American Academy of Nurse Practitioners Certification Program
OTR	Occupational Therapist Registered	NBCOT	National Board for Certification in Occupational Therapy
PA-C	Physician Assistant, Certified	NCCPA	National Commission on the Certification of Physician Assistants
PCNS	Pediatric Clinical Nurse Specialist	ANCC	American Nurses Credentialing Center
PfMP	Portfolio Management Professional	PMI	Project Management Institute
PgMP	Program Management Professional	PMI	Project Management Institute

Credential	*Full Name*	*Organization Acronym*	*Organization Full Name*
PHCNS-BC	Public/Community Health Clinical Nurse Specialist	ANCC	American Nurses Credentialing Center
PMHCNS-BC	Adult Psychiatric-Mental Health Clinical Nurse Specialist, Board Certified	ANCC	American Nurses Credentialing Center
PMHCNS-BC	Child/Adolescent Psychiatric-Mental Health Clinical Nurse Specialist, Board Certified	ANCC	American Nurses Credentialing Center
PMHNP	Psychiatric-Mental Health Nurse Practitioner	ANCC	American Nurses Credentialing Center
PMI-ACP	PMI-Agile Certified Practitioner	PMI	Project Management Institute
PMI-PBA	PMI Professional in Business Analysis	PMI	Project Management Institute
PMI-RMP	PMI Risk Management Professional	PMI	Project Management Institute
PMI-SP	PMI Scheduling Professional	PMI	Project Management Institute
PMP	Project Management Professional	PMI	Project Management Institute
PNP	Pediatric Nurse Practitioner	ANCC	American Nurses Credentialing Center
RN-BC	Registered Nurse, Board Certified	ANCC	American Nurses Credentialing Center
RNC	Registered Nurse, Certified	NCC	National Certification Corporation
SANE-A	Sexual Assault Nurse Examiner, Adult/Adolescent	IAFN	International Association of Forensic Nurses

Credential	Full Name	Organization Acronym	Organization Full Name
SANE-P	Sexual Assault Nurse Examiner, Pediatric	IAFN	International Association of Forensic Nurses
SNP-BC	School Nurse Practitioner	ANCC	American Nurses Credentialing Center
SSCP	Systems Security Certified Practitioner	$(ISC)^2$	International Information Systems Security Certification Consortium

*This credential will sunset December 31, 2018.

II. Degrees

Designation	Full Name
AA	Associate of Arts
AAA	Associate of Applied Arts
AAB	Associate of Applied Business
AAS	Associate of Applied Science
AAS (R)	Associate of Applied Sciences in Radiography
AAS/ADN	Associate of Applied Science/Associate Degree Nursing
AAT	Associate in Applied Technology, Associate of Arts in Teaching
AB	Associate of Business
ABA	Associate of Business Administration
ABS	Associate in Business Science
ADN	Associate Degree in Nursing
AHS	Associate of Health Science
AIM	Applied Information Management

Designation	Full Name
ALA	Associate of Liberal Arts
AOT	Associate in Occupational Technology
APRN	Advance Practice Registered Nurse
APT	Associate in Physical Therapy
ARM	Associate in Risk Management
AS, ASc	Associate of Science
ASCIS	Associate of Science in Computer Information Systems
ASCNT	Associate of Science in Computer Network Technology
ASDH	Associate of Science in Dental Hygiene
ASMA	Associate of Science in Medical Assisting
ASN	Associate of Science in Nursing
ASPT	Associate of Science in Physical Therapy
ASR	Associate of Science in Radiography
ASW	Associate Clinical Social Worker
AT	Associate of Technology
ATR	Art Therapist Registered
AuD	Doctor of Audiology
AyD	Doctor of Ayurvedic Medicine
B Comm	Bachelor of Commerce
BA	Bachelor of Arts
BABA	Bachelor of Arts of Business Administration
BAC	Baccalaureate Addictions Counselor
BAE, BAEd	Bachelor of Arts in Education
BAS	Bachelor of Applied Science
BBA	Bachelor in Healthcare or Business Administration

Designation	Full Name
BBE	Bachelor of Biosystems Engineering
BD	Bachelor of Divinity
BDS	Bachelor of Dental Surgery
BDSc	Bachelor of Dental Science
BE	Bachelor of Education
BHS	Bachelor of Health Science
BHSA	Bachelor of Health Service Administration
BLD	Bioanalyst Laboratory Director
BMT	Bachelor of Medical Technology
BN	Bachelor of Nursing
BOT	Bachelor of Occupational Therapy
BPH	Bachelor of Public Health
BPharm	Bachelor of Pharmacy
BPHS	Bachelor of Professional Health Science
BPod	Bachelor of Podiatry
BPT	Bachelor of Physical Therapy
BS, BSc	Bachelor of Science
BSBA	Bachelor of Science in Business Administration
BSBME	Bachelor of Science in Biomedical Engineering
BScN, BSN	Bachelor of Science in Nursing
BSCS	Bachelor of Science in Computer Science
BSEd	Bachelor of Science in Education
BSHCA	Bachelor of Science in Healthcare Administration
BSMicr	Bachelor of Science in Microbiology
BSPT	Bachelor of Science in Physical Therapy

Designation	Full Name
BSRT	Bachelor of Science in Radiography
BSSW	Bachelor of Science in Social Work
BSW	Bachelor of Social Work
BSwE	Bachelor of Software Engineering
BTh, ThB	Bachelor of Theology
BVSC	Bachelor of Veterinary Science
CCC	Certificate of Clinical Competency
D	Diploma
DA	Doctor of Arts
DAOM	Doctor of Acupuncture and Oriental Medicine
DBA	Doctor of Business Administration
DC	Doctor of Chiropractic
DCH	Doctor of Clinical Hypnotherapy
DCL	Doctor of Cannon Law, Doctor of Civil Law
DCLS	Doctor of Clinical Lab Science
DD	Doctor of Divinity
DDM	Doctor of Dental Medicine
DDS	Doctor of Dental Surgery
DEd	Doctor of Education
DHM	Doctor of Homeopathic Medicine
DIS	Doctor of Information Security
DM	Doctor of Management, Doctor of Music
DMA	Doctor of Musical Arts
DMD	Doctor of Dental Medicine, Doctor of Medical Dentistry
DMin	Doctor of Ministry

Designation	Full Name
DMT	Doctor of Medical Technology
DNE	Doctor of Nursing Education
DNP	Doctor of Nursing Practice
DNS, DNSc, DSN, DScN	Doctor of Nursing Science
DO	Doctor of Ostheopathy
DOS	Doctor of Ocular Science, Doctor of Optical Science
DP	Doctor of Podiatry
DPH, DrPH	Doctor of Public Health
DPhC	Doctor of Pharmaceutical Chemistry
DPM	Doctor of Podiatric Medicine
DPT	Doctor of Physical Therapy
Dr	Doctor
DrPH	Doctor of Public Health
DS, DSc, ScD, SD	Doctor of Science
DSC	Doctor of Surgical Chiropody
DScD	Doctor of Science in Dentistry
DScPT	Doctor of Science in Physical Therapy
DSCS	Doctorate of Science in Computer Science
DSP	Doctor of Surgical Podiatry
DSSc	Doctor of Social Science
DSTh, STD	Doctor of Sacred Theology
DSW	Doctor of Social Welfare, Doctor of Social Work
DTh, ThD	Doctor of Theology
DVM	Doctor of Veterinary Medicine
EdD	Doctor of Education

Designation	*Full Name*
EdS	Education Specialist
JD	Doctor of Laws, Doctor of Jurisprudence, Juris Doctor
LAC, LicAc	Licensed Acupuncturist
LACMH	Licensed Associate Counselor of Mental Health
LCPC	Licensed Clinical Professional Counselor
LCSW	Licensed Clinical Social Worker
LD	Licensed Dietician
LDTC	Learning Disabilities Teacher Consultant
LL	Bachelor of Laws
LLD	Doctor of Laws
LLM	Master of Laws
LMFC	Licensed Marriage Family Counselor
LMFT	Licensed Marriage/Family Therapist
LPC	Licensed Professional Counselor
LPN	Licensed Practical Nurse
LSW	Licensed Social Worker
LVN	Licensed Vocational Nurse
MA	Master of Arts
MAC	Master of Acupuncture, Master Addictions Counselor
MAEd	Master of Arts in Education
MAGD	Master of Academy of General Dentistry
MAcOM	Master of Acupuncture and Oriental Medicine
MAT	Master of Arts in Teaching
MBA	Master of Business Administration

Designation	Full Name
MC	Master of Counseling
MCAT	Master of Creative Arts in Therapy
MCD	Master of Communication Disorders
MCS	Master of Computer Science
MD	Doctor of Medicine
MDiv	Master of Divinity
MDS	Master of Dental Surgery, Master of Dental Science
MEd	Master of Education
MFT	Marriage and Family Therapist, Master of Family Therapy
MHA	Master of Health Administration
MHS	Master of Health Science, Masters in Human Services
MHSA	Master of Health Services Administration
MISM	Master of Information Systems Management
MN	Master of Nursing
MNA	Master of Nurse Anesthesia
MNS	Master of Nutrition Science
MP	Master of Psychotherapy
MPH	Master of Public Health
MPharm	Master of Pharmacy
MRad	Master of Radiology
MRC	Master of Rehabilitation Counseling
MS/MSc	Master of Science
MSBME	Master of Science in Biomedical Engineering
MSBMS	Master of Science in Basic Medical Sciences
MSC	Master of Science in Counseling

Designation	Full Name
MSCIS	Master of Science in Computer Information Systems
MSCS	Master of Science in Computer Science
MSD	Master of Science in Dentistry
MSFS	Master of Science in Forensic Science
MSHA	Master of Science in Health Administration
MSHI	Master of Science in Health Informatics
MSIS	Master of Science in Information Systems
MSN	Master of Science in Nursing
MSOT	Master of Science in Occupational Therapy
MSPAS	Master of Science in Physician Assistant Studies
MSPH	Master of Science in Public Health
MSRD	Master of Science Registered Dietician
MSS	Master of Social Science, Master of Social Service
MSSE	Master of Science in Software Engineering
MSSLP	Master of Science in Speech Language Pathology
MSW	Master of Social Work
MSwE	Master of Software Engineering
MTh	Master of Theology
MusD, DMus	Doctor of Music
ND	Doctor of Naturopathy
NP	Nurse Practitioner
OD	Doctor of Optometry
OT, OTR	Occupational Therapist, Occupational Therapist Registered

Designation	Full Name
PA	Physician Assistant
PharmD	Doctor of Pharmacy
PhB	Bachelor of Philosophy
PhD	Doctor of Philosophy
PsyD	Doctor of Psychology
PsyM	Master of Psychology
PT	Physical Therapist, Physiotherapist
PTA	Physical Therapy Assistant
RD	Registered Dietician
RDA	Registered Dental Assistant
RDH	Registered Dental Hygienist
RDN	Registered Dietician Nutritionist
RMA	Registered Medical Assistant
RN	Registered Nurse
RNA	Registered Nursing Assistant
RNBSN	Registered Nurse Bachelor of Science Nursing
RNC	Registered Nurse Certified
RNMSN	Registered Nurse Master of Science Nursing
RPh	Registered Pharmacist
RRA	Registered Radiology Assistant
RRT	Registered Respiratory Therapist, Registered Radiologic Technologist
RT	Registered Technologist, Radiological Technologist, Respiratory Therapist
SLP	Speech Language Pathologist
SScD	Doctor of Social Science
STB	Bachelor of Sacred Theology

III. Professional Fellowships/ Honors Designations

Designation	Full Name
FAAFP	Fellow of the American Academy of Family Physicians
FAAN	Fellow of the American Academy of Nursing
FACC	Fellow of the American College of Cardiology
FACEP	Fellow of the American College of Emergency Physicians
FACHE	Fellow of the American College of Healthcare Executives
FACMI	Fellow of the American College of Medical Informatics
FACMPE	Fellow of the American College of Medical Practice Executives
FACP	Fellow of the American College of Physicians
FAMIA	Fellow of the American Medical Informatics Association
FASCP	Fellow of the American Society of Clinical Pathologists
FCAP	Fellow of the College of American Pathologists
FCHIME	Fellow of the College of Healthcare Information Management Executives
FHAPI	Honorary Fellow, Association for Pathology Informatics
FHFMA	Fellow of the Healthcare Financial Management Association
FHIMSS	Fellow of the Healthcare Information and Management Systems Society
FIEEE	Fellow of the Institute of Electrical and Electronics Engineers
FNLM	Friends of the National Library of Medicine
LCHIME	Lifetime College of Healthcare Information Management Executives

(Continued)

Designation	Full Name
LFHIMSS	Life Member and Fellow of the Healthcare Information and Management Systems Society
SHIMSS	Senior Member of the Healthcare Information and Management Systems Society
SMIEEE	Senior Member of the Institute of Electrical and Electronics Engineers

Acronyms

A

AA	Attribute authority
AAA	Authentication, authorization, and accounting
ABAC	Attribute-based access control
ABC	Activity-based costing
ABC codes	Alternative billing codes
ACA	Affordable Care Act
ACB	Authorized Certification Body (see ATCB)
ACDF	Access control decision function
ACG	Ambulatory care group
ACI	Access control information
ACID	Atomicity, consistency, isolation, and durability
ACK	General acknowledgment message
ACL	Access control list
ACO	Accountable care organization
AD	Active directory
AD	Addendum
ADE	Adverse drug event
ADG	Ambulatory diagnostic group
ADPAC	Automated data processing application coordinator
ADR	ADT response message
ADR	Adverse drug reaction
ADSL	Asymmetric digital subscriber line
ADT	Admission, discharge, and transfer
AE	Adverse event/adverse experience
AE Title	Application entity title
AEF	Access control enforcement function
AHC	Academic health center
AHT	Average handling time/average handle time
AI	Artificial intelligence
AIDC	Automatic identification and data capture

AIMS	Anesthesia information management system
AIS	Automated information system
ALOS	Average length of stay
ALU	Arithmetic logic unit
AMR	Ambulatory medical record
ANN	Artificial neuron network
APACHE	Acute physiology and chronic health evaluation
APC	Ambulatory payment class
APG	Ambulatory patient group
API	Application program interface
APMs	Alternative payment model
APT	Advanced persistent threat
ARI	Access to radiology information
ARP	Address resolution protocol
ARRA	American Recovery and Reinvestment Act of 2009
ASA	Average speed of answer
ASCII	American standard code for information interchange
ASN	Abstract syntax notation
ASO	Administrative services only
ASP	Active server pages
ATCB	Authorized testing and certification body
ATM	Asynchronous transfer mode
AUC	Appropriate use criteria
AUI	Attachment unit interface
AUP	Acceptable use policy
AVR	Analysis, visualization, and reporting

B

B2B	Business-to-business
B2B2C	Business-to-business-to-consumer
B2C	Business-to-consumer
BA	Business associate
BAN	Body area network
BASIC	Beginner's all-purpose symbolic instruction code
BAT	Filename extension for a batch file
BCMA	Bar code medication administration
BCP	Business continuity plan
BEC	Business email compromise
BH	Behavioral health
BHOM	Behavioral health outcome management
BIA	Business impact analysis

BIOS	Basic input output system
BLE	Bluetooth low energy
BPA	Blanket purchasing agreement
BPM	Business process management
BPS	Bits per second
BRE	Business rules engine
BRFSS	Behavioral Risk Factor Surveillance System
BTRIS	Biomedical Translational Research Information System
BYOC	Bring your own cloud
BYOD	Bring your own device

C

CA	Certificate authority
CA	Corrective action
CAD	Computer-aided detection
CAH	Critical-access hospital
CAL	Computer-assisted learning
CAP	Common alerting protocol
CAP	Corrective action plan
CASE	Computer-assisted software engineering
CAT	Computerized axial tomography
CATH	Cardiac catheterization workflow
CBL	Computer-based learning
CC	Chief Complaint
CCC	Clinical care classification
CCD	Continuity of care document
C-CDA	Consolidated clinical document architecture
CCDS	Common Clinical Data Set
CCO	Chief compliance officer
CCM	Chronic care management
CCMM	Continuity of Care Maturity Model
CCO	Chief compliance officer
CCR	Continuity of care record
CD	Committee draft
CD	Compact disk
CDA	Clinical document architecture
CDMA	Code division multiple access
CDPD	Cellular digital packet data
CDR	Clinical data repository / Clinical data registry
CD-ROM	Compact Disk, read only memory
CDS	Clinical decision support

CDS	Core Data Services
CDSS	Clinical decision support system
CDT	Current dental terminology
CDW	Clinical data warehouse
CE	Coded element
CEHRT	Certified EHR Technology
CEN	European Committee for Standardization
CERT	Computer emergency response team
CF	Conditional formatting/coded formatted element
CGI	Common gateway interface
CHAP	Challenge handshake authentication protocol
CHG	Charge posting
CHIP	Children's Health Insurance Program
C-HOBIC	Canadian Health Outcomes for Better Information and Care
CHPL	Certified Health IT Product List
CHV	Consumer health vocabulary initiative
CIA	Confidentiality/integrity/availability
CIO	Chief informatics officer
CIO	Chief information officer
CIS	Clinical information system
CISC	Complex instruction set computer processor
CM	Composite message/composite data type
CMD	Command
CMET	Common message element type
CMIO	Chief medical informatics officer
CMIO	Chief medical information officer
CMYK	Cyan, magenta, yellow, and black
CNCL	Canceled
CNIO	Chief nursing informatics officer
CNIO	Chief nursing information officer
COAS	Clinical observations access service
COB	Close of business
COB	Coordination of benefits
CORBA	Common object request broker architecture
COW	Computer-on-wheels
CP	Certificate policy
CPC	Comprehensive Primary Care Initiative
CPC+	Comprehensive Primary Care Plus Initiative
CPOE	Computerized practitioner order entry
CPR	Computer-based patient record
CPRS	Computer-based patient record system
CPS	Certification practices statement
CPT	Current procedural terminology

CPU	Central processing unit
CQL	Clinical Quality Language
CQM	Clinical quality measure
CRA	Countermeasure response administration
CRM	Customer relationship management
CRUD	Create, read, update, and delete
CSIRT	Computer Security Incident Response Team
CSMA/CD	Carrier sense multiple access with collision detection
CSO	Chief security officer
CSU/DSU	Channel sharing unit/data service unit
CT	Consistent time
CTI	Computer telephony integration
CTIO	Chief technology innovation officer
CTO	Chief technology officer
CTS	Common terminology services
CU	Control unit
CUI	Concept unique identifier
CVE	Common vulnerabilities and exposures
CVS	Concurrent versions system
CWE	Coded with exceptions
CWE	Common weakness enumeration
CxO	Corporate executives or C-level or C-Suite
CY	Calendar Year

D

DaaS	Data as a service
DAF	Data access framework
DAG	Directed acyclic graph
DApp	Decentralized application
DAM	Domain analysis model
DBA	Database administrator
DBMS	Database management system
DCM	Detailed clinical models
DCM	Dynamic case management
DDI	Design, develop, implement
DDL	Data definition language
DEEDS	Data elements for emergency department systems
DFD	Data flow diagram
DHCP	Data host configuration protocol
DI	Diagnostic imaging
DICOM	Digital imaging and communications in medicine

DLC	Data link control
DLL	Dynamic link library
DLT	Distributed ledger technology
DMA	Direct memory access
DME	Durable medical equipment
DML	Data manipulation language
DNS	Domain name server
DNSSEC	Domain name system security extension
DOS	Disk operating system
DPI	Dots per square inch
DRAM	Dynamic random access memory
DRG	Diagnosis related group
DS4P	Data segmentation for privacy
DSA	Digital signature algorithm
DSG	Document digital signature
DSL	Digital subscriber line
DSL	Domain-specific language
DSLAM	Digital subscriber line access multiplexer
DSM	Diagnostic and Statistical Manual of Mental Disorders
DSML	Directory services markup language
DSMO	Designated standard maintenance organization
DSRIP	Delivery System Reform Incentive Payment
DSSS	Direct sequence spread spectrum
DSTU	Draft standard for trial use
DSU	Data service unit
DSU/CSU	Data service unit/channel service unit
DT	Date data type (YYYY-MM-DD)
DTD	Document type definition
DTE	Data terminal equipment
DTR	Data terminal ready
DTR	Draft technical report
DUA	Data use agreement
DVD	Digital video disk or digital versatile disk

E

e-[text] or e-text	Electronic text
E-1	European digital signal
EAI	Enterprise application integration
EAP	Extensible authentication protocol
EAV	Entity-Attribute-Value
EBB	Eligibility-based billing

EBCDIC	Extended binary coded decimal interchange code
EC	Eligible clinician
EC	Electronic commerce
ECN	Explicit congestion notifier
eCQI	Electronic clinical quality improvement
eCQM	Electronic clinical quality measures
eCommerce	Electronic commerce
ED	Encapsulated data
ED	Evidence documents
EDC	Electronic data capture system
EDDS	Electronic document digital storage
EDI	Electronic data interchange
EDI gateway	Electronic data interchange gateway
EED	Early event detection
EDXL	Emergency data exchange language
EDXL–HAVE	Emergency data exchange language–hospital availability exchange
EEPROM	Electronically erasable programmable read-only memory
E-GOV	The "E-Government Act of 2002"
EHR	Electronic health record
EIDE	Enhanced or extended integrated drive electronics
EIN	Employer identification number
EIP	Enterprise information portal
EIS	Enterprise information system
eLTSS	Electronic long-term care support services
eMAR	Electronic medication administration record
EMC	Electronic media claims
EMI	Electromagnetic interference
EMPI	Enterprise master patient index
EMR	Electronic medical record
EMRAM	Electronic medical record adoption model
EMSEC	Emanations security
EN	European standard
ENP	European nursing care pathways
EOA	Enhanced Oversight Accountability Rule
EOB	Explanation of benefits
EOP	Explanation of payment
ePA	Electronic prior authorization
EPCS	Electronic prescriptions for controlled substances
ePHI	Electronic protected health information
ePHR	Electronic personal health record
ERA	Electronic remittance advice
ERD	Entity relationship diagram

ERDA	Emergency respond data architecture
ERISA	Employee Retirement Income and Security Act of 1975
ERP	Enterprise resource planning
ESS	Executive support system
ETL	Extraction, transformation, loading
EUA	Enterprise user authentication
EULA	End user license agreement
Extended ASCII	Extended American standard code for information interchange

F

FACA	Federal Advisory Committee Act
FAQ	Frequently asked questions
FAR	False acceptance rate
FCOE	Fiber channel over Ethernet
FDDI	Fiber distributed data interface
FFP	Federal financial participation
FFS	Fee-for-service
FHIR	Fast healthcare interoperability resources
FIFO	First in, first out
FIPS	Federal information processing standard
FISMA	Federal Information Security Management Act
FQDN	Fully qualified domain name
FQHC	Federally qualified health center
FTP	File transfer protocol

G

GB	Gigabyte
GBps	Gigabits per second
GDPR	General Data Protection Regulation
GELLO	Guideline expression language, object oriented
GIF	Graphics interchange format
GIG	Global information grid
GIGO	Garbage in, garbage out
GSM	Global system for mobile communications
GUDID	Global unique device identification database
GUI	Graphical user interface
GUID	Global unique identifier

H

HAN	Health alert network
HCPCS	Healthcare Common System Coding System
hData	A specification for exchanging electronic health data
HEDIS	Healthcare effectiveness data and information set
HIE	Health information exchange
HIEx	Health insurance exchange
HIO	Health information organization
HIPAA	Health Insurance Portability and Accountability Act of 1996
HIS	Health information system
HISP	Health information service provider
HIT	Health information technology
HITECH Act	Health Information Technology for Economic and Clinical Health Act
HITAC	Health Information Technology Advisory Committee
HL7	Health Level Seven
HQMF	Health Quality Measure Format
HTML	Hypertext markup language
HTTP	Hypertext transfer protocol
HTTPS	HTTP Secure
HUD	Heads-up display
Hz	Hertz

I

I/O	Input/output device
IAM	Identity access management
ICC	Integrated circuit chip
ICD	International Classification of Diseases
ICIDH	International Classification of Impairments, Disability, and Health
ICMP	Internet control message protocol
ICO	Initial coin offering
ICR	Intelligent call routing
ICR	Intelligent character recognition
ICU	Intensive care unit
IDM	Identity digital management
IDMS	Identity management system
IDN	Integrated delivery network
IDR	Intelligent document recognition
IDS	Integrated delivery system

IGP	Interior gateway protocol
IHE	Integrating the Healthcare Enterprise
IIF	Information in identifiable form
IIS	Immunization information systems
IIS	Internet information systems
IKE	Internet key exchange
ILD	Injection laser diode
iOS	iPhone operating system
IoT	Internet of things
IP	Internet protocol
IPA	Independent practice association
IPsec	Internet protocol security
IPX/SPX	Internetwork packet exchange/sequence packet exchange
IRC	Internet relay chat
IrDA	Infrared Data Association
IRM	Information resource management
IRQ	Interrupt request line
ISA	Interoperability Standards Advisory
ISDN	Integrated service digital network
ISO/TC 215	International Organization for Standardization (ISO) Technical Committee for Health Informatics
ISP	Internet service provider
ITMRA	Information Technology Management Reform Act
IVR	Interactive voice response

J

JAD	Joint application development
JCR	Joint Commission Resources
JFS	Journaling file system
JPEG	Joint photographic experts group
JSON	JavaScript Object Notation
JTC	Joint Technical Committee

K

KAS	Clinical Decision Support (CDS) Knowledge Artifact Specification
KB	Kilobyte
Kbps	Kilobits per second
KHz	Kilohertz

L

LAN	Learning and Action Network
LAN	Local area network
LASA	Look alike/sound alike
LAT	Local area transport
LDA	Latent Dirichlet allocation
LDAP	Lightweight directory access protocol
LDO	Large dialysis organization
LIFO	Last in, first out
LIP	Licensed independent practitioner
LIS	Laboratory information system
LLC	Logical link control
LOE	Level of effort
LOI	Letter of intent
LOINC	Logical observation identifiers names and codes
LOTO	Lock out/Tag out
LPDR	Longitudinal patient disease registries
LQS	Lexicon query service
LRI	Lab results interface
LSC	Life Safety Code
LTC	Long-term care
LTCF	Long-term care facility
LTPAC	Long-term and post-acute care
LTSS	Long-term services and support
LU	Logical unit
LUN	Logical unit number
LVT	Low-volume threshold
LWBS	Left without being seen

M

MAC	Mandatory access control
MAC	Message authentication code
MAC address	Media access control address
MACRA	Medicare Access and CHIP Reauthorization Act 2015
MAN	Metropolitan-area network
MAO	Maximum acceptable/allowable outage
MAU	Media access unit
Mb	Megabit
MBDS	Minimum basic data set
Mbps	Megabits per second

MDA	Model-driven architecture
MDI	Medical device interface
MDI-X port	Medium dependent interface crossover
MDM	Master data management
MDM	Medical document management message
MDM	Mobile device management
MDS	Minimum data set
MedDRA	Medical Dictionary for Regulatory Activities
MEDS	Minimum emergency data set
MeSH	Medical subject heading
mHealth	Mobile health
MHz	Megahertz
MIB	Medical information BUS
MIME	Multipurpose Internet mail extensions
MIPS	Merit-based incentive payment system
MIS	Management information system
MITA	Medicaid information technology architecture
MLM	Medical logic model
MMIS	Medicaid management information system
MOLAP	Multidimensional online analytical processing
MOU	Memorandum of understanding
MPEG	Motion picture expert group
MPI	Master patient index
MPP	Massively parallel processing
MSA	Master services agreement
MSAU	Multiple station access unit
MSO	Management service organizations
MTBF	Mean time between failures
MTTD	Mean time to diagnose
MTTR	Mean time to repair
MU	Meaningful use
MUX	Multiplexer, multipleXer, or multipleXor

N

NAC	Network access control/network admission control
NAS	Network attached storage
NAT	Network address translation
NCPDP	National Council for Prescription Drug Programs
NDC	National Drug Code
NDIS	Network driver interface specification
NEDSS	National Electronic Disease Surveillance System

NEMSIS	National Emergency Medical System (EMS) Information System
NFS	Network file system
NHII	Nationwide Health Information Infrastructure
NHRIC	National Health-Related Items Code
NIC	Network interface card
NIC	Nursing intervention classification
NLP	Natural language processing
NMB	National member body
NMDS	Nursing minimum data set
NMMDS	Nursing management minimum data set
NOC	Network operation center
NOC	Nursing outcome classification
NOI	Notice of intent
NPF	National provider file
NPI	National provider identifier
NSF	National standard format
NSP	Network service provider
NSSN	National standards system network
NUMA	Nonuniform memory architecture
NWIP	New work item proposal

O

OASIS	Outcome and Assessment Information Set
OAuth	Open Authorization
OC	Optical carrier
OCR	Optical character recognition
OCSP	Online certificate status protocol
ODA	Open document architecture
ODBC	Open Database Connectivity
ODS	Operational data store
OEID	Other entity identifier
OID	Object identifier
OLAP	Online analytical processing
OLE	Object linking and embedding
OLTP	Online transaction processing
OM	Outbreak management
OOA	Out of area
OON	Out of network
OOP	Object-oriented programming
OOP	Out of pocket

ORB	Object request broker
OS	Operating system
OSI	Open systems interconnection
OWL	Web ontology language

P

P2P	Peer-to-peer
PACS	Picture archiving and communication systems
PAN	Personal-area network
PAP	Password authentication protocol
PAS	Publicly available specification
PC	Personal computer
PCB	Printed circuit board
PCDH	Patient Centered Data Home™
PCDS	Patient care data set
PCMH	Patient-centered medical home
PCP	Primary care provider
PDC	Primary domain controller
PDF	Portable document format
PDMP	Prescription drug monitoring program
PDP	Policy decision point
PEP	Policy enforcement point
PHI	Protected health information
PHIN	Public health information network
PHIN-MS	Public health information network-messaging system
PHMT	Personal health management tool
PHR	Personal health record
PIDS	Person identification service
PIM	Platform independent model
PIN	Personal identification number
PING	Packet Internet groper
PIP	Policy information point
PIV	Personal identification verification
PIX	Patient identifier cross-referencing
PKC	Public key certificate
PKI	Public key infrastructure
PMP	Point-to-multipoint communication
PNDS	Perioperative nursing data set
PNG	Portable network graphics
POP3	Post office protocol
POP	Point-of-presence

POSIX	Portable open systems interface
PPACA	Patient Protection and Affordable Care Act
PPO	Preferred provider organization
PPP	Point-to-point protocol
PPTP	Point-to-point tunneling protocol
PRAM	Parameter RAM
PRG	Procedure-related group
PROM	Programmable read-only memory
PULSE	Patient Unified Lookup System for Emergencies
PVBM	Physician value-based modifier
PVC	Permanent virtual circuit

Q

QA	Quality assurance
QAPI	Quality assessment performance improvement
QASP	Quality assurance surveillance plan
QC	Quality control
QCDR	Qualified clinical data registry
QDM	Quality data model
QE	Quality entity
QHP	Qualified health plan
QI	Quality improvement
QIDAM	Quality improvement domain analysis model
QIIO	Quality improvement and innovation organization
QIN/QIO	Quality innovation network – Quality improvement organizations
QIO	Quality improvement organization
QMF	Query management facility
QMR	Quick medical reference
QMRT	Quality Measures Reporting Tool
QMS	Quality management system
QoS	Quality of service
QP	Qualified professional
QP	Qualifying APM participant
QPP	Quality Payment Program
QPS	Quality positioning system
QR codes	Quick response codes
QRDA	Quality reporting data architecture
QRUR	Quality and resource use report
QUICK	Quality information and clinical knowledge

R

RA	Registration authority
RAD	Rapid application development
RAID	Redundant array of independent disks
RAM	Random access memory
RAS	Remote access server
RBAC	Role-based access control
RDBMS	Relational database management system
RDF	Resource description framework
REC	Regional extension center
REST	Representational state transfer
RFI	Request for information
RFID	Radio frequency identification
RFP	Request for proposal
RGB	Red, green, blue color model
RHIO	Regional health information organization
RIM	Reference information model
RIS	Radiology information system
RISC	Reduced instruction set computer
RM	Records management
RMI	Remote method invocation
RM-ODP	Reference model for open distributed processing
RMON	Remote network monitor
ROI	Release of information
ROI	Return on investment
ROLAP	Relational online analytical processing
ROM	Read-only memory
RPO	Recovery point objective
RTF	Rich text format
RTLS	Real-time location service
RTM	Reference terminology model
RTO	Recovery time objective
RVU	Relative value unit

S

S/MIME	Secure MIME
SaaS	Software as a service
SAML	Security assertion markup language
SAN	Storage area network
SATA	Serial advanced technology application
SATAN	Security administrator tool for analyzing networks
SBAR	Situation–background–assessment–recommendation

SCOS	Smartcard operating system
SCSI	Small computer system interface
SCUI	Smartcard user interface
SDLC	System development lifecycle
SDO	Standards development organization
SDoH	Social determinants of health
SDXC	Secure digital extended capacity
SEC	Security
SET	Secure electronic transmission
SFTP	Secure file transport protocol
SGML	Standardized generalized markup language
SIG	Special interest group
SIMM	Single in-line memory module
SLIP	Serial line Internet protocol
SME	Subject matter expert
SMP	Symmetric multiprocessing
SMS	Short message service
SMTP	Simple mail transfer protocol
SNA	System network architecture
SNMP	Simple network monitoring protocol
SNMP	System network management protocol
SNOMED–CT	Systematized nomenclature of medicine–clinical terms
SOA	Service-oriented architecture
SOAP	Simple object access protocol
SONET	Synchronous optical network
SOP	Standard operating procedure
SOW	Statement of work
SPD	Summary plan description
SPOOL	Simultaneous peripheral operation online
SQL	Structured query language
SRAM	Static random access memory
SSH	Secure shell
SSL	Secure socket layer
SSO	Single sign-on
STP	Shielded twisted pair
SVC	Switched virtual circuit

T

TC	Technical committee
TCO	Total cost of ownership
TCP/IP	Transmission control protocol/Internet protocol
TDR	Time-domain reflectometer

TELNET	TELecommunications NETwork
TFTP	Trivial file transfer protocol
TGE	Token generation event
TIFF	Tagged image file format
TKIP	Temporal key integrity protocol
TLS	Transport layer security
TOC	Transitions of care
TPA	Third-party administrator

U

UART	Universal asynchronous receiver transmitter
UDDI	Universal description, discover, and integration
UDI	Unique device identifier
UDP	User datagram protocol
UI	User interface
UID	Unique identifier
UM	Utilization management
UMDNS	Universal medical device nomenclature system
UML	Unified modeling language
UMLS	Unified medical language system
UMS	Unified messaging system
UNC	Universal naming convention
UPI	Unique patient identifier
UPS	Uninterruptible power supply
URI	Uniform resource identifier
URL	Uniform resource locator
USB	Universal serial bus
USCDI	U.S. Core Data for Interoperability
USHIK	United States Health Information Knowledgebase
UTP	Unshielded twisted pair

V

VAN	Value-added network
VAX	Virtual address extension
VBC	Value-based care
VBID	Value-based insurance design
VBP	Value-based payment
VDT	View, download, transmit
VISN	Veterans Integrated Service Network
VistA	Veterans Health Information Systems Technology Architecture

VM	Value modifier
VM	Virtual machine
VMR	Virtual machine record
VoIP	Voice over Internet protocol
VPN	Virtual private network
VRAM	Video RAM or video random access memory
VRML	Virtual reality modeling language
VRS	Voice response system
VRU	Voice response unit
VSA	Virtual SAN appliance
VSM	Value stream mapping

W

WAN	Wide area network
WAP	Wireless application protocol
WASP	Wireless application service provider
WAV or WAVE	Waveform audio format (.wav)
WCF	Windows Communication Foundation
WEP	Wired equivalent privacy
WG	Work group
WI	Web interface
Wide SCSI	Wide small computer system interface
WLAN	Wireless local area network
WORM	Write once, read many times
WOW	Workstation on wheels
WPA	Wi-Fi protected access
WSDL	Web services description language
WWW	World Wide Web
WYSIWYG	What you see is what you get
WYSIWYP	What you see is what you print

X

XDS	Cross-enterprise document sharing
XML	Extensible markup language
XSL	Extensible stylesheet language

Z

ZLE	Zero latency enterprise

References

1. National Institute of Standards and Technology. Computer Security Resource Center. Available at: https://csrc.nist.gov/glossary. Last accessed July 2018.
2. TechTarget. Available at: whatis.techtarget.com. Last accessed April 2018.
3. How to Select a Practice Management System. American Medical Association. Available at: https://www.ama-assn.org/practice-management/how-select-practice-management-system. Last accessed September 2018.
4. Business Dictionary. Available at: www.businessdictionary.com. Last accessed April 2018.
5. *ANA Scope and Standards of Nursing Informatics Practice*, 2nd *Ed.*
6. IT Terminology. Available at: http://www.consp.com/it-information-technology-terminology-dictionary. Last accessed April 2018.
7. Wikipedia. Available at: www.wikipedia.org. Last accessed July 2018.
8. *The Free Online Dictionary of Computing. Available at:* http://foldoc.org/. *Denis* Howe, *Ed. Last accessed April* 2018.
9. Health Level Seven (HL7). Available at: http://www.hl7.org/. Last accessed July 2018.
10. HIMSS Analytics. Available at: www.himssanalytics.org. Last accessed April 2018.
11. Oracle. Available at: www.oracle.com. Last accessed April 2018.
12. Office of the National Coordinator for Health Information Technology (ONC). Available at: http://healthit.gov/. Last accessed July 2018.
13. Department of Homeland Security. Available at: www.dhs.gov. Last accessed April 2018.
14. Knowledge Base. Indiana University. Available at: https://kb.iu.edu/d/aiuv. Last accessed August 2018.
15. Explore Terms: A Glossary of Common Cybersecurity Terminology. NICCS. Available at: https://niccs.us-cert.gov/glossary. Last accessed April 2018.
16. IT Law Wiki. Available at: //itlaw.wikia.com/. Last accessed April 2018.
17. National Committee on Vital and Health Statistics (NCVHS). Available at: www.ncvhs.hhs.gov. Last accessed April 2018.
18. Investopedia. Available at: www.investopedia.com. Last accessed April 2018.
19. ANSI. American National Standards Institute. Available at: https://www.ansi.org. Last accessed July 2018.
20. Health Insurance Portability and Accountability Act (HIPAA). Available at: https://www.hipaa.com/. Last accessed July 2018.
21. CloudPatterns.org. Arcitura Education, Inc. Available at: http://www.cloudpatterns.org/. Last accessed July 2018.
22. ACHC. Available at: https://achc.org. Last accessed July 2018.

23. HCSC. Health Care Glossary. Available at: http://www.hcsc.com/glossary.html. Last accessed April 2018.
24. ISO/TS 22600-3. HealthCare Information Privilege Management & Access Control P-3 (terms only). Available at: www.iso.org. Last accessed April 2016.
25. Access Control Information. IBM. Available at: https://publib.boulder.ibm.com/tividd/td/ITIM/SC32-1149-02/en_US/HTML/im451_poag45.htm. Last accessed April 2018.
26. Centers for Medicare & Medicaid Services (CMS). Available at: www.cms.gov. Last accessed July 2018.
27. Integrating the Healthcare Enterprise. Available at: www.ihe.net. Last accessed April 2018.
28. American Health Information Management Association (AHIMA). Available at: www.ahima.org. Last accessed April 2018.
29. *Merriam Webster Dictionary*. Available at: www.merriam-webster.com. Last accessed July 2018.
30. Microsoft Docs. Microsoft Available at: https://docs.microsoft.com/en-us. Last accessed July 2018.
31. VA National Center for Patient Safety (NCPS). Available at: www.patientsafety.va.gov. Last accessed April 2018.
32. Office of Disease Prevent and Health Promotion. Available at: http://health.gov. Last accessed April 2018.
33. What is a background process? Unix & Linux. Available at: http://unix.stackexchange.com/questions/82934/what-is-a-background-process. Last accessed September 2018.
34. RACGP: Royal Australian College of General Practitioners (RACGP) RACGP College House, 1 Palmerston Crescent, South Melbourne, Victoria 3205.
35. U.S. Health and Human Services. Available at: www.hhs.gov. Last accessed April 2018.
36. International Organization for Standardization (ISO).1, ch. de la Voie-Creuse CP 56 CH-1211 Geneva 20, Switzerland. Available at: www.iso.org. Last accessed April 2018.
37. Vistapedia. Available at: http://vistapedia.net. Last accessed April 2018.
38. Venes, D. (2013) Taber's Cyclopedic Medical Dictionary, 22nd Edition. F.A. Davis Company.
39. Webopedia. Available at: www.webopedia.com. Last accessed August 2018.
40. Sengstack, P and Boicey, C. (2015) Mastering Informatics: A Healthcare Handbook for Success. Indianapolis: Sigma Theta Tau International.
41. Food and Drug Administration. Available at: http://www.fda.gov. Last accessed July 2018.
42. TermWiki. Available at: www.termwiki.com/EN:application_entity_title_%28AE_title%29. Last accessed April 2018.
43. Report on Uniform Data Standards for Patient Medical Record Information (2000). National Committee on Vital and Health Statistics (NCVHS). Available at: https://www.ncvhs.hhs.gov/wp-content/uploads/2014/08/hipaa000706.pdf. Last accessed July 2018.
44. Dictionary.com. Last accessed August 2018.
45. Pfleeger, C. and Pfleeger, S. (2003). *Security in Computing*. New Jersey: Pearson Education, Inc. 2003. Last accessed April 2018.
46. CIGNA. www.cigna.com. Last accessed August 2018.

47. Douglas, J. R., & Ritter, M. J. (2011). Implementation of an Anesthesia Information Management System (AIMS). *The Ochsner Journal*, 11(2), 102–114. Available at https://www.ncbi.nlm.nih.gov/pmc/articles/PMC3119212/.

48. Mastrian, K.G. and McGonigle, D. (2017). *Informatics for Health Professionals*. Burlington, MA: Jones & Bartlett Learning.

49. OECD Library. Available at: http://www.oecd-ilibrary.org. Last accessed April 2018.

50. University of Missouri. Available at: http://bppm.missouri.edu/chapter2/2_140.html. Last accessed April 2018.

51. Test Strategy: Alpha vs. Beta Testing. Centercode. Available at: http://www.centercode.com/blog/2011/01/alpha-vs-beta-testing/. Last accessed April 2018.

52. Techopedia. Available at: www.techopedia.com. Last accessed April 2018.

53. Healthcare Information and Management Systems Society (HIMSS). Available at: www.himss.org. Last accessed April 2018.

54. Ancillary Care Services. Available at: http://www.anci-care.com/about2.html. Last accessed April 2018.

55. Definitions. 45 CFR § 160.103 (2004).

56. Encyclopedia. Available at: www.encyclopedia.com. Last accessed April 2018.

57. Infoway. Available at: www.infoway-inforoute.ca. Last accessed April 2018.

58. History of APACHE. Available at: www.salon.com. Last accessed April 2018.

59. University of Victoria (UVIC). www.uvic.ca. Last accessed August 2018.

60. The Free Dictionary. Available at: http://encyclopedia2.thefreedictionary.com/ Last accessed August 2018.

61. World Wide Web Consortium (W3C) Portal to Glossaries. Available at: www.w3.org/Glossary. Last accessed April 2018.

62. OpenEHR. Available at: www.openehr.org. Last accessed August 2018.

63. ISO/IS #13606-1. Electronic health record communication—Part 1: Reference model (terms only). Available at: www.iso.org. Last accessed April 2018.

64. Federal CIO Council. Available at: www.cio.gov/resources. Last accessed July 2018.

65. Coiera E. (2003). *Guide to Health Informatics*, 2nd ed. Arnold, London.

66. Informatics & Nursing: Opportunities & Challenges. Web supplement, 2003 Last accessed April 2018.

67. Pharmacy Benefits Management Services. U.S. Department of Veterans Affairs. Available at: https://www.pbm.va.gov/. Last accessed July 2018.

68. Microsoft. Available at: www.microsoft.com. Last accessed April 2018.

69. TechDifferences. Available at: https://techdifferences.com/. Last accessed July 2018.

70. Goossen, W. T. F. (2014). Detailed Clinical Models: Representing Knowledge, Data and Semantics in Healthcare Information Technology. *Healthcare Informatics Research*, 20(3), 163–172. http://doi.org/10.4258/hir.2014.20.3.163

71. Online Learning. Geek Interview. Available at: http://www.learn.geekinterview.com/. Last accessed July 2018.

72. ISO/IS #17090-1. Public Key Infrastructure-1 Framework and Overview (terms only). Available at: www.iso.org. Last accessed August 2018.

73. Tech Terms. Available at www.techterms.com. Last accessed April 2018.

74. International Engineering Consortium. www.iec.org. Last accessed July 2018.

75. ISO/TS 17117 (revision). Criteria for the Categorization and Evaluation of Terminological Systems (terms only). www.iso.org. Last accessed April 2018.

76. ISO/IS #17115. Vocabulary for Terminological Systems (terms only). www.iso.org. Last accessed April 2018.

77. SNOMED. International Health Terminology Standards Development Organization (IHTSDO). Gammeltory 4, 1. 1457 Copenhagen K, Denmark. www.ihtsdo.org. Last accessed April 2018.

78. Clemmer, L. "Information Security Concepts: Authenticity." (2010). Bright Hub. Available at: http://www.brighthub.com/computing/smb-security/articles/31234.aspx. Last accessed July 2018.

79. HIPAA Regulations. HIPAA Survival Guide. Available at: http://www.hipaasurv ivalguide.com/hipaa-regulations/. Last accessed July 2018.

80. CDC Centers for Disease Control. www.cdc.gov. Last accessed July 2018.

81. Advance Directives: Definitions. Patients Rights Council. Available at: http://www. patientsrightscouncil.org/site/advance-directives-definitions/. Last accessed July 2018.

82. Open Source Initiative. Available at: https://opensource.org/faq. Last accessed August 2018.

83. Incidents of Ransomware on the Rise. April 29, 2016. Federal Bureau of Investigation Available at: https://www.fbi.gov/news/stories/incidents-of-ransomware-on-the-rise. Last accessed August 2018.

84. Answers. Available at: www.answers.com. Last accessed August 2018.

85. Promoting Mental Health. (2005). A World Health Organization Report. WHO. Available at: http://www.who.int/mental_health/evidence/MH_Promotion_Book. pdf. Last accessed August 2018.

86. American Medical Informatics Association (AMIA). Available at: www.amia.org/. Last accessed July 2018.

87. ANSI/ASIS SPC.1-2009 Organizational Resilience: Security preparedness, and con- tinuity management systems. www.ansi.org. Last accessed August 2018.

88. ECQI Resource Center. Office of the National Coordinator for Health Information Technology. Available at https://ecqi.healthit.gov/ecqm-tools-key-resources. Last accessed July 2018.

89. IBM. www.ibm.com. Last accessed July 2018.

90. ISO 9241-11:2018 Ergonomics of human-system interaction – Part 11: Usability: Definitions and concepts. Available at: https://www.iso.org/standard/63500.html. Last accessed August 2018.

91. Castellino, Ronald A. "Computer aided detection (CAD): An overview." Available at: http://www.ncbi.nlm.nih.gov/pmc/articles/PMC1665219/. Last accessed July 2018.

92. American Hospital Association. Available at: www.aha.org. Last accessed August 2018.

93. Federal Emergency Management Agency. www.fema.gov/. Last accessed August 2018.

94. Agency for Healthcare Research and Quality (AHRQ). Available at: www.ahrq.gov. Last accessed July 2018.

95. Health Insurance Terms Glossary. Joint Learning Network. Available at: http://www. jointlearningnetwork.org/technical-initiatives/information-technology/glossary. Last accessed August 2018.

96. Medicine Net. Available at: www.medicinenet.com. Last accessed September 2018.

97. Vocabulary.com. Available at: https://www.vocabulary.com/. Last accessed August 2018.

98. Software Testing Support. Available at: https://www.quia.com/jg/1181678list.html. Last accessed August 2018.

99. Cause and Affect Analysis. USAID ASSIST Project. Available at: https://www.usa idassist.org/resources/cause-and-effect-analysis. Last accessed August 2018.

100. Hansche, S. (2005). *Official (ISC)² Guide to the CISSP-ISSEP CBK*. Boca Raton, FL: Taylor and Francis Group, LLC.
101. Clinical Care Classification System. Available at: www.sabacare.com. Last accessed August 2018.
102. The Open Clinical Project. Available at: www.openclinical.org. Last accessed August 2018.
103. ASTM. Available at: www.astm.org. Last accessed August 2018.
104. ISO/TR 22221. Good Principles and Practices for a Clinical Data Warehouse (terms only). www.iso.org. Last accessed August 2018.
105. CEN/ISSS e-Health Standardization Focus Group. Available at: www.who.int/cla ssifications/terminology/prerequisites.pdf. Last accessed August 2018.
106. Software Engineering Institute. Carnegie Mellon University. Available at: https://ww w.sei.cmu.edu/about/divisions/cert/index.cfm. Last accessed August 2018.
107. English Oxford Living Dictionary. 2018. Definition: Artificial Intelligence. Available at: Last accessed: https://en.oxforddictionaries.com. August 2018
108. Office Support. Microsoft. Available at: https://support.office.com/en-us/. Last accessed July 2018.
109. Telecom Glossary. Alliance for Telecommunications Industry Solutions (ATIS). Available at: http://www.atis.org/glossary/. Last accessed: July 2018.
110. Canadian Health Outcomes for Better Information and Care. Available at: http://c-h obic.cna-aiic.ca/about/default_e.aspx. Last accessed August 2018.
111. Robert Wood Johnson Foundation. www.rwjf.org. Last accessed August 2018.
112. Consumer Health Vocabulary - Synopsis. NIH National Library of Medicine. Available at: https://www.nlm.nih.gov/research/umls/sourcereleasedocs/current/C HV/. Last accessed August 2018.
113. HIPAA Glossary. www.wedi.org. Available at: https://www.wedi.org/docs/resources/ hipaa-glossary-download.pdf?sfvrsn=0. Last accessed July 2018.
114. Public Health Data Standards Consortium. www.phdsc.org. Last accessed August 2018.
115. Rosenbloom, S.T., Miller, R.A., Johnson, K.B. et al. (2008). A model for evaluating interface terminologies. *JAMIA*. 15:1; 65–76.
116. Analytics Insights. SAS. Available at: https://www.sas.com/en_us/insights/analytics. html. Last accessed: July 2018.
117. National Institute for Standards Technology (NIST). Available at: www.nist.gov/ healthcare/index.cfm. Last accessed August 2018.
118. Object Management Group. Available at: http://www.omg.org/. Last accessed August 2018.
119. Ohio Administrative Code: 5101:3 Division of Medical Assistance, Chapter 5101:3-1 General Provisions, 2007.
120. ISO/IS 21549-7:2016. Patient Health Card Data Part 7 E-Prescription to Med Data (terms only). Available at: www.iso.org. Last accessed August 2018.
121. Behavioral Health Care Services (BHCS). Available at: http://www.acbhcs.org/ hippa-glossary/#C. Last accessed August 2018.
122. Community of Interest/Community of Practice. MITRE. Available at: https:// www.mitre.org/publications/systems-engineering-guide/enterprise-engineering/e nterprise-governance/communities-of-interest-andor-community-of-practice. Last accessed August 2018.

123. Medical Dictionary. Available at: http://medical-dictionary.thefreedictionary.com/. Last accessed July 2018.

124. ISO/TR 28380-1. IHE Global Standards Adoption—Part 1 The Process (terms only). Available at: www.iso.org. Last accessed August 2018.

125. Information Security Management Guidelines for Telecommunications, based on ISO/IEC 27002. ITU-T Study Gp 17 TD 2318.

126. Organization for Economic Co-operation and Development. Available at: www.oecd.org. Last accessed August 2018.

127. The City University of New York. Available at: www.cuny.edu. Last accessed August 2018.

128. Benefits of Computer on Wheels Solutions in Healthcare. Available at: http://www.remedi-tech.com/4-benefits-of-computer-on-wheels-solutions-in-healthcare/. Last accessed August 2018.

129. Government Technology. Available at: http://www.govtech.com/. Last accessed August 2018.

130. HL7 Definition. Caristix. Available at: http://hl7-definition.caristix.com:9010/Default.aspx?version=HL7%20v2.5.1&dataType=CWE. Last accessed August 2018.

131. ISO 18308:2011 Health informatics—Requirements for an electronic health record architecture. Available at: www.iso.org. Last accessed August 2018.

132. Kissel, R. (2013). *Glossary of Key Information Security Terms.* National Institute of Standards and Technology. Available at: http://dx.doi.org/10.6028/NIST.IR.7298r2.

133. Reference. Available at: https://www.reference.com. Last accessed August 2018.

134. Slavic Cowen, P. and Moorhead, S. (2014). *Current Issues in Nursing.* St. Louis: Elsevier Health Sciences.

135. *Cambridge Dictionary.* Available at: https://dictionary.cambridge.org/us/. *Last accessed July* 2018.

136. McGonigle, D. and Mastrain, K. (2012). *Nursing Informatics and the Foundation of Knowledge.* Boston: Jones and Bartlett Publishing.

137. IT Law Wiki. Available at: http://itlaw.wikia.com/wiki/. Last accessed August 2018.

138. Welcome to the Argonaut Project. HL7. Available at: http://argonautwiki.hl7.org/index.php?title=Main_Page. Last accessed: July 2018.

139. ARRA Economic Stimulus Package. HITECH Answers. Available at: https://www.hitechanswers.net/about/about-arra/. Last accessed: July 2018.

140. Richesson, R.L. and Krischer, J. (2007). Data standards in clinical research: Gaps, overlaps, challenges and future directions. *JAMIA.* 14:6; 687–696.

141. Tag Management 101. Signal. Available at: http://www.signal.co/resources/tag-management-101/. Last accessed August 2018.

142. Gartner Group. Available at: www.gartner.com/it-glossary. Last accessed August 2018.

143. Description Logics. Available at: http://www.obitko.com/tutorials/ontologies-semantic-web/description-logics.html. Last accessed August 2018.

144. Diagnostic Imaging. Medicine Plus. US National Library of Medicine. Available at: https://www.nlm.nih.gov/medlineplus/diagnosticimaging.html. Last accessed August 2018.

145. NIST. Available at: https://xlinux.nist.gov/dads//HTML/dictionary.html. Last accessed August 2018

146. Digital Signature Standard. July 2013. Information Technology Laboratory. National Institute of standards and Technology. Gaithersburg, MD. Available at: http://nvlpubs.nist.gov/nistpubs/FIPS/NIST.FIPS.186-4.pdf. Last accessed August 2018.

147. WEDI Healthcare Secure Messaging Workgroup. Available at: https://www.wedi.org/docs/resources/15-things-to-know-about-direct-messaging.pdf?sfvrsn=0. Last accessed August 2018.

148. Dictionary. I Six Sigma. Available at: www.isixsigma.com. Last accessed July 2018.

149. Disease Staging. Thomas Jefferson University. Available at: https://www.jefferson.edu/university/skmc/research/research-medical-education/Disease_Staging.html. Last accessed August 2018.

150. PC Magazine. Available at: http://www.pcmag.com/encyclopedia. Last accessed July 2018.

151. Diagnostic and Statistical Manual of Mental Disorders (DSM–5). American Psychiatric Association. Available at: https://www.psychiatry.org/psychiatrists/practice/dsm/dsm-5. Last accessed August 2018.

152. National Information Standards Organization. Available at: http://www.niso.org/. Last accessed August 2018.

153. Federal Standard 1037C. Institute for Telecommunication Sciences. Available at: http://www.its.bldrdoc.gov/fs-1037. Last accessed August 2018.

154. Deployment Resources. US Department of Transportation. Available at: https://www.standards.its.dot.gov/DeploymentResources/BriefStroll. Last accessed August 2018.

155. An Overview of Average Speed of Answer in the Call Center. (2014). TalkDesk. Available at: https://www.talkdesk.com/blog/an-overview-of-average-speed-of-answer-in-the-call-center/. Last accessed July 2018.

156. New World Encyclopedia. Available at: www.newworldencyclopedia.org. Last accessed August 2018.

157. Oasis. Available at: www.oasis-open.org. Last accessed August 2018.

158. United States Congress. Available at: www.house.gov. Last accessed August 2018.

159. American Society for Quality. http://asq.org. Last accessed August 2018.

160. Clinger-Cohen Act of 1996. Available at: www.cio.gov. Last accessed August 2018.

161. Legal Definitions and Legal Terms Defined. USLegal. Available at: http://definitions.uslegal.com/. Last accessed July 2018.

162. Hauenstein, L., Gao, t., Sze, T.W., Crawford, D., Alm, A. and White, D. (2006). A cross-functional service-oriented architecture to support real-time information exchange in emergency medical response. *Conference Proceedings of the IEEE Engineering, Medicine, Biology and Society*; Suppl: 6478–6481.

163. Masic, I., Miokovic, M., & Muhamedagic, B. (2008). Evidence Based Medicine – New Approaches and Challenges. *Acta Informatica Medica*, 16(4), 219–225. http://doi.org/10.5455/aim.2008.16.219-225

164. Mulyar, N., Van der Aalst, W.M.P., and Peleg, M. (2007). A pattern-based analysis of clinical computer–interpretable guideline modeling languages. *JAMIA*. 14:6; 781–797.

165. Van der Aalst, W.M.P., Hofstede, A.H.M., Russell, N. et al. Control Flow Patterns 2003, 2006. Available at: http://www.workflowpatterns.com/patterns/control. Last accessed August 2018.

166. How Stuff Works. Available at: http://computer.howstuffworks.com/. Last accessed July 2018.

167. American College of Physicians. Available at: www.acponline.org. Last accessed August 2018.

168. Federal Information Processing Standards Publications (FIPS PUBS). Available at: http://www.nist.gov/itl/fips.cfm. Last accessed August 2018.

169. Linktionary. Available at: www.linktionary.com. Last accessed August 2018.

170. Cryptography Docs. Available at: https://cryptography.io/en/latest/. Last accessed July 2018.

171. HL7 Standards Product Brief—GELLO (HL7 Version 3 Standard: Gello: A Common Expression Language, Release 2). (n.d.). Available at: http://www.hl7.org/i mplement/standards/product_brief.cfm?product_id=5. Last accessed August 2018.

172. National Human Genome Research Institute. Available at: https://www.genome.gov/ 19016904/faq-about-genetic-and-genomic-science/. Last accessed August 2018.

173. Business Intelligence. Available at: http://businessintelligence.com/. Last accessed August 2018.

174. Hubspot. Available at: http://blog.hubspot.com/. Last accessed August 2018.

175. Kulikowski, C. A., Shortliffe, E. H., Currie, L. M., Elkin, P. L., Hunter, L. E., Johnson, T. R., Williamson, J. J. (2012). AMIA Board white paper: definition of bio-medical informatics and specification of core competencies for graduate education in the discipline. *JAMIA*, 19(6), 931–938. http://doi.org/10.1136/amiajnl-2012-001053

176. Biosurveillance. National Association of County and City Health Officials (NACCHO). Available at: http://archived.naccho.org/topics/emergency/biosurveill ance/. Last accessed July 2018.

177. Apple's HealthKit Is Finally Here—After Bugs, Botches, and Boatloads of Apple Hype." *Forbes*. Available at: http://www.forbes.com/sites/dandiamond/2014/09/26/ apples-healthkit-finally-arrives-after-bugs-botches-and-boatloads-of-apple-hype/ #4340d67e1bec. Last accessed April 2018.

178. Blockchain Basics. Lisk. Available at: https://lisk.io/academy/blockchain-basics. Last accessed July 2018.

179. National Committee for Quality Assurance. Available at: http://www.ncqa.org/hedis-quality-measurement. Last accessed August 2018.

180. Best Practices for HISPs. DirectTrust. Available at: https://www.directtrust.org/wp-content/uploads/2017/05/DirectTrust-One-Pager-05.12.2017.pdf. Last accessed August 2018.

181. Data Warehouse. Health Resources and Services Administration. Available at: http:// www.datawarehouse.hrsa.gov/topics/topics.aspx. Last accessed July 2018.

182. National Quality Forum. Available at: www.qualityforum.org. Last accessed July 2018.

183. Office of Biomedical Translational Research Informatics. National Institutes of Health. Available at: https://btris.nih.gov/. Last accessed July 2018.

184. World Health Organization (WHO). Available at: www.who.org. Last accessed August 2018.

185. International Council of Nurses (ICN). Available at: www.icn.ch. Last accessed August 2018.

186. Landis, Jared. (2014). Post-Acute Care Cheat Sheet: Integrated Delivery Networks. Advisory Board. Available at: https://www.advisory.com/research/post-acute-care-collaborative/members/resources/cheat-sheets/integrated-delivery-networks. Last accessed August 2018.

187. Mancini, J. What the Heck is Intelligent Document Recognition? (2016) Association for Information and Image Management International. Available at: http://info.aii m.org/digital-landfill/what-the-heck-is-intelligent-document-recognition. Last accessed July 2018.

188. Archives. Info.SSL.com. Available at: https://info.ssl.com/glossary. Last accessed July 2018.

189. Department of Biomedical Informatics. Columbia University. Available at: www. dbmi.columbia.edu. Last accessed August 2018.

190. Best Health Tech Infographics of 2014—HIT Consultant." (n.d.). Available at: http://hitconsultant.net/2015/01/12/25-best-health-tech-infographics-of-2014/. Last accessed August 2018.

191. Object-Oriented Programming Concepts. Adobe. Available at: https://www.ado be.com/devnet/actionscript/learning/oop-concepts/objects-and-classes.html. Last accessed July 2018.

192. Hovenga, E.J.S and Mantas, J. (2004). *Global Health Informatics Education.* Washington DC: IOS Press.

193. Substance Abuse and Mental Health Services Administration. Available at: http:// www.integration.samhsa.gov/. Last accessed August 2018.

194. IEEE Standards Association. Available at: https://standards.ieee.org/findstds/stan dard/1012-2012.html. Last accessed August 2018.

195. *Making Government Work: Electronic Delivery of Federal Services.* 1993. Washington, DC: Diane Publishing Co.

196. *Mosby's Dental Dictionary*, 2nd edition. Copyright 2008 Elsevier, Inc.

197. Clinical Observation. National Information Center on Health Services Research and Health Care Technology (NICHSR). U.S. National Library of Medicine. Available at: https://www.nlm.nih.gov/nichsr/usestats/clinical_observation.html. Last accessed July 2018.

198. ISBT 128. Available at: https://iccbba.org/. Last accessed August 2018.

199. ITIM Groups. IBM. Available at: https://publib.boulder.ibm.com/tividd/td/ITIM/ SC32-1149-02/en_US/HTML/im451_poag70.htm. Last accessed August 2018.

200. Glossary of Defense Acquisition Acronyms and Terms. Available at: https://dap.dau. mil/glossary/Pages/Default.aspx. Last accessed November 2016.

201. JSON. http://www.json.org/. Last accessed August 2018.

202. Arnold S. (Ed.). (2008). *Guide to the Wireless Medical Practice: Finding the Right Connections for Healthcare.* Chicago: HIMSS.

203. Lifewire. Available at: https://www.lifewire.com. Last accessed July 2018.

204. Abdelhak, M., Grostick, S., and Hanken, M. (2013). *Health Information: Management of a Strategic Resource.* St. Louis, MO: Elsevier Inc., 2012.

205. Tomsho, Greg. (2015). *Guide to Networking Essentials.* Boston: Cengage Learning, 2016.

206. Logical Observation Identifiers Names and Codes (LOINC). Available at: http:// www.loinc.org. Last accessed August 2018.

207. Woolf, S. H., Grol, R., Hutchinson, A., Eccles, M., and Grimshaw, J. (1999). Potential benefits, limitations, and harms of clinical guidelines. *BMJ*, 318(7182), 527–530.

208. HL7 Resources. (n.d.). Corepoint Health. Available at: http://corepointhealth.com/ resource-center/hl7-resources. Last accessed August 2018.

209. American Academy of Pediatrics. Available at: https://medicalhomeinfo.aap.org/Pag es/default.aspx. Last accessed August 2018.

210. Deloitte LLP. Available at: www.deloitte.com. Last accessed August 2018.

211. Lundy, K.S. and Bergamini, A. (2003). *Essentials of Nursing Informatics*. Sudbury, MA: Jones & Bartlett Publishers.

212. Definition of Master Services Agreement. Chron. Available at: http://smallbusiness.chron.com/definition-master-services-agreement-40141.html. Last accessed August 2018.

213. Understanding Management Services Organizations (MSOs). Physicians Practice Available at: http://www.physicianspractice.com/practice-models/understanding-management-services-organizations-msos. Last accessed August 2018.

214. National Council on Prescription Drug Programs (NCPDP). Available at: www.ncpdp.org. Last accessed August 2018.

215. National Emergency Medical Services Information System (NEMSIS). National Highway Traffic Safety Administration. Available at: www.nemsis.org. Last accessed August 2018.

216. NIC Overview. University of Iowa College for Nursing Centers. Available at: http://www.nursing.uiowa.edu/cncce/nursing-interventions-classification-overview. Last accessed August 2018.

217. The OMAHA System. Available at: www.omahasystem.org/systemo.htm. Last accessed August 2018.

218. Healthcare.gov. Available at: https://www.healthcare.gov/glossary/. Last accessed July 2018.

219. Technology Modeling. Enterprise Architecture Solutions. Available at: https://www.enterprise-architecture.org/techology-architecture-tutorials. Last accessed July 2018.

220. SPARC. Available at: http://sparcopen.org/open-access/. Last accessed August 2018.

221. Hickey, J. and Brosnan, C. (2016) *Evaluation of Health Care Quality for DNPs*, Second Edition. New York: Springer Publishing Company.

222. Cognitive Computing Definition. Cognitive Computing Consortium. Available at: https://cognitivecomputingconsortium.com/definition-of-cognitive-computing/. Last accessed July 2018.

223. Computer Basics. Goodwill Community Foundation, Inc. Available at: http://edu.gcflearnfree.org/en/computerbasics/. Last accessed August 2018.

224. Health Information Access Layer. eHealth Ontario. Available at: https://www.ehealthblueprint.com/en/documentation/chapter/health-information-access-layer-hial. Last accessed July 2018.

225. State of Tennessee Office of eHealth. Available at: http://tn.gov/ehealth. Last accessed August 2018.

226. Lehpamer, H. (2012). *RFID Design Principles*, Second Edition. Norwood, MA: Artech House.

227. Eck, D. (2014) Introduction to Programming Using Java, Version 7.0. Available at: http://math.hws.edu/javanotes/index.html. Last accessed July 2018.

228. Plain Text. The Linux Information Project. Available at: http://www.linfo.org/plain_text.html. Last accessed August 2018.

229. Joint Commission (formerly Joint Commission on Accreditation of Healthcare Organizations). Available at: www.jointcommission.org. Last accessed July 2018.

230. Kaiser Family Foundation. Available at: www.kff.org. Last accessed July 2018.

231. All of Us. *National Institutes of Health*. Available at: https://allofus.nih.gov/. Last accessed August 2018.

232. OECD. (2016). *OECD Health Policy Studies: Better Ways to Pay for Health Care*. Paris: OECD Publishing. http://dx.doi.org/10.178/9789264258211-en.

233. Office of the Australian Information Commissioner. Australian Government. Available at: https://www.oaic.gov.au/. Last accessed August 2018.

234. Information Systems Audit and Control Association. (2015). *CISA Review Manual*, 26th ed.

235. National Center for Biotechnology Information. U.S. National Library of Medicine. Available at: www.ncbi.nlm.nih.gov/search. Last accessed August 2018.

236. Hasman, A. (1995). *Education and Training In Health Informatics in Europe.* Washington, DC: IOS Press.

237. Stockburger, David W. "Introductory Statistics: Concepts, Models, and Applications." 2013. Available at: http://www.psychstat.missouristate.edu/IntroBook3/sbk.htm. Last accessed August 2018.

238. RISC Architecture. Stanford University. Available at: https://cs.stanford.edu/people/eroberts/courses/soco/projects/risc/whatis/index.html. Last accessed August 2018.

239. Andison, M. and Moss, J. (2007) "What Nurses Do: Use of the ISO Reference Terminology Model for Nursing Action as a Framework for Analyzing MICU Nursing Practice Patterns." *AMIA Annual Symposium Proceedings 2007*; 2007: 21–25. Available at: http://www.ncbi.nlm.nih.gov/pmc/articles/PMC2942066/. Last accessed August 2018.

240. The Serial ATA International Organization. Available at: http://sata-io.org. Last accessed August 2018.

241. Mayo Clinic College of Medicine. Available at: www.mayo.edu. Last accessed August 2018.

242. DoD Net-Centric Data Strategy. Department of Defernse. Available at: http://dodcio.defense.gov/Portals/0/Documents/DIEA/Net-Centric-Data-Strategy-2003-05-092.pdf. Last accessed August 2018.

243. Conformance Assessment Process. Device Language Message Specification (DLMS) User Association. Available at: http://www.dlms.com/conformance/conformancetestmaintenance/index.html. Last accessed July 2018.

244. ISO/TS 22220. Identification of Subjects of Health Care (terms only). Available at: www.iso.org. Last accessed August 2018.

245. MITRE. Available at: www.mitre.org. Last accessed August 2018.

246. Center for Connected Health Policy. Available at: http://cchpca.org/. Last accessed June 2018.

247. Overview of Conformance Testing. National Institute of Standards and Technology (NIST). Available at: https://www.nist.gov/itl/ssd/information-systems-group/overview-conformance-testing. Last accessed July 2018.

248. ECRI Institute. www.ecri.org. Last accessed August 2018.

249. Chilmark Research. Understanding Connected Health. Orion Heath. Available at: https://orionhealth.com/us/knowledge-hub/reports/understanding-connected-health/. Last accessed July 2018.

250. International Organisation for Standardization. Available at: https://www.iso.org. Last accessed July 2018.

251. Usability Testing. Usability.gov. Available at: http://www.usability.gov/how-to-and-tools/methods/usability-testing.html. Last accessed August 2018.

252. United States Health Information Knowledgebase. Available at: www.ushik.org. Last accessed July 2018.

253. Oxford Reference. Available at: http://www.oxfordreference.com. Last accessed July 2018.

254. Continua Design Guidelines. Personal Connected Health Alliance. Available at: https://www.pchalliance.org/continua-design-guidelines. Last accessed July 2018.

255. US Department of Veterans Affairs. Available at: https://www.data.va.gov/dataset/vet erans-health-information-systems-and-technology-architecture-vista. Last accessed July 2018.

256. What is CORBA? OIAS. Available at: http://www.ois.com/Products/what-is-corb a.html. Last accessed August 2018.

257. Dalhio, H.S. and Singh, J. (2010). VoIP signal processing in digital domain. *IUP Journal of Electrical & Electronics Engine*ring. 3(4); 38–43.

258. Infolific. Available at: https://infolific.com. Last accessed August 2018.

259. Goodbole, N.S. (2004). *Software Quality Assurance: Principles and Practice.* Pangbourne, UK: Alpha Science Intl Ltd. p. 288.

260. Patel, M., Asch, D., and Volpp, K. "Wearable Devices as Facilitators, not Drivers, of Health Behavior Change." *Journal of the American Medical Association.* 313(5). Available at: http://jama.jamanetwork.com/article.aspx?articleid=2089651.

261. Research. Health Information Privacy. U.S. Department of Health and Human Services. Available at: https://www.hhs.gov/hipaa/for-professionals/special-topics/r esearch/index.html Last accessed September 2018.

262. What's the difference between wet, digital and electronic signatures? Laserfiche. Available at: https://www.laserfiche.com/ecmblog/whats-the-difference-between-w et-digital-and-electronic-signatures/. Last accessed August 2018.

263. X.25: Interface between Data Terminal Equipment (DTE) and Data Circuit-terminating Equipment (DCE) for terminals operating in the packet mode and con-nected to public data networks by dedicated circuit. International Telecommunications Union. Available at: https://www.itu.int/rec/T-REC-X.25-199610-I/en. Last accessed August 2018.

264. About X12. X12. Available at: http://www.x12.org/about/asc-x12-about.cfm. Last accessed August 2018.

265. What is Zigbee? Zigbee. Available at: http://www.zigbee.org/what-is-zigbee/. Last accessed August 2018.

266. Certificate Policies. U.S. Department of Treasury. Available at http://pki.treas.gov/ cert_policies.htm. Last accessed July 2018.

267. Ameerican Medical Association. Available at: https://www.ama-assn.org/. Last accessed July 2018.

268. Dong, J. (2007). *Network Dictionary.* Javvin Technologies.

269. Unified Medical Language System (UMLS) Glossary. National Library of Medicine. Available at: https://www.nlm.nih.gov/research/umls/new_users/glossary.html. Last accessed July 2018.

270. Decentralized Applications – dApps. Blockchain Hub. Available at: https://blockch ainhub.net/decentralized-applications-dapps/. Last accessed July 2018.

271. The Year of DApps. (2018). Medium. Available at: https://medium.com/the-mission /2018-the-year-of-dapps-dbe108860bcb. Last accessed July 2018.

272. What is a data subject? EU GDPR Compliant. Available at: https://eugdprcompliant. com/what-is-data-subject/. Last accessed July 2018.

273. Your Dictionary. Available at www.yourdictionary.com. Last accessed July 2018.

274. Shortliffe, E and Perreault, L. (2013). *Medical Informatics: Computer Applications in Health Care and Biomedicine,* Second Edition. New York: Spring Science and Business Media.

275. Design Develop Implement. Available at: https://ddiprogram.org/. Last accessed July 2018.

276. Karris, S. (2009). *Networks: Design and Management.* Fremont, CA: Orchard Publications.

277. Deep Learning. Available at: http://deeplearning.net/. Last accessed July 2018.

278. Juniper TechLibrary. Juniper Networks. Available at: https://www.juniper.net/documentation/. Last accessed July 2018.

279. Computed Radiography vs. Digital Radiography. JPI Healthcare Solutions. Available at: http://www.jpihealthcare.com/computed-radiography-cr-and-digital-radiography-dr-which-should-you-choose/. Last accessed July 2018.

280. The Present and Future of Digital Therapeutics. (2017). Noteworthy – The Journal Blog. Available at: https://blog.usejournal.com/the-present-and-future-of-digital-therapeutics-954c121fdf20. Last accessed July 2018.

281. What is a distributed ledger? CoinDesk. Available at: https://www.coindesk.com/information/what-is-a-distributed-ledger/. Last accessed July 2018.

282. CDISC. Available at: www.cdisc.org. Last accessed July 2018.

283. TechnologyUK. Available at: https://www.technologyuk.net. Last accessed July 2018.

284. MACRAnyms: Acronyms and Terms Related to MACRA. American Academy of Family Physicians. Available at: https://www.aafp.org/practice-management/payment/medicare-payment/macra-101/acronyms.html. Last accessed July 2018.

285. Electronic Data Capture. Parexel. Available at: https://www.parexel.com/solutions/informatics/electronic-data-capture. Last accessed July 2018.

286. PUBLIC LAW 107 - 347 - E-GOVERNMENT ACT OF 2002. Government Publishing Office. Available at: https://www.gpo.gov/fdsys/pkg/PLAW-107publ347/content-detail.html. Last accessed July 2018.

287. IGI Global. Available at: https://www.igi-global.com/dictionary/. Last accessed July 2018.

288. What is an electronic signature? CEF Digital. Available at: https://ec.europa.eu/cefdigital/wiki/pages/viewpage.action?pageId=46992760. Last accessed July 2018.

289. European Standards. DIN. Available at: https://www.din.de/en/din-and-our-partners/din-in-europe/european-standards. Last accessed July 2018.

290. CoverMyMeds. Available at: https://www.covermymeds.com/main/. Last accessed July 2018.

291. Practice Fusion. Available at: https://www.practicefusion.com. Last accessed July 2018.

292. Porterfield, A., Engelbert, K., & Coustasse, A. (2014). Electronic prescribing: improving the efficiency and accuracy of prescribing in the ambulatory care setting. *Perspectives in Health Information Management*, 11(Spring), 1g.

293. Resource Center. Lucidchart. Available at: https://www.lucidchart.com/pages/resource-center. Last accessed July 2018.

294. Ethereum. Available at: https://ethereum.org/. Last accessed July 2018.

295. Hawkins, R. C. (2005). The Evidence Based Medicine approach to diagnostic testing: practicalities and limitations. *Clin Biochem Rev*, 26(2), 7-18. https://www.ncbi.nlm.nih.gov/pubmed/16278748

296. Thammasak, Rujirayanyong, Shi, Jonathan J. (2005). A project-oriented data warehouse for construction. *Automation in Construction*, Elsevier.

297. Building a dimensional data model. IBM Knowledge Center. IBM. Available at: https://www.ibm.com/support/knowledgecenter/en/SSGU8G_12.1.0/com.ibm.whse.doc/ids_ddi_360.htm Last accessed March 2018.

298. Fat Protocols. (2016) Union Square Ventures. Available at: http://www.usv.com/blog/fat-protocols. Last accessed July 2018.

299. Definitions specific to Medicaid. 42 CFR 400.203 (2011).

300. RP Photonics Consulting. Available at: https://www.rp-photonics.com/consulting.html. Last accessed July 2018.

301. Salesforce Help. Salesforce. Available at: https://help.salesforce.com/. Last accessed July 2018.

302. Shortliffe, Edward. H., Cimino, James, J. (2014). *Biomedical Informatics: Computer Applications in Health Care and Biomedicine,* Third Edition. Springer. 942.

303. Gantt. Available at: http://www.gantt.com. Last accessed July 2018.

304. What is a Gateway and What does it do? WhatIsMyIPAdress.com. Available at: https://whatismyipaddress.com/gateway. Last accessed July 2018.

305. EU GDPR Portal. Available at: https://www.eugdpr.org/. Last accessed July 2018.

306. Grid Computing Info Centre. Available at: http://www.gridcomputing.com. Last accessed July 2018.

307. GS1 US. Available at: https://www.gs1us.org/. Last accessed August 2018.

308. GUID.one. Available at: http://guid.one/guid. Last accessed July 2018.

309. Woodard, Robert. (2015) Biomed Cyber Survey. Bureau of Industry and Security. U.S. Department of Commerce. Available at: https://www.bis.doc.gov/index.php/documents/pdfs/1231-biomed-cyber-survey-pdf/file. Last accessed September 2018.

310. Northcutt, S. Hash Functions. Security Laboratory. SANS Technology Institute. Available at: https://www.sans.edu/cyber-research/security-laboratory/article/hash-functions. Last accessed July 2018.

311. Definition. Trend Micro. Available at: https://www.trendmicro.com/vinfo/us/security/definition/a. Last accessed July 2018.

312. Blackwood, R. and Curie, C (2016). Study design for assessing effectiveness, efficiency and acceptability of services including measures of structure, process, service quality, and outcome of health care Public Health Action Support Team. Available at https://www.healthknowledge.org.uk/public-health-textbook/research-methods/1c-health-care-evaluation-health-care-assessment/study-design-assessing-effectiveness. Last accessed July 2018.

313. Wolfram MathWorld. Available at: http://mathworld.wolfram.com/. Last accessed July 2018.

314. The state of your health insurance marketplace. HealthInsurance.org. Available at: https://www.healthinsurance.org/state-health-insurance-exchanges/. Last accessed July 2018.

315. Resources. Pacific Health Information Network (PHIN). Available at: http://phin-network.org/resources/. Last accessed July 2018.

316. Smart Card Primer. Secure Technology Alliance. Available at: https://www.securetechalliance.org/smart-cards-intro-primer/. Last accessed July 2018.

317. About Hyperledger. The Linux Foundation. Available at: https://www.hyperledger.org/about. Last accessed July 2018.

318. What is individually identifiable information? University of Miami Health System. Available at: http://privacy.med.miami.edu/faq/privacy-faqs/what-is-individually-identifiable-health-information. Last accessed July 2018.

319. Data vs. Information. Diffen. Available at: https://www.diffen.com/difference/D ata_vs_Information. Last accessed July 2018.

320. *Encyclopaedia Britannica*. Available at: https://www.britannica.com/. Last accessed July 2018.

321. The 7 Components of a Clinical Integrated Network. (2012). *Becker's Hospital Review*. Available at: https://www.beckershospitalreview.com/hospital-physician-rel ationships/the-7-components-of-a-clinical-integration-network.html. Last accessed July 2018.

322. Support Center. Symantec. Available at: https://support.symantec.com/en_US.html. Last accessed July 2018.

323. Compiled vs. Interpreted Languages. Vanguard Software Corporation. Available at: http://www.vanguardsw.com/dphelp4/dph00296.htm. Last accessed July 2018.

324. Nivedita, S., Padmini, R., Shanmugam, R. (2012). TCP/IP: The Internet Layer Protocol. InformIT. Pearson Education. Available at: http://www.informit.com/articl es/article.aspx?p=29578&seqNum=5. Last accessed July 2018.

325. Parr, B. February 2011. IPv4 & IPv6: A Short Guide. Mashable. Available at: https://ma shable.com/2011/02/03/ipv4-ipv6-guide/#ibtu68q9uOq9. Last accessed August 2018.

326. Engineering in Medicine & Biology Society. IEEE. Available at: http://standard s.embs.org/healthcare-informatics/. Last accessed July 2018.

327. JASON Defense Advisory Panel Reports. Available at: https://fas.org/irp/agency/ dod/jason/. Last Accessed July 2018.

328. Joint Commission Resources. Available at: https://www.jcrinc.com. Last accessed July 2018.

329. JIRA. Atlassian. Available at: https://www.atlassian.com/software/jira. Last accessed July 2018.

330. What is DBMS. Available at: http://whatisdbms.com/what-is-join-and-its-types-i n-dbms/. Last accessed July 2018.

331. What is a Ledger? My Accounting Course. Available at: https://www.myaccountingc ourse.com/accounting-dictionary/ledger. Last accessed July 2018.

332. Sugumaran, V. (2014) *Recent Advances in Intelligent Technologies and Information Systems*. Hershey, PA: IGI Global.

333. Dojat, M., Niessen, W., Kennedy, D. (2017) *MAPPING: Management and Processing of Images for Population Imaging*. Frontiers Media SA.

334. Level of Effort (LOE). Project Management Knowledge. Available at: https://project-management-knowledge.com/definitions/l/level-of-effort-loe/. Last accessed July 2018.

335. Stutman, H. (2010). "A Longitudinal Medical Record is Key to Clinical Decision Support." Clinical Innovation + Technology. Available at: https://www.clinical-inno vation.com/topics/ehr-emr/longitudinal-medical-record-key-clinical-decision-supp ort. Last accessed July 2018.

336. Computer Terms, Dictionary and Glossary. Computer Hope. Available at: https:// www.computerhope.com/jargon.htm. Last accessed July 2018.

337. Control of Hazardous Energy Lockout/Tagout. (2002). Occupational Safety & Health Administration (OSHA) 3120. Available at: https://www.osha.gov/Publicati ons/3120.html. Last accessed July 2018.

338. Longitudinal Pediatric Data Resource. Newborn Screening Translational Research Network (NBSTRN). Available at: https://www.nbstrn.org/research-tools/longitu dinal-pediatric-data-resource. Last accessed July 2018.

339. McCall, N. (2001). "Long Term Care: Definition, Demand, Cost, and Financing. Who Will Pay for Long Term Care?" *Health Administration Press*. Available at: http://www.ache.org/PUBS/1mccall.pdf. Last accessed July 2018.

340. Glossary. LongTermCare.gov. U.S. Department of Health and Human Services. Available at: https://longtermcare.acl.gov/the-basics/glossary.html. Last accessed July 2018.

341. Machine Readable Travel Documents MRTD MRZ MRP explained (2014). Honeywell. Available at: https://support.honeywellaidc.com/s/article/Machine-Readable-Travel-Documents-MRTD-MRZ-MRP-explained. Last accessed July 2018.

342. Glossary. Continuity Compliance. Available at: https://www.continuitycompliance.org/glossary/. Last accessed July 2018.

343. The Network Encyclopedia. Available at http://www.thenetworkencyclopedia.com. Last accessed July 2018.

344. Grober, E. D., and Bohnen, J. M. A. (2005). Defining medical error. *Canadian Journal of Surgery*, 48(1), 39–44.

345. Saranummi, N. (2005). *Regional Health Economies and ICT Services: The PICNIC Services*. Washington, DC: IOS Press.

346. Ingram, D. "What is a Management Information System?" (2018). Chron. Available at: http://smallbusiness.chron.com/management-information-system-2104.html. Last accessed July 2018.

347. The Moving Picture Experts Group. Available at: https://mpeg.chiariglione.org. Last accessed July 2018.

348. Gliklich RE, Dreyer NA, Leavy MB, editors. Registries for Evaluating Patient Outcomes: A User's Guide [Internet]. 3rd edition. Rockville (MD): Agency for Healthcare Research and Quality (US); 2014 Apr. 17, Managing Patient Identity Across Data Sources. Available at: https://www.ncbi.nlm.nih.gov/books/NBK208618/

349. KPI Library. Available at: http://kpilibrary.com/kpis. Last accessed July 2018.

350. What is the difference between unicast and multicast streams?" Visionary Solutions. Available at: http://www.vsicam.com/_faq/what-is-the-difference-between-unicast-and-multicast-streams/. Last accessed July 2018.

351. The Interactive Glossary: Defining the Net. WebsiteBuilders.com. Available at: https://websitebuilders.com/how-to/glossary/. Last accessed July 2018.

352. McCarthy, D. B., Propp, K., Cohen, A., Sabharwal, R., Schachter, A. A., and Rein, A. L. (2014). Learning from Health Information Exchange Technical Architecture and Implementation in Seven Beacon Communities. *EGEMS*, 2(1), 1060. http://doi.org/10.13063/2327-9214.1060

353. NoSQL Databases. Basho. Available at: http://basho.com/resources/nosql-databases/. Last accessed July 2018.

354. Yegulalp, S. (2017) "What is NoSQL? NoSQL databases explained." InfoWorld. Available at: https://www.infoworld.com/article/3240644/nosql/what-is-nosql-nosql-databases-explained.html. Last accessed July 2018.

355. Nutrition Informatics. Academy of Nutrition and Dietetics. Available at: http://www.eatrightpro.org/~/media/eatrightpro%20files/practice/scope%20standards%20of%20practice/practicepaper-nutrition_informatics-final.ashx. Last accessed July 2018.

356. How to Configure OCSP Stapling on APACHE and Nginx". DigitalOcean. Available at https://www.digitalocean.com/community/tutorials/how-to-configure-ocsp-stapling-on-apache-and-nginx. Last accessed July 2018.

357. What is ODA?" Available at http://xml.coverpages.org/odanovl0.html. Last accessed July 2018.

358. Health Plan Identifier (HPID) and Other Entity Identifier (OEID). Military Health System. Available at https://www.health.mil/Military-Health-Topics/Business-Suppo rt/HIPAA-Transactions-Code-Sets-Identifiers/Identifiers/Health-Plan-Identifier-a nd-Other-Entity-Identifier. Last accessed July 2018.

359. Browne, G. (2004). *Website Indexing: Enhancing Access to Information within Websites.* Adelaide, South Australia: Auslib Press.

360. HealthInsurance.Org. Available at: https://www.healthinsurance.org/glossary/out-of-network-out-of-plan/. Last accessed July 2018.

361. User Interface. HN Computing. Scottish Qualifications Authority. Available at: https:// www.sqa.org.uk/e-learning/COS101CD/page_04.htm. Last accessed July 2018.

362. Oregon Association of Hospitals and Health Systems. Available at: http://oahhs.org. Last accessed July 2018.

363. Information Resources Management Association. 2016. Public Health and Welfare: Concepts, Methodologies, Tools and Applications. Hershey, PA: IGI Global.

364. Glossary. SLAC National Accelerator Laboratory. Stanford University. Available at: https://www.slac.stanford.edu/comp/unix/gnu-info/bison_14.html. Last accessed July 2018.

365. Yeoman G, Furlong P, Seres M, et al. (2017) Defining patient centricity with patients for patients and caregivers: a collaborative endeavor. BMJ Innovations Published Online First: doi:10.1136/bmjinnov-2016-000157

366. Fong, D. (2018) Patient-centric Technology Improves Access, Efficiency and Quality of Care. Wolters Kluwer. Available at: http://www.wolterskluwercdi.com/blog/pat ient-centric-technology/. Last accessed July 2018.

367. Patient Centered Data Homes. Strategic Health Information Exchange Collaborative (SHIEC). Available at: https://strategichie.com/initiatives/pcdh/. Last accessed July 2018.

368. Defining the PCMH. Agency for Healthcare Research and Quality. U.S. Department of Health & Human Services. Available at: https://pcmh.ahrq.gov/page/defining-pcmh. Last accessed August 2018.

369. Adobe. Available at: https://acrobat.adobe.com/us/en/. Last accessed July 2018.

370. Personal Connected Health Alliance. Available at: https://www.pchalliance.org. Last accessed July 2018.

371. ICT Standards for Procurement. European Commission. Available at: https://joinup. ec.europa.eu/collection/ict-standards-procurement/interoperability-and-portability. Last accessed July 2018.

372. Edition - Standard for Information Technology--Portable Operating System Interface (POSIX(R)) Base Specifications, Issue 7. IEEE. Available at: https://ieeexplore.ieee.org/ document/7582338/. Last accessed August 2018.

373. Quality Payment Program. Centers for Medicare and Medicaid Services (CMS). Available at: https://qpp.cms.gov/mips/overview. Last accessed: July 2018.

374. Quality Assurance Surveillance Plan (QASP). Defense Acquisition University (DAU). Available at: https://www.dau.mil/acquipedia/Pages/ArticleDetails.aspx?aid =07612fab-5891-4078-abfc-a6a7ca2b8c0a. Last accessed July 2018.

375. Basics of Quality Improvement. American Academy of Family Physicians (AAFP). Available at: https://www.aafp.org/practice-management/improvement/basics.html. Last accessed July 2018.

376. ISO 9001:2015. Quality management systems – Requirements. Available at: www. iso.org. Last accessed July 2018.

377. Regulations. Occupational Safety and Health Administration (OSHA). Available at: https://www.osha.gov/pls/oshaweb/owadisp.show_document?p_table=STANDAR DS&p_id=10618. Last accessed July 2018.

378. Peters, D. (2009). *Improving Health Service Delivery in Developing Countries: From Evidence to Action*. Washington, DC: World Bank Publications.

379. Quality Management Principles. ISO. Available at: https://www.iso.org/files/live/sites/isoorg/files/archive/pdf/en/pub100080.pdf. Last accessed August 2018.

380. Terminology and Classifications. NHS Digital. Available at: https://digital.nhs.uk/services/terminology-and-classifications. Last accessed July 2018.

381. ISTQB Certification Exam. Software Testing Genius. Available at: http://www.software-testinggenius.com/. Last accessed July 2018.

382. Reliability and Validity. UC Davis. Available at: http://psc.dss.ucdavis.edu/sommerb/sommerdemo/intro/validity.htm. Last accessed July 2018.

383. Remote Patient Monitoring. Center for Connected Health Policy. Available at: http://www.cchpca.org/remote-patient-monitoring. Last accessed August 2018.

384. Eliciting, Collecting, and Developing Requirements. MITRE. Available at: https://www.mitre.org/publications/systems-engineering-guide/se-lifecycle-building-blocks/requirements-engineering/eliciting-collecting-and-developing-requirements. Last accessed July 2018.

385. Phaal, R., Farrukh, C., Probert, D. "Technology roadmapping—A planning framework for evolution and revolution." *Technological Forecasting and Social Change*. Volume 71, Issues 1–2, 2004, Pages 5-26, ISSN 0040-1625. https://doi.org/10.1016/S0040-1625(03)00072-6.

386. Rolstadas, A. 2012. *Computer-Aided Production Management*. Norway: Springer Science & Business Media.

387. What SATAN is. Porcupine. Available at: http://www.porcupine.org/satan/summary.html. Last accessed July 2018.

388. Institute for Healthcare Improvement. Available at: www.ihi.org. Last accessed August 2018.

389. What is a Scatter Plot? Chartio. Available at: https://chartio.com/learn/dashboards-and-charts/what-is-a-scatter-plot/. Last accessed July 2018.

390. Mayes, K., Markantonakis, K. 2017. *Smart Cards, Tokens, Security and Applications*, 2nd Edition. Switzerland: Springer.

391. Cohen, F. 2010. *Fast SOA: The Way to Use Native XML Technology to Achieve Service Oriented Architecture Governance, Scalability and Performance*. New York: Morgan Kaufmann Publishers.

392. Hughes, A. (2017). "Definition of Security Compromise." Bizfluent. Available at: https://bizfluent.com/about-6567858-definition-security-compromise.html. Last accessed July 2018.

393. Hornun-Prahauser, V., Behrendt, W., Benari, M. Developing further the concept of ePortfolio with the use of Semantic Web Technologies. Available at: http://citeseerx.ist.psu.edu/viewdoc/download?doi=10.1.1.83.8494&rep=rep1&type=pdf. Last accessed August 2018.

394. Defined Term. Available at: https://definedterm.com. Last accessed August 2018.

395. Tomsho, G. (2016). *Guide to Operating Systems*, 5th Edition. United States: Cengage Learning.

396. Cao, L. (2015). *Metasynthetic Computing and Engineering of Complex Systems*. London: Springer.

397. Spacey, J. (December 2016). "What is Session Management?" Simplicable. Available at: https://simplicable.com/new/session-management. Last accessed August 2018.

398. Risk Communication. World Health Organization. Available at: http://www.who. int/risk-communication/simulation-exercises/terms-definitions/en/. Last accessed August 2018.

399. Matlis, J. (2000). "Symmetrical Multiprocessing." *Computer World.* IDG. Available at: https://www.computerworld.com/article/2588624/network-servers/symmetrical--multiprocessing.html. Last accessed August 2018.

400. What Software Architecture Is and What It Isn't." Software Architecture in Practice, Second Edition. Available at: http://www.ece.ubc.ca/~matei/EECE417/BASS/ch0 2lev1sec1.html#ch02fn01. Last accessed August 2018.

401. Software Testing Support. Available at: https://www.quia.com/jg/1181678list.html. Last accessed August 2018.

402. What is SSL? SSL.com. Available at: http://info.ssl.com/article.aspx?id=10241. Last accessed August 2018.

403. ISO/IEC Guide 2:2004 Standardization and related activities—General vocabulary. ISO. Available at: https://www.iso.org/standard/39976.html. Last accessed August 2018.

404. Rognehaugh, R. (1998). *The Managed Health Care Dictionary.* Maryland: Jones & Bartlett Learning.

405. Center for Excellence in Primary Care. UCSF. Available at: https://cepc.ucsf.edu/. Last accessed August 2018.

406. Garfinkel, S., Spafford, G. (2002). *Web Security, Privacy & Commerce.* California: O'Reilly Media, Inc.

407. Shiri, A. (2012). *Powering Search: The Role of Thesauri in New Information Environments.* Information Today, Inc.

408. SNOMED Glossary. Available at: https://confluence.ihtsdotools.org/display/DO CGLOSS/SNOMED+Gloassry. Last accessed August 2018.

409. The Concept of Train-the-Trainer." eLeap. Available at: https://www.eleapsoftware. com/exploring-the-train-the-trainer-model-the-what-why-and-hows/. Last accessed August 2018.

410. Kiel, J. (2006). *Information Technology for the Practicing Physician.* New York: Springer-Verlag.

411. Dunning, D. "What is a Computer Trapdoor?" Techwalla. Available at: https://www. techwalla.com/articles/what-is-a-computer-trapdoor. Last accessed August 2018.

412. What is Utilization Management? America Physical Therapy Association. Available at: http://www.apta.org/WhatIsUM/. Last accessed August 2018.

413. Croskerry, P., Cosby, K. 2009. *Patient Safety in Emergency Medicine.* Philadelphia: Lippincott Williams & Wilkins.

414. Frequently Asked Questions. Unicode. Available at: http://unicode.org/faq/utf_bom. html. Last accessed August 2018.

415. What is Value-Based Healthcare? (2018). NEJM Catalyst. Available at: https://catalyst. nejm.org/what-is-value-based-healthcare/. Last accessed July 2018.

416. FamiliesUSA. Available at: https://familiesusa.org. Last accessed August 2018.

417. Intermountain Healthcare Opens New Hospital – Without a Building or Walls. (2018). Intermountain Healthcare. Available at: https://intermountainhealthcare.org/ news/2018/02/intermountain-healthcare-opens-new-hospital-without-a-building-or-walls/. Last accessed July 2018.

418. Veterans Integrated Service Network (VISN). Association for Healthcare Volunteer Resource Professionals (AHVRP). Available at: http://www.ahvrp.org/about/visn. shtml. Last accessed July 2018.

419. Veterans Health Administration. U.S. Department of Veterans Affairs. Available at: https://www.va.gov/health/aboutVHA.asp. Last accessed July 2018.

420. Palmer, D. (2018). What is malware? Everything you need to know about viruses, Trojans and malicious software. ZD Net. Available at: https://www.zdnet.com/art icle/what-is-malware-everything-you-need-to-know-about-viruses-trojans-and-malic ious-software/. Last accessed July 2018.

421. Benefits of Workstations on Wheels in Healthcare. (2017). Add on Data. Available at: https://www.addondata.com/2017/09/benefits-of-workstations-on-wheels-in-hea lthcare/. Last accessed July 2018.

422. Chapple, M., Littlejohn Shinder, D., Tittel, E. (2002). TICSA Training Guide. Indianapolis: Pearson IT Certification.

423. Access Control Policy and Implementation Guides. Computer Security Resource Center. NIST. Available at: https://csrc.nist.gov/Projects/Access-Control-Policy-an d-Implementation-Guides. Last accessed August 2018.

424. Public Welfare – Accounting of disclosures of protected health information. 45 CFR 164.528 (2011).

425. Miller, D., Mancuso, P. (2008). MCITP 70-623 Exam Cram: Supporting and Troubleshooting Applications on a Windows Vista Client for Consumer Support Technicians. Indianapolis: Pearson IT Certification.

426. Business Email Compromise. (2017). Public Service Announcement. Federal Bureau of Investigation. Available at: https://www.ic3.gov/media/2017/170504.aspx. Last accessed September 2018.

427. Notice 2014-21. Internal Revenue Service. Available at: https://www.irs.gov/pub/irs-drop/n-14-21.pdf. Last accessed September 2018.

428. Transition Planning. (2006). ProjectManagment.com. Available at: https://www.projectm anagement.com/wikis/233094/Transition-Planning. Last accessed September 2018.

429. Common Attack Pattern Enumeration and Classification. MITRE. Available at: https://capec.mitre.org/index.html. Last accessed September 2018.

430. Chronic Care Management Toolkit. American College of Physicians. Available at: https://www.acponline.org/system/files/documents/running_practice/payment_c oding/medicare/chronic_care_management_toolkit.pdf. Last accessed July 2018.

431. Kessler, K. "Enhanced ABAP Development with Core Data Services (CDS)." (2015) SAPinsider. Available at: https://sapinsider.wispubs.com/Assets/Articles/2015/October/ SPI-enhanced-ABAP-development-with-Core-Data-Services. Last accessed July 2018.

432. Fiks, A. G. (2011). Designing computerized decision support that works for clinicians and families. *Current Problems in Pediatric and Adolescent Health Care*, 41(3), 60–88. http://doi.org/10.1016/j.cppeds.2010.10.006

433. ISO/IEC 15417:2007 Information technology — Automatic identification and data capture techniques — Code 128 bar code symbology specification. Available at: www.iso.org. Last accessed August 2018.

434. What is Data Linkage? Data Linkage Western Australia. Available at: https://www. datalinkage-wa.org.au/what-is-data-linkage. Last accessed August 2018.

435. Indiana University IT Support Center Knowledge Base. Available at: https://kb.iu. edu/d/aiau. Last accessed December 2018.

436. "What is DAG?" Medium. Available at: https://medium.com/nakamo-to/what-is-dag-distributed-ledger-technology-8b182a858e19. Last accessed December 2018.

437. "Patient Unified Lookup System for Emergencies." Sequoia Project. Available at: https://sequoiaproject.org/pulse/. Last accessed December 2018.

438. "Smart Contracts." Blockchain Hub. Available at: https://blockchainhub.net/smart-contracts/. Last accessed December 2018.

439. MassChallenge HealthTech. "A Digital Health Collaborative" Medium. Available at: https://medium.com/@MassChallengeHT/a-digital-health-collaborative-a4f633dc9118. Last accessed December 2018.

440. Provost, P., Johns, M., Palmer, S. (2018) Procuring Interoperability: Achieving High-Quality, Connected, and Person-Centered Care. National Academy of Medicine. Available at: https://nam.edu/wp-content/uploads/2018/10/Procuring-Interoperability_web.pdf. Last accessed December 2018.

Index

T